# The good
# web site
## guide 2005

GRAHAM EDMONDS

 HarperCollins*Publishers*

An Imprint of HarperCollinsPublishers
77–85 Fulham Palace Road,
Hammersmith, London W6 8JB
www.harpercollins.co.uk

Published by HarperEntertainment 2004
1

ISBN 0 00 719083 2
Set in News Gothic

Printed and bound in Great Britain by Clays Ltd, St Ives plc

Designed by Staziker Jones, Cardiff

# Introduction

Welcome to the fifth edition of the Good Web Site Guide and we've sold over 250,000 copies to date. This edition is fully updated, all the sites have been checked and rechecked and I've added over 500 more. The book now contains some 5,000 sites in all.

I review the very best sites in each category, then look for those sites that offer something unique or have features that make them stand out and recommend those too. I also list alternatives, especially in the popular genres such as music, shopping or finance. Essentially I concentrate on what's really useful and would like to encourage people to see the Internet as a tool like any other and not be intimidated by it. This year I've expanded a couple of important new sections, firstly Disability Information, here the Internet is particularly useful and you can find a huge amount of information and help. Secondly, Education which is vastly improved thanks to several teachers who have suggested sites. History has also been strengthened and reorganised.

New sections include Science Fiction, English Usage and, to reflect the latest Internet trends, Blogging and Social Networking.

So what else has changed in a year since the last edition? Generally, standards have improved, consequently sites that would have been award winning two years ago are now seen as the norm. We've changed our rating system to reflect this. One notable area of improvement are the government run sites which are generally well-designed, useful and efficient. Quality is still a big issue, the costs and time involved in maintaining a good site are sometimes prohibitive so that many sites don't seem to be updated as frequently as they should be, while others just die through lack of interest and funding. Still hundreds of sites go live every day showing that creativity and entreprenurialism are alive and kicking on the Net.

Lack of time and resources often result in site names (URLs) being turned over to directories, search engines or even adult entertainment sites. Please do let me know if you find any major changes to the sites recommended in this book, I can assure you that all the reviews are accurate at the time of writing this book. Send comments to: **goodwebsiteguide@hotmail.com**

## Keeping safe

Some people are worried about using their credit card to shop
on the Net. In theory it's safer than giving credit card details
over the phone, because on most sites the information is
encrypted. Before giving out card details, check that you are on
a secure line, a small padlock icon will appear on your toolbar,
and the http:// prefix will change to https://. Providing you shop
from UK sites, you are fully covered by the same fair trade laws
that cover every form of shopping in the UK, but buying from
abroad could have some risks attached. If in doubt, shop from
reputable firms and known brand names. Check out our
Security section on page 351.

There's still a great deal of concern about cookies. A cookie is
the popular name of a file which holds some information about
your machine and, only if you give it out, about you. They have
a sinister reputation but they enable web site owners to monitor
traffic and find out who is visiting their sites. In theory,
this means they can tailor their content to their customers
or provide a better service. If you're worried about cookies,
you can easily delete them or set your computer not to receive
them. Be aware however, that many sites do need cookies
to function, especially shopping sites.

## Using the book

### Ratings

Standards are now so high that nearly all the sites included
in the book follow the key rules on web design, however some
deserve extra recognition. We've introduced five new ratings
which are outlined below. The hope is that sites awarded these
merit ratings will display them on their home pages.

  Watch out also for the general GWSG logo. Sites can
show this to indicate that they have been featured
in this book. Inclusion shows that they've met high
standards and gives recognition to their work.

 **Information merit** – this is awarded when the site content goes
beyond normal expectations and provides a level of information
that is exceptional.

 **Service merit** – given to those sites who offer something unique
or something that otherwise you'd have to pay for; it's not a
reflection of how good the staff are or how quickly they deliver.

 **Design merit** – given to those sites that ignore the web site
sausage factory approach to design and produce something
definitive or use the technology in an original way.

 **Fun merit** – for those sites that are unexpectedly good fun
to use and see.

**GWSG Top Site Award** – reserved for those exceptional sites
that offer a combination of quality design, service and content.

**Origin** – a site's country of origin is not always obvious.
This can be important, especially if you are buying from abroad.
There may be restrictions or taxes that aren't obvious at the time
of purchase. Also information that is shown as general may
apply to one part of the world and not another. For instance,
gardening advice on a US site may not be appropriate in the UK.

I'm not pretending to be a judge and jury, these ratings are just
my opinion, that of a customer and consumer. If you have any
suggestions as to how I can improve the Good Web Site Guide
or have a site you think should be included in the 2006 edition
then please e-mail me at **goodwebsiteguide@hotmail.com**

# Acknowledgements

I'd just like to end in thanking a few important people:

Firstly, a big thank you to all those people who have written in with suggestions and sites for me to check out, over 100 sites have been included in the book as a result of people e-mailing me. Also to anyone who bought the first books and the booksellers who supported them.

To the excellent team at HarperCollins.

All my many friends and colleagues for their support and suggestions.

Especially to Deborah Gray for her great patience and excellent advice and ever increasing contributions to the book, may she get that Mac.

And to Michaela for all else that matters.

For Oliver.

# Aircraft and Aviation

**www.flyer.co.uk**                                                            UK

### AVIATION IN THE UK

A well-established portal with comprehensive news, views and
information about the world of aviation from the *Flyer Magazine*
site. There's a good section on aviation links, a club and school
guide and info on how to buy and sell an aircraft, classified ads
and even free Internet access.

**www.flightinternational.com**                                   UK

### AVIATION NEWS

An online version of the best selling magazine with articles,
information and news all laid out in a slick site. It basically
gives you a taster of what's in the mag and you have to
subscribe to get the best out of it; however, there's good
information on events, a bookshop and a jobs section.

*Other sites from specialist magazines:*
**www.airspacemag.com** – the magazine of the Smithsonian
Air and Space Museum has a few really interesting articles,
but not much else.
**www.airpictorial.com** – another site plugging the magazine,
its got some news stories, and you can buy aircraft schematic
plans too.
**www.flightjournal.com** – one of the better sites in that you get
quite a lot of content, and good design too.
**www.pilotweb.co.uk** – probably the best of the flying mag sites
interesting content, a good, easy to use design and lots of
information too.
**www.womanpilot.com** – awful design, but some interesting
articles here from a magazine devoted to women pilots.

**www.aeroflight.co.uk**

### AVIATION ENTHUSIASTS                                          UK

This site attempts to offer an 'information stop' for all aviation
enthusiasts. It's clearly laid out and has details on international
air forces, a section on the media including specialist books
and bookshops, a discussion forum, as well as details of air
shows and museums.

**A**

## www.f4aviation.co.uk                                           UK
*AIR SCENE UK*
A weekly e-zine provided by F4 Aviation, a group of dedicated
enthusiasts, this site has lots of information, nostalgia,
links to related sites and personal flying accounts. It's also
got an air show listing with reports, previews and some
good photography.

## www.landings.com                                              US
THE BUSIEST AVIATION HUB IN CYBERSPACE
A huge amount of information on offer from this site including
the latest news, history, a route planner, stories and masses
of links; use the directory to navigate this massive site.

## www.airliners.net                                             UK
AIRLINERS
With nearly 500,000 photos, this is a huge site, it has a good
search facility and should appeal to photographers as well as
plane spotters. It also offers a shop, news, chat, links and a
huge amount of information. See also **www.airlinerworld.com**
which is better than the usual magazine spin off site; you can
buy merchandise and chat to other enthusiasts, there's a small
gallery too.

## www.zap16.com                                                 US
PLANES, PICS AND FACTS
Excellent site that offers fact sheets and pictures on both
military and civil aircraft. There's also news, links and air
show information. Beware annoying pop-up ads.

## www.raf.mod.uk                                                UK

ROYAL AIR FORCE
This site features lots of information on the RAF – you can
locate a display or fly past, find career advice, check out a
squadron or get technical information. The history section
is particularly good with data covering aircraft from the very
first planes to the latest illustrated by a gallery of pictures;
however, the time-line section still only reaches 1989.
See also **www.rafmuseum.org.uk** for the sites dedicated to
the museums at Hendon and Cosford.

## www.wpafb.af.mil/museum                    US

US AIR FORCE MUSEUM
A superbly detailed site with masses of data on the aircraft and
their history from the first planes to space flight. The archive
section is particularly good with features on particular types
of aircraft and weapons, with information about how they
were developed.

## http://theaerodrome.com                    UK

FIRST WORLD WAR
Devoted to the aircraft and aces of the First World War,
this site offers lots of background information, personal
experiences and details about the pilots who fought above
the trenches. For an emerging site on Second World War
aircraft try **www.compsoc.man.ac.uk/~wingman/** while at
**www.fighter-collection.com** you can find out about the
remaining airworthy 'war birds' in Europe.

## www.vintageaircraft.org                    US

VINTAGE AIRCRAFT ASSOCIATION
Events, information, photos plus details of the Association and
what it does are all here on this utilitarian site; however, it's a
little slow to download. There is a shop selling a wide range of
merchandise but special arrangements have to be made for
those outside the US.

*See also:*
**www.battle-of-britain.com** – an overview of the battle,
the aircraft and those who fought in it.
**www.battleofbritain.net** – home of the Battle of Britain
Historical Society.
**www.fighter-planes.com** – an overview of all fighter planes
from 1930 to date with specifications and some photos.
**www.nucleus.com/~ltwright/lanc_1.htm** – a detailed history
of the Lancaster bomber.
**www.spitfiresociety.demon.co.uk** – all you need to know
about Spitfires.
**www.thunder-and-lightnings.co.uk** – a site devoted to British
post war military aircraft, with lots of detail, although it hasn't
been updated for a while.

A

## www.janesonline.com    UK

### JANES

Janes is the authority on defence forces world-wide and for a price you can buy books and CD-ROMs which contain all the information you'll ever need about the world's military might. You have to register to get anything out of it, but there are a number of free newsletter options, anything else, you have to pay for. It's a little stingy really, but I suppose they are protecting their assets.

## www.airdisaster.com    US

### NO.1 AVIATION SAFETY RESOURCE

A rather macabre site that reviews each major air crash, and looks into the reasons behind what happened. It's not for the squeamish, but the cockpit voice recordings and eyewitness accounts make fascinating, if disturbing, reading. There are some really annoying pop-up adverts on this site, which spoils the visit. See also **www.aaib.gov.uk** for the Air Accident Investigation Branch which has a monthly bulletin with details of crashes and current investigations.

## www.aviationconsumer.com    US

### EQUIPMENT RATED

A consumer site dedicated to the aviation world with reviews and tests done on everything from planes to sunglasses.
To get the best out of it you need to subscribe. Unfortunately, the dull layout makes it tedious to use in some respects.

## www.gliderpilot.net    UK

### GLIDER PILOT NETWORK

Weather, news, links and information on all forms of gliding, plus chat and classified ads. You need to register to get the best out of the site.

## www.iac.org    US

### AEROBATICS

The site of the International Aerobatic Club and the place to go for information on the sport. See also **www.aerobatics.org.uk** for the British Aerobatic Association.

*Other aviation sites worth checking out:*

**http://avia.russian.ee** – an overview of the world's helicopters, not updated for a year or so though.

**http://hotairballooning.com** – an American site devoted to hot air ballooning.

**http://luchtvaart.pagina.nl** – a Dutch site offering a huge number of aviation-related links.

**www.aerostationery.co.uk** – maps for aviators.

**www.babo.org.uk** – the British Association of Balloon Operators.

**www.globalaircraft.org** – a vast site with information primarily on US aircraft with lots of information and interactivity.

**www.risingup.com** – general portal site with useful links.

**www.ulflyingmag.com** – oddly designed, but informative site on ultra light flying.

# Antiques and Collectibles

*The Internet is a great place to learn about antiques, it's also full of specialist sites run by fanatical collectors. If you want to take the risk of buying over the Net, then the best prices are found on the big auction sites such as Ebay and icollector.*

## www.antiques.co.uk                                              UK

FIND AND BUY ONLINE

An attractive and well-designed site, which is basically an online showroom dedicated to most aspects of art and antiques. The emphasis is on quality, experts vet all items and you can arrange viewings too. There's also a news and reviews section with interesting articles on the latest fashionable antiques. Value for money is, of course, purely subjective.

## www.atg-online.com                                              UK

*ANTIQUES TRADE GAZETTE*

A comprehensive and wide-ranging site covering all aspects of antique buying from auctions to dealers and classified advertising. You need to register to get the best out of it though.

## www.antiquesbulletin.co.uk                                UK

### INTERACTIVE WORLD OF ANTIQUES

A well laid out site with good information and links to more specialist sites and dealers. It aims to be comprehensive and does a great job, there are details on auctions, advice on buying and selling, and a bookshop. You can also buy and sell from the site. To access the articles archive, you need to purchase a site licence. See also **www.theantiquesdirectory.co.uk** which is good for links and information, but an unattractive and waywardly designed site.

## www.invaluable.com                                       UK

### ART MARKET INTELLIGENCE

The aim of this site is to provide 'impartial electronic information on antiques, fine art and premium collectables to dealers, private buyers, museums and other institutions'. It proves to be a great resource providing contact details and links to hundreds of dealers, catalogues and auction houses world-wide. Use the 'ideal' section to search dealers' stock. The links section is particularly good.

## www.antiquesworld.co.uk                                  UK

### AN ALADDIN'S CAVE FOR THE ENTHUSIAST

Catch up on the latest news, obtain details on major and local fairs and events, book a course or indulge your interests by linking to a specialist online retailer or club. You can't buy from this site but the links and information are very good.

## www.antiquestall.com                                      UK

### ONLINE ANTIQUES STALL

A no-nonsense site devoted to selling antiques at fixed prices rather than by auction. There's a good search facility and each item has a picture and details of shipping.

## www.antiquegems.net                                       UK

### ANTIQUE JEWELLERY

A fine site from a Birmingham dealer and restorer with a good selection of gems and jewellery as well as watches and a selection of bargains. You can't buy online but there's a contact service for the pieces that you're interested in.

A

## www.dmgantiquefairs.com                                    UK

FOR THE LARGEST ANTIQUES FAIRS
DMG run the largest fairs in the UK. Their attractive site gives
details of each fair, including dates, location and local tourist
information. For a site that simply lists antiques and collector's
fairs in date order with links to organiser's web sites go to
**www.antiques-web.co.uk/fairs.html**

## www.portobelloonline.com                                   UK

THE PORTOBELLO ROAD
The traders from London's well-known antiques market have
got together a great site which not only gives information
about Portobello Road itself, but also offers excellent links
and a directory.

## www.lapada.co.uk                                           UK

ASSOCIATION OF ART AND ANTIQUE DEALERS
Get information on their fairs, advice on buying and selling
antiques, learn how to care for your antiques as well as useful links.

## www.bada.org                                               UK

BRITISH ANTIQUE DEALER'S ASSOCIATION
Attractive and informative listing site for antique dealers in the
UK, grouped in 16 categories, it's easy to find a specialist in a
particular area of interest. There's also information on their
events and lots of advice on buying antiques.

## www.bafra.org.uk                                           UK

THE BRITISH ANTIQUE FURNITURE RESTORER'S
ASSOCIATION
If you have an antique that is in need of restoration, then this
is a useful place to visit as it helps you find the right restorer.
Apart from the usual links page, there's also information and
articles on caring for antiques and how find a course if you
want to become a restorer.

## www.antique-furniture.co.uk                                UK

EUROPE'S LARGEST SELECTION
An attractive site from a specialist dealer offering a wide range
of furniture to choose from, good photography and the promise
of a high level of service to match.

A

## www.collectiques.co.uk                                     UK
### COLLECTIBLES
Despite its fairly naff name, Collectiques is a good resource if
you're searching for information or that elusive piece for your
collection. It covers an impressive array of areas of interest from
toys to models, kits and architectural antiques, it's easy to use
and it's great for background info and links.

## www.collectorcafe.com                                      UK
### ONLINE COLLECTING COMMUNITY
A portal site which is great for classified ads links, articles and
chat covering most of the major areas of collecting.

## www.worldcollectorsnet.com                                 US
### BY COLLECTORS FOR COLLECTORS
Great for discussion groups, collector's message boards and
general chat about collecting. There's also a good online
magazine plus plenty of advice and links. See also
**www.collectors.com** which is great for Americana and
also **www.collectingchannel.com**

## www.finds.org.uk                                           UK
### THE PORTABLE ANTIQUITIES SCHEME
An interesting site devoted to volunteered archaeological and
antiquity finds made by individuals who offer to register them
so that they can be researched properly.

# Ceramics

## www.studiopottery.com                                      UK

### THE POTTERY STUDIO
Divided into 3 sections: pots, potters and potteries, this site gives
information on the history of studio pottery. It's a huge site with
over 4,600 pages and it's continually being updated. Everything
is cross-referenced with good explanations and photographs.

## www.claricecliff.com                                       UK
### THE FIRST LADY OF CERAMIC DESIGN
A must for fans of Clarice Cliff pottery. There is information
on auctions, biographical details, patterns, shapes; also a
newsletter and forum for related chat. The site offers
reproductions and related merchandise for sale.

**www.chinasearch.uk.com**                                         UK
> REPLACING LOST CHINA
> A company specialising in finding china to match services and
> lost pieces, they also buy unwanted tableware. The site is easy
> to use and they have over 1 million pieces in stock so they
> should be able to help.

# Apple Mac Users

*The following sites specialise in Apple Mac technology and programs.*
*See also the general sections on Computers, Software and Games*
*that may also have relevant information.*

**www.apple.com** or **www.uk.euro.apple.com**                      US

> HOME OF THE ORIGINAL
> Get the latest information and advances in Apple computers at
> this beautifully designed site. You can buy from the Applestore but
> don't expect huge discounts, although they do offer finance deals.

**www.ihateapple.com**                                              US
> IF YOU REALLY DON'T LIKE APPLE
> An entertaining anti-Apple web site devoted to 'debunking' and
> exposing Apple faults – it's actually quite informative and funny too.

## Hardware

**www.cancomuk.com**                                                UK
> APPLE MAC HARDWARE AND SOFTWARE
> A messy site offering a wide selection of hardware, peripherals
> and software all developed for Apple computers. There are plenty
> of deals and free delivery on all orders over £200 before VAT.

**www.macwarehouse.co.uk**                                          UK
> GREAT PRICES ON MACS
> Part of the Microwarehouse group, they specialise in mail order
> supply with a reputation for excellent service. Good prices and
> a wide range make this a good first port of call if you need a
> new PC or an upgrade.

**A**

*See also:*
**www.macassist.co.uk** – buy the Mac that's right for you.
**www.macreviewzone.com** – more reviews and buying help.

# Software

## www.versiontracker.com                                    US

SOFTWARE FOR MACS
A software specialist that's a great place for downloading the
latest programs, it has a huge selection and many are free.
You have to subscribe to get the best out of it, but it's well
worth the effort.

*See also:*
**www.macupdate.com** – good for the latest hot software
and updates.
**www.mac-upgrade.com** – news, reviews and how to upgrade
your Mac.
**www.theapplecollection.com** – a huge site with lots of
information and downloads but principally a collection of all
things sporting the apple logo.

# Information and help

## www.macintouch.com                                        US

THE ORIGINAL MAC NEWS AND INFORMATION SITE
If you have a Mac then this is the site for you. It has lots of
information, bug fixes and software to download, but it is a
little overwhelming and it takes a while to get your bearings.
Once you've done that, for the Mac user this site is invaluable.

## www.macinstruct.com                                       US

LEARN ABOUT MACS
A site dedicated to free tutorials on all aspects of using an
Apple Mac, they are well written and the site's unfussy design
seems to suit the subject.

*See also the following:*
**www.applelust.com** – a site devoted to forums discussing all
things Apple.
**www.everymac.com** – another good guide to the world of
Macintosh.

**www.macaddict.com** – very comprehensive, one for the experts.
**www.macfixit.com** – fix your problems.
**www.macinstein.com** – which has a good directory, even a quiz.
**www.maclaunch.com** – the latest news.
**www.macnn.com** – the Mac News network, lots of ratings.
**www.macobserver.com** – more news, tips and forums.
**www.macrumors.com** – a great place to find the latest information and ideas about what could be on the way from Apple, good for tips too.

## Music for Macs

*Here's a selection of sites that offer the Mac owner a place to go to download the latest digital music files. Please be aware that downloading some types of files may be illegal.*

### www.apple.com/itunes
HOME OF THE I-POD
A huge amount of material to choose from including the latest tunes, classics and audio books, prices vary enormously and it's not always easy to find what you're looking for, but the choice is excellent.

*Other places to look:*
**www.limewire.com** – a file-sharing program that is suitable for Mac users, more stable than some.
**www.macband.com** – a well-categorised site covering free music donated by bands.
**www.macidol.com** – news, discussions, free downloads and even an album.
**www.macjams.com** – an Apple Garage band community site.
**www.macmusic.org** – keep up to date with the latest music news, software and hardware. There's over 3,000 music-related links and also forums and advice.
**www.mp3-mac.com** – a huge selection here covering every category of music and a wide selection of software too.

## Games for Macs

*Here are some great sites to help you if you feel restricted by having an Apple Mac.*

A

**www.macgamer.com**                                                US
   MAC GAMER MAG
   A very good online magazine with all the usual features
   we've come to expect: news, reviews, links and even a few
   giveaways. It's all neatly packaged on an attractive website.

**www.macgamefiles.com**                                            US
   MAC GAME FILE LIBRARY
   To quote them 'Macgame files.com is the one-stop source for
   Macintosh game files. The web site features lively libraries of
   Macintosh demos, shareware, updaters, tools, add-ons, and
   more'. And they're right; it's a very useful site with some really
   good games and software.

**www.insidemacgames.com**                                          US
   *IMG* MAGAZINE
   A magazine devoted to Mac games where you can find the
   latest demos, updates for the games, loads of shareware
   games, news and reviews.

# Architecture

**www.greatbuildings.com**                                          US
   ARCHITECTURE ONLINE
   This US-oriented site shows over 800 buildings and features
   hundreds of leading architects, with 3D models, photographic
   images and architectural drawings, commentaries,
   bibliographies and web links. It's all well packaged, easy to
   use and you can search by architect, building or location.

**www.skyscrapers.com**                                             US

   SKYSCRAPERTASTIC!
   This really entertaining and award-winning site has nearly
   82,000 skyscrapers listed from over 500 cities, and more are
   being added constantly. There are also features; chat and
   you can search by region as well as by architect or building.
   The only fault is that there's lots of extraneous information
   that can clutter the site.

**www.architecture.com**                                     UK

THE ROYAL INSTITUTE FOR BRITISH ARCHITECTS
A massive site from the RIBA with some 250,000 pages on
all aspects of architecture including history, jobs, events and
features on great buildings.

**www.buildingconservation.com**                             UK

CONSERVING ASSETS
They claim to be the online information centre for the
conservation and restoration of historic buildings, churches,
gardens and landscapes; the site seems to live up to its billing
providing plenty of quality information and links.

*Also check out the following sites:*
**www.aabc-register.co.uk** – the register of architects accredited
in building conservation.
**www.archibot.com** – news and forums dedicated to all
things architectural.
**www.archidose.org** – an entertaining and informative weekly
magazine devoted to contemporary architecture run by an
American expert.
**www.architectureforall.com** – a collaborative venture between
the Victoria & Albert Museum and the RIBA to promote
understanding of architecture.
**www.arcspace.com** – photos, opinions and features on the
most important architects and their work.
**www.artandarchitecture.co.uk** – An initiative to promote
interaction between artists and architects. This site makes for
interesting reading and whatever your opinions on the projects
themselves, it certainly sparks debate and the imagination.
**www.retropolis.net** – Art Deco architecture, a labour of love.
**www.spab.org.uk** – home of the charity The Society for the
Protection of Ancient Buildings.

# Art and the Arts

*One of the best things about the Internet is the ability to showcase*
*things that otherwise would be quite obscure or inaccessible.*
*Now working artists to show their wares to excellent effect and we can*
*view their art before we buy. In addition, we can now 'visit' some of*
*the world's great galleries and museums. Here are the best sites for*
*posters, online galleries, museums, cartoons, exhibitions, showcases*
*for new talent and how to get the best clip-art for your own use.*

A

# Resources and encyclopedias

**www.artlex.com**                                                          US

THE VISUAL ARTS DICTIONARY
From abbozzo to zoomorphic, there are over 3,300 definitions
of art-related terms with links to related articles on other sites.
The cross-referencing is excellent.

**www.artcyclopedia.com**                                              CANADA

THE FINE ART SEARCH ENGINE
A popular resource for finding out just about anything to do
with art, it's quick, nicely designed and informative. At time of
writing they had indexed 1,200 leading arts sites, and offer
links to an estimated 125,000 works by 7,500 different artists.

**www.accessart.org.uk**                                                    UK

MAKING ART ACCESSIBLE
A really good, colourful site dedicated to helping students,
children and teachers get to grips with the art world and the
meaning behind art. There are good online workshops on topics
such as sculpture, use of colour and photography.

**http://wwar.com**                                                         US

THE WORLD-WIDE ART RESOURCE
This is an effective search vehicle with links to artists,
exhibitions, galleries and museums, it now offers up over
91,000 works of art from over 22,000 'masters'. Plenty of
pop-up adverts spoil it though.

**www.artchive.com**                                                        UK

MARK HARDEN'S ARTCHIVE
Incredible, but seemingly the work of one art fanatic, this
superb site not only has an excellent art encyclopaedia, but also
the latest art news and galleries with special online exhibitions.
The quality of the pictures is outstanding. There's also a
section on theory and good links. For more links try
**www.chart.ac.uk/vlib**

*See also:*
**www.abcgallery.com** – Olga's Gallery is hugely informative and well illustrated.
**www.askart.com** – a massive directory on art and artists, US-oriented.
**www.finearthistory.com** – a clear and easy to navigate art encyclopedia.

# Art in the UK

**www.culture.gov.uk**                                      UK

> THE GOVERNMENT'S VIEW
> A dense site giving information on how the Government is supporting the arts and museums. There are plenty of facts, figures and reports to download, as well as links and information on libraries, the creative industries and even sport.

**www.design-council.org.uk**                              UK

> PROMOTING THE EFFECTIVE USE OF DESIGN
> This good-looking site effectively promotes the work of The Design Council through access to their archives of articles on design and details of their work with government; also gives feedback on design issues.

**www.artguide.org**                                       UK

> THE ART LOVER'S GUIDE TO BRITAIN AND IRELAND
> Organised by artist, region, exhibition or museum with more than 4,500 listings in all. This site is easy to navigate with a good search engine and cross-referencing making it simple to find out about events in a particular region, aided by annotated maps.

# Art styles, periods, schools, most popular artists and countries

**www.impressionism.org**                                  US

> LEARN ABOUT IMPRESSIONISM
> An overview of the movement with a tutorial all contained on a well-illustrated site.

A

## www.surrealism.co.uk    UK
### ONLINE GALLERY
Not as way out as you'd expect, this site gives an overview of surrealism and features contemporary artists. The online gallery is OK without being that exciting, but as a showcase it works.

## www.graffiti.org    UK
### THE WRITING ON THE WALL
If you're fascinated by graffiti, then here's the place to go – it's got a gallery of the best examples, history and links to other graffiti sites.

## www.the-artists.org    UK
### 20TH CENTURY ART
This site is easy to use, with minimalist design and details of every major artist of the last century.

## www.dlc.fi/~hurmari/preraph.htm    UK

### PRE-RAPHAELITES
An exhaustive listing of sites and links to pages on the Pre Raphaelites, their paintings, lives and even those who posed for them.

*Sites featuring the top artists:*
**http://arthistory.about.com/library/blartists.htm** – biographies of over 150 artists plus loads of art history information.
**www.chez.com/renoir/indexe.html** – Renoir
**www.daliuniverse.com** – Dali
**www.lucidcafe.com/library/96jun/gauguin.html** – Gauguin
**www.hansholbein.nl** – Holbein
**www.mark-rothko.com** – Rothko
**www.marmottan.com** – Monet
**www.mos.org/leonardo** – Da Vinci
**www.musee-matisse-nice.org/** – Matisse
**www.tamu.edu/mocl/picasso** – Picasso
**www.vangoghgallery.com** – Van Gogh.

## www.asianart.com                                    US

ART IN ASIA

All you need to know on Asian art. Basically, it covers all
the major cultures in four sections; Exhibitions, Articles,
Associations and Galleries. It's not very well cross-referenced,
which makes it hard to navigate, although there is a pretty
good search engine.

## www.lonker.net/art_african_1.htm                    US

AFRICAN ART

A good-looking site dedicated to mainly sub-Saharan cave
and rock paintings. It's well illustrated and authoritative,
there's also a sister site on Aboriginal Art at
**www.lonker.net/art_aboriginal_1.htm**

# The major museums and galleries

## www.museums.co.uk                                   UK

MUSEUM SEARCH

MuseumNet is a simple search engine which allows you to
search either by subject or location, each entry has a short
description and a map. There's also industry information and
a jobs page for those who want to work in a museum.

## www.museumstuff.com                                 US

MUSEUM GATEWAY

An outstanding portal devoted to American museums.
There's information on virtually any topic you can name plus
thousands of links to specialist sites and museums. They also
provide a list of museum shops, chat rooms and forums plus
links to the fun sections on museum sites.

## www.24hourmuseum.org.uk                             UK

OPEN ALL HOURS

Run by the Campaign for Museums, this site aims to give high
quality access to the UK's galleries, museums and heritage sites
– and it succeeds. The graphics are clear, it's easy to use and
really informative. There are a selection of online exhibitions,
web features, a museum finder, links, news and a link to
**www.show.me.uk**, which is the sister site for children.

**A**

**www.tate.org.uk** UK

THE ARCHETYPAL GALLERY SITE
A real treat with excellent design and quality pictures, the site
covers all the Tate galleries and offers information about
exhibitions, relevant articles, webcasts and also a good shop.

**www.nationalgallery.org.uk** UK

THE NATIONAL COLLECTION
A very comprehensive site, with sections on the permanent
collection and exhibitions. There's also a shop with a wide
range of books and gifts as well as information for schools and
the outreach programme. For access to the all the Scottish
National Galleries on a similar site, go to **www.natgalscot.ac.uk**
who have a similarly informative and enjoyable site.

**www.thebritishmuseum.ac.uk** UK

ILLUMINATING NEW CULTURES
Whether you explore the world's cultures with interactive
mapping, understand and educate yourself or just browse the
collection, this is a beautifully illustrated site. The online shop
stocks a selection of gifts and goods based on museum
artefacts. Delivery cost depends on weight of purchases.
Parents will appreciate the family online tour and children's
compass, a museum guide for children. They also arrange
museum tours.

**www.npg.org.uk** UK

THE NATIONAL PORTRAIT GALLERY
With over 27,000 works on view, this is one of the biggest
online galleries. It shows the most influential characters in
British history portrayed by artists of their time. You can search
by sitter or artist, and buy the print. The online shop offers gifts
plus pictures with options on print size, framing and delivery,
including overseas.

**www.royalacademy.org.uk** UK

WHERE ART IS MADE, SEEN AND DEBATED
An interestingly designed and modern gallery site with all the
information you need on the Royal Academy as well as ticket
information and a shop. There's support for schools, colleges
and teachers, plus information and previews of exhibitions.

## www.vam.ac.uk

UK   VICTORIA & ALBERT MUSEUM
The world's largest museum has a plain functional web site, with information on visiting, learning and how you can help support the museum. The online shop offers gifts, reproductions and books. You can also explore the museum virtually, visiting most of the galleries with back-up information explaining their exhibits plus details of what they contain.

## www.moma.org                                                US

THE MUSEUM OF MODERN ART IN NEW YORK
A comprehensive and minimally attractive site that covers the collection and offers much in the way of information on the works and artists. There's also an excellent gift shop, although shipping to the UK is expensive. It can be quite slow at times.

## www.metmuseum.org

US   THE METROPOLITAN MUSEUM OF ART IN NEW YORK
A very stylish site, featuring lots of great ideas, with quality illustrations and photographs, you can view any one of 6,500 exhibits, have a taster by taking the director's tour, become a member, or visit a special exhibition. The shop offers a great range of products, many exclusive, and there's a handy gift finder service. Delivery costs to the UK depend on how much you spend.

## www.si.edu                                                  US

THE SMITHSONIAN
A fairly cluttered site but once you get used to it there's a huge amount of information on every major aspect of art plus sections on science and history. There's the magazine too.

## www.courtauld.ac.uk                                         UK

COURTAULD COLLECTION
A minimally illustrated site with details of the collection plus educational resources and information on the gallery. It's a shame that more of the art isn't available to view on the site.

A

## www.louvre.fr                                               FRANCE

FRANCE'S TREASURE HOUSE
Similar to the UK's National Gallery site: there's a virtual tour
where you can view the collection and learn about its history,
you can also check out the latest exhibitions and buy advance
tickets. The shop has some interesting items, delivery to the
UK starts at 12.95 Euros.

## www.guggenheim.org                                          US

VANGUARDS OF ARCHITECTURE AND CULTURE
There is the promise of a unique virtual museum, but while
we wait, the other four – Berlin, Bilbao, Venice, New York
and Las Vegas can be visited here. You can find out about
exhibitions and collections, projects, tours, events and
developmental programs, while membership entitles you to
free entry and a store discount. The store is stocked with a
wonderful selection of unusual goods and gifts, and is not
bad value, though delivery to the UK starts at £18.

## www.hermitagemuseum.org                                     RUSSIA

THE STATE HERMITAGE MUSEUM
Another beautifully presented museum site with features on
the highlights of the collection with a section of superb digital
photographs, details of the museum itself, exhibitions and an
education centre.

## www.artgalleries-london.com                                 UK

GUIDE TO LONDON'S TREASURES
An attractive site that offers a directory of the capital's
museums, galleries and relevant links to related sites.

# Clipart

*These sites are loaded with pop-ups and advertising, which is really
irritating, you may just try Google (**www.google.co.uk**), which has an
excellent image search facility. If you know of a site that is ad free
please let me know.*

**www.clipart.net**                                                    US

A

> THE PLACE TO START IF YOU NEED CLIP-ART
> A clip-art search facility, you should quickly find the perfect
> image. Many linked sites have free art for use, otherwise cost
> varies enormously depending on what you want.
>
> *See also:*
> **www.321clipart.com** – some 12,000 images.
> **www.barrysclipart.com** – a huge resource with hundreds
> of categories.
> **www.clipartcastle.com** – sections on photos and animation
> as well as clip art. Registration is a right pain though.

## Cartoons and drawing

**www.cartoonbank.com**                                                US

> WORLD'S LARGEST CARTOON DATABASE
> Need to find a cartoon for a particular occasion? Then there's
> a choice of over 20,000 mostly from *New Yorker* magazine.
> You can send e-cards, but they only supply products to the US.
> For a massive set of links to cartoon and humorous
> sites then try the excellent Norwegian search site
> **www.cartoon-links.com**

**www.cartoon-factory.com**                                            US

> BUYING CARTOON CELS
> Buy cartoon cels, mainly from Disney and Warner cartoons;
> you can search by subject or artist. Delivery is expensive,
> although they are flexible about payment. See also the Open
> Directory Project's section on Animation. It offers over 17,000
> links at **http://dmoz.org/arts/animation**.

**www.drawingpower.org.uk**                                            UK

> THE BIG DRAW
> A bid to get us all drawing, the Big Draw happens every
> October and here you can get encouragement and details
> on events and programs.

**A**

# Buying art

### www.artrepublic.co.uk                                         UK

BOOKS, POSTERS AND WHAT'S ON WHERE

A nicely designed, easy-to-use site with thousands of art
posters and prints to choose from. There is also an option to
have posters framed and free shipping world-wide. There is also
a glossary of art terms and biographical data on an impressive
number of artists. What's on world-wide provides details of the
latest exhibitions, competitions and travel information for over
1,250 museums around the world.

### www.onlineposters.com                                         UK

POSTER SHOPS ONLINE

Simply a ranked list of shops that sell posters, from the
generalist to the very specialised retailers.

### www.barewalls.com                                             US

INTERNET'S LARGEST ART PRINT AND POSTER STORE

This site backs its claim with a huge range, it's also excellent
for gifts and unusual prints and posters but be aware that the
shipping costs are high – $29 for the UK. There's also a gift
voucher scheme. See also **www.art.com** which is excellent
and does a great line in movie posters as well as art.
Delivery is expensive.

### www.postershop.co.uk                                          UK

FINE ART PRINTS AND POSTERS

There are over 22,000 prints and posters available to buy,
covering the work of over 3,900 artists. There's also a framing
service and a good user-friendly search facility where you can
search by subject as well as artist. In the museum shop there's
a range of art-related gifts to choose from. Delivery costs £4
for the UK.

### www.totalposter.com                                           UK

GET THE BIG PICTURE

Excellent poster store, specialising in photographic posters with
a very wide selection. Extra services include: printing up your
own photos to poster size, plus pictures of recent key
sporting and news events in their 'Stop Press' section.
Delivery costs vary.

## www.easyart.com                                             UK

### FINE ART PRINTS AND POSTERS

Excellent art shop selling posters, limited editions, photographs
and etchings. They provide inspiration too with advice on the
best place to hang art in your home and a custom art section
where you can turn pictures of your friends into pop icons.

## www.eyestorm.com                                            UK

### BUYING CONTEMPORARY ART

A really attractive and well-designed site, which showcases
contemporary art and photography, you can buy online as well.

## www.whitecube.com                                           UK

### WHITE CUBE GALLERY

This outstandingly designed site showcases top artists in an
original way and highlights what can be done when web site
development technology is used at its best. Although influential
in developing the careers of some of the best artists working
today, you can buy art here at reasonable prices too.

*Other online art showcase sites and stores worth visiting:*
**www.artandparcel.com** – messy site that boasts the largest
gallery on the web.
**www.artlondon.com** – well designed art store with an
emphasis on the UK, value for money and quality.
**www.artuk.co.uk** – a slightly confusing site but well worth
a visit as there's some interesting art and articles.
**www.axisartists.org.uk** – a very good showcase site for
contemporary artists with lots of content and information as
well as links and exhibitions. It claims over 17,000 pieces of
work by over 4000 artists.
**www.britart.com** – good-looking site concentrating on the work
of 400 British artists.
**www.fineart.co.uk** – the home of the Fine Art Trade Guild.
**www.modernbritishartists.co.uk** – a gallery and shop catering
for those of us who love and covet the work of modern British
artists, including those from early in the last century.
**www.newartportfolio.com** – another showcase site for new
artists with an intriguing design, offering plenty of information
and a money back guarantee – useful if you find you can't live
with your purchase after all.

A

**www.artloss.com**                                          US

THE ART LOSS REGISTER
The register of stolen and lost art featured thefts and recoveries
makes for interesting if rather sad reading.

## Creating art

**www.kurzweilcyberart.com**                                 US

CYBER ART
Once you download the program, watch in fascination as art is
created for you as a screen saver. It's free and great fun too.

**www.saa.co.uk**                                            UK

THE SOCIETY FOR ALL ARTISTS
Help, advice, forums, tuition and a good shop make this a
useful site for any artist amateur or professional. There's also a
gallery if you're looking for art to buy. Additional services and
discounts are on offer for those who join.

**www.watercolor-online.com**                                US

ALL FORMS OF WATERCOLOUR
Very good site devoted to all aspects of watercolour painting;
it has tutorials, advice, links and provides a good place to start
when searching for information on the subject.

*For more watercolour sites try:*
**http://painting.about.com/cs/watercolours/index.htm** –
pages of advice from the excellent **www.about.com**
**www.paintdoodles.com** – an interactive course on CD-Rom.
**www.wasp-art.skynow.co.uk** – a simple online course
by Peter Saw.

**www.simplypainting.com**                                   UK

FRANK CLARK
Learn how to paint with leading art teacher Frank Clark, the site
has free lessons, tips plus a shop and gallery.

# Astrology

A

**www.astrology.com**                                                UK

ALL ABOUT ASTROLOGY

A very comprehensive site offering free advice from the stars,
you can buy a personalised reading and chart, or just browse
the more general horoscopes. You can find celebrity horoscopes
too, and learn about the history and techniques of astrology.
See also **www.horoscope.co.uk** home of Horoscope Magazine.

**www.live-astro.com**                                               UK

RUSSELL GRANT

Now is your chance to buy a horoscope from a real celebrity,
costs range from £3.99 upwards. This site has been expanded
to include dream interpretations, tarot and other astrological
resources as well as the various horoscopes.

**www.easyscopes.com**                                               US

ASTROLOGY SEARCH ENGINE

Here you can get as many different free horoscopes as you
can handle, the site contains direct links to the daily, weekly,
monthly and yearly horoscopes for each zodiac sign. You just
have to select your zodiac sign and you are presented with a
large list of horoscopes to choose from. It's amazing how
different they all are for the same sign!

**www.lovetest.com**                                                 US

ARE YOU COMPATIBLE?

It's a bit long winded to use but enter your birthday and your
partner's and you get a compatibility score based on the star
signs. There are also quizzes, chat, classified ads, links,
not forgetting the love test thermometer.

*See also:*

**www.astro.com** – comprehensive offering with every major
aspect of astrology covered and explained.
**www.astro-eclipse.co.uk** – a basic site with an overview of the
subject plus links and forum pages.
**www.freewillastrology.com** – good-looking site with lots of
predictions about future events, usual star signs and much
more from astrologer Rob Brezsny.
**www.thezodiac.com** – a fairly amateur site but it's clear and
easy to use with lots of fun astrological things to do.

A

# Auctions and Classified Ads

*Before using these sites be sure that you are aware of the rules and regulations surrounding the bidding process, and what your rights are as a seller or purchaser. If they are not properly explained during the registration process, then use another site. They should also offer a returns policy as well as insurance cover. Whilst there are plenty of bargains available, not all the products on offer are cheaper than the high street or specialist vendor; it's very much a case of buyer beware. Having said that, once you're used to it, it can be fun, and you can save a great deal of money.*

### www.ukauctionhelp.co.uk                                        UK

HELP WITH USING AUCTIONS

A site dedicated to giving the low down on auctions. It's informative and genuinely helpful – shame about the design, which makes it difficult to use and it's cluttered with lots of adverts.

### www.bidxs.com                                                   US

AUCTION SEARCH ENGINE

An attempt to allow you to search the auction sites for your wanted items, you can search by category, price or by item. It's quite slow but useful nonetheless.

### www.ebay.co.uk                                                  UK

YOUR PERSONAL TRADING COMMUNITY

With over 3 million items you are likely to find what you want here. The emphasis is on collectibles and it is strong on antiques of all sorts, although if it's sellable, it's sure to be here. There is a 24-hour support facility and automatic insurance cover on all items up to £120. Previous clients have reviewed each person who has something to sell, that way you can check up on their reliability.

### www.ebid.co.uk                                                  UK

NO CHARGE TO LIST AN ITEM

Divided into auctions, wanted and swap sections. The auctions can easily be accessed and browsed; its strengths are in computing, electronics and music, although there has been a great increase in the number of collectibles available.

## www.icollector.com                                               US

### REDEFINING THE ART OF COLLECTING

An attractive site bringing together the wares of some 350
auction houses and dealers, icollector is an ambitious project
that works well. The emphasis is on art, antiques and
collectibles. Be sure that the auction house you're dealing with
ships outside the US.

## www.qxl.com                                                UK/EUROPE

### A PAN-EUROPEAN AUCTION COMMUNITY

This wide-ranging site offers anything from airline tickets
and holidays to cars, collectibles and electronics (in several
languages). The quality of merchandise seems better than most
sites. Another site worth checking out is **www.CQout.co.uk**
it has over 6,000 lots, a wide selection of categories and
a nice design.

## www.sothebys.com                                               UK/US

### QUALITY ASSURED

Details of their auctions and information on what they do,
plus you can buy catalogues and search for items that may
be coming up for sale.

## www.christies.com                                                 UK

### FOR THOSE WITH DEEP WALLETS

Christies have a classic site with info on their programme of
auctions and on how to buy and sell through them, but you
can't carry out transactions from the site. The LotFinder service
searches their auctions for that special item – for a fee.
There's also a good specialist bookstore and lots of information
on how to buy and sell.

## www.bid-up.tv/                                                    UK

### BID UP.TV

The site related to the digital TV show is a temperamental one.
On the face of it, it's easy to use and find the products you're
interested in, but it went down regularly when we used it.

A

## www.ad-mart.co.uk UK

AWARD WINNING
Excellent design and ease of use makes this site stand out;
there are fourteen sections, all the usual suspects plus personal
ads, boating and pets. See also **www.nettrader.co.uk** which is
also really well designed and easy to use.

## www.exchangeandmart.co.uk UK

*EXCHANGE & MART*
Everything the paper has and more – great bargains on a
massive range of goods found using a good search facility,
all packaged on a bright, easy-to-use site. It is split into three
major sections: home and leisure, motoring and business.

## www.loot.com UK

FREE ADS ONLINE
Over 75,000 ads make Loot a great place to go for a bargain.
It's an interesting site to browse with seventeen sections
covering the usual classified ad subjects supplemented by
areas featuring students, jobs, accommodation and personals.

# Beauty

*Beauty product retailers are popular on the Internet, so we've featured a few of the best ones for advice, help and shopping!*

## www.beautyconsumer.com                                        UK

### COMPLETE GUIDE TO SKIN CARE

An excellent web site with help and information on all forms of skin care as well as beauty tips and product information, there's even a section especially for men. Two people experienced in the field put it together and the information is very easy to access.

## www.avonshop.co.uk                                            UK

### SHOP WITHOUT THE DROP

A very good online shop from the traditional leaders in direct selling of cosmetics, with clear design and lots of offers.

## www.lookfantastic.com                                         UK

### LOOK FANTASTIC

Not as much fun as it was when it started, but it's still a well-designed online retailer offering some really good discounts, while shipping costs start at £2.50. It also offers advice guides on how to use make-up, shampoo and conditioners, in fact virtually everything a girl needs – it's war out there after all.

## www.fragrancenet.com                                          US

### WORLD'S LARGEST DISCOUNT FRAGRANCE STORE

A massive range of perfumes for men and women, every brand is represented and there are some excellent offers. However, the site is American with shipping costs from $19 dollars and more depending on what you buy. See also **www.perfumeshopping.com** who offer 1,000 perfumes and fragrances from a well-designed UK-based site and the eponymous **www.halfpriceperfumes.co.uk**

## www.directcosmetics.com                                       UK

### WIDE RANGE AND THE BEST PRICES

They claim to offer a wide range of perfumes with up to 90% off UK recommended retail prices plus other big brand name cosmetics. The site is quick and easy-to-use and the offers are genuine; however, delivery costs £3.95.

**B**

## www.avon.uk.com UK

AVON CALLING
A very good-looking and easy to use site with a wide range of cosmetics available, they also sell health products and lingerie, you can also have a chat in the café and learn about their campaign against breast cancer.

*See also:*
**www.allbeautyproducts.com** – excellent site from the Allcures camp.
**www.beautynaturals.com** – attractive all round beauty site.
**www.beautyserve.com** – home of the Guild of Professional Beauty Therapists
**www.beautyspy.com** – a German company with a nice site and a good range, all the prices are in Euros but it seems good value, watch out for the shipping costs though.
**www.benefitcosmetics.com** – trendy cosmetics from the US, worth it to be different…
**www.buycosmeticsdirect.com** – a wide range and lots of offers, jewellery as well as cosmetics.
**www.cosmetics.com** – American skincare specialists.
**www.creativenailplace.com** – specialist shop covering nail art and beauty.
**www.magicmakeup.co.uk** – great for special offers
**www.makeupalley.com** – reviews, chat and products all on make-up.
**www.perfuma.com** – another shop with a wide range of perfumes, gifts and beauty products, and a good men's section.
**www.skinstore.com** – good-looking US site selling premium skincare products.

## Hair

## www.ukhairdressers.com UK

HAIR STYLES DATABASE
Some 1000 styles illustrated including celebrity styles and virtual makeovers, also with advice and fortune telling.

*See also:*
**www.folica.com** – great US site on hair care.
**www.salonweb.com** – hair care products and advice.

# The High Street online

## www.bodyshop.co.uk                                                        UK

> ISSUES, SELF-ESTEEM AND COSMETICS
> Balancing the rights of the under-privileged with the demands
> of a commercial cosmetics company. There is good product
> information but you can't buy online.

## www.lush.co.uk                                                            UK

> SOAP WITHOUT THE SCENT
> Lush offer a wide range of soaps and associated products from
> their site, it's easy to shop and if you like their soap but find the
> smell of the high street shops overpowering, then it's perfect.
> Postage & packing starts at £3.95.
>
> *See also:*
> **www.spacenk.co.uk** – nicely designed store featuring their
> excellent cosmetics.
> **www.wellbeing.com** – strong offering from Boots, easier to
> shop than the real store!

# *Blogging*

*Keeping a web log or 'Blog' is one of the more recent Internet crazes;
it allows you to effectively set up your own site cheaply and to a high
standard. Its commonest form is that of an online diary covering a
specific interest, usually with lots of links to related web sites. Pages are
added chronologically and there's usually a facility for visitors to leave
comments; some blogs are very informative and entertaining. They are
particularly useful for keeping up to date with friends and family.
Here are some sites that can help you on your way and give you all
the advice you're likely to need.*

## www.blogger.com                                                          US

> THE MOST POPULAR
> The original Blogger's site, now owned by Google, it's easy-
> to-use and free, there are step-by-step instructions and plenty
> of support.

*Other sites and software to help you on your way:*

**http://radio.userland.com** – easy-to-use and with lots of features, software for those lacking technical skills.

**www.20six.co.uk** – here you can even send photos to your blog via a mobile, the site is nicely designed but it won't stay free for long.

**www.blogarama.com** – a directory of around 1,000 blogs.

**www.blogwise.com** – a directory of over 14,000 blogs.

**www.livejournal.com** – the most straight forward and communal of the blogging systems, now with over 2 million users.

**www.mac.com** – home of iBlog, an expensive but slick way of blogging for Apple Macs only.

**www.moveabletype.org** – one for the more advanced user, but if you take the time to learn how to use it, it will offer some features for customising your blog.

**www.onlineblog.com** – from the *Guardian*, a blog covering the latest in technology and the Internet.

# Books and Booksellers

*Books were the first products to be sold in volume over the Internet, and their success has meant that there are many online booksellers, all boasting about the speed of their service and how many titles they can get. In the main, the basic service is the same wherever you go, just pick the bookshop that suits you.*

### www.bookbrain.co.uk                                   UK

BEST PRICES FOR BOOKS

All you do is type in the title of the book and Bookbrain will search out the online store that is offering it the cheapest (including postage). You then click again to get taken to the store to buy the book – simple. It's also worth checking out the American site **www.bestbookbuys.com** and **www.booktracker.co.uk** who offer a similar service.

### www.books.co.uk                                       UK

THE BOOKSHOPS RATED

An overview of online booksellers and their service rated, it's great for links and a good way to find a specialist. See also **www.book-shops.net** which is more of a directory.

# Booksellers

## www.amazon.co.uk                                                    UK

### MORE THAN JUST A BOOKSTORE
Amazon is the leading online bookseller and most online
stores have followed their formula of combining value with
recommendation. Amazon has spent much on providing a
wider offering than just books and now has sections for music,
gifts, travel, games, software and DVD/video. It also offers an
auction service, there's an excellent kids' section aimed at
parents, and you can download e-books to read on your PC or
handheld computer. It also offers used goods for sale via third
party retailers which can offer great value for money. For books,
there are better prices elsewhere, although they have the odd
very good offer. See also **www.waterstones.co.uk** who have
abandoned their site in favour of Amazon, as has Borders
**www.borders.com**

## www.bol.com                                                        UK

### THE EURO-BOOKSELLER
Owned by Bertlesmann the German media giant, you can get
access to books in seven European countries. Slightly dull,
it appeals to the true book lover with lots of recommendations,
although it has plenty of offers. Like Amazon it has expanded
to include music, video, DVD and games.

## www.ottakars.co.uk                                                 UK

### E-MAIL A BOOKSTORE
Ottakars' site is clear and easy to use with some nice personal
touches; it offers a mix of store information, recommendation,
competitions and they offer free online magazines on a variety
of genres that are very entertaining. There's a web page for
each store giving information on the locale and events, and
while there are no facilities to buy books from the site,
unusually you can e-mail your local store to see if they have
the book you want.

B

## http://bookshop.blackwell.co.uk                                    UK

### NOT JUST FOR ACADEMICS AND THE SERIOUS MINDED

Blackwells are best known for academic and professional books, but their site offers much more, with the emphasis on recommendation and help finding the right book rather than value for money; however, free delivery on orders over £25. For more academic books, a good place to try is **www.studentbookworld.com**

## www.swotbooks.co.uk                                                UK

### LOW COST BOOKS FOR CLEVER DICKS

A fun bookshop aimed at students that offers DVDs and music too. It also has one of the best e-book shops around. The site could be made easier to navigate though.

## www.countrybookshop.co.uk                                          UK

### YOUR LOCAL BOOKSHOP

It may not offer the cheapest books, but it's easier and more enjoyable to use than many sites and there's free delivery on orders over £25.

## www.greenmetropolis.com                                            UK

### GOING GREEN

An interesting take on the bookselling theme, here all (mainly good condition second hand) books are one price and there's a donation towards planting a tree. You can sell your books at this site too. Great idea, we hope it catches on.

## www.bn.com                                                         UK

### THE WORLD'S BIGGEST BOOKSELLER

Barnes and Noble's site boasts more books than any other online bookseller. In style it follows the other bookshops with an American bias, and looks very similar to Amazon. It has a good out-of-print service; you can also buy software, prints and posters as well as magazines and music. Unusual features include an online university where you can take courses in anything from business to learning a language.

## www.powells.com
US

MASSIVE

A huge and impressive site which is well designed and relatively easy to use, Powells seems to occupy most of Portland in Oregon and for once the cost of shipping isn't prohibitive for UK customers. A good place to go if you're looking for something unusual.

## www.bookpeople.co.uk
UK

INCREDIBLE DISCOUNTS

Offers a limited range of discounted books with up to 75% off the r.r.p. It's strong on children's titles and certain types of fiction, but low on recommendations. Some books vary from shop editions – using cheaper paper or are paperback editions. Delivery is free if you spend over £25, plus point-based loyalty scheme.

## http://bookclubsuk.com
UK

BOOK CLUBS

Basically a guide to some 35 book clubs, how to join and get the best out of them. The site is pretty basic but is easily navigable.

# Specialist booksellers and sites

*The following sites specialise in one form or genre of book:*
**www.compman.co.uk** – computer manuals.
**www.crimetime.co.uk** – good overview of what's going on in the crime fiction world.
**www.dancebooks.co.uk** – if you need a book on dance here's where to start.
**www.firstbookshop.com** – one of the few to offer book tokens.
**www.gamblingbooks.co.uk** – excellent selection from the High Stakes bookshop.
**www.poems.com** – home of Poetry Daily.
**www.poetrybooks.co.uk** – the poetry book society.
**www.soccer-books.co.uk** – features over 1,000 books on football.
**www.stanfords.co.uk** – excellent site from the UK's leading travel and map retailers.

# Second hand books and book finding

**www.abebooks.com**                                              UK

ADVANCED BOOK EXCHANGE
A network of some 12,000 independent booksellers from
around the world claiming access to 50 million used, rare, and
out-of-print books; just use the excellent search engine to find
your book and they'll direct you to the nearest bookseller.

**www.booklovers.co.uk**                                          UK

QUALITY SECOND HAND BOOKS
If you can't find the book you want, then this is worth a try.
There is an excellent search facility or you can leave them a
request. They will then give you a quote if you want to sell a
book or arrange a swap. There's also an events listing for
book fairs.

*See also:*
**www.bibliofind.com** – a search engine from Amazon devoted
to second hand and rare books.
**www.bookfinder.com** – a more detailed search facility than
Bibliofind and you can use it in French, German and Italian.
**www.hp-bookfinders.co.uk** – UK-based book finding service
with an easy to use site.
**www.shapero.com** – a specialist in natural history and travel-
related second-hand books.

# Audio books

**www.audiobooks.co.uk**                                          UK

THE TALKING BOOKSHOP
Specialists in books on tape, they have around 6,000 titles in
stock and can quickly get another 10,000. They also stock CDs
but no MP3s yet. Search the site by author or reader, as well
as by title. There are some offers, but most stock is at full
price with delivery being £2 per order. Also uses the address
**www.talkingbooks.co.uk**. See also **www.isis-publishing.co.uk**
who have thousands of unabridged audio books, and more in
the way of CDs.

*See also:*
**www.audiobooksforfree.com** – well they're not all free and the site is quite slow, but there's a good deal of choice.
**www.payperlisten.com** – a pay as you go service which saves a huge amount on the usual audio book formats.

# E-books

**www.free-ebooks.net**                                                        US
### E-BOOKS FOR FREE
A straightforward site devoted to making the most of free e-books with recommendations and the encouragement to produce your own e-book.

*See also:*
**http://digitalmediastore.adobe.com** – lots available but you have to have the Adobe reader to access them.
**www.bartleby.com/ebook** – lots of classics and other free books to choose from.
**www.fictionwise.com** – a massive range of e-books to choose from non-fiction as well as fiction and they seem to cover all the formats too.
**www.netlibrary.com** – awkward to use but a huge selection.

# Literature and authors

**http://promo.net/pg/**                                                        US

### PROJECT GUTENBERG
This is one of the most famous Internet projects ever and one of the first web sites to post free e-books. There are over 6,000 listed. You can't do it justice in a small review, suffice to say it's well worth a visit for any book lover. If you're hooked on it, then there is the chance to become a volunteer proof-reader too.

*See also:*
**http://onlinebooks.library.upenn.edu** – over 20,000 books to download with a huge bias towards American titles, it's especially strong on history.
**www.questia.com** – claiming to be the world's biggest online library with over 47,000 books and 370,000 journals and other articles, you have to subscribe though some content is free.

**www.literature-awards.com**                                    US

BOOK AWARDS
A comprehensive listing of the major book awards throughout
the world, who won them and why they exist.

**http://classics.mit.edu**                                      US

THE CLASSICS ONLINE
A superb resource offering over 440 free books to print or
download, there's also a search facility and help with studying.
See also **www.bibliomania.com**

**www.shakespeare.sk**                                           UK

COMPLETE WORKS
This is a straightforward site featuring the complete writings of
Shakespeare, including biographical details and a glossary
explaining the language of the time.

*See also:*
**www.bronte.org.uk** – home of the Parsonage Museum in
Haworth with information about the place and an overview of
the Brontes and their lives.
**www.dickensmuseum.com** – home of the Dickens Museum in
London with details about what you can see and links.
**www.janeausten.co.uk** – the Jane Austen Centre in Bath with
a good online magazine offering information on everything from
fashion to biographical details.
**www.hardysociety.org** – The Thomas Hardy Society with good
contextual links.
**www.lang.nagoya-u.ac.jp/~matsuoka/Bronte.html** – all you
need to know about the Bronte sisters and more.
**www.mss.library.nottingham.ac.uk/dhl_home.html** –
D H Lawrence resources at The University of Nottingham.
**www.pemberley.com** – a pretty obsessive site devoted to
everything Jane Austen with discussion groups too.
**www.yale.edu/hardysoc** – award winning site on
Thomas Hardy.

# Reading Groups

## www.bookgroup.info                                           UK

READING GROUP GUIDE
An attractive and informative site on how run a book group and
choose titles with an archive of titles and how they've rated
them. There's also a forum and a directory is promised.

*See also:*
**http://readers.penguin.co.uk** – run by Penguin books you can
get discounts for your group and use the directory, but you have
to register first.
**www.readinggroupguides.com** – an American site offering
information and guidance on books and how to run a
reading group.
**www.readinggroups.co.uk** – a neat site run by publisher
Harper Collins with news, advice and competitions.

# Children's books

## www.cool-reads.co.uk                                        UK

CHILDREN'S BOOK REVIEWS
Books for 10- to 15-year olds, reviewed by 10- to 15-year olds.
An outstanding site both for its design and content. The books
are well categorised and reviewed using a star rating system.
If you're stuck for something to read, then a trip here is well
worthwhile. There are also games, quizzes and chat.

## www.achuka.co.uk                                            UK

CHILDREN'S BOOKS
Achuka are specialists in children's books and offer a
comprehensive listing of what's available. There's plenty of
information on the latest news and awards as well as reviews,
author interviews, a chat section and links to booksellers.
For shopping you are directed to Amazon.

*Other children's book sites:*
**www.carolhurst.com** – good design and great for book reviews.
**www.centreforthechildrensbook.org.uk** – opening in 2005
in Newcastle.
**www.childrensbookshop.com** – very traditional site from
a shop based in Hay on Wye.

B

**www.ucalgary.ca/~dkbrown/** – home of the excellent Children's Literature Web Guide.

**www.ukchildrensbooks.co.uk** – basically a list of links to sites listed by author, illustrator, publisher and a miscellaneous section.

**www.usbourne.com** – good interactive site from this specialist publisher.

**www.wordpool.co.uk** – good advice on what to read.

**www.wordsofdiscovery.com** – a children's bookshop that stocks books aimed at giving children a positive and more spiritual view on life.

**www.worldbookday.com** – find out about this great event that happens every March.

## Resources for writers

### www.author.co.uk                                    UK

FOR AUTHORS EVERYWHERE

A good place to start if you think you've got a book in you (haven't we all?) with sections, articles and links to help. Worth a visit even for experienced authors. With a slightly messy site **www.writersservices.com** offers just as much, if not more, help and advice.

*See also:*

**www.thenewwriter.com** – online magazine for writers.

**www.theromancereader.com** – lots of romantic reviews and links.

## Best publisher websites

**www.bloomsbury.com** – home of Harry Potter and the Scott's Miscellany's.

**www.dk.com** – excellent site from one of the leading reference publishers, some good offers too.

**www.harpercollins.co.uk** – a wide ranging site from the publishers of this book with sections on Tolkein and plenty of celebrities as well as fiction and reference.

**www.madaboutbooks.co.uk** – a cool site from Hodder Headline.

**www.penguin.co.uk** – a bright and breezy site from Penguin with plenty to see, information on author events and readers groups too.

**www.randomhouse.co.uk** – nice design but unreliable site from one of the biggest publishers.

## Other book-related sites worth checking out

**www.bookaid.org**                                            UK

BOOKS FOR CHARITY
A charity dedicated to giving unwanted books to places where
books are scarce and needed. Find out about their activities and
how you can get involved.

**www.bookcrossing.com**                                       UK

RELEASE A BOOK
Step 1 – read your book, Step 2 – say what you think about the
book on the site with a reference number, Step 3 – release the
book, give it to a friend or leave it somewhere. You can then get
e-mails from anyone who reads the book.

# *Broadband*

*As access to ADSL or broadband becomes common, more and
more sites are cropping up to cater for those lucky enough to
have it. Here are some useful sites where you can start your
broadband experience.*

**www.broadband-help.com**                                     UK

ALL YOU NEED TO KNOW
A good place to start, here you'll find advice and reviews all
dedicated to help you make the most out of your broadband
experience. See also **www.adslguide.org.uk**, which is just as
informative albeit from a less attractive site.

**www.broadbandchecker.co.uk**                                 UK

BROADBAND AVAILABILITY
A neat and easy to use site; you just type in your postcode and
phone number and the site will tell you whether broadband
is available in your area. You can also compare providers'
prices too.

B

## www.siteforsites.com                                          US
### BROADBAND SEARCH
A simple search engine devoted to those sites that are aimed at broadband users, it's very easy to use and it's well categorised.

## www.dslreports.com                                            US
### SITE REVIEWS
A horrible site to use but it features hundreds of broadband sites with reviews, some of which are quite amusing.
See also **www.razav.com** for a great selection of sites.

## www.broadbandweek.com                                         UK
### ALL THE LATEST DEVELOPMENTS
Keep abreast of all the latest technology and increasing download speeds at this business-like site.

## www.broadband-television.com                                  US
### STREAMING TV
A huge range of channels available to view including music as well as TV, you have to download the free software but the results are generally worth the effort – it's the choosing that is the difficult part.

*Other sites worth checking out are:*
**www.broadband4britain.co.uk** – information from this broadband pressure group.
**www.bt.com/broadband** – all the latest from British Telecom.
**www.low-cost-broadband.com** – find the best deal in your area.

# Cars

*Whether you want to buy a car, check out your insurance or even arrange a service, it can all be done on the Net. If you want to hire a car see page 471.*

## Motoring organisations

**www.dvla.gov.uk**                                                    UK

DRIVER AND VEHICLE LICENSING AGENCY
Excellent for the official line in motoring, the driver's section has details on penalty points, licence changes and medical issues. The vehicles section goes through all related forms and there's also a 'What's New' page. It's clearly and concisely written throughout and information is easy to find.

**www.rmif.co.uk**                                                     UK

RETAIL MOTOR INDUSTRY FEDERATION
A rich source of information covering all aspects of buying and selling cars for both industry and consumers alike. It's great as a starting place if you want to find out about legislation and the latest news, it also has an excellent links section.

**www.smmt.co.uk**                                                     UK

SOCIETY OF MOTOR MANUFACTURERS & TRADERS
The SMMT support the British motor industry by campaigning and informing the trade and public alike. Here you can get information on topics like the motor show and the tax regime based on exhaust emissions, as well as links to other industry sites.

**www.theaa.co.uk**                                                    UK

THE AA
A very comprehensive motoring site with a route planner, new and used car info, travel information, insurance quotes, shop and a car data checking facility.

**www.rac.co.uk**                                                      UK

THE RAC
A much clearer site than the AA's, with a very good route planner and traffic news service. There's also information about buying a car, getting the best finance and insurance deals and a small shop.

**www.greenflag.co.uk**                                              UK

GREEN FLAG

The usual route planner and car buying advice all packaged on a nice-looking and very green site, there's a particularly good section on European travel and motoring advice. Arranging a quote for breakdown cover is quite complicated. See also **www.internationalbreakdown.com** who offer a wide range of cover across the UK and Europe.

# Car information and buying guides

**www.autoindex.org**                                               US

WORLD CAR CATALOGUE

An amazing directory of the world's car makers illustrated by some 35,000 pictures. There is detailed information on each manufacturer and what they produce. You can search by maker, country, category or body style.

**www.carsurvey.org**

CAR REVIEWS BY THEIR OWNERS                                          UK

Don't let the basic design fool you, this is an impressive collection of reviews on hundreds of cars, by those most important people – their owners. It's easily searchable and genuinely useful if you're looking for unbiased opinion.

**www.carkeys.co.uk**                                               UK

INFORMATION SERVICE STATION

A wide-ranging magazine-style site with lots of data on current and new models as well as launch reviews and motoring news.

**www.carnet.co.uk**

ONLINE CAR MAGAZINE                                                 UK

Car Net is a well designed and fun site with the latest news and new car reviews as well as feature micro-sites and links to deals on cars and insurance, statistics (on over 6,000 cars) and classifieds. You can also visit the specialist forums and have a go at the trivia quizzes.

C

## www.hoot-uk.com    UK

IT'S A HOOT!

A fun, simple site with a marque-by-marque news listing and the latest headlines. There are also sections with car tests, some good writing and chat at the aptly named 'Gas Station'.

## www.womanmotorist.com    US

MOTORING ISN'T JUST FOR MEN

A well laid out and interesting magazine-style site that dispels the myth that motoring is just for men. Lots of advice, buying information, a glossary and car reviews.

## www.parkers.co.uk    UK

REDUCING THE GAMBLE

The premier buying guide with a premier site, this covers all the information you'll need to select the right car for you. There are five sections: Pricing – a complete list of cars from 1982 and what you should be paying. Choosing – advice on the right car for you. Buying – with details of used cars and finance deals. Guides – consumer guides on insurance, warranties, breaking down, MOTs, etc. Advice – legal, important contacts and chat. See also **www.glass.co.uk** who offer similar information but their site is poor.

# Magazine sites

## www.autoexpress.co.uk    UK

THE BEST MOTORING NEWS AND INFORMATION

Massive database on cars, with motoring news and features on the latest models, you can check prices too. It also has classified ads and a great set of links. You have to register to get access to most of the information; lots of advertising makes the site a bit annoying to use.

## www.whatcar.co.uk    UK

*WHAT CAR* MAGAZINE

A neatly packaged, one-stop shop for cars with sections on buying, selling, news, features and road tests, there's a cars for sale section and an easy-to-use search facility.

### www.autocarmag.com                                      UK

*AUTOCAR* MAGAZINE
A fine site from this popular weekly with plenty of interactive
features including videos and even a blogging service, there are
news, reviews, advice and shopping too.

## TV tie-in sites

### www.topgear.beeb.com                                     UK

TOP GEAR
A new look site to go along with the new TV series, it has
everything you'd expect along with features on new and
used cars, competitions, classifieds and a shop. See also
**www.bbc.co.uk/lifestyle/motoring/** which is great for advice
on buying and owning.

### www.4car.co.uk                                           UK

DRIVEN
News, sport, reviews, advice, chat and games – it's all here,
and you can find out what's been and is being featured on their
main motoring programmes.

## Traders and car finding services

### www.motortrak.com                                        UK

USED CAR SEARCH
A hi-tech site where, in theory, you can find the right used car.
Just follow the search guidelines and up pops your ideal car!
It's easy to use and very fast.

### www.autobytel.co.uk                                     US/UK

WORLD'S LEADING CAR BUYING SERVICE
The easy way to buy a car online, just select the model you
want then follow the online instructions, they've improved
information on used and nearly new cars and will get quotes
from local dealers. All cars featured have detailed descriptions
and photos. There's also financial information and
aftercare service.

## www.oneswoop.co.uk
UK

SMART WAY TO BUY

A straightforward and very popular site that concentrates on making the process of buying a car as painless as possible, you can choose a car through one of three methods: buy what's available quickly; have a bit more choice; or be really picky. There are also some good special offers and a finance section.

## www.jamjar.com
UK

DIRECT LINE

One of the most hyped sites for car buying, Jam Jar is a big investment for Direct Line Insurance and they want to make it work well. The design is OK, and if you persevere there are some fantastic offers. They're also improving the service by branching into other merchandise related to driving, such as personal leasing and insurance.

*For more car buying information and cars for sale try:*
**http://uk.cars.yahoo.com** – the excellent Yahoo has a used car search engine, car comparison facility and directory.
**www.autolocate.co.uk** – great for links, good new car guide and review section, also good for used cars.
**www.autolocate.co.uk** – Ireland's leading online car retailer and auction house.
**www.autoseek.co.uk** – thousands of cars for sale, great for links.
**www.autotrader.co.uk** – claiming to be Britain's biggest car showroom with 260,000 listed. Nice, clear design.
**www.broadspeed.com** – car import specialists with a nicely designed and fast site.
**www.carseller.co.uk** – free advertising if selling and good links.
**www.carsource.co.uk** – great for data and online quotes, lots of cars for sale.
**www.carsupermarkets.co.uk** – a useful list of the UK's car supermarkets with lots of information and how to find them.
**www.cartalk.com** – a good US magazine site.
**www.contracthireandleasing.co.uk** – a portal site for all the UK's contact and leasing companies.
**www.eurekar.com** – lots of deals from this specialist importer.
**www.fish4cars.co.uk** – over 150,000 cars on their database, plus hundreds of other vehicles. Comprehensive.
**www.new-car-net.co.uk** – informative and well illustrated car review site.

**www.savemoneyoncars.co.uk** – bright and breezy site with lots of deals and information on buying a car cheaply.

**www.showroom4cars.com** – bright, brash and fast.

**www.topmarques.co.uk** – luxury vehicles only, some 6,000 for sale.

**www.vanbuy.co.uk** – vans and more vans of all shapes and sizes.

**www.virgincars.com** – good savings and speedy delivery and nice design.

**www.wannavan.com** – specialist in supplying vans for business and personal use.

## www.carpricecheck.com                                    UK

WHERE TO GET THE BEST DEAL

If you can't be bothered with trawling around the different car dealers, just put in the model you want and after you've given a few details 'Car price Check' will get back to you with the best deal. See also the car price checker at **www.uk.kelkoo.com**

## www.hpicheck.com                                         UK

DON'T BE RIPPED OFF...

Before you buy a second-hand car it's wise to pay out £35.95 on an HPI check, which will tell you about what mileage the car should have, whether it's been in an accident or damaged and also if there's any outstanding finance against it.

## www.ukstolencars.co.uk                                   UK

ARE YOU DRIVING A STOLEN CAR?

A simple and free search of the UK stolen cars database offering helpful information and advice.

# For disabled motorists

## www.ddmc.org.uk                                          UK

DISABLED DRIVERS MOTOR CLUB

A campaigning site from the DDMC who are devoted to improving the lot of disabled motorists. It has lots of useful information and you can find out about and support their latest campaigns. See also **www.dda.org.uk** home of the Disabled Drivers Association who work along the same lines.

**www.motability.co.uk**    UK

GET MOBILE
A scheme for helping disabled people get mobile by contract
hiring a car, the site is very clear and easy to use too.

*See also:*

**www.aixam.co.uk** – a leading supplier of quadricycles and
adapted cars.

**www.dft.gov.uk** – the Department for Transport.

**www.motability.royalsun.co.uk/fullsite/index.html** –
a motability scheme from an insurance company.

# Cheaper and greener fuels

**www.est-powershift.org.uk**    UK

CONVERTING TO CLEANER FUELS
A well put together and informative site aimed at encouraging
drivers to shift to cleaner fuels such as LPG, you can find
out how to convert your car, where the fuel stations are and
the latest government information such as grants and
future proposals.

**www.spongecars.com**    UK

LPG CONVERSIONS
Excellent overview and information site covering all aspects
of converting a car to LPG, an explanation of what it is,
how to get a conversion quote and the latest news.

*See also:*

**www.bath.ac.uk/~en2bwp/gaspower.htm** – learn about
gas-powered cars.

**www.evuk.co.uk** – not just milk floats and golf carts,
it's serious stuff, the electric car business.

**www.lpga.co.uk** – information from the Liquid Petroleum
Gas Association.

**www.toyota.co.uk/prius** – home of the successful hybrid
electrical petrol car.

# Car registrations

**www.dvla-som.co.uk**                                                           UK

CHERISHED AND PERSONALISED NUMBERS
Here's the first port of call if you want that special number
plate. They sell by auction but there's plenty of help and you
search for un-issued, select registrations in both new and old
styles. Order over the phone using their hotline.

*For more sites try:*
**www.alotofnumberplates.co.uk** – good search engine,
over 5 million combinations.
**www.statreg.co.uk** – lots of cheap plates.
**www.newreg.co.uk** – the first online directory of cherished
registration marks.

# Insurance

*Most of the general finance sites (page 121) and motoring
organisations (page 53) will offer links to insurance companies,
but these are worth a try.*

**www.easycover.com**                                                            UK

CAR INSURANCE
Quotes from a large number of insurance suppliers, you just fill
in the form, and they get back to you with a quote.

*See also:*
**www.cheapest-motor-insurance.co.uk**
**www.eaglestar.co.uk**
**www.swinton.co.uk**
**www.diamond.co.uk** and **www.girlmotor.co.uk** – specialists in
insurance for women drivers who are statistically a safer bet.

# Looking after and repairing your car

**www.ukmot.com**                                                                UK

M.O.T.
Find your nearest M.O.T. test centre, get facts about the test
and what's actually supposed to be checked, there's also a
reminder service. You can also run an HPI check from the site
and find out about the foibles of specific models.

**www.carcareclinic.com**                                    UK

LOOKING AFTER YOUR CAR
If you need advice with car repairs or faults, then help is at
hand here. There are discussion forums on all sorts of problems
and, if you post a message or ask for advice, there's always
someone to answer. They also provide a glossary of terms and
a good set of links. See also **www.autosite.com/garage/
garmenu.asp**, which is from a large American site, here you
can find a maintenance encyclopaedia.

**www.haynes.co.uk**                                         UK

HAYNES MANUALS
Unfortunately they've stopped the download service, so now
you have to buy the books – there's 2,500 available so there
should be one for you.

## Car accessories and kits

**www.halfords.com**                                         UK

DRIVING DOWN PRICES
A fairly wide range of products for your car and bike at good
prices and sold from a very good site, there's advice and a store
locator too.

**www.autofashion.co.uk**                                    UK

ACCESSORISE YOUR CAR
An entertaining site where you can buy body kits and
accessories for many makes of car, including custom made.

**www.modify.co.uk**                                         UK

COMPREHENSIVE LISTING SERVICE
An outstanding source for information on those companies that
can help you improve your car. There's a directory of specialists
– everything from tuners to insurance, articles on how to
modify your motor and lastly statistics on virtually every
modern car.

*See also:*
**www.autostore.co.uk** – specialists in car storage solutions,
slow site though.
**www.caralarms-security.co.uk** – every type of car alarm and
security device.

C

**www.gttowing.co.uk** – for tow bars, roof racks and trailers, good site.

**www.motech.uk.com** – specialists in performance enhancement.

**www.roofbox.co.uk** – roof boxes and most other storage solutions.

**www.saveanddrive.co.uk** – another storage specialist.

## www.caraudiocentre.com
UK

### IN CAR AUDIO SYSTEMS

Here you can get loads of advice and offers on a wide range of stereos with a price promise and low delivery costs.

See also **www.toade.com** who have a highly interactive site and can also supply security, multi-media and navigation equipment on top of audio, and **www.incar-discount.co.uk** who specialise in CD changers.

# Specialist car sites

## www.classicmotor.co.uk
UK

### FOR CLASSIC CARS

By far the best classic car site. Design wise it's a jumble (it's better to use the no frames version), but it's comprehensive, including clubs, classifieds and books; here you can buy anything from a car to a headlight bulb.

*See also:*

**www.classic-car-directory.com** – which is a well categorised links site.

**www.hireaclassiccar.com** – classic car hire specialist.

**www.kitcar.com** – US-oriented and a messy site, but a huge amount of information.

**www.kit-cars.com** – home of *Kit Cars* magazine.

**www.kitcars.org** – UK site being redeveloped at time of our visit.

**www.motorbase.com** – a growing site with lots of potential, good for links but a little slow.

**www.vintage-car-world.com** – a German-owned site offering news, event information and classifieds.

**www.pistonheads.com**                                          UK

SPEED MATTERS
Pistonheads is a British site dedicated to the faster side of
motoring and is great for reviews of the latest cars and chat.
It's passionate and very informative.

**www.krbaker.demon.co.uk/britcars**                             UK

HISTORY OF BRITISH CARS TO 1960
An amateur site with a good make-by-make history of the
British car industry, it includes a glossary and information on
tax and other historical references. Unfortunately it's not
well illustrated.

**www.conceptcar.co.uk**                                         UK

AUTOMOTIVE DESIGN
A really interesting, comprehensive and well laid out site
devoted to car design and new concepts, it's great for links
and you can tell that it's used by the industry itself.

# Learning to drive

**www.learners.co.uk**                                           UK

LEARNER'S DIRECTORY
The point of this site is to help you find the right driving school,
just type in your postcode and the schools will be listed along
with helpful additional information such as whether they have a
female instructor or that they train for motorway driving. There
is plenty of supplementary information on things like theory
tests and how to buy a car.

**www.2pass.co.uk**                                              UK

THEORY AND PRACTICAL TESTS
A learner driver's dream, this site helps with your tests in giving
advice, mock exams plus other interesting snippets of
information such as why the British drive on the left. There are
also articles on driving abroad, on motorbikes and driving
automatics. There's also plenty of fun with top stories, quizzes
and crash of the month.

C

### www.driving-tests.co.uk                                    UK
THE DSA
Get the official line from the Driving Standards Agency where
you can book an online driving theory test, get advice for
learners and instructors and learn about government schemes
to promote better driving. For the Highway Code faithfully
reproduced as a website and more theory tests go to
**www.highwaycode.gov.uk**

*See also:*
**www.bsm.co.uk** – one of the UK biggest driving schools.
**www.iam.org.uk** – home of the Institute Of Advanced Motorists.
**www.roadcode.co.uk** – Highway Code for young people.

## Driving issues

### www.speed-trap.co.uk                                      UK
THE SPEED TRAP BIBLE
While not condoning speeding, this site gives the low down on
speed traps, the law and links to police forces. There's even
data on the types of cameras used and advice on dealing with
the courts and police. However, remember that they are
sponsored by a speed trap detector company. See also
**www.speedcamerasuk.com**

### www.parkingticket.co.uk                                   UK
PARKING PROBLEMS
This site gives details regarding parking regulations and free
advice on how to challenge a parking ticket that you feel has
been issued unfairly. For those wanting up-to-date information
on how to keep one step ahead of over-zealous parking
attendants, there is a free monthly e-zine.

### www.abd.org.uk                                            UK
CAMPAIGNING FOR THE DRIVER
The Association of British Drivers aims to be the lobbying voice
of beleaguered drivers in the UK. Here you can find out
about their campaigns against speed traps, speed limits,
the environment and the road infrastructure.

**www.vosa.gov.uk**                                    UK
> VEHICLE AND OPERATOR SERVICES AGENCY
> A government body covering all aspects of the Traffic Area
> Network and the Vehicle Inspectorate, it also has links to other
> government campaigns and transport related bodies. See also
> **www.dft.gov.uk**

C

**www.rospa.co.uk/cms/**                               UK
> ROYAL SOCIETY FOR THE PREVENTION OF ACCIDENTS
> An excellent site from ROSPA with loads of information about
> road safety with fact sheets available on most issues and
> problems that affect every driver and pedestrian. See also
> **www.cic.cranfield.ac.uk** where all the crash testing goes on.

**www.reportroadrage.co.uk**                           UK
> ROAD RAGE ISSUES
> A site supported by the RAC that looks into every aspect of road
> rage, including its causes and how to prevent it. There's lots of
> advice, stories and information to help you become a safer and
> calmer driver.

**www.secureyourmotor.gov.uk**                         UK
> SECURITY TIPS FOR MOTORISTS
> Pretty straightforward site detailing the best steps to guard
> against your car, bike or truck being stolen. You can take tests
> to see how secure your car is or test your security knowledge.

**www.cclondon.com**                                   UK
> LONDON CONGESTION CHARGES
> All you need to know about the congestion charge and how
> to pay it.

# Celebrities

*Find your favourite celebrities and their web sites using these sites.*
*A word of caution though – there are many celebrity search engines*
*available on the web and while it's easy to find your favourite,*
*it's also very easy to unwittingly access adult-orientated material*
*through them.*

C

### www.celeblink.com                                          US

LINKS TO THE STARS

Just about the best celebrity directory in terms of lack of advertising and dodgy links. There are also some good articles, gossip and entertainment news.

### www.celebhoo.com                                          US

FOR EVERYTHING CELEBRITY

A very good fan site directory plus information, birthdays, chat and gossip.

### www.thespiannet.com                                        UK

ACTORS AND ACTRESSES

Lots of actors and actresses listed with links and details including e-mail addresses. It's also a good resource for aspiring thespians.

*See also:*
**www.celebrity-link.com** – nearly 9,000 celebrities listed.
**www.celebsites.com** – huge listing of some 20,000 celeb sites.

### www.celebrityemail.com                                     US

E-MAIL THE STARS

E-mail addresses to over 22,000 of the world's most famous people. It's quite biased towards Americans but give it a try anyway, you might get a reply.

### www.debretts.co.uk                                         UK

POSH CELEBRITY GOSSIP

An excellent site from Debretts who have been tracking the lives of celebrities for many years longer than the likes of *OK* and *Hello*. There are sections on people in the news plus a good celebrity search engine. There are also sections on the royal family, a guide to the season, charities and a fun search section where you can match birthdays.

### www.hellomagazine.com                                      UK

THE WORLD IN PICTURES

Hello magazine's web site features pictures and articles from current and previous issues with loads of celebrities. You can't search by celebrity but you can have fun trawling through the pictures.

## www.eonline.com                                    US

E!
Entertainment Online features all the latest gossip mainly
oriented towards the US and Hollywood in particular.
It's fun and irreverent and has a reputation for being first with
the news.

## www.glamourmagazine.co.uk                          UK

LOSE YOURSELF IN GLAMOUR
Gossip, fashion, beauty tips, chat, competitions and, of course,
celebrities are the mainstay of *Glamour* magazine's site.
Its main function though is to plug the real magazine.

## www.famousnamechanges.com                          US

WHO WAS WHO
Find out what name celebrities where born with and what
they changed it to – great for trivia quizzes.

## www.amiannoyingornot.com                           US

VOTE FOR MOST ANNOYING CELEBRITIES
You can spend ages on this site; it's easy to vote and fun to
use. Each celeb gets a page with biographical details and
reasons why they could be annoying or not…

## www.mugshots.com                                    US

WHEN IT ALL GOES WRONG
This could only happen in America, see mug shots of the
rich and famous when, once in a while, they break the law.
There's also a serious side with sections covering national
US events and the FBI's most-wanted list. Ghoulish but
fascinating too.

## www.thesmokinggun.com                               US

FINDING THE SLEAZE – ALLEGEDLY
Devoted to finding skeletons in cupboards, Smoking Gun
has everything from confidential documents and incriminating
evidence to mug shots. If your favourite celeb has done
something wrong, even a small thing, it'll be here.

### www.bbc.co.uk/celebdaq
UK

CELEBRITY STOCK EXCHANGE
The BBC's Celebrity Stock Exchange show now lives on in the form of this website. It monitors the rise and fall of many celebrities and allocates a stock 'price' to them – it's fun to see who's on the up and who's on the slide. See also the Hollywood Stock Exchange at **www.hsx.com**

# Charities

*The Internet offers a great opportunity to give to your favourite charity or support a cause dear to your heart. There are so many that we're unable to list them all, but here are some top sites with directories to help you find the ones that interest you. For charity cards see page 199 and for health-related charities see page 206.*

## Charity information

### www.charitychoice.co.uk
UK

ENCYCLOPAEDIA OF CHARITIES
A very useful and well-put together directory of charities with a good search facility and a list in over 30 categories. There's also the excellent 'Goodwill Gallery' where you can post up a service or a donation you're willing to give to charity.

### www.caritasdata.co.uk
UK

CHARITIES DIRECT
A support site for charities with information on how to raise funds and run a charity, there's also a good directory of UK charities and you can rank them by expenditure, revenue and fund size.

### www.charitycommission.gov.uk
UK

THE CHARITY COMMISSION
The Charity Commission's mission is to give the public confidence in the integrity of charities in England and Wales, and their site lists over 180,000 charities. There's also lots of advice for charities, a list of their publications and links to related sites.

## www.charitynet.org UK

INFORMATION ON THE NON-PROFIT WORLD
A useful database covering charities and non-profit
organisations world-wide, it has sections on education,
government, IT, legal issues and jobs too.

*See also:*
**www.bcconnections.org.uk** – businesses can find out how they
can get involved in charity donations and charities can find out
how they can get businesses involved in their work.
**www.charities.org** – information about American charities.
**www.charitychoice.co.uk** – a well-categorised search engine
devoted to charities around the world.
**www.helplines.org.uk** – the Telephone Helplines Association.

# Giving

## www.justgiving.com UK

GIVE EFFECTIVELY
A newsy and informative site devoted to making the process
of giving to charity as easy as possible, whether you're an
individual donor, charity or a company. The site is divided into
three sections: Fundraise, Donate and Sponsor, so you can
go directly to the area that interests you. See also
**www.allaboutgiving.org**, which is especially informative about
unusual ways of donating such as using tax and shares.

## www.thehungersite.com US

CLICK AND GIVE
Just one click and you'll donate a cup of food to the world's
hungry via registered sponsors, a brilliant idea and one that
works – over 42 million cups were donated in 2003. Sign up
and they'll send you a reminder to visit every weekend.
There are also sister sites for breast cancer, saving rain forests
and animal rescue. See also **www.freedonation.com**, which
has similar aims and works along the same lines.

## www.careinternational.org.uk UK

HELPING THE WORLDS POOREST
Care are all about helping the world's most stricken people,
here you can learn about their work and donate.

C

*See also:*

**www.50ways.org** – an outstanding American site devoted
to ways of giving money to save the world's children
from suffering.

**www.buildaschool.org** – just click to contribute to building
schools in developing countries.

**www.charitychallenge.com** – raise money for your chosen
charity by taking an adventure holiday through
Charity Challenge.

**www.ecpat.net** – working to eliminate all forms of child abuse.

**www.givewater.org** – help the get water to where it's
most needed.

**www.sendacow.org.uk** – get livestock to those who really need
it in East Africa.

**www.warchild.co.uk** – devoted to helping victims of war and
conflict, excellent site design too.

# Chat

*There are literally thousands of chat sites and rooms on the web
covering many different topics. However, this is the area of the Net
that people have the most concerns about. There have been loads
of cases where people have been tricked into giving out personal
information and even arranged unsuitable meetings. But at its best,
a chat program is a great way to keep in contact with friends,
especially if they live miles away. So chat wisely by following our top
tips for keeping safe.*

## CHAT – OUR TOP TIPS

1     Be wary, just like you would be if you were visiting any
new place.
2     Don't give your e-mail address out without making sure that
only the person you're sending it to can read it.
3     People often pretend to be someone they're not when they're
chatting; unless you know the person, assume that's the case
with anyone you chat with online.
4     Don't meet up with anyone you've met online – keep your
online life separate. Chances are they'd be a let down anyway,
even if they were genuine.
5     If you like the look of a chat room or site, but you're not sure
about it, get a recommendation first.

6   If you want to meet up with friends online, arrange a time and place beforehand.
7   If you don't like someone, just block 'em.
8   Check out the excellent **www.chatdanger.com** (see below) for more info on how to chat safely.

C

## www.chatdanger.com                                                    US

KEEP SAFE IN CHAT ROOMS
A great site devoted to the perils of using chat rooms, full of advice and sensible information, it can be a little slow though, but it's worth persevering.

*The following are the major chat sites and programs:*

## www.aim.com                                                           UK

AOL INSTANT MESSENGER
One of the most popular, it's pretty safe and anyway you can easily block people who are a nuisance, or just set it up so that only friends can talk to you.

## http://web.icq.com                                                    US

ICQ – I SEEK YOU
There are lots of chat rooms here. It's quick and easy to use combined with a mobile phone. There are lots of features such as games, money advice, music and lurve.

## http://communities.msn.com/people                                     US

MICROSOFT MSN MESSENGER
Easy to use, but it can be confusing as Microsoft are so keen for you to use other parts of their massive site that you'll often find yourself suddenly transferred. The best bet is to customise it so that there's no mistake.

## www.mirc.com                                                          US

IRC – INTERNET RELAY CHAT
Recently improved and updated, this remains a straightforward chat program that is easy to use. Generally it's been overtaken by the likes of MSN and AOL, but some web sites may opt to use it.

### www.trillian.cc
US

COMMUNICATE WITH FLEXIBILITY AND STYLE
Trillian enables connections to all the major chat programs
through one interface. The reader looks good and you can
personalise it too. An excellent idea that works well.

### www.paltalk.com
US

VERSATILITY
A feature laden system with everything from video conferencing
to instant messaging – all free!

### www.habbohotel.com
UK

FOR UK TEENS
Lots of recommendation from users has meant the inclusion of
this site in the book, flexibility, fun graphics and an excellent
monitoring policy make it popular.

# Children

*There's been a continuing growth in the number of sites in this
category. You can save pounds on children's clothes and toys by
shopping over the Net; it's easy and the service is often excellent
because the sites are put together by people who really care. The
Internet is also an excellent way to educate and entertain children.
They are fascinated by it and quickly become experts. Listed here are
some of the best sites anywhere. For ideas for days out with children
see the British travel listings page 459, for educational sites see page
99 and for parenting concerns see page 304.*

## Shopping for children

### www.toy.co.uk
UK

FIND THAT TOY
A very useful toy search engine, you can search by type,
company or age. Once searched, it lists the toys with details,
price and where you can buy it online.

## www.elc.co.uk                                         UK

### EARLY LEARNING CENTRE

A well-designed and user-friendly site that offers a wide range
of toys for the under-fives in particular, it's strong on character
products and traditional toys alike. Delivery costs £3.95 per
order, free if you spend over £75, and you can expect goods to
arrive in 5 days.

## www.hamleys.co.uk                                     UK

### FINEST TOY STORE IN THE WORLD

Hamley's has improved its site and you can search for toys by
gender, price or age. There's also an okay selection of character
areas within the store as well as the more traditional range,
which is their main strength. Children can leave a wishlist
on the site and they do a birthday reminder service.
Delivery starts at £4.95.

## www.toysrus.co.uk                                     UK

### NOT JUST TOYS

Good site with all the key brands and 'in' things you'd expect
– you can even buy a mobile phone. Has links to key
toy manufacturer's sites and a sister site called
**www.babiesrus.co.uk** which covers younger children.
Delivery is £3.90 for the UK.

## www.thetoyshop.com                                    UK

### THE ENTERTAINER

The online spin-off from the Entertainer high street stores;
it offers much in the way of bargains and this bright and breezy
site is easy to navigate. You can search by toy, age, price or
category. Shipping to the UK is £3.95 flat rate while
international rates vary.

## www.newcron.com                                       UK

### CHARACTER PRODUCTS

Newcron has taken over the Character Warehouse site to
produce an online store that offers a wide range of mainstream
and unusual character products. You can search by character,
product or price; delivery starts at £3.99. See also
**www.shop4toys.co.uk** which has a similar offer.

C

### www.woodentoysonline.co.uk                    UK
WOODEN TOYS
A wide range of wooden and innovative toys here covering lots
of categories and types, all on a well-categorised and easy to
use site.

### www.outdoortoysdirect.co.uk                    UK
UK    LOW PRICES ON OUTDOOR TOYS
Excellent value for money with free delivery, a money back
guarantee, plus a wide range of goods. The selection consists of
everything from trampolines to swings, slides and play houses.
To complete your outdoor experience you can always pay a visit
to **www.kiteshop.co.uk** who offer a wide range of kites and
advice from an excellent site.

### www.krucialkids.com                    UK
ALL ABOARD THE KRUCIAL KIDS EXPRESS
Annoying name, but not an annoying site. It specialises in
developmental toys for children up to eight years old, providing
detailed information on the educational value of each of the
200 or so toys. The prices aren't bad either. Delivery begins
at £1.95 and is free if you spend over £60. For educational
toys see also **www.ticktocktoys.co.uk** and also
**www.mulberrybush.co.uk** who specialise in toys for under 12s.

### www.mailorderexpress.com                    UK
SHOP IN THE COMFORT OF YOUR HOME
Excellent toy store with games and models too. Shop by brand
or by category, with some good prices and special offers.
The design is a little old fashioned but effective nonetheless.

*Other sites worth a visit are:*
**www.drtoy.com** – a quirky American site run by someone who
has reviewed and rated some 2,000 products for children.
**www.huggables.co.uk** – specialists in teddies and other cute
soft toys.
**www.modelmegastore.co.uk** – excellent for models of all type,
especially remote control cars, shipping is good value.
**www.orchardtoys.co.uk** – specialists in fun, educational toys.
**www.theoldtoyshop.com** – mainly vintage and collectible toys.
**www.totalrobots.com** – all sorts of robots, probably one for
dads really.

**www.toycentre.com** – a sparse site with some good prices, most brands represented.
**www.toyopia.co.uk** – a toy shop that has a fun design and a good range to choose from too.
**www.toysdirecttoyourdoor.co.uk** – good design, specialists in Brio among other things.
**www.toywiz.com** – an American site where you can get unusual and new toys, even those that are no longer produced. Toys are generally cheaper but shipping is costly.

## Products other than toys

### www.jojomamanbebe.co.uk                                        UK

FASHIONABLE MOTHERS AND THEIR CHILDREN
Excellent for everything from maternity wear and designer children's clothes to gifts for newborn babies. Also has sections on toys, maternity products and special offers. All the designs are tested and they aim to be comfortable as well as fashionable. Delivery costs £3.95, free if collected from the warehouse in Newport. For baby wear try
**www.overthemoon-babywear.co.uk** who include a section on natural fibre clothing with free postage in the UK.

### www.gltc.co.uk                                                UK

THE GREAT LITTLE TRADING COMPANY
A good-looking site offering a wide range of child safety products, furniture and baby equipment, you can search the site by age and by product category. Delivery starts at £3.95.

### www.urchin.co.uk                                              UK

WORTH HAVING A BABY FOR
Urchin has a wide range of products and have won awards for their catalogue business. You'll find: cots and beds, bathtime accessories, bikes, clothes, for baby, travel goods, toys and things for the independent child who likes to personalise their own room. They boast a sense of style and good design, and they succeed. Also have a bargains section. Delivery is £4.50 per order with a next day surcharge of £3.

# Things to do

**www.mamamedia.com**                                               UK

THE PLACE FOR KIDS ON THE NET
This versatile site has everything a child and parent could want,
there is an excellent selection of interactive games, puzzles and
quizzes, combined with a great deal of wit and fun. Best of all,
it encourages children to communicate by submitting a
message and gets them voting on what's important to them.
There's a superb 'Grown-ups' section with information on
getting the best out of the Net with your children.

**www.bonus.com**                                                  US

THE SUPER SITE FOR KIDS
Excellent graphics and masses of genuinely good games make
a visit to Bonus a treat for all ages. There are quizzes and
puzzles, with sections offering a photo gallery, art resource and
homework help. Access to the web is limited to a protected
environment. Shame about the pop-ups and advertising.

**www.yucky.com**                                                  US

THE YUCKIEST SITE ON THE INTERNET
Find out how to turn milk into slime or how much you know
about worms – yucky lives up to its name. Essentially this is
an excellent, fun site that helps kids learn science and biology.
There are guides for parents on how to get the best out of the
site and links to recommended sites. Try this URL if you can't
get access on the usual one **http://yucky.kids.discovery.com**

**www.wonka.com**                                                  UK

THE WILD WORLD OF WONKA
Ingenious site sponsored by Nestlé with great illustrations and a
fun approach, it has several sections all with lots of interactivity,
as well as an online club. There's the Invention Room with lots
of trivia, Planet Vermes is about space, Loompaland takes you
into the animal kingdom, and so on. You can also send
postcards and get involved in competitions. They're always
adding new stuff, so it keeps kids' interest alive.

## www.switcheroozoo.com                                    UK

MAKE NEW ANIMALS
Over 6,500 combinations of animals can be made at this very
entertaining web site, you need Shockwave and a decent PC
for it to work effectively.

## www.magictricks.co.uk                                    UK

THE UK'S LEADING ONLINE MAGIC TRICKS STORE
A magic store chock full of tricks, sets and accompanying
equipment. You can send in suggestions for new tricks and even
find a magician. There's also a section on TV magicians and
a bookstore. P&P is free when you spend over £20. See also
**www.magicweek.co.uk** which is well-designed but more adult.

*Other activity sites worth checking out:*
**http://web.ukonline.co.uk/conker** – The Kids Ark – Join
Captain Zeb gathering material on the world, strange animals,
myths and facts – before it all disappears.
**www.24hourmuseum.org.uk/24kids.html** – good quality,
(if a little boring) online educational kids' content from the
24-hour Museum site with interactive journeys, a Harry Potter
trail and arts activities.
**www.alfy.com** – excellent with lots of games and plenty of
things to do and see.
**www.badgeplanet.co.uk** – a great site where you can buy and
also design your own badges.
**www.ex.ac.uk/bugclub** – bugs and creepy crawlies for all ages.
**www.globalgang.org.uk** – a Christian Aid sponsored activity
and magazine site mainly covering world issues.
**www.headbone.com** – part of Bonus with chat and games.
**www.hotwheels.com/kids** – a good-looking, but slow site from
a model car maker that has some good features and games.
Needs latest Flash Player to work.
**www.kiddonet.com** – download the interactive play area for
games and surfing in a safe environment. Masses to do and
good links. Largely aimed at girls.
**www.kids.warnerbros.com** – a links page to their children's
productions, when you consider what they produce, it's a
shame they can't do more.
**www.kidscastle.si.edu** – a pretty average kids' educational
magazine site from the Smithsonian Museum. Useful
for homework.

**www.kidscom.com** – play games, post a message on the message board and write to a pen friend (unfortunately the safe chat lines are open during our night-time). A bit dull.

**www.kidsdomain.com** – masses to download, from colouring books, music demos and homework help and games. Split into three age ranges.

**www.kidsjokes.co.uk** – over 12,000 jokes...

**www.kidskorner.net** – great use of cartoons to introduce and play games – stealthily educational.

**www.kidsreads.com** – an American site all about kids' books, with games and quizzes. Good for young Harry Potter fans.

**www.kzone.com.au** – excellent activity site from Australia.

**www.lego.co.uk** – games, product information, adventures with their leading characters, lots of interactive features make this site something of a gem.

**www.lemonadegame.com** – how much lemonade can you sell? Learn about market forces in this oddly fascinating game.

**www.matmice.com** – create your own web site home page and add it to the internet the easy way.

**www.missdorothy.com** – The good-looking *Dot* comic, which has loads of activities and is fun to use. Takes a while to download and you need the latest Flash downloads to get the best out of it.

**www.neopets.com** – look after a multitude of virtual pets, play games and even trade them.

## TV, book and character sites

### www.citv.co.uk                                          UK

CHILDREN'S ITV

Keep up-to-date with your favourite programmes and talk to the stars of the shows. There's lots to occupy children here including chat with fellow fans, play games, find something to do, enter a competition, e-mail a friend and join the club.

### www.nickjr.com                                          UK

THE NICKELODEON CHANNEL

Ideal for under-eights, this has a good selection of games and quizzes to play either with an adult or solo. The 'Red Rocket Store' has an excellent selection of merchandise, but beware of shipping costs. For activities aimed at a wider age range check out **www.nick.co.uk** where there is chat, gossip, games and plenty of background info on the shows.

## www.sesamestreet.com                                    UK
### THE CHILDREN'S TELEVISION WORKSHOP
Enter Elmo's world which is very colourful, with lots to do.
There are games to play, art and music to create and friends
to talk to. There's plenty for parents too.

## www.bbc.co.uk/cbbc                                       UK
### CHILDREN'S BBC
Lots of activities here, you can catch up on the latest news,
play games and find out about the stars of the programs.
There are also web guide links to other recommended children's
sites. See also **www.bbc.co.uk/cbeebies** which is for the very
young with printable colouring pages, stories and games.

## www.bbc.co.uk/newsround                                 UK
### KEEP UP TO SPEED
One of the best bits of CBBC is Newsround, here you can get
all the latest news, do quizzes, chat and join their club.

## www.disney.com                                          US
### WHERE THE MAGIC LIVES
A mega site that is split into eight sections:
1   Entertainment – details of films, activities and a Disney A–Z.
2   Kids Island Home – lots of games and music.
3   Playhouse – games and character sites for younger children.
4   Blast – the online kids' club.
5   Family fun – party planners, recipes and craft ideas.
6   Vacations – Information on the theme parks.
7   Shopping – the Disney store and auctions.
8   Main Street – more retail opportunities.

The British version **www.disney.co.uk** is more compact with
less about vacations and more emphasis on activity. You should
be aware that it's very commercial with lots of pop-up adverts
and we even found it difficult to move on to other sites after
loading it, you have to close the browser.

C

### www.cooltoons.com
UK

RUGRATS, STRESSED ERIC AND MORE

Each character has their own section where you can find lots to do and see. There's also an eight-step guide on how to become an animator. The store has all the related merchandise.

### www.foxkids.co.uk
UK

FOX TV

All the characters and shows are featured on this bright and entertaining site with added extras like a games section, competitions, a sports page and a magazine. There's also a shopping facility where you earn Brix by using the site, they can then be spent on goodies in the 'Boutik'. The graphics can be a little temperamental.

### www.aardman.com
UK

HOME OF WALLACE AND GROMMIT

This brilliant site takes a while to download but it's worth the wait. There's news on what the team are up to, links to their films, e-cards, a shop and an inside story on how it all began.

### www.gosh.org
UK

HOME OF PETER PAN

A good site from Great Ormond Street Hospital's charity with a section devoted to Peter Pan – all proceeds from the sale of the books go to hospital. There's also lots to do on the site with competitions, links and information about the hospital itself.

### www.guinnessrecords.com
UK

GUINNESS WORLD RECORDS

An outstanding site that offers much in the way of entertainment with footage of favourite records and informative sections on key areas of record breaking such as sport, nature, the material world and human achievements.

*Here's where the best children's characters and shows hang out:*
Action Man – **www.actionman.com** and
**www.thunderbirdsonline.com**
Angelina Ballerina – **www.angelinaballerina.com**
Animal Ark – **www.animalark.co.uk**
Art Attack – **www.artattack.co.uk**
Artemis Fowl – **www.artemisfowl.co.uk**

Asterix the Gaul – **http://www.asterix.tm.fr/**
Bagpuss – **www.smallfilms.co.uk/bagpuss**
Barbie – **www.barbie.com**
Batman – **www.batmantas.com** (animated series)
Batman – **www.batmanbeyond.com**
Beano – **www.beano.co.uk**
Beyblade – **www.beyblade.com**
Bill and Ben –
**www.bbc.co.uk/cbeebies/characterpages/billandben**
Bob the Builder – **www.bobthebuilder.org**
Boohbahs – **www.boohbah.com**
Buffy – **www.buffy.com** and **www.buffyguide.com**
Danger Mouse – **www.dangermouse.org**
Dragonball Z – **www.dragonballz.com** or **www.dbzgtlegacy.com**
Fimbels – **www.bbc.co.uk/cbeebies/fimbles**
Goosebumps – **www.scholastic.com/goosebumps**
Lemony Snicket – **www.lemonysnicket.com**
Letter Land – **www.letterland.com**
Mary Kate and Ashley – **www.marykateandashley.com**
Mr Men – **www.mrmen.com**
Noddy – **www.noddy.com**
Paddington – **www.paddingtonbear.co.uk**
Pokemon – **www.pokeland.yorks.net** or **www.pokemon.com**
Roald Dahl – **www.roalddahlclub.com**
Robot Wars – **www.robotwars.co.uk**
Spiderman – **www.spiderman.sonypictures.com** or
**www.spiderman.com**
Teletubbies – **www.teletubbies.com**
Thomas the Tank Engine – **www.thomasthetankengine.com**
Thunderbirds – **www.thunderbirdsonline.co.uk**
Tintin – **www.tintin.be**
Toontown – **www.toontown.com**
Tweenies – **www.bbc.co.uk/tweenies**
Winnie the Pooh – **www.winniethepooh.co.uk**
Yu-Gi-Oh – **www.yugiohkingofgames.com**

## Harry Potter

*Harry Potter deserves a special mention and with loads of web sites springing up, here are the official and some of the best unofficial ones.*

### www.bloomsbury.com/harrypotter                                    UK

WHERE IT ALL BEGAN
You have to enter using a secret password known only to
witches and wizards everywhere, then you get to find out all
about the books, meet JK Rowling and join the Harry Potter
club. 'Howlers and Owlers' – e-mail insults and compliments
– is great, but don't worry if you're a 'Muggle', all is explained.

### www.scholastic.com/harrypotter                                    UK

HARRY AMERICAN STYLE
Here's wizard trivia, quizzes, screensavers, information about
the books and an interview with JK Rowling, all on a fairly
boring web site.

### http://harrypotter.warnerbros.co.uk                               UK

HARRY IN THE MOVIES
An outstanding site offering the latest news on the films plus
downloads and lots of other activities, you can chat, shop for
Harry merchandise and play games.

### www.mugglenet.com                                                  US

THE ULTIMATE HARRY POTTER SITE
An excellent fan site put together by some teenage fans, it has
features on the books and the films plus links, games and the
latest news. The Wall of Shame is particularly entertaining.

## Search engines and site directories

### www.yahooligans.com                                                US

THE KID'S ONLINE WEB GUIDE
Probably the most popular site for kids, yahooligans offers
parents safety and kids hours of fun. There are games, articles
and features on the 'in' characters, education resources and
sections on sport, science, computing and TV. It has an
American bias.

### www.ajkids.com                                                     US

ASK JEEVES FOR KIDS
A search engine aimed at children, it's simple, safe and is
excellent for homework enquiries and games.

**www.fkbko.co.uk**                                    UK

FOR KIDS BY KIDS ONLINE
Part of an EU-funded project designed to make surfing the net
safe for children, it has chat, e-mail, surfing and search
facilities and the excellent design makes it easy to use too.

*See also:*
**www.familyfriendlysearch.com** – a simple search engine that
searches several of the major directories kids' sections.
**www.infoplease.com** – good for homework.
**www.ipl.org/div/kidspace** – the children's section of the Internet
Public Library, useful for homework as it's quite oriented to
education sites.
**www.kidsclick.com** – a poorly designed directory of some
5,000 child oriented sites.
**www.kidsseek.co.uk** – a messily designed search engine that
allows UK-only searches.
**www.kidtastic.com** – safe search for kids.

# Christmas

*Sites to give some seasonal cheer and also help you prepare for
the big day.*

**www.christmas.com**                                  US

CELEBRATING CHRISTMAS AROUND THE WORLD
A good directory of stores and sites devoted to all aspects
of Christmas, it has a strong American bias though.

*Other Christmassy sites worth checking out:*
**www.christmas-carols.net** – lyrics for all the best-known carols.
**www.christmasrecipe.com** – every Christmas recipe you'll ever
likely to need.
**www.emailsanta.com** – too lazy to send a letter, well now you
can e-mail Santa.
**www.howstuffworks.com/christmas** – all your questions about
the advent season answered including the eternal question
'Why is Christmas sometimes spelled Xmas?'
**www.noradsanta.org** – track Santa as he makes his way
around the skies.

C

### www.northpole.com                                                 US
SANTA'S SECRET VILLAGE
A very good activity site for children and adults too, with
everything from educational activities to shopping.

### www.christmas.co.uk                                               US
RAISE FUNDS FOR CHARITY
A bright and entertaining site where you can give to certain
charities and shop for presents too.

### www.christmastimeuk.com                                           UK
CHRISTMAS SHOP
Selling all you could possibly need during the festive season,
this shop has a wide range and an e-mail service if you want
something specific. Delivery charges vary according to what you
buy and where you are.

*See also:*
**www.christmaslightseurope.com** – exterior light store with a
big Christmas section.
**www.thechristmaslightscompany.co.uk** – a lights specialist
both indoor and out.

# Competitions

### www.loquax.co.uk                                                  UK
THE UK'S COMPETITION PORTAL
This site doesn't give away prizes but lists the web sites that
do. There are hundreds of competitions featured, and if you
own a web site they'll even run a competition for you. There are
daily updates and special features such as 'Pick of the Prizes'
which features the best the web has to offer, with links to the
relevant sites.

*See also:*
**www.compaholics.co.uk** – competitions and gambling too,
heavy on the advertising.
**www.myoffers.co.uk** – a slow site with, as the name suggests,
lots of offers.
**www.prizemagic.co.uk** – humorous site from a person who has
won over £100,000 in competitions.

**www.theprizefinder.com** – offer a wide range of prizes in lots of categories, you have to register though.
**www.theprizefinder.com** – excellent site, they claim someone actually won £1,000,000 there.
**www.wincompetitionprizes.co.uk** – a minimalist approach from this site who appear to go for quality rather than quantity.

# Computers

*It's no surprise that the number one place to buy a computer is the Internet. With these sites you won't go far wrong, and it's also worth checking out the price checker sites on page 321 before going shopping and checking the software sites on page 367. Mac users should also check out the section on Apple Macs on page 19.*

## Information and reviews

### www.itreviews.co.uk                                    UK

START HERE TO FIND THE BEST
IT Reviews gives unbiased reports, not only on computer products, but also on software, games and related books. The site has a good search facility and a quick visit may save you loads of hassle when you come to buy.

### www.pcadvisor.co.uk                                    UK

EXPERT ADVICE IN PLAIN ENGLISH
A derivative from *PC Advisor* magazine, the site offers much in the way of reviews and information on how to find the best PC. It also allows you to pick up advice from experts on technical queries. There's a games room, a place from which you can download programs and a consumer section where you can air your praises and gripes.

*See also:*
**www.byte.com** – one for those who know something about computer technology.
**www.compshopper.co.uk** – good for reviews and information also links to Dabs (see below) for shopping.
**www.computerweekly.com** – fairly dull site but informative on all aspects of computing.

**www.cnet.com** – product reviews aplenty, also has downloads and shopping links.

**www.streettech.com** – opinions and personal reviews with attitude from several experts.

**www.zdnet.co.uk** – very good reviews section at this large and diverse site.

## Stores

**www.pcworld.co.uk**                                                UK

THE COMPUTER SUPERSTORE

A very strong offering from one of the leading computer stores with lots of offers and star buys. They sell a wide range of electronics from cameras to the expected PCs and peripherals.

**www.simply.co.uk**                                                 UK

SIMPLY DOES IT

An award-winning site and company that offers a wide range of PCs and related products, their strengths are speed, quality of service and competitive prices. They also sell mobile phones.

**www.dabs.com**                                                     UK

500,000 CUSTOMERS LATER…

One of the most successful online computer product retailers, with a very good reputation for service, there are loads of offers and a wide range of goods. It's a big site and not that easy to navigate, but there are rewards for those who persevere in the guise of dabspoints, which can be converted to airmiles.

**www.easyetrader.co.uk**                                            UK

EASY

Well designed and attractive site from a retailer who specialises in computers and accessories. It also offers up the latest computing news and links to company sites.

**www.tiny.com**                                                     UK

LATEST TECHNOLOGY AT UNBEATABLE PRICES

A businesslike site that includes all the details you'd need on their range of computers and peripherals for home and office use. Tiny are the UK's largest computer manufacturer and have a history of reliability and good deals. Shipping costs vary according to what you buy and where you live.

## www.totalpda.co.uk
UK

PERSONAL DIGITAL ASSISTANT'S
Good-looking site specialising in PDAs and related products
with a wide range and some good bargains. See also
**www.expansys.com** who have some very good offers.

*PC manufacturers' site addresses:*
Apple – **www.apple.com**
Dell – **www.dell.co.uk**
Elonex – **www.elonex.co.uk**
Evesham – **www.evesham.com**
Gateway – **www.gateway.com/uk**
Hewlett Packard – **www.hp.com/uk**
Time – **www.timecomputers.com**
Viglen – **www.viglen.co.uk**

# Computer accessories

## www.planetmicro.co.uk
UK

ACCESSORISE YOUR PC
Much in the way of add-ons for PCs and essential equipment
that can enable you to get more out of your computer, or keep
an old PC going. Good design and some good pricing too.

*See also:*
**www.cityPCspares.co.uk** – a very wide range from cables
to computers.
**www.dreamdirect.co.uk** – good-looking site mainly selling
software but also with an OK range of PC accessories
and equipment.
**www.keytools.com** – a great site devoted to providing
equipment that is easy to use.
**www.tonik.co.uk** – excellent computer consumables store with
free delivery in the UK.

## www.cex.co.uk
UK

COMPUTER EXCHANGE
Computer Exchange buy and sell used electronics, computers
and games. The process is pretty straightforward, so if you have
an old PC give them a call.

## Information on repairing and upgrading your PC

*The following sites are useful if you want to keep up with the latest developments, need help when your PC goes wrong or just need to learn something:*

**www.pcmech.com**                                                              US
> PC MECHANIC
> Plain English explanations of all the bits that make up a computer, it's easy to follow and use with lots of background information and support. Excellent.

> **www.compinfo.co.uk** – a bewildering number of computer related links all set out in a large directory.
> **www.driverguide.com** – advice on finding and installing the right drivers for your PC.
> **www.help.com** – part of the high quality CNET site it has the most up-to-date information on new products and articles and advice. It assumes some knowledge.
> **www.maximumpc.co.uk** – lots of tutorials, useful programs to download and reviews galore.
> **www.pcpitstop.com** – a host of programs to get your PC running on top form. They can even test how well your PC is running and offer advice on how to improve its performance.
> **www.wired.com** – all the latest news and product information.

## *Consumer information and advice*

*A new section following requests from readers, these sites help with the latest consumer law and provide answers or give guidance on what to do if you've been wronged.*

**www.which.net**                                                              UK

> WHICH? MAGAZINE
> Excellent spin-off from the magazine with everything from consumer advice to product reviews. You need to be a member to get the best out of it.

## www.consumers.gov.uk UK

### THE CONSUMER GATEWAY

A consumer advice site run by the government that offers links
and information across all the major areas where issues occur
from cars, to shopping to home improvements. A good place to
start if you have issues you feel strongly about.

*See also:*

**www.adviceguide.org.uk** – the old Citizens Advice Bureau
offers a wide range of tips and advice on the most common
problems and how to solve them, plus how to get in touch if
you have specific issues.

**www.bbc.co.uk/watchdog** – lots of information on the back of
the TV program with legal FAQs, example letters for complaints
and specific features.

**www.ciao.co.uk** – independent product reviews on a wide
range of categories.

**www.consumer-rights.org.uk** – handy hints and tips all
designed to ensure that you to get the best service.

**www.consumerworld.org** – an American site with a huge
number of useful links.

**www.ethicalconsumer.org** – a UK-based site devoted to listing
those companies whose environmental and social track records
are less than envious.

**www.howtocomplain.com** – find out how to make a complaint
at this easy-to-follow site, which even provides specially
designed forms to make your complaint even more effective.

**www.oft.gov.uk** – home of the Office of Fair Trading.

**www.streettech.com** – honest reviews on the latest technology.

**www.tomshardware.com** – a popular and messy but very
information heavy site full of advice and help with the most
common problems and issues facing the computer user.

**www.tradingstandards.gov.uk** – the Trading Standards site
offers a wealth of information on safety and legislation for
businesses, education establishments and consumers.

# Crime

*This section continues to expand. It is intended to be of help to victims of crime or it may even help solve one. Hopefully you won't need it.*

C

## www.police.uk                                                    UK

THE POLICE ONLINE

Here you can notify the police of minor crimes and get essential information on the organisation and how it works. There are sections on specific crimes or appeals, recruitment and information on related organisations. The site is easy to navigate and use.

*See also:*

**www.cia.gov** – the Central Intelligence Agency.
**www.crb.org.uk** – Criminal Records Bureau helps employers with criminal records information amongst other services.
**www.fbi.gov** – the Federal Bureau of Investigation.
**www.interpol.com** – the fight against international crime.
**www.nationalcrimesquad.police.uk** – the fight against organised crime.
**www.pca.gov.uk** – the Police Complaints Authority.

## www.cjsonline.org                                               UK

THE CRIMINAL JUSTICE SYSTEM

A helpful site that tells what happens when someone gets arrested, and provides information about the trial procedure, how a court works and what you need to do if you're a witness. There's a guide to who does what in the legal profession and a section on related links. See also the Crown Prosecution Service at **www.cps.gov.uk**

## www.crimestoppers-uk.org                                        UK

KEEP 'EM PEELED

Information on the Crimestoppers trust and how you can get involved in their fight against crime with information on the latest campaign and initiatives, links and, of course, their phone number 0800 555 111. See also **www.crimereduction.gov.uk** which has been set up by the government to become the number one resource for the crime prevention practitioner.

## www.localhomewatch.co.uk    UK
### NEIGHBOURHOOD WATCH
A directory of neighbourhood watch schemes by county with
advice on preventing crime and how you can set up a
neighbourhood watch scheme in your area. See also
**www.crimeconcern.org.uk** who give advice on helping to
reduce crime and also the fear of crime in local communities.

## www.victimsupport.com    UK
### VICTIM SUPPORT
An independent charity that supports the victims of crime
throughout the UK with help and advice. It also advises witnesses
on the justice system and campaigns for equal opportunities.
You can also find out about how you can help or give funds.

## www.fraud.org    US
### NATIONAL FRAUD INFORMATION CENTER
Find out about the many ways you can be defrauded and how
to spot a fraud on the Internet.

*See also:*
**www.fraudbureau.com** – a consumer-oriented scam-listing
service, you can search for specific complaints and add your
experiences too.
**www.fraudforum.org** – have your say about fraud and catch
the latest news.
**www.quatloos.com** – a listing of all sorts of scams and
fraudulent practises; an entertaining and educational read.
**www.scambusters.com** – more help on scams and annoyances
on the Internet.

## www.dumbcriminalacts.com    US
### THE STUPIDEST CRIMINALS
Here you can find out about the daftest criminal acts in history
and have a good laugh at their expense, some are truly
unbelievable and sadly it does lack a bit of credibility as it
doesn't always list the source of the stories. See also
**www.dumbcrooks.com** which is a bit low tech but the stories
are more detailed.

# Cycles and Cycling

*See page 464 for cycling holidays and tours and page 380 for information on cycling as a sport.*

**C**

### www.cycleweb.co.uk                                                   UK

THE INTERNET CYCLING CLUB
A great attempt to bring together all things cycling. Aimed at a general audience rather than cycling as a sport, it has masses of sections and links on everything from the latest news to clubs, shops and holidays.

*See also:*
**www.a-nelson.dircon.co.uk/cyclingprelycra** – cycling as it used to be before the Lycra-clad hordes took to the roads, nicely done and with a great nostalgic feel.
**www.bikemagic.com** – forums on hot bike topics, reviews of equipment, buying advice, classifieds, the latest news, links and an events calendar.
**www.bikeweek.org.uk** – find out about Bike Week which is in mid-June.
**www.ctc.org.uk** – the National Cyclist's Organisation's site offers lots of information on all aspects of the hobby and the benefits associated with getting on your bike.
**www.cycling.uk.com** – great for cycling links.
**www.newtocycling.co.uk** – help for those who are new to cycling from Izzy Sez with advice and links too.
**www.procycling.com** – a magazine devoted to professional cycling, pretty basic design but it covers all the latest news.
**www.tandem-club.org.uk** – a pretty basic site devoted to the world of the tandem with discussion groups, classifieds, buying advice, events and a newsletter.

## Buying a bike

### www.bicyclenet.co.uk                                                 UK

UK'S NUMBER 1 ONLINE BICYCLE SHOP
Great selection of bikes and accessories, there's also good advice on how to buy the right bike and assembly instructions on all that they sell. Delivery is free for bikes and orders in excess of £50. See also **www.cyclestuff.co.uk** who have a good range of accessories, as does the wonderfully named **www.wiggle.co.uk**

# Dance

*Here are a few sites for those who dance or think they can...*

### www.danceart.com

DANCE!
A slightly messy but enthusiastic site centred on the dance
scene, it has lots of links, articles and interviews.

*See also:*

**http://scarecrow.caps.ou.edu/~hneeman/dance_hotlist.html** –
a hotlist of dance sites.

**www.dancebooks.co.uk** – where to go for specialist dance titles.

**www.dancescape.com** – a good Canadian dance magazine site.

**www.dancesport.uk.com** – the UK ballroom dancing scene
covered.

**www.dancing-times.co.uk** – *Dancing Times* and *Dancing Today*.

**www.folkdancing.org** – home of the Folk Dance Association.

**www.irishdancing.com** – a cheery site from International Irish
Dancing magazine.

**www.istd.org** – home of the Imperial Society of Teachers
of Dancing.

**www.pearldata.co.uk/dance/paul/cool.htm** – good for dancing-
related links.

**www.rad.org.uk** – the Royal Academy of Dance.

**www.the-ballet.com** – a good e-zine all about ballet.

**www.young-dancers.org** – dedicated to helping teenagers learn
to dance.

# Dating

*Using the Net has become an accepted means to meet people, but
be careful about how you go about meeting up; many people aren't
exactly honest about their details. If in doubt, err on the side of
caution. See also the new section on Social Networking on page 366.*

### www.onlinedatingmagazine.com

AN AUTHORITATIVE INSIGHT
An excellent magazine site devoted to all aspects of dating with
site reviews, tips, articles and advice. It is well designed and up
to date, there are even some cartoons and it's all written in a
chirpy style.

**www.wildxangel.com**                                        UK

THE LOW DOWN
An American site that tells it like it is and gives advice about
using chat and dating sites, it also gives awards for the best
ones and there are links too. Although the advice is sound it's
a little out of date and you should also check out **www.dating-agencies-uk.co.uk/dating-tips.htm** where there's lots of good
advice. See also the attractive **www.topdatingtips.com**

**www.thedatingportal.com**                                  US

DATING LINKS
A portal devoted to dating sites; they are well categorised but it is
geared towards the US market. See also **www.datingbind.com**
and for the UK **www.dating-agencies-uk.co.uk**

**www.uksingles.co.uk**                                      UK

FOR ALL UK SINGLES
Not just about dating, this site is devoted to helping you get the
most out of life. There are several sections: accommodation,
sport and activities, holidays, help for single parents, and
listings for matchmaking and dating services. All the companies
that advertise in the directories are vetted too.

**www.faceparty.com**                                        UK

BIGGEST PARTY ON EARTH
A combination of dating agency, party organiser and chat site.
You download your details and photo to create your own profile,
then just join in.

*Here are some additional sites, there's not much to choose
between them, it's all a matter of taste. All are secure and
allow you to browse and participate in relative safety:*
**www.dateline.co.uk** – 30 years experience at the dating game
gives Dateline lots of credibility and it's a good site too, easy to
use and reassuring.
**www.datingdirect.com** – claims to be the UK's largest agency
with over one million members, the site is not as sophisticated
as some, though they seem to have lots of success stories.
**www.dinnerdates.com** – one of the longest established and
most respected dining and social events clubs for unattached
single people in the UK; find out how you can get involved here.
**www.directdating.com** – one of the most popular dating sites
with over 1 million members.

**www.idealpartner.net** – a personality profiling approach to finding a partner.

**www.ivorytowers.net** – where unattached alumni and undergraduates from the 'leading' universities get together.

**www.love-exchange.co.uk** – upmarket profiles for busy professionals, you can chat without revealing your proper e-mail address.

**www.match.com** – leading site in the US, get your profile matched to someone or join in the chat, there's an excellent magazine too.

**www.nomorefrogs.com** – find your perfect partner using psychometric testing.

**www.singles121.com** – good site, easy to use with, on the whole, good quality photos.

**www.speeddater.co.uk** – the latest dating craze covered for the UK and especially London.

**www.udate.com** – US site for over-25s only, an attractive site with a good search facility.

### www.soyouvebeendumped.com                                UK

HOW TO COPE...
An interesting way to help yourself after you've split up, lots of advice and help to get you through it all.

# Disability Help and Information

*In this expanded section you'll find sites that may help if you are disabled or care for someone with a disability. It's also worth checking your local council's site as they tend to have good local information on the help that is available in your area.*

## Information and advice

### www.disability.gov.uk

UK THE GOVERNMENT'S VIEW
Information and help on rights for the disabled with links to related departments. You can't help thinking that there could have been more information across a broader spectrum.
See **www.dwp.gov.uk/lifeevent/benefits/index.htm** for an index of benefits and services available.

**www.bcodp.org.uk**                                                      UK

THE BRITISH COUNCIL OF DISABLED PEOPLE
An action-oriented site that has information on how the council works, useful articles and helpful information. It shows how you can get involved whether you are disabled or not, and most importantly, how you can contribute.

*For more advice check out the following sites:*
**www.abilitynet.org.uk** – excellent regional database offering help whatever your situation.
**www.dialuk.org.uk** – the Disability Advice Network.
**www.disabilityresources.org** – an American site devoted to resources available on the Internet.
**www.makoa.org** – another US site, not a good design, but a huge number of links all the same.
**www.youreable.com** – great for news, features and jobs.

# Independent living

**www.dlf.org.uk**                                                        UK

THE DISABLED LIVING FOUNDATION
A charity devoted to helping people who need equipment to live life to the full. This excellent site has information on how to choose the best equipment, masses of links to self-help groups, a bookshop, training information and of course a section on how you can contribute.

*See section on motability under Cars page 58 as well as:*
**www.disabledgo.info** – a directory of places that have good access and businesses that are sympathetic to disabled people.
**www.e-accessibility.com** – a monthly newsletter largely aimed at people with sight problems, it concentrates on various aspects of technology and computing.
**www.independentliving.co.uk** – equipment and advice on making life easier.
**www.keytools.com** – an excellent site from a company specialising in providing computer accessories.
**www.mobilitywarehouse.com** – excellent range of products and an attractive and user friendly site
**www.motability.co.uk** – the scheme that helps you contract hire a car or powered wheelchair or scooter.
**www.sunrisemedical.com** – a wide range of products and links, some only available abroad, the site is slow too.
**www.wheelchair-travel.co.uk** – self drive wheelchairs and cars for hire.

# Children

**www.ncb.org.uk/cdc/**                                    UK

> COUNCIL FOR DISABLED CHILDREN
> From the National Children's Bureau, this site is basically
> a forum devoted to helping parents and children cope with
> disability. It's a good starting point if you need information,
> but it's not an easy site to navigate so patience is required.
> See also **www.childcarelink.gov.uk** and **www.cafamily.org.uk**
> where you can find advice on caring for a disabled child.

# Students and education

**www.techdis.ac.uk**                                    UK

> HELP FOR STUDENTS WITH A DISABILITY
> A site containing masses of help and information designed
> to enable disabled students to have the opportunity to learn
> effectively. Most of it is free, so an excellent resource. See also
> **www.skill.org.uk** who help promote opportunities for post-16
> year olds in education and **www.nasen.org.uk** the National
> Association for Special Educational Needs.

# Jobs

**www.jobability.com**                                    UK

> LEADING JOB SITE FOR DISABLED PEOPLE
> A straightforward site designed to help disabled people find
> employment; it covers the UK by region plus opportunities in
> the rest of the world. There's also advice on careers and how
> to find a job. See also who have a good jobs section.

> *See also:*
> **www.opportunity.org.uk**
> **www.rehab.ie/uk**
> **www.remploy.co.uk**
> **www.shaw-trust.org.uk**
> **www.yourable.com**

# Rights and having your say

**www.drc-gb.org** UK

> DISABILITY RIGHTS
> A helpful site offering links and views on rights issues for the
> disabled. The site doesn't always load properly and it's not easy
> to find your way around, but useful nonetheless – at least
> there's a search facility.

**www.disabilityview.co.uk** UK

> DISABILITY VIEW
> Inspired by the magazine of the same name, this site sets out
> to be the best source of information for all those who have to
> cope with a disability, and it largely succeeds. There are loads
> of links and useful sections such as travel, guides, sports and
> an events guide. See also **www.disabilitynow.org.uk**

**www.webequality.org.uk** UK

> DISABILITY EQUALITY TRAINING
> Working with employers to enable disabled people to get
> employed and stay employed. There's masses of practical
> advice and even a quiz to start you off.

# For carers

**www.carers.gov.uk** UK

> FOR THOSE WHO CARE
> A barely useful resource from the government for carers,
> there are links and details of their policies concerning care.
> For more useful sites go to **www.aqu.co.uk/carers** and also
> **www.caringmatters.dial.pipex.com** all of which have articles,
> chat and useful links.

# Keeping in touch

**www.disabledunited.com** UK

> THE MEETING PLACE
> A sort of Friends Reunited, but much more as it offers
> information on travel, links, chat, forums and lastly dating.

*Do-It-Yourself is now under Home and DIY on page 228.*

# Education

*Using the Internet for homework or study has become one of its primary uses; these sites will help enormously, especially alongside the reference and encyclopaedia sites listed on page 329. There is also a section aimed at students on page 403.*

## Homework help

**www.bbc.co.uk/education** UK

E

GET EQUIPPED FOR LIFE
Good-looking site covering learning at school, college and adult education. Each section tends to be tied to a particular programme rather than subject, but there is masses here and the quality of content is particularly good. The revision sections are excellent.

**www.brainpop.com** US

LEARN BY ANIMATION
A wonderful example of how the Internet should be used. Here you can download animations that cover and explain specific aspects of maths, health, technology, science, English and more. The site is American but very useful for UK students too.

**www.cln.org/int_expert.html** US

ASK AN EXPERT
This site lists almost a hundred sites by subject, including somewhere you can ask an expert your homework question – what a doddle! North American bias though.

**www.discoveryschool.com** US

ANSWERS TO HOMEWORK, FREE
This huge database is one of the biggest online homework sites, with some 700 links to a variety of reference sites and the provision to ask questions too. Layout has been improved and you can more easily access the information, it also has an excellent clip art gallery.

**www.examaid.co.uk** UK

COPING WITH EXAMS
Not a great web site but it does give an insight into how students cope with exams (or not) and how to help get through them successfully.

### www.happychild.org.uk
UK

PROJECT HAPPY CHILD
A mess of a site but one that aims to provide an index of educational resources for schools, parents and children. There's loads to see and do and it does a good job of highlighting charities for example, but the poor design gets in the way of its objectives. Well worth a visit, but be patient.

### www.homeworkelephant.co.uk
UK

LET THE ELEPHANT HELP
Rightly considered one of the top educational sites with some 5,000 resources and straightforward layout, all aimed at helping children achieve great results. There's help with specific subjects, hints and tips, help for parents and teachers. The agony elephant is great if you get really stuck. It's constantly being updated, so worth checking regularly.

### www.homeworkhigh.co.uk
UK

LEARN WITH CHANNEL 4
Split into six learning sections: history, geography, science, maths, English and languages. There's also news and a chat room plus a personal help section that covers topics like bullying. They even provide teachers online for live sessions to help you out. You can ask questions, track down lots of information and chat with fellow homework sufferers. All in all, this is one of the better-looking homework sites. Excellent.

### www.kevinsplayroom.co.uk
UK

AWARD WINNING PORTAL
An excellent site which is put together with the heavy involvement of pupils. It's won numerous awards and is a favourite among teachers and pupils alike. It has over 2,000 approved sites and they are well categorised. There's also a translation service and a links page for teachers.

### www.learn.co.uk
UK

LEARN WITH THE *GUARDIAN*
A curriculum-based site that has much to offer in terms of content. They work closely with schools and it shows; that and access to the *Guardian* content means this is one of the best sites from which to learn. The down side is that it's all a bit clinical and not much fun.

## www.learningalive.co.uk                                    UK

FOR PRIMARY AND SECONDARY
The 'Living Library' is a useful resource for homework help for
both primary and secondary students while 'Pathways' provides
over 4,000 links to a variety of reference sites. There are loads
of resources for teachers too.

## www.livinglibrary.co.uk                                    UK

MULTI-MEDIA RESOURCES
Interesting design and plenty to choose from for both teachers
and pupils alike, it's split into primary and 11+ sections, you
can either browse by topic or use the search facility, there's also
a tips section for teachers too.

## www.parentlink.co.uk                                       UK

HELPING YOUR CHILD
A site written by teachers aimed at helping parents to help their
children by preparing them for the classroom, very useful
although it concentrates on numeracy and literacy.

## www.schoolsnet.com                                         UK

THE EDUCATION SUPER SITE
An incredibly impressive site that covers all aspects of
education; there are school and site guides, jobs pages, book
and computer shops, information on revision and exams, the
latest news and, of course, plenty of chat. Parents and students
should go to **www.educate.org.uk**, which is part of the same
site but with loads of helpful information and advice.

## www.schoolzone.co.uk                                       UK

UK'S TOP EDUCATIONAL SEARCH ENGINE
With over 40,000 sites and bits of resource all checked by
teachers, Schoolzone has masses of information. It is clearly
designed and easy to use with all the sites summarised and
reviewed. There is free software to download, plus homework
help, career advice, teacher support (they do need it
apparently) and much more. Don't be put off by the
confusing layout; it's worth sticking with. See also
**www.ukeducationguide.co.uk** who offer hundreds of links
and **www.thelighthouseforeducation.co.uk**

## Pre-school and infant education

### www.underfives.co.uk                                                    UK

WEB RESOURCE FOR PRE-SCHOOL
Loads of things to do and see here, from games and activities
to download, to help and advice for parents. Like the best
educational sites its educational bias is not obvious or
overwhelming, the tone is just right, it's also simple to use
and fast.

### www.enchantedlearning.com                                              UK

FROM APES TO WHALES
It's messy, uncool and largely aimed at young children, but there's
loads of good information and activities hidden away, especially on
nature. Use the search engine to find what you need.

### www.thebigbus.com                                                       UK

HOORAY FOR THE BIG BUS!
Excellent animation and content make this stand out, although
it can be a little slow and you have to subscribe to the CD
magazine to get the best out of it (you get a free demo one
as a trial). Excellent for younger children.

## Primary

### www.atschool.co.uk                                                      UK

PRIMARY EDUCATION
Specialising in Key Stage 1 and 2, this site is fun as well as
educational and, while the content is strong, you do have to
subscribe. Rates start at £9.99 for a quarterly subscription.
This site does seem quite slow, so probably one for the
broadband users.

### www.edontheweb.com                                                      UK

HELP WITH SATS
Written by a teacher, this site is designed to help children pass
their SAT exams. It's lively and well written with lots of
activities too.

## www.gridclub.com

UK

FOR 7 TO 11 YEAR OLDS
An excellent site which is backed by the government and
several high profile contributors including Channel 4. It uses
entertaining educational games to do most of it tutoring but
there are links to the more traditional stuff available too. It's
been built with safety in mind and it encourages children
proactively. All in all, what an educational site should be.

## www.samlearning.com

UK

EXAM REVISION
SAM stands for self-assessment and marking, on this brilliant
site you can do just that, it has mock exams covering every
major subject and key stage plus GCSE and A level. There are
top tips on taking exams and the chance to win some great
prizes when you register. There is a 14-day free trial then there
are various payment options. See also **www.courseshop.co.uk**
who offer a wide range of courses from GCSE upwards.

# Secondary

*These sites are aimed at secondary-aged students. If you can't find
what you are looking for here, don't forget our sections on Art,
English usage, History, Nature and environment, Reference, Religion,
Science and Space all of which are extremely helpful when it comes
to homework.*

# Biology

## www.exam.net

UK

A LEVEL BIOLOGY
Good site with all you're likely to need to pass this A level,
it has lots of interactive features including video clips.

# Design

## www.3d-i.org

US

DESIGN
A beautifully designed site on design and it's many forms in
particular fashion, architecture and product design. It aids the
student by enabling them to have a go at designing products
plus advice on the basic principles.

# English

### www.courseworkbank.co.uk UK

ESSAY HELP
Claiming to be the UK's largest database of quality essays by students from 14 year olds to those at university, they cover a wide variety of subjects and there's no charge but beware that teachers are familiar with this resource too! See also the American **www.sparknotes.com** who offer their range of study guides free to download if you register.

### www.englishresources.co.uk UK

ENGLISH
Hundreds of free resources available here, it's very useful for revision and for teachers too with a good search engine and sections aimed at each secondary school age range. See also our new section on English usage on page 111.

## History

### www.schoolhistory.co.uk UK

HISTORY REVISION
An excellent site devoted to helping students learn and revise history with quizzes and many free resources, also has lessons and worksheets for teachers too.

## Languages

### www.frenchrevision.co.uk UK

FRENCH REVISION
Lots of interactive exercises at most levels of French for students aged 11 to 18. There are also useful links and past papers to have a go at.

## Maths

### http://mathworld.wolfram.com US

MATHS WORLD
An outstanding site devoted to the world of mathematics. It explains the complexities really well and is great for homework. It also has sections on chemistry, physics and astronomy. See also the comprehensive **http://tcaep.co.uk/maths/index.htm** and also **www.mathsisfun.com**

E

# Post-16 and adult education

**www.ngfl.gov.uk**                                              UK

THE NATIONAL GRID FOR LEARNING
The official government education site with sections on every
aspect of learning. There's something for everyone, whatever
your needs. It is particularly good for info on further and adult
education. There are also details on school web sites, a features
section that covers news and events, plus advice on Internet
safety. See also **www.lsc.gov.uk** home of the Learning and
Skills Council which provides education for over-16 year olds.

**www.learndirect.co.uk**                                        UK

ADULT LEARNING
A government-backed site that aims to bring education to
everyone whatever their needs. The site explains the
background to the initiative plus details of courses and how you
can find one that meets your requirements. There's also help for
businesses and a jobs advice section.

*See also:*
**www.city-and-guilds.co.uk** – vocational qualifications with over
500 from which to choose.
**www.coursesuseek.com** and **www.want2learn.com** – sister
sites devoted to offering a wide variety of online courses.
**www.lifelonglearning.co.uk** – an informative government site
aimed at helping people with further education ambitions.
**www.niace.org.uk** – a non-government organisation formed to
'support an increase in the total numbers of adults engaged in
formal and informal learning in England and Wales; and at the
same time to take positive action to improve opportunities and
widen access to learning opportunities for those communities
under-represented in current provision'.
**www.support4learning.org.uk** – a wide-ranging resource aimed
at helping people support their education needs in a more
holistic way.
**www.wea.org.uk** – the Worker's Educational Association helps
provide learning opportunities for everyone but especially those
who had missed out or been disadvantaged in some way.

# National Curriculum and government policy

**www.nc.uk.net**                                                    UK

NATIONAL CURRICULUM REVEALED
Very detailed explanation of the National Curriculum and
prescribed standards.

*See also:*
**www.ace-ed.org.uk** – help for parents at the Advisory Centre
for Education. **www.becta.org.uk** – information on technology
and ICT education.
**www.dfes.gov.uk** – The Department for Education and Skills,
if you want a more overall picture on education.
**www.dfes.gov.uk/parents/discover** – for parents who want to
be proactive in their child's education.
**www.parentcentre.gov.uk** – well, more information from the
Government on supporting children's learning.
**www.ngfl.gov.uk** – National Grid for Learning, outstanding for
links. Some very good content too.
**www.ofsted.gov.uk** – The Office for Standards in Education,
if you have a problem go here first.
**www.qca.org.uk** – more information on the national curriculum.
**www.sqa.org.uk** – for information on the Scottish
education system.

## Specialist education publishers

*Below are listed some of the key education publishers, they often
have competitions, online help and free books.*

**www.activerevision.com** – from Harper Collins, at this site you
can test yourself to see how likely you are to pass your exams.
It then recommends which books would help you to get a pass.
**www.bbc.co.uk/revisewise** – excellent section for those doing
their National Tests.
**www.cgpbooks.co.uk** – a basic online shop with details of their
popular study guides, which you can buy online.
**www.hodderheadline.co.uk** – one of the biggest education
publishers offers a fairly staid but useful site. Teachers can
order inspection copies of their books.
**www.letts-education.co.uk** – excellent site with lots of
resources, news and explanatory notes about their books.
Plus the Letts Challenge for schools and shop.

**www.nelsonthornes.co.uk** – a typical publishing site with good background on their titles and how to order them. Some books are available as online resources if you register.

# Teacher Resources

**www.theteachernet.co.uk**

ALL A TEACHER NEEDS
An excellent site that pulls together all the education resources that a teacher is likely to need from advice on how to use the Internet to getting a job and, of course, forums; there's even a certificate generator.

*See also:*
**www.byteachers.org.uk** – a collection of useful websites created by teachers for teachers.
**www.eteach.com** – recruitment for teachers.
**www.everythingeducation.org** – like an education swap shop this site brings education and business together. A great place to find equipment for schools at a decent price.
**www.learninginfo.com** – excellent site aimed at helping those with learning disabilities.
**www.literacymatters.co.uk** – a good resource site for teachers on literacy from pre-school to year 7.
**www.primarygames.co.uk** – educational games supported by the National Curriculum.
**www.primaryresources.co.uk** – excellent place to go for free lessons, ideas and worksheets.
**www.primaryworksheets.co.uk** – a straightforward site listing work sheets for primary school teachers.
**www.qualityteachingresources.co.uk** – similar to the Teacher Net but aimed at Primary school and student teachers.
**www.teachingtables.co.uk** – work sheet generation and times table help.
**www.tes.co.uk** – educational resources and news from the *Times Educational Supplement*.

# Electrical Goods, Gadgets and Appliances

*This section covers stores that sell the usual electrical goods but also offer a bit more in terms of range, offers or service. There's also the odd spy camera and gadget shop.*

## www.comet.co.uk                                                                 UK

### ALWAYS LOW PRICES, GUARANTEED

A pretty messy site these days with masses of offers on the front page, having said that it's a great place to view the widest range of goods at excellent prices.

## www.dixons.co.uk                                                               UK

### OFFERS GALORE

The Dixons site has plenty of offers and reflects what you'd find in their stores very well. It has a similar but slightly wider product range to Comet, with an additional photographic section. Delivery costs vary.

## www.richersounds.com                                                           UK

### LOWEST PRICES GUARANTEED

Despite the fact this site wouldn't win design awards, bargain hunters will want to include this site on their list, it's similar to the other electrical goods retailers but with a leaning towards music and TVs, with plenty of offers and advice. There is a search facility and the products are obviously good value, delivery charges vary depending on what you buy, although products are delivered within 5 working days.

## www.maplin.co.uk                                                               UK

### ELECTRONICS CATALOGUE

Maplin is well established and it's a bit of an event when the new catalogue is published. Now you can always have access to the latest innovations and basic equipment at this well put together site. It features the expected massive range with free delivery for orders over £30; they've recently introduced a collection point service, for £2.50 you can have your goods delivered to a local late night store for out-of-hours collection.

## www.electricshop.co.uk                                    UK
### BETTER PRODUCTS, BETTER PRICES
A good-looking but slightly messy site with a huge range of
electrical goods with offers too. The site is easy to use and has
a good search facility and it's a combination of all these factors
that make it stand out.

*See also:*

**www.24-7electrical.co.uk** – which is well designed and looks
strong on customer service judging by the number of times they
ask you to contact them.

**www.discount-appliances.co.uk** – excellent range of kitchen
appliances but awful site design, having said that product
pictures are good.

**www.electricaldiscountuk.co.uk** – a pretty straightforward site
with some good offers and a wide range.

**www.empiredirect.co.uk** – a busy-looking site with lots of
offers and a wide range.

**www.pure-digital.com** – specialists in digital products such as
radios, PC, audio and home entertainment.

**www.rtwodesign.ndirect.co.uk** – good-looking site from this
kitchen specialist.

**www.searchappliance.co.uk** – well illustrated store from this
kitchen appliance specialist.

**www.vacuumcleanersdirect.co.uk** – some 200 models to
choose from and a range of other goods besides, some great
prices too.

**www.we-sell-it.co.uk** – is also worth a visit for good prices on
kitchen and other domestic appliances.

## www.appliancespares.co.uk                                UK
### FIX IT YOURSELF
Ezee-Fix has thousands of spare parts for a massive range of
products, nearly all illustrated, including fridges, cookers,
microwaves, vacuum cleaners, etc. All it needs is online fitting
instructions, and more details on the products, and it would
be perfect.

## www.flyingtoolbox.com                                    UK

### IF YOU CAN'T FIX IT YOURSELF

With Flying Toolbox you can find someone to repair your faulty
item. Type in your location and details of the repair and they
will provide a list of repairers in your area with information on
charges and a rating from previous customers. Good though it
is, could it be just a way of selling insurance policies?

## www.bull-electrical.com                                  UK

### FOR THE SPECIALIST

Fascinating to visit, this mess of a site offers every sort of
electronic device, from divining rods to radio kits to spy
cameras. There are four basic sections:

1. Surplus electronic – scientific and optical goods,
   even steam engines.
2. Links to specialist shops – such as spy equipment
   and hydroponics.
3. Free services.
4. Web services – shopping cart technology, for example.

## www.innovations.co.uk                                    UK

### NEW TECHNOLOGY

Several hundred innovative, unusual or just plain daft items for
sale, all on a neat web site, the best bit is probably the gift
wizard, which helps you find the perfect gift when you're stuck
for something to buy. Other places for technology geeks to get
their kicks are **www.thegadgetshop.co.uk** who have free
delivery on orders over £10 and a free returns policy,
**www.firebox.com** for a really wide range of gadgets amongst
other boy's toys.

## www.simplyradios.com                                     UK

### RADIOS SPECIALIST

An excellent site devoted to radios and the first place to go if
you want something groovy or the latest thing in digital.

# English Usage

*With the success of the book Eats, Shoots and Leaves, English grammar, punctuation and usage have come under the spotlight and it seems there's even more pressure to get it right. If you're not sure where apostrophes go or what a noun or pronoun is, then these sites can help. If it is a dictionary you're after, those are found on page 332.*

## www.learnenglish.org.uk                                    UK

LEARNING ENGLISH
An excellent site from the British Council primarily aimed at those for whom English is a second language but it has a huge amount of information for students and those who just want brush up.

*See also:*
**www.apostrophe.fsnet.co.uk** – learn how to use and misuse them at home of the Apostrophe Protection Society.
**www.cogs.susx.ac.uk/local/doc/punctuation/node00.html** – a guide to punctuation from Sussex University.
**www.dailygrammar.com** – grammar lessons and quizzes.
**www.englishclub.net** – learn and teach English with the help of this comprehensive site.
**www.english-zone.com** – an American site and directory devoted to learning English; it's useful, but you have to register.
**www.gramster.com** – a free program to help with your grammar.
**www.plainenglish.co.uk** – the plain English campaign and their fight to make everything clear.
**www.soundofenglish.org** – English pronunciation.
**www.stpt.usf.edu/pms** – punctuation made simple.
**www.ucl.ac.uk/internet-grammar** – a free online course about English grammar aimed at university undergraduates but useful nonetheless.
**www.usingenglish.com** – a solid English language learning site.

# E-mail

*Here's a selection of the best free e-mail providers, there are hundreds to chose from, but hopefully these sites should help you find the one that's right for you, whether you're after efficiency or a trendy @ moniker.*

## www.fepg.net                                                    US

### FREE E-MAIL PROVIDERS GUIDE
Here's the place to start, it lists over 1,400 providers in 85 countries, including over 40 from the UK, so it's pretty comprehensive. It tends to just list them with a few details but there are recommended sites too. There's also a news section and forums.

## www.sneakemail.com                                              US

### SNEAK E-MAIL
Sneak e-mail provides an e-mail protection service whereby you can maintain a level of anonymity, stop spam or unsuitable e-mails getting to you, avoid unwanted soliciting or prevent others from selling your e-mail address to marketing companies, for example.

## www.twigger.co.uk                                               UK

### ANYWHERE IN THE WORLD
An excellent service that enables you to use your chosen e-mail address wherever you may be. One advantage is that you can see attachments before you download them onto your PC. The service is subscription based.

## www.emailaddresses.com                                          US

### E-MAIL ADDRESS DIRECTORY
A useful directory of e-mail services and programs to help you manage your e-mail and mail to your site if you own one, there are also tips on how to find an e-mail address and a directory of address directories. See also **www.web-email-addresses.com** a very good directory with site and software reviews

## www.spamcop.com                                                 US

### STOP SPAM
Spam is a term used to describe unsolicited commercial e-mail, we all get bombarded by it and at this site you can download a useful little program that will help you minimise it. See also **www.stopspam.org www.qurb.com** and **www.spaminspector.com**

# E-zines

*E-zines are the magazines of the web and there are millions of them, some with great content and quality writing. Here are some of the best reviewed along with a couple of sites that can help you find one that you like. You should be aware that many contain adult or pornographic material.*

**http://zinos.com**                                                              US

> E-ZINE DIGEST AND DATABASE
> A well-categorised site with information and reviews of some of the world's best e-zines, it's attractive and easy to find what you're looking for but not that comprehensive. See also **www.ezineseek.com** who have some 8,000 categorised and also **www.ezine-dir.com** who offer almost 3,000.

## Three of the best

**www.salon.com**                                                              US

> *SALON*
> An outstanding magazine offering a wide range of articles and topics with quality contributors and excellent writing. It's entertaining and witty covering the latest news and in depth features on current topics.

**www.theregister.co.uk**                                                              US

> *THE REGISTER*
> An opinionated and newsy e-zine devoted to the technology and computing worlds – it describes itself as 'biting the hand that feeds IT'. It's not an easy read but it's very authoritative.

**www.theonion.com**                                                              US

> AMERICA'S FINEST NEWS SOURCE
> A great send-up of American tabloid newspapers, this is one of the most visited sites on the Internet and easily one of the funniest.

# Fashion and Accessories

*The big brands have never been cheaper. Selling fashion and designer gear is another Net success, as customers flock to the great discounts that are on offer. Many people still prefer to try clothes on before buying, but the good sites all offer a convenient returns policy.*

## Fashion

**www.fuk.co.uk**                                                            UK

> FASHION UK
> All you ever need to know about the latest in UK and world fashion, updated daily. There's a good links library, competitions, chat and, of course, shopping. It's all packaged into a really attractive site, which initially looks cluttered but is OK once you get used to it.

**www.vogue.co.uk**                                                          UK

> THE LATEST NEWS FROM BRITISH VOGUE
> An absolute must for the serious follower of fashion. There's the latest catwalk news and views, and a handy who's who of fashion. There's also a section on jobs, and you can order a subscription too.
>
> For a similar experience try **www.elle.com** or the slightly less fashion-oriented but more fun **www.cosmomag.com** For access to the top designers' most recent collections and a glimpse at what could be available in the shops the following season try **www.firstview.com**

**www.ftv.com**                                                          FRANCE

> FASHION TV
> The 24-hour fashion station, so popular in gyms and bars, has a good site offering the latest from around the world. Features include video clips, radio interviews with designers plus links, gossip and horoscopes.

## www.net-a-porter.com                                                                  UK

### PRET A PORTER

A great-looking site that is easy to use with information on the
latest fashions, plus catwalk reports and shopping where you
can browse by designer or product type. Delivery costs vary
according to what you buy. For an alternative try
**www.theclothesstore.com** who also have a good selection
of clothes and accessories.

## www.fashionmall.com                                                                   US

### FASHION STORE DIRECTORY

A huge number of stores listed by category, packed with offers
and the latest new designs. Most stores are American and their
ability to deliver outside the US and delivery charges vary
considerably. The site is well-designed and easy to browse.

## www.fashion.net                                                                       US

### GUIDE TO FASHION

A good fashion search engine and directory with the added
advantage that it carries the latest fashion news too.

## www.yoox.com                                                                          UK

### TOP DESIGNERS

Great-looking site with top offers from the top designers, it's
well laid out and easy to navigate with a good returns policy.
You can search by designer or category and the quality of the
photos is good. Offers range from a few pounds to
massive discounts.

## www.haburi.com                                                                        UK

### CUT-PRICE DESIGNER CLOTHES FOR MEN AND WOMEN

Not a big range of clothes but excellent prices. Clear,
no-nonsense design makes the site easy to use.

## www.apc.fr                                                                         FRANCE

### FRENCH CHIC FROM APC

Unusual in style and for something a little different APC's site
is worth a visit. Delivery is expensive in line with the clothes,
which are beautifully designed and well presented. For more
of the French look go to **www.redoute.co.uk**

## www.gap.com                                          US

FOR US RESIDENTS ONLY
A clear, uncluttered design makes shopping here easy if
you live in the United States! For UK residents it's window-
shopping only.

## www.next.co.uk                                       UK

THE NEXT DIRECTORY
The online version of the Next catalogue is available including
clothes for men, women and children as well as products for
the home. Prices are the same as the directory, next day
delivery is £3.50 and return of unwanted goods is free.
You can order the full catalogue for £3.50.

## www.extremepie.com                                   UK

EXTREME FASHION FROM EXTREME SPORTS
A brand led selection of clothes from the world of BMX, surf,
skate and other so called sports. The site is excellent with clear
visuals and delivery costs start at £2.95.

## www.pop-boutique.com                                 UK

BUY SOMETHING THAT'S ALREADY OUT OF DATE!
A fantastic site devoted to fashion chic from the 60s, 70s and
80s, it can be a little slow but worth the wait if you're into the
period. It also sells accessories and offers a good set of
related links.

*See also:*
**www.kitschshop.co.uk** – who offer lots beside just clothes.
**www.retrorebels.co.uk** – quirky and streetwise.

## www.badfads.com                                      US

IT SHOULD NEVER HAVE HAPPENED...
An entertaining site featuring the Bad Fad Museum full of clothes,
events and collectibles that maybe we'd be better off not
remembering. The whole is a fun reminiscence of the 70s and 80s.

*Other fashion sites worth a peek...*
**www.east.co.uk** – they don't sell from the site but the clothes
look great.
**www.fashionangel.com** – excellent directory and portal for
fashion related links.

**www.fashionguide.com** – US-oriented fashion gossip and tips.
**www.fashionplanet.com** – New York-oriented fashion magazine and store.
**www.girlonthestreet.com** – home to a New York trend agency with some top tips and a sneak preview on what's coming up.
**www.girlprops.com** – another New York-based site with masses of accessories to choose from. Delivery is expensive to the UK though.
**www.hintmag.com** – a well designed fashion e-zine with regular features, news and links. The photography is especially good.
**www.japanesestreets.com** – the latest on Japanese street fashion.
**www.lucire.com** – another fashion magazine, this one is well thought of and it covers everything from catwalk style to skincare.
**www.monsoon.co.uk** – good illustrations and online store, combined with Accessorize.
**www.oasis-stores.com** – good-looking site with information on the latest trends.
**www.toastbypost.co.uk** – good mail order catalogue with the latest designs.

*Top designers*
**www.alexandermcqueen.net** – Alexander McQueen
**www.armaniexchange.com** – cheap Armani
**www.bensherman.co.uk** – Ben Sherman
**www.chanel.com** – Chanel
**www.christian-lacroix.fr** – Christian Lacroix
**www.dior.com** – Dior
**www.gucci.com** – Gucci
**www.hugo.com** – Hugo Boss
**www.jpgaultier.fr** – Jean Paul Gaultier
**www.karenmillen.com** – Karen Millen
**www.kenzo.com** – Kenzo
**www.paulsmith.co.uk** – Paul Smith
**www.tedbaker.co.uk** – Ted Baker
**www.tommy.com** – Tommy Hilfiger

# General clothes stores

## www.arcadia.co.uk                                           UK

THE UK'S LEADING FASHION RETAILER
The Arcadia Group has over 1,200 stores in the UK and the web sites are accessible, easy to use and offer good value for money. Each site has its own personality that reflects the high street store. Delivery charges vary.

**www.burton.co.uk** – Burton
**www.dorothyperkins.co.uk** – Dorothy Perkins
**www.evans.ltd.uk** – Evans
**www.missselfridge.co.uk** – Miss Selfridge
**www.outfitfashion.com** – Outfit
**www.topman.co.uk** – Topman
**www.topshop.co.uk** – Topshop
**www.wallis-fashion.com** – Wallis

## www.zoom.co.uk                                          UK

### MORE THAN JUST A SHOP
This is an excellent magazine-style site, with lots of features
other than shopping, such as free Internet access and e-mail.
Shopping consists of links to specialist retailers. You can enter
prize draws and there are a number of exclusive offers as well.
Not always the cheapest, but an entertaining shopping site.

## www.kaysnet.com                                         UK

### KAYS CATALOGUE
Massive range combined with value for money is the formula
for success with Kays. While they lead with clothes there are
plenty of other sections outside of that: jewellery, home
entertainment, toys, etc. They offer free 48-hour delivery,
£2.95 for next day delivery.

## www.freemans.co.uk                                      UK

### FREE DELIVERY IN THE UK AND GOOD PRICES
A similar site to Kays, not the full catalogue but there's a wide
range to choose from including top brands. Split into five major
sections; women, men, children, home and sports, they offer
free delivery for UK customers. There are also prizes to be won,
a special features on topical themes and information on how to
get the full catalogue.

*See also:*
**www.aboundonline.com** – a catalogue site with a very good
choice and offers a style guide and outfit finder service.
**www.grattan.co.uk** – for Grattan's catalogue.
**www.littlewoods-online.com** – wide selection of across
the range.

# Specialist clothes stores

## www.asseenonscreen.com                                      UK
### BUY WHAT YOU SEE ON FILM OR TV
Now you can buy that bit of jewellery or the cool gear that
you've seen your favourite TV or film star wearing, As Seen on
Screen specialises in supplying just that. You can search by star
or programme; it isn't cheap but you'll get noticed. They also
have a handy gift ideas section if you're looking for inspiration.

## www.bloomingmarvellous.co.uk                                UK
### MATERNITY WEAR
The UK's leading store in maternity and babywear has an
attractive site that features a good selection of clothes and
nursery products. There are no discounts on the clothes, but
they do have regular sales with some good bargains. Delivery in
the UK is £3.95 per order.

## www.shoe-shop.com                                           UK
### EUROPE'S BIGGEST SHOE SHOP
A massive selection of shoes and brands to chose from, the site
is nicely designed with good pictures of the shoes, some of
which can be seen in 3-D, a facility they are expanding.
Delivery is included in the price and there's a good
returns policy.

*See also:*
**www.britfoot.com** – home of the British Footwear Association.
**www.centuryinshoes.com** – an excellent overview of the
development of shoes in the last century.
**www.cosyfeet.com** – a good site devoted to extra roomy
footwear and socks!
**www.office.co.uk** – neat site design from this High
Street retailer.
**www.shoesdirect.co.uk** – straightforward with some
good offers.
**www.shoetailor.com** – a huge range from this popular specialist.
**www.voodooshoes.com** – great name and quite fashion oriented.

# Underwear and lingerie

## www.figleaves.com                                                    UK

MORE THAN JUST A FIG LEAF

Fig Leaves has become a big Internet success with a huge
range of lingerie from most major designers with plenty of offers
and on an easy-to-use site. They have a free delivery and free
return option too.

*See also:*

**www.assetsco.co.uk** – for men's underwear.
**www.kiniki.com** – more men's underwear.
**www.legsonline.com** – a UK specialist with a wide range.
**www.littlewomen.co.uk** – solutions for little women.
**www.rigbyandpeller.com** – for up-market lingerie.
**www.victoriassecret.com** – for designer style.

# Accessories and jewellery

## www.jewellers.net                                                    UK

THE BIGGEST RANGE ON THE NET

Excellent range of products, fashion jewellery, gifts, gold and
silver, the watch section is particularly strong. There is also
information on the history of gems, the manufacturers and
brands available. Delivery to the UK is free for orders over £50,
and there is a 30-day no quibble returns policy.

*Also check out:*

**www.geraldonline.com** – a wide range of jewellery and
watches from Gerald Ratner and associates.
**www.jewellerycatalogue.co.uk** – guarantee low prices.
**www.madaboutjewellery.com** – costume jewellery with
designer style.
**www.tateossian.com** – great contemporary jewellery and
accessories

## www.topbrands.net                                                    UK

WATCH HEAVEN

A large range of watches including Swatch, Casio, G Shock,
Baby G and Umbro are available here. The site is fast and
easy-to-use, but a better search facility would save time.
Delivery is free for the UK, but prices appear to be similar to
the high street.

# Finance, Banking and Shares

*The Internet is proving to be a real winner when it comes to personal finance, product comparison and home share dealing, with these sites you will get the latest advice and may even make some money.*

## General finance information sites, directories and mortgages

**www.fsa.gov.uk**                                                    UK

FINANCIAL SERVICES AUTHORITY
The regulating body that you can go to if you need help with your rights or if you want to find out about financial products; it will also help you to verify that the financial institution you're dealing with is legitimate. See also **www.oft.gov.uk** for the Office of Fair Trading and its informative site.

**www.financial-ombudsman.org.uk**                                   UK

FINANCIAL OMBUDSMAN SERVICES
When you have a complaint about a financial service this is a good point of call for sensible advice and help on how to go about getting a fair hearing.

**www.find.co.uk**                                                    UK

INTERNET DIRECTORY FOR FINANCIAL SERVICES
Access to thousands of financial sites; split into nine sections: loans, credit cards, insurance, mortgages, investment, banking and saving, life and pensions, information and advice, business services share dealing and some hints on best buys. Superb. See also **www.financelink.co.uk**

**www.ft.com or www.ftyourmoney.com**                                 UK

*FINANCIAL TIMES*
FT.com offers up to date news and information. The 'Your Money' section is biased towards personal finance.
Although it looks daunting, it is easy-to-use and provides sound, independent advice for everyone.

### www.fool.co.uk                                     US

THE MOTLEY FOOL
Finance with a sense of fun, The Fool is exciting and a real
education in shrewdness. It not only takes the mystery out of
share dealing but gives great advice on investment and personal
finance. You need to register to get the best out of it.

### www.thisismoney.com                               UK

MONEY NEWS AND ADVICE
Easy-to-use, reliable, 24-hour financial advice from the Daily
Mail group. It has loads of information on all aspects of
personal finance and is particularly good for comparison tools,
especially mortgages, and there's a good 'Ask the
Experts' section.

### www.iii.co.uk                                      UK

INTERACTIVE INVESTOR INTERNATIONAL
Now known as Ample, the emphasis is on investment and
share dealing with some personal finance thrown in. It retains
the interactivity of the original site but with some additional
investment information. Also can be reached through
**www.ample.com**

### www.blays.co.uk                                    UK

BLAYS GUIDES
Excellent design and impartial advice make the Blays guide a
must visit site for personal finance. Click on the 'MoneyExpert'
section for personal finance information. It has all the usual
suspects: mortgages, savings etc, plus very good sections for
students. There's also a comparative section for utilities.

### www.moneynet.co.uk                                 UK

IMPARTIAL AND COMPREHENSIVE
Rated as one of the best independent personal finance sites,
it covers over 100 mortgage lenders, has a user-friendly search
facility plus help with conveyancing and financial calculators.
It now also covers medical and life insurance well too.

*For other similar sites go to:*
**www.advfn.com** – a really ugly site but comprehensive, if you
can put up with the design.
**www.adviceonline.co.uk** – independent financial advice on a
logically designed site.

**www.bbc.co.uk/yourmoney** – outstanding and ever changing site from the BBC, best for keeping up to date with the latest financial news.

**www.digitallook.com** – one of the leading providers of financial information, excellent site.

**www.marketplace.co.uk** – 'independent' advisers from Bradford and Bingley help you make the right financial choices from mortgages to investments and pensions.

**www.moneybrain.co.uk** – a slick site offering a wide range of financial products and independent advice.

**www.moneyfacts.co.uk** – a no-nonsense information site that shows the cheapest and best value financial products with lots of authority, it's also a comparatively fast site and less tricky than some. It also covers annuities and offshore banking.

**www.moneysupermarket.com** – a very good all-rounder with help in most of the important areas of personal finance; good site layout and lots of practical advice add to the package.

**www.sexymoney.co.uk** – a good attempt at making money fun, in reality it offers solid advice on most aspects of finance.

## www.unbiased.co.uk                                              UK

### FIND AN INDEPENDENT FINANCIAL ADVISER
A good independent financial adviser is hard to come by, if you need one, then here's a good place to start. Just type in your postcode and the services you need and up pops a list of specialists in your area. See also **www.financialplanning.org.uk** for the Institute of Financial Planning and **www.sofa.org** for the Society of Financial Planners, both sites give information on how to get a financial adviser and plan your finances.

## www.quote-engine.com                                            UK

### BEST VALUE CREDIT
A guide to help you find the best deals on credit cards and loans. It's easy enough to use and there are online forms as well as links. It also covers insurance and household bills.

# Mortgage specialists

## www.charcoalonline.co.uk                                        UK

### JOIN CHARCOAL
This established mortgage adviser owned by Bradford & Bingley offers over 500 mortgages from over 45 lenders. There are also sections on pensions, investments and insurance.

*It's worth shopping around so check out these sites too:*

**www.endowmentaction.co.uk** – from *Which?* magazine here you can find out what to do if you think you've been miss-sold an endowment policy.

**www.mortgageman.co.uk** – aimed at the self-employed or those having difficulty getting a mortgage from the usual lenders, or with CCJs.

**www.mortgagepoint.co.uk** – geared towards first time buyers and those with a less than perfect credit history.

**www.mortgageshop.com** – independent financial advice about which is the best mortgage for you, a somewhat messy site though.

**www.mortgages-online.co.uk** – good independent source of information.

**www.yourmortgage.co.uk** – *Your Mortgage* magazine.

## www.mortgagecode.org.uk                                    UK

MORTGAGE CODE COMPLIANCE BOARD
The role of the mortgage board is to ensure that consumers are protected. They have a code of conduct that the lenders sign up to and they back that up by continually monitoring them. The site is packed with sensible information and help.

# Insurance

## www.insurancewide.com                                     UK

HOME OF INSURANCE ON THE WEB
Claiming to be the fastest way to get insurance cover, they offer a wide range of insurance policies covering life, travel, transport, home and business.

## www.easycover.com                                         UK

UK'S BIGGEST INDEPENDENT INSURANCE WEB SITE
Here you can get a wide range of quotes just by filling in one form. The emphasis is on convenience and speed.

## www.warrantydirect.co.uk                                  UK

EXTENDED WARRANTIES
Here you can get cover for the important things in life, your car, appliances and your computer.

*Other sites worth checking out:*

**www.eaglestardirect.co.uk** – a sparse but useful site from one of the market leaders.

**www.elephant.co.uk** – instant quotes on a wide selection of policies although they mainly specialise in car insurance.

**www.inspop.com** – choose the specially selected policy and buy online.

**www.insurance.co.uk** – another comparison site backed by Lloyds TSB.

**www.morethan.com** – hyped with the 'Where's Lucky' ads, this site is from Royal Sun Alliance and it's good for quotes in most areas including pets.

**www.quotelinedirect.co.uk** – quotes on a wide range of insurance areas.

**www.soreeyes.co.uk** – a wide range of policies and options.

**www.theaa.com/services/insuranceandfinance** – AA Insurance covers travel, cars and home.

**www.ukinsuranceguide.co.uk** – a good place to find specialist insurers.

*For advice on insurance or problems with insurance:*

**www.abi.org.uk** – Association of British Insurers, lots of advice on all aspects of insurance plus industry information.

**www.gisc.co.uk** – General Insurance Standards Council, where to go if you have a problem, it is responsible for a code of conduct amongst insurers. Some sections are available in Welsh.

# Investing and share dealing

### www.charlesschwab.co.uk                                      US

CHARLES SCHWAB EUROPE

Although you'll need to register and put up a deposit, this is the biggest and probably the most reliable Internet share dealer for the UK. You can trade online from various different accounts depending on how much you trade and your level of expertise.

*Any of the following are worth checking out, they are all good sites, each with a slightly different focus, so find the one that suits you:*

**www.apcims.co.uk** – home of the Association of Private Client Investment Managers and Stockbrokers and a usefully informative site to boot.

**www.barclays-stockbrokers.co.uk** – good value for smaller share deals and possibly the best for beginners.

**www.cofunds.co.uk** – have more control over your investments and savings.

**www.deal4free.com** – unusual and highly rated dealing site offering spread betting, share dealing and currency trading. You need a good understanding of finance to get the best out of it.

**www.earningswhispers.com** – the latest hot stock picks and earnings news.

**www.ethicalinvestment.org.uk** – if you want to invest your money in business that has a moral conscience, then here's the site that will lead you in the right direction.

**www.etrade.com** – a well-designed share trading site.

**www.freequotes.co.uk** – an all singing and dancing site with the latest share information, tips and links to related and important sites.

**www.fundsnetwork.co.uk** – an online investment superstore with a huge range of options.

**www.gni.co.uk** – award winning trading and investment site, good design.

**www.hemscott.com** – one of the more comprehensive offerings with good use of other technologies such as SMS.

**www.investorschronicle.co.uk** – this established magazine offers a useful site for share information and dealing, especially good for data on medium-sized and large companies.

**www.invest-trees.com** – profits from investing in woodlands.

**www.itsonline.co.uk** – a well-designed site that concentrates on explaining and campaigning for investment trusts.

**www.morningstar.co.uk** – a very dense site with huge amounts of information, part of its service is to collate and interpret the output of financial journalists, which must be a job in itself.

**www.nsandi.com** – National Savings and Investments.

**www.sharepeople.com** – owned by American Express, it has a nice design, is easy to use with lots of explanation on how it all works. Costs vary depending on the size of trade.

**www.sharexpress.co.uk** – the Halifax share dealing service that is a good beginner's site and charges competitively.

**www.tdwaterhouse.co.uk** – slightly more expensive than Barclays, but still quite good value, well designed with good information to back it all up.

**www.trustnet.co.uk** – all you need to know about investing in trusts.

## www.investmentguide.co.uk                                    UK

FOR THOSE WHO GO IT ALONE

An outstanding site that gives you access to three books from Harold Baldwin which are regularly updated and contain high quality information regarding share dealing and other investments; suitable for beginners or experts. Some information is by subscription.

*See also*:

**www.aitc.co.uk** – an excellent guide and advice site to Investment Trusts.

**www.citywire.co.uk** – advice and analysis from a well regarded source, some information is subscription only.

**www.hargreaveslansdown.co.uk** – a wide-ranging site with lots of investment options and advice on where to put your hard earned cash.

**www.investmentuk.org** – home of the Investment Management Association where you can find out about how the investment industry is managed, works with government, as well as some useful advice.

**www.investopedia.com** – described as the investment education site, it's packed with information and helps to navigate the investment minefield.

# Pensions

## www.pensionsorter.com                                        UK

FIND A PENSION

Excellent site if you need help around the pensions minefield, with lots of jargon-free and independent information. It tells you how to buy one, how much you should be paying and advice on what you should be saving if you want a golden retirement.

## www.pensionguide.gov.uk                                      UK

KNOW YOUR OPTIONS

An impartial guide to pensions from the government, which aims to help you choose the right option, there's also information for employers and current pension holders. Also check out **www.thepensionservice.gov.uk** – the Department for Work and Pensions represents the government line on pensions and gives good advice and the latest news.

## www.essentialpensions.co.uk                                      UK

FREE GUIDE TO UK PENSIONS
While the site wouldn't win any design awards, it is very useful and offers a comprehensive overview of most types of pension plus a calculator and a service that traces old and neglected schemes.

*For more information on pensions see:*
**www.dwp.gov.uk** – the government's advice site from the Dept of Work and Pensions with information on benefits and services.
**www.opas.org.uk** – the Office of the Pensions Advisory Service helps when things go wrong.
**www.opra.gov.uk** – the Occupational Pensions Regulatory Authority ensures pension schemes are run properly.
**www.pensioncalculator.org.uk** – a useful and detailed site on calculating your pension.
**www.PensionsNetwork.com** – good site dedicated to bringing you the best value stakeholder pensions. It's easy to use and comes with a good pensions calculator.
**www.sippdeal.co.uk** – advice on how to invest your pension in a Self Invested Personal Pension.
**www.sipp-provider-group.org.uk** – informative site on SIPP.

# Banks and building societies

## www.bankfacts.org.uk                                             UK

BRITISH BANKERS ASSOCIATION
Answers to the most common questions about banking, advice about Internet banks, the banking code and general information. There's also a facility that helps you resurrect dormant accounts. See also **www.bankingcode.org.uk** where you can find details of the standards of service that all the banks have signed up to. For information on building societies go to the Building Society Association at **www.bsa.org.uk** and also the portal site **www.buildingsocieties.com** which offers a useful regional guide.

*Here are the high street and Internet banks, building societies and the online facilities they currently offer:*
**www.abbey.com** formally **www.abbeynational.co.uk** the re-launched service offers a wide range of online financial services. For their trendy internet bank go to the sharper designed Cahoot at **www.cahoot.com** which offers similar services.

**www.alliance-leicester.co.uk** – a bright comprehensive service offering mortgages, insurance and banking.

**www.banking.hsbc.co.uk** – straightforward and easy-to-use site offering online banking alongside the usual services from HSBC, like most other big banks they've also launched a trendier Internet bank called **www.firstdirect.co.uk** which offers all the expected features plus WAP banking from an impressive site.

**www.bankofscotlandhalifax.co.uk** formerly **www.bankofscotland.co.uk** – this is now the Halifax site with extra clutter; for details see below.

**www.barclays.co.uk** – one of the original innovators in Internet banking, they offer an exhaustive service covering all aspects of personal and small business banking.

**www.citibank.co.uk** – very impressive site with a complete Internet personal banking service with competitive rates. Citibank have few branches and this is their attempt at a bigger foothold in the UK.

**www.co-operativebank.co.uk** – acknowledged as the most comprehensive of the banking sites – and it's easy to use. Excellent, but they have also launched the trendier and more competitive Smile banking site **www.smile.co.uk** which is aimed at a younger audience. Both offer ethical and green options.

**www.egg.co.uk** – A new-look site with banking, insurance, investment advice even shopping.

**www.halifax.co.uk** – comprehensive range of services via an easy-to-use and well-designed site and you'll find a great deal of advice and information all clearly explained. Their Internet-only banking offshoot is called Intelligent Finance, which is excellent and can be found at the memorable **www.if.com**

**www.lloydstsb.co.uk** – combined with Scottish Widows, Lloyds offer a more rounded and comprehensive financial service than most. The online banking is well established and efficient. They provide help for small businesses and some Welsh language support too.

**www.nationwide.co.uk** – a much slicker design than the old Nationwide site, they offer a complete online banking service as well as loans and mortgages.

**www.natwest.com** – NatWest offer both online and share dealing, with good sections for students and small businesses. It's got a nice design, and it's straightforward to use.

**www.newcastlenet.co.uk** – a nice-looking and easy-to-use site from one of the smaller banking/building societies, offering all the usual services including online mortgage applications.
**www.standardchartered.com** – good-looking and user-friendly site from this small bank.
**www.virgin-direct.co.uk** – access to Virgin's comprehensive financial services site featuring a share dealing service, pension advice, banking, mortgages and general financial advice. There's help for the visually impaired as well.
**www.woolwich.co.uk** – online banking plus all the other usual personal financial services make the Woolwich site a little different.
**www.ybs.co.uk** – a good all-rounder from the Yorkshire Building Society.

## www.switchwithwhich.co.uk                                    UK

SWITCH BANK ACCOUNTS EASILY
*Which?* magazine's site devoted to a campaign to encourage people to switch to less costly bank accounts. There is advice on the best account for you and how to move your account to the recommended one painlessly.

## Tax

## www.inlandrevenue.gov.uk                                     UK

TALK TO THE TAXMAN
The Inland Revenue has a very informative site where you can get help on all aspects of tax. You can even submit your tax return over the Internet and there's a good set of links to other government departments.

## www.tax.org.uk                                               UK

CHARTERED INSTITUTE OF TAXATION
A great resource, they don't provide information on individual questions but they can put you in touch with a qualified adviser. It's a good place to start if you have a problem with your tax.

## http://listen.to/taxman                                      UK

THE TAX CALCULATOR
Amazingly fast, just input your gross earnings and your tax and actual earnings are calculated.

**www.etax.co.uk**                                                    UK
> USEFUL DOWNLOADS
> An attractive and easy-to-use site with helpful downloads of
> spreadsheets and forms from this Kent specialist.

# Business

**www.economist.com**                                                 UK
> *THE ECONOMIST* MAGAZINE
> The airports' best-selling magazine goes online with a wide-
> ranging site that covers business and politics world-wide.
> You can get access to the archive and also their excellent
> country surveys. If you're in business you need this in your
> favourites box. See also **www.businessweek.com** who offer
> a wide range of business news and information.

**www.startinbusiness.co.uk**                                         UK
> AN ONLINE BUSINESS STARTER KIT
> An excellent portal site on all things to do with business
> including a good guide to help you start a business. There are
> plenty of links plus listings of businesses for sale, property,
> services and potential opportunities.

**www.businessadviceonline.org.uk**                                   UK
> BUSINESS ADVICE
> An excellent resource whether you're starting out or want to
> improve an existing business. There are sections on choosing
> the right IT systems, contracts, selling techniques and
> much more.

**www.hoovers.com**                                                   UK
> COMPANY RESEARCH
> Get basic information on any UK and US company plus related
> links and advice, a very useful research tool. See also
> **www.carolworld.com** – Company Annual Reports Online,
> a useful free service.
>
> *See also:*
> **www.business-ethics.com** – encouraging the right sort of
> corporate responsibility.
> **www.bvca.co.uk** – the public face of venture capitalism.
> **www.businesslink.org** – the National Business Advice Service
> has a comprehensive site backed up by a hotline.

**www.clearlybusiness.com** – offers the same information as above but is a more commercial affair.

**www.companies-house.gov.uk** – a useful site if you want to research companies with assess to information and guidance on most aspects of business and the regulations surrounding it. Here you can check-up on whether companies really exist or not.

**www.whichfranchise.com** – a slightly messy site that offers the information you need on all the available franchises in the UK, and how to go about getting one.

## www.uk.sage.com                                             UK

BUSINESS SOFTWARE

If you need accounting software to solve virtually any sort of problem or provide a new service, you should find it here. Sage has a good reputation for helping small businesses.

## www.asiannet.com                                            US

BUSINESS INFORMATION ON ASIA

Market information, news, services and links all geared to the main Asian markets each of which has a feature site. There are company profiles as well as an online shop where you can contact companies to get product samples.

# Credit checking

## www.checkmyfile.com                                         UK

IS YOUR CREDIT GOOD?

For just under a tenner you can get a basic online credit rating on yourself, or if you pay more, they'll send you a more detailed report. Very useful and informative, they even keep updating your file for a yearly sum. You can also work out your likely credit score using their online calculator for free. Data protection is guaranteed too.

*See also these sites that offer similar information and services:*
**www.callcredit.plc.uk** – get your credit file sent for £2.
**www.equifax.co.uk** – get a full detailed credit report for £8.25 online.
**www.experian.co.uk** – get a credit report sent for £2.

# Debt management

**www.nacab.org.uk**                                                    UK

CITIZENS ADVICE BUREAU
Often the first port of call for people with debt issues, the site
offers useful information and the latest campaigns. There's a
search facility to find your nearest office and a link to
**www.adviceguide.org.uk** which contains basic advice and
information on your rights.

*See also:*
**www.cccs.co.uk** – a charity dedicated to helping people get
out of debt.
**www.debtadvicecentre.co.uk** – lots of useful advice and
information on what to do if you find yourself in debt;
excellent for links.
**www.debtcounsellors.co.uk** – specialists in advising people
on what to do if they get into financial difficulty and dealing
with creditors.
**www.nationaldebtline.com** – a free debt help service with
useful links.

# Miscellaneous

**www.young-money.co.uk**                                               UK

ONLINE MONEY GAME SHOW
Combines general knowledge and financial games aimed at
turning the little ones into the financial whiz-kids of the future.
There's a lot that most adults can learn from the site as well
– it's a fun way of learning about the world of finance. You need
Shockwave for it to work. See also **www.moneychimp.com**
who offer a basic explanation on most aspects of finance.

**www.ifs.org.uk**                                                      UK

INSTITUTE OF FISCAL STUDIES
Independent analysis of all things financial especially the tax
system, surprisingly interesting but a pretty dull site.

**www.paypal.com**                                                      UK

SEND AND RECEIVE MONEY ONLINE
A genuinely useful service, especially for small businesses and
online auction junkies, it's very easy and straightforward to use.
There's a directory of over 42,000 web sites that use PayPal
and details of how your site can get involved.

## www.moneysavingexpert.com UK

SAVE ON EVERYTHING
Saving money guides to almost every thing we pay out on,
from credit cards to utilities, this is an extremely useful site
from TV and radio pundit Martin Lewis.

# Finding Someone

*Following the success of Friends Reunited, there's been a massive
explosion of sites dedicated to finding old friends and colleagues.
Here we've listed all the best sites, and also the place to go to find
a phone number, contacts for business and the home.*

## Directory sites

### www.yell.co.uk UK

UK BUSINESS DIRECTORY
Basically a search engine and directory devoted to businesses.
The online Yellow Pages is a very handy site to have in your
favourites list, it's easy-to-use and you can download the
toolbar on to your browser to make it even more convenient.
You can even get your search results shown on a map.
See also **www.bigyellow.com** for the US.

### www.scoot.co.uk UK

THE SIMPLE WAY TO FIND A BUSINESS
Register, type in the person's name or profession then hit the
Scoot button and the answer comes back in seconds. Oriented
towards finding businesses but useful nonetheless. There's also
a cinema finder.

### www.thomweb.co.uk UK

THE ANSWER COMES OUT OF THE BLUE
Thomson's offer an impressive site and provide local directories
online. It's divided up into five major categories:

1. A business finder – search using a combination of name, type
   of business or region.
2. People finder – track down phone numbers and home or e-mail
   addresses.
3. Comprehensive local information – available on the major cities
   and regions.

4.    News.
5.    Net search and directory.

**www.bt.com/directory-enquiries**                                    UK
BRITISH TELECOM DIRECTORY
The way to cut those bills to directory enquiries. You're given
free access to 10 enquiries per day, but you can have another
200 free searches per month if you register. For a full overview
of BT services including checking up and paying your phone
bill go to **www.bt.com**

*See also:*
**www.addresses.com/intl-directories.php** – another list of
international directories.
**www.anywho.com** – straightforward American-oriented search
site with an international section.
**www.infospace.com** – another good search engine with yellow
(business) and white (people) pages sections, it offers much
more though including a good web directory.
**www.royalmail.co.uk** – The mail may have a silly name
nowadays but this site offers a useful address finder and you
can track your recorded deliveries too.
**www.ukphonebook.com** – simple to use, quick with a
no-nonsense design, also has mapping, a business finder and
lots of adverts.

**www.192.com**                                                       UK
THE UK'S LARGEST DIRECTORY SERVICE
Plenty available for non-fee payers such as people and business
finders, directories and route planning. There are also various
subscription options, providing access to other databases such
as the electoral role, company reports and the UK-info CD.

# Finding old friends

**www.friendsreunited.co.uk**                                         UK
THE ONE STOP SITE TO REUNITE
Once the UK's most visited web site, a phenomenal success
story and millions of people have made contact with old friends
using the site. The read only service is free, but access to the
full service costs £7.50. For that you get access to the schools
and workplace data base and the ability to contact people
through the site. It's very easy to use and you'll quickly
lose yourself.

*See also:*

**www.disabledunited.com** – dedicated to uniting disabled people.

**www.friend-ships.com** – find that person you met on a cruise.

**www.gradfinder.com** – good site covering many of the world's schools and universities.

**www.scoutsreunited.co.uk** – find your old scouting buddies here.

**www.reunitelostfriends.co.uk** – a nicely designed site with some unusual sections such as 'lost sweethearts' and 'mothers groups'.

*Some similar sites dedicated to re-uniting old service colleagues:*
**www.armedforcesfriends.co.uk**
**www.forcesreunited.org.uk**
**www.servicepals.com**
**www.the-ex-forces-network.org.uk**

*Try also:*

**www.adoptionlink.co.uk** – helping those adopted to find their roots

**www.ariadne.ac.uk/issue20/search-engines/#lycos** – another page of tips, advice and links on finding people using the Internet.

**www.arielbruce.com** – Ariel Bruce is an ex-social worker with a good track record of finding missing people.

**www.find-someone.com** – a very commercial US site offering software for sale that may help track someone down.

**www.journalismnet.com/people** – a tips sheet that contains links and advice on how to find people.

**www.missing-you.net** – free message posting designed to help find lost friends thought to be in the UK.

**www.peopletracer.co.uk** – people traced for a fee – from £24.95.

**www.reunite.org** – helping families who have suffered the trauma of child abduction.

## www.andys-penpals.com                                    UK

FIND A PENPAL

A site devoted to penpals around the world. It's easy to use and free; there are also links to similar sites and a chat room.

# Flowers

## Sending flowers

### www.interflora.co.uk                                    UK

TURNING THOUGHTS INTO FLOWERS
Interflora can send flowers to over 140 countries, many on the
same day as the order. They'll have a selection to send for
virtually every occasion and they offer a reminder service.
The service is excellent, although they are not very up front on
delivery costs, which can be high. If you can't get what you
need here then try **www.teleflorist.co.uk** who offer a
similar service.

### www.flyingflowers.com                                   UK

EUROPE'S LEADING FLOWERS BY POST COMPANY
Freshly picked flowers flown from Jersey to the UK from £8.99.
All prices include delivery and you save at least £1 on all
bouquets against their standard advertised off-line prices.
They'll also arrange next day delivery in the UK. The site is
simple and there's a reminder service just to make sure you
don't forget anyone.

### www.clareflorist.co.uk                                  UK

STYLISH BOUQUETS AND PRETTY PICTURES
Easy-to-use site with good customer services and free delivery
to UK with surcharge for same day delivery. Cost reflects the
sophistication of the flowers.

### www.daisys2roses.com                                    UK

MAKE YOUR OWN BOUQUET
A simple, step-by-step approach to making up a bouquet of
your choice. You can select from a large range of flowers and
there's help to get you started, you can even search by flower
type. Delivery is free in the UK.

## Flower arranging

**www.paula-pryke-flowers.com**                                    UK

> LIVE YOUR LIFE IN COLOURS
> A bright and well laid out site from one of the UK's premium
> flower arrangers. There are details of her books and designs,
> which you can order.
>
> *See also:*
> **www.jane-packer.co.uk** – another top celebrity with a site
> offering limited information; however, it does come with a
> contact e-mail.
> **www.nafas.org.uk** – informative, if dull site from the National
> Association of Flower Arrangement Societies.
> **www.silkflowerarranging.com** – learn how to arrange silk
> flowers successfully.
> **www.thegardener.btinternet.co.uk** – details on how to achieve
> the perfect flower arrangers garden.

# Food and Drink

*Whether you want to order from the comfort of your own home,
indulge yourself, find the latest food news or get a recipe, this
collection of sites will fulfil your foodie desires. It features
supermarkets, online magazines and information sites, specialist food
retailers, vegetarian and organic stockists, drinks information and
suppliers, where to go for kitchen equipment and help in finding
the best places when eating out.*

## Supermarkets and general food stores

**www.iceland.co.uk**                                             UK

> FROZEN FOOD SPECIALIST DELIVERS
> Iceland's online service is considered one of the best with
> nearly all of the UK covered. Easy to navigate, but can be
> ponderous to use. Your order is saved each time, which then
> acts as the basis for your next order. Information on the
> products is good, and there's a wide range available; orders
> must be £40 or more. They also offer deals on
> home appliances.

## www.waitrose.com

### IF YOU ARE REALLY INTO FOOD
Waitrose is offering a very good comprehensive and well designed site that oozes quality, so it's a pleasure to do your grocery shopping online. You can buy wine, gifts, organics and some John Lewis products. In addition it also has all the features you'd expect from an ISP, articles and recipes in their *Illustrated Food* magazine including information on food-related campaigns and organic issues, an excellent gift shop, plus party, flowers and travel sections and even one on competitions and puzzles. See also the excellent **www.ocado.com** who, in partnership with Waitrose, offer a delivery service to mainly the south of England – one to watch.

## www.tesco.co.uk

### THE LIFESTYLE SUPERSTORE
This functional site has a comprehensive offering, there's a wide range of goods on offer though, including electrical goods, clothes and books. There's also a section on personal finance, other shops, parenting advice and healthy living. Offers now abound with some great savings all aimed at capturing your e-mail address and future custom. As if echoing Tesco's movement away from selling just food, groceries do not seem to be the major function of this site anymore.

## www.sainsburys.co.uk

### NOT JUST GOOD TASTE
Sainsbury's site is sparser than Tesco, with the emphasis being on good food, cooking, recommendation and taste, and of course the Nectar loyalty card. The facility to place an advance order at their Calais store, which you can then pick up, and pay for in France, will appeal to those who wish to save time on their booze run.

## www.somerfield.co.uk

### MEGADEALS
The emphasis is firmly on offers but there's also a recipe finder, wine guide and essential food facts. The kid's section includes food-based science experiments, recipes and a quiz. Delivery covers most of the UK and it's free if you spend more than £25, provided you live near enough to the store.

F

### www.asda.co.uk                                              UK

PERMANENTLY LOW PRICES
There's lots of information about the company and what it
stands for plus links to its online shop. There are also sections
on financial services, health and offers. Delivery is £4.25,
but free if you spend more than £99.

### www.safeway.co.uk                                           UK

FOR THE FAMILY WITH YOUNG CHILDREN
A good all-rounder, the Safeway site provides much in the way
of information on lifestyle subjects including cookery advice,
recipes, a drinks guide and advice on healthy eating. There's no
online shopping though there is information on savings and
their cheap petrol scheme. As Safeway has a new owner at
time of writing, this may change soon.

### www.heinz-direct.co.uk                                      UK

DELIVERING MORE THAN 57 VARIETIES OF FOOD
To get the best value for money it's best to order in bulk, as
delivery charges can be high. It can be very slow to use and
is split into product feature sections: Weightwatchers, canned
grocery, Heinz and Farley's baby food, hampers, and sauces
and pickles.

### www.homefarmfoods.com                                       UK

DELICIOUS FROZEN FOOD DELIVERED FREE
Good selection of frozen foods and huge range of ready meals
with a good use of symbols indicating whether the product is
low fat, microwavable, vegetarian etc. With free delivery, it's
especially good value, and there is no minimum order. See also
**www.foodhall.co.uk** who have a good selection of specialist
stores to choose from.

### www.farmersmarkets.net                                      UK

NATIONAL ASSOCIATION OF FARMERS' MARKETS
A farmers' market sells locally produced goods; locate your
nearest market or get advice on how to set one up.

### www.freedomfood.co.uk                                       UK

RSPCA FARM ASSURANCE
Details of a scheme from the RSPCA to improve conditions for
farm animals. The site shows where you can buy these
products, lists producers and has some recipes too.

# African cuisine

## www.betumi.com
GHANA

### TRADITIONAL AND CONTEMPORARY
Recipes, information and links on Africa and its food, it also has some charitable aspects.

*See also:*
**http://africafood.tripod.com** – some recipes at this site promoting an African cookery book.
**www.boykie.co.uk/south-african-cuisine.htm** – South African cuisine.
**www.afrol.com/Categories/Culture/recipes.htm** – West African recipes.
**www.khound.com/topics/africanr.htm** – a bit of a mess but a good overview of African cookery by country and region plus information on its derivatives too.

# Asian and Indian cookery

## www.curryhouse.co.uk
UK

### EVERYTHING YOU NEED TO KNOW ABOUT CURRY
Curryholics can get their fill of recipes, recommendations, taste tests, interviews with famous chefs and a restaurant guide, good for links too.

*See also:*
**www.curryguidenet.co.uk** – a good-looking site with a good range of recipes and restaurants.
**www.currypages.com** – an Indian Restaurant guide although none of our local ones were listed!
**www.currysauce.com** – get all the sauces delivered and still win a year's supply.
**www.gcosta.co.uk/curryclub** – join Pat Chapman's famous curry club, access recipes and buy his range of ingredients.
**www.redhotcurry.com/food_and_drink/index.htm** – excellent food and drink section from the well-known British Asian portal.

**www.straitscafe.com**                                    SINGAPORE
RECIPES FROM SINGAPORE
A straightforward site with lots of recipes not only from
Singapore, but from Southeast and East Asia including Japan
and China, there's also a good set of links and a useful glossary
at the 'pantry'. For Indonesian cooking go to the enjoyable
Henks Hot Kitchen which can be found at **www.indochef.com**

**www.japanweb.co.uk**                                          JAPAN
JAPANESE CUISINE
An interesting and growing site covering the basics of Japanese
cooking along with recipes and a UK restaurant guide. It also
has a glossary and tips on etiquette. 'Itadakimasu' as they say.
See also **www.yosushi.com** who offer a hi-tech site that
features their restaurants and a sushi-ordering service to
selected areas, but you need Internet Explorer to get it to work.

**www.thaicuisine.com**                                            US
RECIPES AND RESTAURANTS
This site offers recipes and ingredient information, though the
restaurant list is only for the US, see also **www.tat.or.th/food/**
which has good background information on Thai food, and
**www.importfood.com/recipes.html** who offer up some
125 recipes.

**www.chinavoc.com/cuisine/index.asp**                             US
CHINESE COOKERY
Lots of tips and background information on Chinese cookery
with advice on techniques and recipes.
**www.chinavista.com/culture/cuisine/recipes.html** is worth
checking out for its list of regional recipes. Our old favourite
**www.chopstix.co.uk** is up and running and looks good,
unfortunately the links are not very reliable.
Also **www.chinatown-online.co.uk** is dedicated to what's going
on in London's China Town; it has an excellent food section.

*See also:*
**www.asiarecipe.com** – a messy, but well-intentioned site with
a range of recipes and ingredients covering the whole of Asia.

# Barbecues

## www.barbecuen.com
US

BARBECUES

In the unlikely event that our weather will be good enough to have a barbecue, then here's a site with all you need to know on the subject. See also the musically enhanced **www.britishbarbecue.co.uk** with 2,250 recipes.

# British and Irish cookery

## www.greatbritishkitchen.co.uk
UK

BRITISH FOOD TRUST

This has an extensive recipe collection, history, chat from celebrity chefs and a kids' recipe collection makes this a much improved site.

*See also:*

**http://pages.eidosnet.co.uk/cookbook/index.html** – a tribute to British cooking with some 50 recipes, the site is pretty dated though.

**www.recipes4us.co.uk** – who have over 2,000 recipes although some are international.

**www.regionalfoodanddrink.co.uk** – a regional guide to the UK's food specialists.

## www.rampantscotland.com/recipes
UK

A WEE FEAST

A very simple site listing a good selection of traditional Scottish recipes. **www.ifb.net/webit/recipes.htm** and **www.scottishrecipes.co.uk** also have a small collection of Scottish recipes.

## www.baxters.co.uk
UK

TRADITIONAL FARE

An old Scottish firm offering their range of soups, jams, sauces, hampers and gift foods online through a well-designed and easy-to-use site; there are also recipes from top chef Nick Nairn. Shipping charges vary according to destination.

**www.tasteofireland.com**                                           UK

> A TASTE OF IRELAND
> Recipes, a restaurant guide and a shop all in one, it's not that
> comprehensive but well worth a visit nonetheless.

**www.red4.co.uk/recipes.htm**                                       UK

> WELSH RECIPES
> Here are over 120 traditional recipes including lava bread,
> wines, cawl and Welshcakes. See also
> **www.hookerycookery.com/welsh-menu.htm** where there's
> a similar list.

**www.tasteofengland.co.uk**                                         UK

> A TASTE OF ENGLAND
> Not much in the way of recipes but it does serve as a portal to
> English farmers and producers, so great for links, though the
> site is a bit of mess.

## Celebrity chefs and TV

*If you can't find what you're looking for on their dedicated websites,
check out* **www.bbc.co.uk/food** *where you'll find a list of over 40 TV
cooks and presenters.*

**www.delia.co.uk**                                                  UK

> DELIA SMITH
> The queen of British cookery has a clean, well-designed site
> with lots of recipes, which can be accessed by the good search
> facility. If you join you get added features such as daily tips,
> competitions and the chance to chat to Delia. There's also a
> section on what Delia is up to and you can ask questions and
> get advice at the cookery school. Last year a shop was added to
> the site, and now there's also travel, gardening and homeware.

**www.jamieoliver.net**                                              UK

> WHAT HE'S ABOUT
> The official site mainly dedicated to Jamie's diary but there's
> also advice on kitchen hassles and links to his restaurant,
> charity and kitchenware. He is gradually adding to the small
> recipe collection.

## www.garyrhodes.com
UK

### GARY RHODES
Recipes, tips and seasonal suggestions here at Rhodes' official site. There's also a good section on the basics and loads of information on entertaining in style all on a nicely designed, if somewhat wishy-washy site.

## www.rickstein.co.uk
UK

### PADSTOW, STEIN AND SEAFOOD
Information on Rick, his restaurants and cookery school all wrapped up in a tidy website. You can also book a table or a room as well as order products from the online deli.

## www.ukfood.tv
UK

### UK FOOD
Very attractive site from this specialist TV channel with lots of recipes, tips and features based on their programming.

## www.foodtv.com
US

### FOOD NETWORK
A rather strange but quite appealing site devoted to American TV cooks. It has some video footage and a search engine that covers 20,000 recipes, plus some good articles.

# Cheese

## www.cheese.com
US

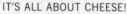

### IT'S ALL ABOUT CHEESE!
A huge resource site with information on over 700 types of cheese. There's advice about the best way to eat cheese, a vegetarian section, a cheese bookshop and links to other cheese-related sites and online stores. You can even find a suitable cheese searching by texture, country or type of milk. They've added a shop, but as it's American it is not very useful to a UK audience. For more cheese information try the attractive Cheesenet site at **http://cheesenet.wgx.com** it has an excellent search facility, or the American Dairy Association's **www.ilovecheese.com** which also offers a cheese guide and lots of recipes.

**www.cheesemongers.co.uk**                                    UK

OPULENT SITE FROM UK'S OLDEST CHEESEMONGERS
Paxton and Whitfield, the royal cheesemongers, provide a very
clear and easy-to-use online shop but charge £10.00 to ship
goods. A superb selection of cheese and luxury produce, with
hampers, cheese kitchen, accessories and wine. A pleasure to
browse and it's tempting to buy; you can also join the
Cheese Society. See also the British Cheese Board at
**www.britishcheese.com** where you can learn about our
cheeses, get some recipes and general cheese propaganda.

**www.teddingtoncheese.co.uk**                                 UK

BRITISH AND CONTINENTAL CHEESEMONGERS
Much-acclaimed site offering over 130 types of cheese at
competitive prices. The sections are split by country and there's
a good system for showing whether the cheese is suitable
for vegetarians, pregnant women, etc. There is also an
encyclopaedia, a selection of wine and other produce; you can
even design your own hamper. When buying you can stipulate
how much cheese you want in grams (150 minimum),
shipping from £7.25 for the UK and a minimum order of £18.

**www.fromages.com**                                        FRANCE

TRADITIONAL FRENCH CHEESE
French cheese available to order and delivered within 24 hours
along with wine recommendations and express shipping from
France. Delivery is included in the price but if you're worried
about cost you probably shouldn't be shopping here.

## Confectionery, cake and chocolate

**www.hotelchocolat.com**                                      UK

DEDICATED TO GOOD CHOCOLATE
An excellent and well-illustrated site from an experienced
retailer, they also offer lots of choice and a wide range of
chocolate-related gifts and you can even buy in bulk! There's
a really good selection facility and the chocolate tasting club.
Delivery to UK included in the price and they will guarantee
that it's delivered by a specified date. Formally called
**www.chocexpress.co.uk**

## www.chocaid.com
UK

### HELP THE HUNGRY
A great site where you can give to charity when you buy gourmet chocolates, they have a good selection and you can choose which good cause your donation goes to.

## www.thorntons.co.uk
UK

### WELCOME TO CHOCOLATE HEAVEN
Thorntons offer a comprehensive and easy-to-use site, with an emphasis on gifts. The range is extensive and they supply world-wide – at a cost. Orders costs start at £4.50 for the UK. There are product sections for continental, premier, gifts and hampers plus flowers and wine. For handmade chocolates try the tempting selections at **www.chocolateschocolates.co.uk** or **www.handmadechocolates.co.uk**

*See also:*
**www.bettysbypost.co.uk** – a wide selection of goodies from this well known Harrogate confectioner.
**www.cadbury.co.uk** – where you can learn all about chocolate plus lots of recipes and play games.
**www.chocolate.co.uk** – home of the Chocolate Society.
**www.cocoaura.com** – high class chocolatier with some very original handmade recipes.
**www.hersheys.com** – tour the famous American factory, good for recipes too.
**www.prestat.co.uk** – hand-made chocolates delivered to your door the next day
**www.virtualchocolate.com** – where you can send virtual chocolate, read chocolate inspired stories and poems.

## www.thecakestore.com
UK

### CAKES, CAKES AND MORE CAKES
Very good online cake store with a huge selection, good prices and you can order a tailor-made cake too. Sadly they only deliver in London and parts of the South East. See also **www.clickthecookie.co.uk** who offer a wide range of cookies and gift options; particularly useful if you want to send themed fortune cookies or a tube of fortune cookie insults.

### www.janeasher.co.uk UK

JANE ASHER CAKES
A pretty workman-like affair, you can order personalised cakes
(London orders only delivered or collected by customer), select
from a range of mail order cakes and you can buy equipment too.

### www.pastrywiz.com US

PASTRY HEAVEN
A general food site with the emphasis on pastry in all its forms,
there are plenty of recipes and links to keep all cake
fans happy.

*See also:*
**www.flourbin.co.uk** – get any number of different types of
flour here.

### www.oldsweetshop.com UK

SWEETS THE WAY THEY USED TO BE...
Sweets from an old fashioned sweet shop, stacked with
favourites like Dolly Mixtures, sugared almonds and Parma
violets, a visit here is a nostalgia trip as much as anything.
Delivery is charged to you at whatever they get charged by
weight. See also **www.sugarboy.co.uk** who offer a wide
range of goodies and **www.aquarterof.com** which is great for
old favourites.

## Diet and nutrition

### www.3fatchicks.com US

THE SOURCE FOR DIET SUPPORT
The awesome Three Fat Chicks have produced one of the best
food web sites. It's entertaining and informative about dieting or
trying to stay healthy. There are food reviews, how to live on
fast food, recipes, links to other low fat sites, a section for
chocoholics, diet tips and 'tool box' which has calorie tables
and calculators; also getting started, on losing weight and how
to get free samples. Check out the fast food guide to get the
nutritional low down on your fast food chain favourites.

## www.cookinglight.com
US

THE BEST FROM COOKING LIGHT MAGAZINE
One of the world's best-selling food magazines, their slow site offers a huge selection of healthy recipes and step-by-step guides to cooking. There are also articles on healthy living.

## www.weightwatchers.co.uk
UK

WELCOME TO WEIGHTWATCHERS UK
A much improved site with more information on how to lose weight, keep motivated, keep fit, chat and, of course, where to find your local group. There's also a shop where you can buy specially selected foods and related diet products – delivery starts at £3.50, free on orders over £60.

## http://atkins-uk.com also http://atkinscenter.com
UK

DR ATKINS
The world's best selling dietician offers a site that gives the background to his low carbohydrate diet and how you can lose weight and get healthy on it. You can shop for Atkins' supplements and foods, delivery begins at £4.95. For another approach try **www.low-carb.com**

## www.mynutrition.co.uk
UK

ONLINE GUIDE TO HEALTHY EATING
Find out what you really should be eating from this cool British site, which has been put together by a professional nutritionist. Its features include an A-Z of ailments and diseases, dietary advice, newsletter, relevant articles and of course shopping. Delivery is £1.50 for the UK.

## www.weightlossresources.co.uk
UK

FAD FREE TOOLS FOR HEALTHY WEIGHT LOSS
Excellent place to go for information on weight loss and diets; you can keep a weight loss diary, find out about exercise, get advice on what to eat and catch up on the latest research. You can also share your experience with others too, you have to register to get the best out of it.

*See also:*
**http://lowfatcooking.about.com** – a well-presented and informative section from the About.com website.
**www.caloriecontrol.org** – low fat information from the Calorie Control Council.

www.coolmeals.co.uk – food facts for kids.

www.cyberdiet.com – a good all rounder with a wide range of advice, including specialist diets.

www.fatfree.com – almost 5,000 recipes, all fat free or very low fat.

www.fatfreekitchen.com – Indian vegetarian and low fat recipes.

www.foodsubs.com – a useful food thesaurus with the added benefit that it offers up low fat substitutes to fatty foods.

www.nutrition.org.uk – home of the British Nutrition Foundation, a site with masses of advice and information, especially useful for parents.

www.realslimmers.com – a well-designed site with good advice and practical help.

www.rosemary-conley.co.uk – all about Rosemary and her healthy lifestyle.

## Special dietary needs

*Also refer to the section on health, page 200.*

### www.diabeticgourmet.com                                     UK

DELICIOUS FOR DIABETICS
Lots of recipes and ideas to make food palatable without endangering your blood sugar levels from Diabetic Gourmet magazine, see also **www.diabetic.com/cookbook** where there's a great archive of recipes.

### www.gfcfdiet.com                                            UK

GLUTEN FREE
The design lets this site down, but it has very good information on gluten free products and food. See also **www.celiac.com** who have some good recipes and **www.glutenfreemall.com** whose temperamental site has lots of information on products, although they don't deliver to the UK at time of writing.

### www.foodag.com                                             UK

E-NUMBERS MADE CLEAR
The food additives guide with information on what additives are bad for you and which are derived from animals.
The ingredients section provides a list of e-numbers in common food groups indicating the nasties to be avoided.

**www.foodallergy.org**                                          US
  ALLERGY AND ANAPHYLAXIS
  A useful site with information and links on food allergies and
  their reactions, it's very much oriented to the US so also try
  **www.anaphylaxis.org.uk/** which is also very helpful and UK-based.

# French food

**www.gourmet2000.co.uk**                                        UK
  LE GOURMET FRANÇAIS
  High quality French ingredients and recipes, combined with a
  nicely designed site and convenient shopping. Delivery is very
  pricey at £7.99 for the minimum £20 order, but once you
  spend £100 it's free.

**http://frenchfood.about.com**                                  US
  FRENCH CUISINE
  **About.com** have created a superb resource at this site with
  a huge amount of data, articles and recipes. Every aspect of
  French cooking seems to be covered from the ingredients to the
  shops and presentation.

  *See also:*
  **www.afrenchkiss.com** – make your own gourmet meals with
  this fun French recipe creation program.
  **www.hertzmann.com/index.php** – French recipes from
  an obsessive…
  **www.manoir.com** – world class recipes from Raymond Blanc
  as well as details of his hotels and restaurants.
  **www.paniers.com** – high quality French food online, for a price.

# Hygiene and food safety

**www.foodsafety.gov/~fsg/fsgadvic.html**                        UK
  FOOD SAFETY
  A government site with basic advice on handling foods in all
  sorts of situations from product-specific advice to helping those
  with special needs; there's also good links to related topics.

  *See also:*
  **www.foodstandards.gov.uk** – home of the Food Standards
  Association who have lots of information on what is safe to eat.
  **www.ourfood.com** – an overview of food science and hygiene.

# Italian food

### www.mangiarebene.net                                          US

EAT WELL
An award-winning site that covers everything to do with Italian
cookery. Its aim is to give a grand tour of Italian cuisine –
and it succeeds, including some 600 recipes in the English
language section, but over 1,600 overall. See also
**http://italy1.com/cuisine** which has good regional cooking and
food information as well as lots of recipes, while for Italian food
shopping try **www.esperya.com**

### www.ilovepasta.org                                          US

US NATIONAL PASTA ASSOCIATION
250 recipes, tips, fast meals and healthy options all wrapped
up in a clear and easy-to-use site. There's also information on
the different types of pasta and advice on the right sauces to
go with them.

### www.getoily.com                                          UK

OLIVE OIL
All you need to know about olive oil, cooking with it, health
benefits and history, oh and you can buy it too, along with a
good selection of other Mediterranean products.

### www.dominos.co.uk                                          UK

PIZZA DELIVERY
Order your pizza online and get it delivered to your home
providing you live near enough to one of their outlets that is.
It's a nicely designed site, which also has a few games if you
get bored waiting.

## Kitchen equipment

### www.lakelandlimited.co.uk                                          UK

EXCELLENT CUSTOMER SERVICE
Lakeland pride themselves on service and it shows, they aim to
get all orders dispatched in 24 hours and delivery on orders
over £40 is free. The product listing for both kitchen and
homeware is comprehensive too.

**www.urbanbar.com**                                                          UK

GLASS AND CLASS
A very attractive site from this glass specialist, the range isn't
large but it's well presented and there are recipes, links and
special offers too.

*See also:*
**www.7day-chef.com** – wide range of equipment and kitchen
accessories and some excellent offers on top brands too.
**www.alessi.com** – a tour round the kitchen design powerhouse that
is Alessi, the best bit is that you can now buy from this site too.
**www.cucinadirect.com** – a very wide range of kitchen
equipment and related products, delivery starts at £4.95.
**www.divertimenti.co.uk** – Divertimenti are also worth a look,
they go for quality and they are good for gifts.
**www.kingsofhagley.co.uk** – excellent cookware shop with lots
of choice and a personal service.
**www.kitchenware.co.uk** – have a good range, with postage for
the UK being £3.95 per order.
**www.pots-and-pans.co.uk** – Scottish company offering kitchen
equipment through a good online store; it's good value but
delivery charges may vary.

## Kosher cookery

**www.koshercooking.com**                                                     UK
JEWISH CUISINE
Lots of recipes and links covering all forms of kosher cookery
and occasions.

**www.totallyjewish.com/food**                                                UK
J-FOOD
Part of the lively Totally Jewish site which gives has a
magazine-style approach to modern Jewish cookery including a
messageboard, restaurant guide, chef's questions and features.
For another more personal recipe collection go to
**http://screamingmeemies.com/eats**

# Luxury food, deli and gift sites

### www.allpresent.com                                                    UK

GIFTS FOR THE DISCERNING
An Amazon-style shop offering gifts in the form of chocolates,
drinks and bakery items such as cakes and biscuits all
beautifully boxed. They also sell flowers and cards; delivery
costs vary according to what you buy.

### www.fortnumandmason.co.uk                                             UK

EXQUISITE GIFTS
A wide range of gift chocolates, hampers and more from one of
the leading luxury stores, UK residents have a wider choice
including condiments, teas and wines. Carriage is £7 for UK
residents unless you're a F&M account holder then it's free
when you spend £50.

*See also:*
**www.champershampers.co.uk** – family-run hamper business.
**www.fifthsense.com** – odd design but a wide range and
good value.
**www.hamper.com** – good design and a wide range of products.
**www.hampers.uk.com** – a wide range of hampers large
and small.
**www.valvonacrolla-online.co.uk** – lots of special food from this
Edinburgh retailer.

## Meat and fish

### www.traditionalbutcher.co.uk                                         UK

A TRADITIONAL BUTCHER
John Miles is based in Herefordshire and knows a thing or two
about meat, you can buy meats and deli products online,
there's a good range and delivery is charged at cost.
They seem to take a great deal of care on quality.

*See also:*
**www.donaldrussell.co.uk** – a butcher who offers a wide range
of other produce as well as meats. The site is well illustrated
and there are recipes too.
**www.swaddles.co.uk** – organic butchers, with other produce
for sale from a good-looking site.

**www.meat-at-your-door.com** – who offers a wide range of meats; delivery cost is £29.38 for up to 20kg in weight.

## www.fresh-fish-online.co.uk                                UK

FRESH FISH DELIVERED

A Devon company who own their own trawlers will deliver overnight so that your fish is very fresh. They also deliver frozen, shell fish and smoked fish. They claim to subsidise delivery costs, so there's a minimum charge of £10. Be aware that this is a speaking webpage, so turn off your sound if you want a silent visit.

## www.martins-seafresh.co.uk                               UK

SOMETHING FISHY

You can order your fish fresh from this messy site which also has recipes and helpful information on things fishy including dealing with shellfish.

# Middle Eastern cookery

## www.al-bab.com/arab/food.htm                             UK

MIDDLE EAST CUISINE

An excellent overview of Arab cuisine from Arab Gateway with links to key sites covering all the major styles. See also the enjoyable Nadia's Middle Eastern Cookery site at **http://twdg.com/cooking/home.html** which is a little out of date but still informative.

## www.arabicslice.com                                       UK

STEP BY STEP ARABIC CUISINE

A well-designed and well-written cookery site featuring the best of Arabic food with simple step-by-step recipes, lots of explanation and illustrations.

## Miscellaneous food sites

### www.leapingsalmon.co.uk UK

STRESS IS FOR OTHER FISH
This well publicised site is about providing creative and
inspirational products to make gourmet cooking fun and
achievable in the home. Each meal kit is created for two people
by a top chef with step-by-step instructions. Order your meal
the day before and it gets delivered overnight so that the food
is as fresh as possible. They deliver anywhere in the UK for
£4.50. Same day delivery is available in London. It really works.

### www.reluctantgourmet.com US

GOURMET COOKING FOR BEGINNERS
Basically a beginner's cookery book, it's well designed and easy
to follow with a glossary, guide to techniques, equipment,
tips and recipes.

### www.cheftalk.com UK

THE FOOD LOVER'S LINK TO PROFESSIONAL CHEFS
Excellent site for articles and discussion about food with tips
and advice from the top chefs. There's a good links section,
recipes and a recommended restaurant guide.

### www.expatboxes.com UK

FOOD PARCELS FOR THOSE LIVING ABROAD
OK so you miss HP sauce, childhood sweet favourites and
proper salad cream, relief is at hand here. You can get your
rations in the form of specially selected hampers or they
will tailor make and shop the high street for you.
Delivery costs are high. For the Scottish equivalent try
**www.scottishfoodoverseas.com**

### www.edible.com UK

YOU CAN EAT IT, HONEST!
All sorts of insects, unusual meat and bugs you can eat, often
mixed with something exotic, the food available here is only for
the culinary brave. The site design is excellent though some
people might find the intro faintly disturbing... See also
**www.eatbug.com** which is more insect oriented.

*Other unusual sites to check out:*

**www.cookingbynumbers.com** – what's in your fridge? Well tick the boxes and this site will give you recipes that help use up whatever's there.

**www.egullet.com** – a messy e-zine devoted to food that has some good articles if you can be bothered to wade through the site.

**www.exploratorium.edu/cooking** – discover the science of cookery at this site which makes fascinating reading.

**www.gti.net/mocolib1/kid/food.html** – a timeline marking the history of cookery through the ages, with links and background information.

**www.lileks.com/institute/gallery** – a very funny site, explore the Gallery of Regrettable Food.

**www.topsecretrecipes.com** – discover what really goes into America's big brand name foods.

# Recipes, general food sites and magazines

## www.kitchenlink.com                                      US

WHAT'S COOKING ON THE NET
A bit clunky to use, but it has so many links to other key foodie sites and food-related sections that it has to be the place to start your online food and drink experience. The design can make it irritating to use and it's got a little slow, but persevere and you'll be rewarded with a resource that is difficult to beat.

*Other American sites worth checking out are these, all have loads of recipes and it's just a matter of finding one you like.*
**www.chef2chef.net** – outstanding professional cookery portal site with masses of links.

**www.cookeryonline.com** – very messy design but pretty comprehensive.

**www.cyber-kitchen.com** – excellent for links and specialised subjects.

**www.foodstop.com** – excellent articles about food.

**www.goodcooking.com**– another excellent food site, with some good food writing.

**www.ichef.com** – good search facility, nice design.

**www.meals.com** – good for meal planning and recipes.

**www.mealsforyou.com** – recipes for solutions: healthy, tasty, nutritional and so on.

**www.netcooks.com** – hundreds of recipes submitted by the public.

**www.recipezaar.com** – the world's smartest cookbook.

**www.ucook.com** – the ultimate cookery shop with recipes added.

**www.yumyum.com** – good fun.

## www.tudocs.com                                                    US

THE ULTIMATE DIRECTORY OF COOKING SITES

The main difference with Tudocs is that it grades each cookery site on its site listing. The listing is divided up into 19 sections, such as meat, beverages, low fat and ethnic. British cookery is in the ethnic section. See also **www.cookingindex.com**

## http://epicurious.com                                             US

FOR PEOPLE WHO EAT

Owned by Condé Nast, this massive site combines articles from their magazines with information generated by the Epicurious team, the site has been tidied up but there's still plenty of advice on topics such as recipes, cooking tips, TV, restaurant reviews, live-chat, forums, wine and kitchen equipment. It's fast, easy to navigate and international in feel.

## www.foodlines.com                                              CANADA

FOR THOSE WITH A PASSION FOR FOOD

It's easy to find the right recipe at this comprehensive site with a modern touch. There are some good recipes, as well as food quizzes and food jokes.

## www.allrecipes.com                                                US

THE HOME OF GREAT RECIPES

This site gets its own review because it's not overly cluttered, it's just got loads of recipes which can be found easily and each is rated by people who have cooked them.

## http://cookbook.rin.ru                                        RUSSIA

COOKERY ART

Really interesting cookery site with all the usual recipe sections but some unusual ones including exotic and erotic!

# Spanish food

**www.spanish-kitchen.co.uk**                                    UK

SPANISH CUISINE
What looks like a thorough walk though of the cuisine with
recipes and explanations of what to expect when you go there.

**www.tenstartapas.com**                                        UK

TOP TAPAS
An exercise in the creation of the best ever tapas by several of the
UK's top chefs. The whole point of it though is actually to get you
interested in Sherry of all things. Still the site looks great.

*See also:*
**www.catacurian.com** – enjoy Catalan cuisine here.
**www.culinaryweeks.com** – Spanish food course in hilariously
bad English.
**www.donquijote.org/culture/recipes** – some good recipes from
this primarily language learning site.
**www.spaintour.com/cusine.htm** – an overview of regional
foods, note the spelling!

# Spices

**www.apinchof.com**                                            US

HERBS AND SPICES
A bit of a mess but it's very informative about a whole range of
herbs and spices with articles from chefs and gardeners, it has
recipes and lots of links to help you out.

*See also:*
**www.ringoffire.net** – a diverse web ring devoted to all that is
hot and spicy.
**www.seasonedpioneers.co.uk** – recipes and spicy foods from
all around the globe, the site could do with an upgrade though.
**www.spiceadvice.com** – useful spice encyclopaedia from this
American spice retailer who doesn't ship outside the US.
**www.thespicebazaar.com** – a good-looking and well laid out
spice store that also sells dried fruits and herbs.

# Vegetarian and organic

### www.organicfood.co.uk                                    UK
A WORLD OF ORGANIC INFORMATION
A very informative site which gives the latest news on organic
food. There are sections on why you should shop organic,
recommendations on retailers, lifestyle tips, shopping and chat.
There are also links to key related sites.

*See also:*
**www.crueltyfreeshop.com** – the animal-friendly superstore who
sell a wide range of products but a limited amount of foodstuffs.
**www.helenbrowningorganics.co.uk** – buying advice, recipes
and an online shop from this Wiltshire organic farmer.
**www.organicdelivery.co.uk** – a good organic food retailer with
some good offers.
**www.swaddles.co.uk** – a wide range of organic food
including meat.

### www.freshfood.co.uk                                     UK
THE FRESH FOOD COMPANY
Another combined supermarket and information site with a
wide range of produce to choose from, this one has a recipe
section too. They have a subscription system, which delivers
your chosen goods on a regular basis. Delivery is covered by a
box scheme, which is like a regular subscription; prices vary
according to your commitment.

### www.vegsoc.org                                           UK
THE VEGETARIAN SOCIETY
This is the official site of the UK branch with sections on news,
new veggies, environment, business opportunities, recipes and
the Cordon Vert school, youth with virtual schoolroom, health,
membership info and online bookstore. Each section is packed
with information written in plain English, and there is a search
engine for information on any veggie topic.

### www.vegweb.com                                           US
VEGGIES UNITE!
If you're a vegetarian this is a great place, though not a great
design. There are hundreds of recipes, plus features, chat and
ideas in the VegWeb newsletter.

**www.vegansociety.com**                                          UK

AVOIDING THE USE OF ANIMAL PRODUCTS
The official site of the Vegan Society, promotes veganism by
providing information, links to other related sites and books.
There is a limited selection of goods in the shop, mostly books
and personal items. For a wider shopping experience go to
**www.veganstore.co.uk** who offer over 800 suitable products.

*See also:*
**www.earthsave.org** – a worthy organisation that promotes
vegetarianism by helping you choose the right way to eat.
**www.living-foods.com** – devoted to the subject of eating only
raw foods.
**www.veggieheaven.com** – UK restaurant guide for vegetarians
and vegans with over 185 listed.

## Drink: non-alcoholic

**www.whittard.co.uk**                                          UK

SPECIALITY TEAS DELIVERED WORLD-WIDE
An excellent site dedicated to their selection of teas and coffees;
it's easy to use and they will ship throughout the world.
Delivery varies according to weight for the UK – free if you
spend £50 or more.

*See also:*
**www.pgmoment.com** – all you need to know about PG Tips.
**www.realcoffee.co.uk** – coffee delivered to your door the day
after roasting from the Roast and Post Coffee company.
**www.redmonkeycoffee.com** – modern online coffee retailer
with free UK delivery.
**www.tea.co.uk** – great-looking site from the Tea Council with
lots of facts and reasons given why we should drink more of
the stuff.
**www.twinings.com** – information on tea and their products too.

## Drink: beer

**www.camra.org.uk**                                          UK

THE CAMPAIGN FOR REAL ALE STARTS HERE
A comprehensive site that has all the news and views on the
campaign for real ale. Sadly, it only advertises its Good Beer
Guide and local versions, with only a small section on the best
beers. Includes sections on beer in Europe, cider and festivals.

**www.realbeer.com** US

THE BEER PORTAL
Over 150,000 pages dedicated to beer, with articles, reviews, links and shopping all wrapped up in a well-designed site.

*See also:*
**www.beerhunter.com** a very good site, home to expert Michael Jackson author of the World Beer Guide.
**www.beersofeurope.co.uk** – a beer store who offer a huge range from which to choose.
**www.protzonbeer.com** – aficionado Roger Protz give his views on beer and pubs.

## Drink: wine and spirits

*There are many web sites selling wine and spirits, the quality of the information in this section is very high. These are some of the best.*

**www.berry-bros.co.uk** or **www.bbr.co.uk** UK

THE INTERNET WINE SHOP
This attractive and award-winning site offers over 1,000 different wines and spirits at prices from £4 to over £4,000. There is a great deal of information about each wine and advice on the different varieties. You can also buy related products such as cigars. Delivery for orders over £150 is free; otherwise it's £10 for the UK. They will deliver abroad and even store the wine for you.

**www.winecellar.co.uk** UK

NOT JUST WINE AND GOOD VALUE
They also sell spirits as well as wine and, while the choice isn't as good as some online wine retailers, Wine Cellar are good value. Use the search facility to find the whole range which isn't obvious from the home page. Delivery is £5.99.

**www.wine-lovers-page.com** US

ONE OF THE BEST PLACES TO LEARN ABOUT WINE
Highly informative for novices and experts alike, this site has it all. There are categories on learning about wine, reading and buying books and tasting notes for some 80,000 wines. Also within the site there's a glossary, a label decoder, a list of Internet wine shops, wine writers archive, wine search engine and much more.

## www.winespectator.com                                         UK

THE MOST COMPREHENSIVE WINE WEB SITE
From *Wine Spectator* magazine you get a site packed with
information. There's news, features, a wine search facility,
forums, weekly features, a library, the best wineries, wine
auctions and travel. The dining section has a world restaurant
guide, tips on eating out, wine matching and a set of links to
gourmet food.

## www.wine-pages.com                                            UK

A GREAT BRITISH NON-COMMERCIAL WINE SITE
Most independently written wine sites are poor, however wine
expert Tom Cannavan has put together a strong offering, which
is updated daily. It's well written, informative and links to other
good wine sites and online wine merchants.

## www.wineanorak.com                                            UK

THE WINE ANORAK
For another good British independent wine site, try the Wine
Anorak, it's just a great wine magazine, with lots of advice,
articles, issues of the day and general information on wines
and regions.

## www.jancisrobinson.com                                        UK

TV WINE EXPERT
Jancis Robinson has a bright site with wine news, tips, and
features on the latest wines and information on her books
and videos.

## www.ozclarke.com                                              UK

OZ ON OZ
Lots about Oz and what he's up to plus information on how to
get his books and CD-ROM. There's also his wine magazine to
browse, which includes tips on tasting, producer profiles, wine
basics and the latest news.

## www.superplonk.com                                            UK

MALCOLM GLUCK
Excellent site from Malcolm Gluck, the author of the Superplonk
books, there are offers and tips on where to buy good value
high quality wines. Sometimes slow to download.

*Other wine sites worth checking out are:*
**www.booths-wine.co.uk** – claims to sell imaginative and distinctive wines.
**www.cephas.co.uk** – superb images of wines and vineyards around the world.
**www.internetwineguide.com** – a good, if advert laden, all rounder.
**www.majestic.co.uk** – lots of offers and a well designed site.
**www.laithwaites.co.uk** – no-nonsense site with lots of offers and a money back guarantee. All wines are illustrated with a picture of the bottle.
**www.vintageroots.co.uk** – excellent for organic wines, spirits and beers.
**www.wineontheweb.com** – good wine magazine with audio features.
**www.wine-searcher.com** – a wine search engine, type in the wine you want and up pops a selection from various retailers from around the world and UK, all suppliers are vetted for quality and service. Pricey.

## www.idrink.com                                                    US

DRINK RECIPES AND COCKTAILS
With over 5,000 drinks recipes you're almost bound to find something to your liking, you have to be a member to get the best out of it though. See also **www.cocktailtime.com** and the comprehensive **www.webtender.com**

## www.barmeister.com                                                US

THE ONLINE GUIDE TO DRINKING
Packed with information on everything to do with drink, there are over 1,700 drink recipes available and about 500 drinking games. If you have another, then send it to be featured in the site.

## www.whiskyweb.com                                                 UK

A WEE DRAM
A comprehensive site for the whisky lover featuring history, information on how whisky is made, links to all the distilleries by region, a list of events and, of course, a shop (phone for delivery rates according to purchase). For a whisky trail around the Speyside distilleries go to **www.ifb.net/webit/whisky.htm**

# Eating out

## www.goodguides.com

HOME OF THE GOOD PUB GUIDE

Once you've registered it has an easy-to-use regional guide to the best pubs, which are rated on food, beer, value, good places to stay and good range of wine. You can also get a listing by award winner. The site hosts the Good Guide to Britain, which is a good resource for what's on where. See also **www.greatbeer.co.uk** one man's passion and guide to over 200 pubs in the UK.

## www.dine-online.co.uk
UK

UK-BASED WINING, DINING AND TRAVEL REVIEW

A slightly pretentious, but sincere attempt at an independent eating-out review website. It has a good and expanding selection of recommended restaurants, covers wine and has some well-written feature articles. It relies heavily on reader recommendation, so there's a good deal of variation in coverage and review quality and some were written some time ago.

## www.theaa.com/getaway/restaurants
UK

AA RESTAURANT SEARCH

Nestled away in the AA site is a little known gem in its hotels section – an excellent regional restaurant guide to the UK. Each of the 4,000 listed is graded and there are comments on quality of food, ambience, an idea of the price and, of course, how to get there.

## www.viamichelin.co.uk
UK

MICHELIN

A revamped site from Michelin with improved route finding and a good restaurant and hotel guide. You may be bothered by intrusive pop-up adverts though.

## www.gofortea.com
UK

TEA TIME

A site devoted to finding the best spots for the traditional British afternoon tea, though it does concentrate on hotels rather than tea shops.

*Other restaurant review sites worth looking at before you go out are:*

**www.conran.com/eat** – a guide to Terence Conran's restaurants with online booking and some special offers, nice design too.

**www.cuisinenet.co.uk** – book online at selected restaurants, nice design.

**www.local-restaurant.com** – good restaurant finder for cities, not so good for country areas.

**www.squaremeal.co.uk** – newsy guide to London's restaurants, it also covers selected ones in the UK.

**www.toptable.co.uk** – co-ordinates free booking at over 1,100 restaurants, nice design too.

**www.ukrestaurantguide.com** – good for links and finding a restaurant but slow and not comprehensive.

# Free Stuff

*Free stuff is exactly what the term suggests, and these are sites whose owners have trawled the Net or been offered free services, software, trial products and so on. It's amazing what you can find but as most sites are American some offers won't apply.*

### www.free.com                                                    US

GET SOMETHING FOR NOTHING
One of the best and largest sites of its type, there are literally hundreds of pages of free goodies waiting to be snapped up. Very wide-ranging and very much geared towards the US, but with over 9,000 links you should find something.

### www.freeinuk.co.uk                                              UK

JUST THE UK
Not just free stuff but also excellent Internet offers from British sites, good design, but not that easy to navigate. The Top ten section is great.

*Other sites worth looking into are these listed below, but most are American so some offers may not apply for the UK.*
**www.1freestuff.com** – one of oldest and probably best categorised.
**www.find-a-freebie.co.uk** – very well categorised and extensive selection.

**www.freeandfun.com** – the usual long list, don't see what's fun about it though.

**www.freebiedot.com** – a huge selection both UK and international.

**www.freebielist.com** – a well-categorised listing – easy to use and good links.

**www.freestuffpage.com** – some really esoteric ones here.

**www.thefreesite.com** – more of the same, nice layout.

**www.thefreezone.co.uk** – an excellent collection of link pages.

**www.totallyfreestuff.com** – massive selection.

*Furniture see under Home and DIY page 228.*

F

# Gambling and Betting Sites

*Gambling sites abound on the Internet and they often use some of the most sophisticated marketing techniques to keep you hooked, new screens pop up as you click on the close button tempting you with the chance to win millions. All the gaming sites are monitored by gaming commissions but above all be sensible, it's easy to get carried away. You should be aware that some carry spyware, programs that monitor your online activity.*

## Gambling and gaming

**www.betgambling.net**                                               US

> THE GAMBLERS PORTAL
> A useful gambling directory, which also offers forums and guides to the various games and sites. Its design isn't great but it is quite comprehensive. See also the less cluttered
> **www.winner.com**

**www.gamblehouse.com**                                               UK

> YOUR ONLINE GAMBLING GUIDE
> A very good place to start, they review online casinos and rank them according to whether they are licensed, make payments quickly, offer good odds, variety and quality of games and lastly customer service. Lots of pop-up adverts though.
>
> *These are the casinos and gambling sites we liked:*
> **www.24ktgoldcasino.com** – good graphics and fast response times make this great fun, but you need a decent PC to download the software. There are 40 or so games and you can either play for fun or for money.
> **www.888.com** – claims to be the world's most popular online casino, great design.
> **www.betasyouclick.com** – A directory with links to web sites from around the world, which offer sports books, casinos, financial spread betting, lotteries and competitions.
> **www.galagames.co.uk** – good graphics, lots of games and less fussy than most.
> **www.gamble.co.uk** – a good directory and review site.

**www.intercasino.com** – easy to use and they've over 70 games to choose from.

**www.pogo.com** – from EA Games lots to choose from, lots of prizes to play for.

# Betting

### www.settle-a-bet.co.uk
UK

BETS EXPLAINED
If you can't tell the difference between a trixie or a yankee and thought spreadbetting was something that went on toast, then this is the site for you. It has (not always simple) explanations of virtually every conceivable type of bet.

### www.oddschecker.co.uk
UK

COMPARE THE ODDS
A great way to ensure you get the best deal from the online bookmakers, you just choose the sport and the event, then you get a read-out of the latest odds given by a selection of bookies – you can click on the bookmaker of your choice to place your bet. It's continually being updated; the site's a must for the committed gambler.

### www.ukbetting.com
UK

LIVE INTERACTIVE BETTING
Concentrating on sports betting, this is a clear, easy-to-use site; take a guest tour before applying to join. You need to open an account to take part, using your credit or debit card, bets are £1 minimum. See also the popular **www.bluesq.com** which offers a similar but possibly slightly broader service, and special bets on things like soap operas and political elections. Also worth a visit is **www.bet365.co.uk** who cover a wide variety of areas and offer some good deals.

### www.mybetting.co.uk
UK

FREE BETTING
My Betting works as a collation site for free bets and offers from bookmakers around the Internet. It takes a minute or so to get used to the design but once you're on board it's easy to get yourself a few free bets, albeit at the price of a registration or two.

### www.racingpost.co.uk                                               UK

*THE RACING POST*
A combination of news, racing and betting on a clear, well-designed site. Also features greyhounds and information on bloodstock.

### www.ladbrokes.co.uk                                               UK

UK'S NUMBER 1 BOOKMAKER
Ladbrokes offer a combination of news, information and sport-related betting with excellent features on racing, golf and the other major sporting events. There's also a casino, lotteries, a specials section where you can bet on politics or big events and, of course, the now ubiquitous poker game.

### www.willhill.com                                                  UK

THE MOST RESPECTED NAME IN BOOKMAKING
The best online betting site in terms of speed, layout and design, it has the best event finder, results service and betting calculator. The bet finder service is also very good and quick. All the major sports are featured and there is a specials section for those out of the ordinary flutters. Betting is live as it happens.

*See also:*
**www.paddypower.com** – a strong site from Ireland's biggest bookmaker with betting on horses, football and other top sports – even politics.
**www.sportingindex.com** – excellent and wide ranging spread betting site with offers and competitions.
**www.victorchandler.com** – horse racing specialist but covers other sports too.

### www.tote.co.uk                                                    UK

BET ON THE HORSES, LIVE
Devoted to horse racing, the Tote fairly successfully attempts to bring you the excitement and feel of live betting online. It explains what the bets mean and has a very good set of links relating to horses and racing.

**www.thedogs.co.uk**                                                    UK

    GONE TO THE DOGS
    Everything you need to know about greyhounds and greyhound
    racing. You can adopt or get advice on buying a dog, find the
    nearest track, get the latest results and learn how to place bets.
    You can't gamble from the site but they provide links.

## Miscellaneous

**www.national-lottery.co.uk**                                           UK

    IT COULD BE YOU
    Find out about Lotto and even play online, there's info on how
    to play and results of Euromillions and instant win games too.
    They also tell you about the good causes that the National
    Lottery supports. If you want to know whether your premium
    bonds are worth anything try **www.nationalsavings.co.uk** you
    need your bondholder number handy.

**www.highstakes.co.uk**                                                 UK

    HIGH STAKES BOOKSTORE
    Books on virtually every aspect of gambling at this minimalist
    site. It also offers selected links and you can order online too.

**www.gamblersanonymous.org.uk**                                         UK

    WHEN THE STAKES GET TOO HIGH...
    Where to go when it all gets too much, a straightforward site
    listing crucial phone numbers and information on how to deal
    with the compulsion.

# Games

*There's a massive selection of games on the Internet, here are just
some of the very best ones, from board games to quizzes to your
everyday 'shoot 'em up' type. There are more games for Macs listed
on page 19.*

*It's worth remembering that before downloading a game from a site it's
wise to check for viruses. If you've not got anti-virus software on your
PC then check out our section on Virus management on page 351.*

*Parents should be aware that some games are quite violent or contain sexual references, so it's as well to check them out before letting your child loose on them.*

# Finding games

### http://gamespotter.com                                      US

GAMES SEARCH ENGINE

A really handy site where you can get links to virtually every type of game whether it be a puzzle or action. Alternatively, you can use the search facility to find something. Each game on the list is reviewed as well.

## Games magazines and information

### www.avault.com                                             US

THE ADRENALINE VAULT

A comprehensive games magazine with demos, reviews and features on software and hardware – good looking too. There's also a good cheats and hints section.

### www.gamespy.com                                           US

GAMINGS HOMEPAGE

Lots here, apart from the usual reviews and features. There are chat and help sections and links to the arcade section with hundreds of demos plus free games to play. See also **www.gamespot.co.uk** which offers lots of info as well.

### www.gamers.com                                            US

A MOMENT ENJOYED IS NOT WASTED

A great-looking site with all the features you'd expect from a games magazine but it has more in the way of downloads and games to play. There is also a chat section and competitions.

### www.happypuppy.com                                        US

GAMES REVIEWED

Happy Puppy has been around a while now reviewing games in all the major formats. Each is given a thorough test, then it's rated and given a review. There are also links to related games sites. It's all packaged on a really good web site which is quick and user-friendly.

## www.gamefaqs.com                                              US

GAMES FREQUENTLY ASKED QUESTIONS
All information is free and donated, there are FAQs and tip
sheets on any number of games, and it seems to be regularly
updated.

## www.game-sector.co.uk                                          UK

FOR THE GAMERS BY THE GAMERS
A very good games review and news site with an interesting
design. There are sections for each type of game player as well
as feedback and forums too.

## http://vgstrategies.about.com                                   US

ABOUT GAMES
An set of information pages from the excellent About.com with
articles and links covering all the likely strategies needed
for gaming.

# Games to play

## www.boxerjam.com                                               UK

ONLINE GAMESHOW
Excellent site devoted to giving the user access to original and
traditional games played online, for cash and prizes.

## www.classicgaming.com                                          US

GAMING THE WAY YOU REMEMBER IT
Probably one for older gamers but there's some good stuff on
here so it's at least worth a look and it's amazing how new
some of the games are.

## www.gamehippo.com                                              US

OVER 1,000 FREE GAMES
Enough to keep you occupied for hours with games of every
type from board to action to puzzles and sports. There's also a
really good set of links to other sites. It's worth checking out
**www.freeloader.com** which has a more modern selection
available, but you have to register and jump through a few
hoops to get them.

*See also the oddly designed* **www.download-game.com** *who also offer a large number including old favourites, and Sean O'Connor's site* **www.windowsgames.co.uk** *where there's a small selection of high quality games to download.*

## www.gamearchive.com                                        UK

### PINBALL MACHINES

A site devoted to pinball machines and similar games put together by real fans. There's also a selection of video games and links to similar sites, however, there are no console games. See also **www.videogames.org**

## www.gamebrew.com                                           US

### CHOOSE YOUR GAME

Gamebrew specialises in Java games and there are some brilliant ones to download and play here, you choose from any six categories from puzzles to casino to arcade.

## http://games.yahoo.com                                     US

### YAHOO!

This popular search engine has its own games section. Here you can play against others or yourself online. The emphasis is on board games, puzzles and quizzes. Games Domain, which previously had its own entry in this guide, is now a section of Yahoo and offers a combination of freebies and competitions and they've recently added a section on mobile games.

## www.graalonline.com                                        UK

### THE GRAAL KINGDOMS

Set in a mythical realm, this is a good multi-player game with lots of levels and a high degree of interactivity and customisation.

## www.worldogl.com                                           US

### ONLINE GAMING LEAGUE

Join a community of gamers who play in leagues for fun. You can play all the major online games and compete in the leagues and ladders if you like. To quote them: 'What matters is that people are meeting and interacting with other people on the Internet via our services and their game'.

## www.planetquake.com
US

### THE EPICENTRE OF QUAKE
Quake is the most popular game played on the Internet, and
this slightly slow site gives you all the background and details
on the game. It's got loads of links and features as well as
reviews and chat.

## www.shockwave.com
US

### SHOCKWAVE GRAPHICS
Shockwave's fantastic site offers much in the way of high
definition games for both action fans and those who prefer to
test their minds a bit; the site also offers films and other useful
programs. You can also subscribe to their online gaming section
with over 60 games choose from.

## www.lysator.liu.se/tolkien-games
SWEDEN

### LORD OF THE RINGS
Get immersed in Tolkien's Middle Earth with some 100 games.
It's got action games, quizzes and puzzles, strategy games and,
of course, role playing games.

## www.wireplay.com
US

### THE GAMES NETWORK
A good online games resource with over 30 to choose from,
the site encourages the players to interact, it has chat rooms
and forums and also organises competitions.

## www.zone.com
US

### MICROSOFT GAMES ZONE
With over 100 games to choose from you shouldn't be
disappointed. They range from board and card games to
multi-player strategy and simulation games to playing for cash.
It's a shame they've done away with what was a good
children's section.

## www.orisinal.com
US

### JUST FOR FUN
A selection of high quality silly and funny games using a very
original and text free format and design.

**www.spaceinvaders.de**                                          GERMANY

SPACE INVADER SHRINE
A fun homage to the original game with history, trivia, tips and
of course you can play the game too.

**www.popcap.com**                                                     US

100% JAVA
An excellent site with very high quality games to download onto
the PC, palm or Mac and also to play on the web.

**www.sodaplay.com**                                                   UK

BUILD YOUR OWN....
A really interesting and different gaming experience. Here you
can design your models and send them to the 'zoo' for display
and use by others. You can race them and exchange them with
friends too.

# Game manufacturers and console games

**www.dreamcast.com**                                                  US

DREAMCAST FROM SEGA
Get the latest information on what's coming, try it out or play
online; you can also get the latest technology.

**http://cube.ign.com**

GAME CUBE
Dedicated to the format, there are lots of reviews, previews and
the latest information on what's coming too.

**www.hasbro.com/games**                                               US

HASBRO GAMES
A commercial site from one of the biggest manufacturers, with
a useful list of what they produce.

**www.nintendo.com**                                                   US

OFFICIAL NINTENDO
Get the latest news from Nintendo and its spin-offs – N64,
Game Boy and Game Cube. There's also information on the
hardware and details of the games new and old. For a site with
wider Nintendo info go to the excellent **www.nintendojo.com**

## http://uk.playstation.com    US

### OFFICIAL PLAYSTATION SITE

Looks good with games information, information on the hardware, previews, new release details and a special features section featuring reviews by well-known gamers. There's also a chat section and a shop.

*Also check out:*
**www.absolute-playstation.com**
**www.playstation.com**
**www.psxextreme.com**

## www.pocketgamer.org    UK

### GAMES FOR POCKET PCS

OK so you've bought your handheld PC, you've impressed the boss, now, what do you really use it for? Oh yes, play games! There's a lot here for most different types of operating systems, if not, then there are links to related sites. Try also **www.handango.com** who, while not a specialist have expanded their games selection and is a much better designed site.

## www.gamespy.com/xbox formerly www.planetxbox.com    US

### XBOX

Part of the Gamespy network, this site gives background on Microsoft's toy, with the latest game news, reviews, demos and previews too. See also **www.xbox.com** and the annoying to load **www.xboxemea.com/playtogether** who offer some exclusive previews.

## www.station.sony.com    US

### SONY ONLINE GAMES

Sony have put together an exceptional site for online gaming, and with over 6 million members, it's one of the most popular. The site is well designed and easy to use and there are lots of games to choose from. Providing you can put up with the adverts, it's a real treat to use.

## www.sega-europe.com    EUROPE

### SEGA

Get the latest news on the latest games and buy them at the store. The site is well designed but it can be irritating waiting for stuff to load if you're on a normal modem.

# Fantasy league and strategy games

## www.dreamleague.com                                         US

PLAY FANTASY SPORT

Dream League offer fantasy games in several sports including
football, Formula 1 and cricket. Even with the sports you can
play foreign leagues. It's easy to register and join in –
and it's free.

## www.fantasyleague.com                                       UK

FANTASY FOOTIE

Be a football manager, play for yourself, in a league, or even
organise a game for your workplace or school. Get the latest
team news on your chosen players and how they're doing
against the rest.

G

## www.thedugout.net                                           UK

CHAMPIONSHIP MANAGER

An excellent site devoted to Championship Manager and soccer
gaming, you can discuss the game, get up to speed with the
latest tactics, get the low down on the players and generally
join in. There are also links to related sites.

## www.primagames.com                                          US

PRIMA

The largest fantasy game publisher offers a site packed
with reviews, demos and articles. You can also buy a book
on virtually every strategy game. See also
**www.strategy-gaming.com** which is pretty comprehensive.

## www.gamesworkshop.com                                       UK

WAR GAMING

A comprehensive offering covering war games including
collecting, painting and gaming itself, there's also forums,
chat and links to the major games. See also **www.britwar.co.uk**
which is good for links and **www.wargames.co.uk** which is
pretty comprehensive.

# Cheats, hints and tips

## www.computerandvideogames.com                                    US

THE CHEAT STATION

Select the console or game type that you want a cheat on, then drill down the menus until you get the specific game or cheat that you want. There are cheats for thousands of games so you should find what you're looking for. If you can't, check out **www.xcheater.com** who have a smaller selection, but you never know your luck.

*See also:*

**www.cheatextreme.com** – great for Play Station cheats.
**www.cheatheaven.com** – a one-stop site for cheats in over 1,200 games covering most consoles. Good search facility, but some annoying adverts and pop-ups.
**www.playstation2-cheats.co.uk** – cheats for PS2.

# Games shops

*If you know which game you want, then it's probably better to use a price checker such as Kelkoo (***http://uk.kelkoo.com***) to find the best price on the game. They will put you through to the store offering the best all round deal. If you want to browse, then these are considered the best online stores for a wide range of games:*

**www.chipsworld.co.uk** – good for Sega and Nintendo. (UK)
**www.game.uk.com** – a good comprehensive offering. (UK)
**www.gameplay.com** – Gameplay is one of the most visited games sites. Once a magazine site, it's now transformed into a well designed store, browsable by platform and good value. (UK)
**www.gamesstreet.co.uk** – part of the Streets Online group one of the top shops on the Internet – good kids' section. Delivery costs start at £1. Good value too. (UK)
**www.telegames.co.uk** – around 5,000 types of game in stock, covering all makes. Also has a bargain section. (UK)
**www.ukgames.com** – excellent range and good prices. (UK)

## Miscellaneous

### www.etch-a-sketch.com                                    UK
REMEMBER ETCH-A-SKETCH?
For those of you who don't remember back that far, Etch-a-Sketch is a rather annoying drawing game. It's been faithfully recreated here and it's still just as difficult to do curves. There are also a few other simple games and some links to children's games sites.

### www.wargames.co.uk                                      UK
WAR GAMES FORUM
All you need to know about war-gaming on one site, albeit a slow one. There are links to specialist traders and to every aspect of the game from figurines to books to software.

### www.tele-actor.net/tele-twister                          US
TWISTER
Yes at set times of the day or night you can play Twister online, well you can vote for what moves the players might take.

## Card and board games

### www.tradgames.org.uk                                     UK
TRADITIONAL GAMES
A history and a guide to traditional games; board games, table games, pub games and lawn games too.

### www.playsite.com                                         US
EASY TO PLAY
A collection of straightforward multi-player online games, specialising in cards, word puzzles and board games.

### www.chess.co.uk                                          UK
ULTIMATE CHESS
Massive chess site that's got information on the game, news and views, reviews and shopping. There are lots of links to other chess sites and downloads. Also info on backgammon, go, poker and bridge.

*See also:*
**www.bcf.org.uk** – for the British Chess Federation.
**www.chessclub.com** – for the Internet Chess club who had over 2,000 players online when we visited, including 19 grandmasters.

## www.gammon.com                                                    US

BACKGAMMON
If you like backgammon, here's the place to start. There are links to live game playing and masses of related information. Also check out **www.bkgm.com**

## www.msoworld.com                                                  US

BOARD GAMES, PUZZLES AND QUIZZES
The ultimate site of its type, there are over 100 board games and masses of quizzes and tests.

## www.monopoly.com                                                  US

MONOPOLY
A pretty boring site, it offers a history plus information on where you can buy, along with tips on how to play and how you can get involved in tournaments. See also **http://uk.mymonopoly.com** where you can create your own personalised game to order.

## www.thehouseofcards.com                                           US

LOADS OF CARD GAMES
Huge number of card games to play and download with sections on card tricks, history, links and word games – there's not much missing here. See also **www.pagat.com** for an alternative.

## www.solitairegames.com                                            US

SOLITAIRE
Play online or download a game onto your PC, there are plenty to choose from and it's quick. There's also a good set of links to other online card games.

## http://bridge.ecats.co.uk                                         UK

BRIDGE RESOURCE
A good place for information on bridge from a software company associated with the game at a high level. See also **www.bridgemagazine.co.uk**

# Crosswords, puzzles and word games

### www.cluemaster.com                                          UK
CROSSWORDS AND WORD PUZZLES
1,000 pages of puzzles, word games and crosswords, all free.
The site is pretty straightforward, although you have to register
to get the best out of it.

### www.crosswordsite.com                                       UK
ALL CROSSWORDS
Hundreds to chose from, with the option either to print off or fill
in online. There are four levels of difficulty with the hardest
being quite tough. See also **www.crossword-puzzles.co.uk**

G

### www.fun-with-words.com                                      US
THE WORDPLAY WEBSITE
Dedicated to amusing English, the Fun with Words site offers
games, puzzles and an insight into the sorts of tricks you can
play with the language.

*Other crossword and puzzle sites worth checking out are
listed below:*
**http://crosswords.about.com** – links and tips from this giant
reference site.
**www.canopia.com** – odd design but a good choice of puzzles
and crosswords.
**www.lovatts.com.au** – plenty to chose from at this
Australian magazine.
**www.puzzleblog.com** – a word game which is a spin-off
of Scrabble.

# Quizzes and general knowledge

### www.thinks.com                                              UK
FUN AND GAMES FOR PLAYFUL BRAINS
Massive collection of games, puzzles and quizzes with
something for everyone, it's easy to navigate and free.

### www.trivialpursuit.com                                      UK
TRIVIAL PURSUIT
A massive disappointment; this is a purely commercial site
geared to selling the various versions of the official game.

## www.mensa.org.uk                                               UK
### THE HIGH IQ SOCIETY
Mensa only admit people who pass their high IQ test – see if
you've got what it takes. The site, which has been upgraded,
has a few free tests and, if eligible, you can join the club.

## www.queendom.com                                              US
### SERIOUSLY ENTERTAINING
Excellent site for all sorts of brain tingling tests, the major
difference is that it also offers personality profiles and
psychometric tests so that they may be useful in getting on in
your career or just keeping your brain healthy see also
**www.emode.com**

*Check out these sites:*
**www.coolquiz.com** – several different types of quiz from sports
to movies and quotes. Nice wacky design. (US)
**www.funtrivia.com** – a massive trivia site with over 600,000
questions. (US)
**www.quiz.co.uk** – a couple of hundred questions in several
unusual categories including kids, nature, food and sport. (UK)
**www.quizyourfriends.com** – a fun quiz creation site.
**www.test.com** – mainly serious tests, but you can find out your
IQ and find out how creative you are. Visit the family section
to take tests on entertainment and sports amongst others.
You have to pay for some of the tests. (US)

# Gardening

*There are lots of high quality British gardening sites, but many of
the best sites are still based in America, so bear this in mind for
tenderness, soil and climate advice. Those recommended give
good general information and good links to specialist sites. Due to
regulations on importing of seeds and plants, these can't be imported
from outside the UK.*

### www.gardenworld.co.uk

UK

THE UK'S BEST

Described as the UK's best garden centre and horticultural site. It includes a list of over 1,000 garden centres, with addresses, contact numbers and e-mail addresses. Outstanding list of links to other sites on most aspects of gardening. Truly comprehensive with sections on wildlife, books, holidays, advice, societies and specialists, it now also has the addition of a link to the RHS plant finder service – excellent.

### www.expertgardener.com

UK

GARDENING COMMUNITY

Essentially a chat site devoted to gardening, but there's advice and articles from award-winning gardeners too, which combined with good design, makes this site stand out. There are links to a good selection of online shops, plus a magazine as well as access to chat rooms and communities on various subjects from urban gardening to plantaholics corner.

### www.gardenweb.com

UK

GARDEN QUESTIONS ANSWERED

Probably the best site for lively gardening debate; it's enjoyable, international, comprehensive and has a nice tone. There are several discussion forums on various gardening topics, garden advice, plant dictionary and competitions. Using the forums is easy and fun, and you're sure to find the answer to almost any gardening question.

### www.kew.org.uk

UK

ROYAL BOTANIC GARDENS

Kew's mission is to increase knowledge about plants and conserve them for future generations. This site gives plenty of information about their work, the collections, features and events. There are also details of the facilities at the gardens, conservation, educational material and lots of links to related sites.

### www.rhs.org.uk

UK

ROYAL HORTICULTURAL SOCIETY

An excellent site from the RHS which features a plant finder service covering some 70,000 plant types, a garden finder and an event finder. There's also advice and information about the RHS, an opportunity to buy advance tickets to their shows and a seed catalogue.

*Other gardening advice and information sites well worth trying are:*

**www.carryongardening.org.uk** – award-winning site with all the usual features plus some celebrity input. Good for links and the idea exchange feature.

**www.e-garden.co.uk** – one of the best; there's lots here for everyone, covering a much wider range of topics and regions than most, all packaged in a compact site.

**www.gardenforum.co.uk** – outstanding gardening forum site, good if you're a novice to using forums and chat sites.

**www.gardenguides.com** – a useful American resource site with loads of information on every aspect of gardening. It has lots of tips, handy guides, and a free online newsletter.

**www.gardenlinks.co.uk** – links to gardening sites over 40 categories, a good place to start searching for something specific.

**www.gonegardening.com** – nice design, wide ranging magazine and shop.

**www.plants-magazine.com** – very good garden magazine, broad in scope but particularly strong on new plants, a vehicle for selling the magazine itself.

## Gardening stores

### www.greenfingers.com                                          UK

COMPREHENSIVE GARDENING

A gardening superstore with many categories and some good offers. There's also plenty in the way of advice and tips, plus an ask the gardener facility.

### www.crocus.co.uk                                              UK

GARDENERS BY NATURE

A good-looking site full of ideas enhanced by excellent photographs, there are some good articles and features, but it's basically a gorgeous shop with thousands of plants and products to choose from and some good offers. Delivery to England and Southern Scotland starts at £5.95 (£1 for seeds), if you live elsewhere you need to contact them to see if delivery is possible for a surcharge.

### www.blooms-online.com
UK

ONE-STOP GARDENER'S RESOURCE
A beautiful site that will supply all your garden needs and
desires. In addition to ordering your seeds and buying your
garden furniture, there's a great plant search where you can
find plants of specific size and colour for that difficult hole
in the border. There are DIY projects, a design service,
a gardener's club and advice. Delivery cost depends on your
order, or you can pick up at their nearest store.

### www.gardentrading.co.uk
UK

GARDENING GIFTS
A well-presented site from a company that specialises in gift
products associated with gardening from furniture to lighting
to small gifts.

*Other gardening shops worth checking out are:*
**www.burncoose.co.uk** – nice design, searchable plant
catalogue with some good offers.
**www.e-garden.co.uk** – nice-looking site with a magazine and
shop, a little slow, but with some good offers.
**www.gardencentre.co.uk** – not a great design but some good
offers and ideas.
**www.glut.co.uk** – the Gluttonous Gardener provides unusual
presents for every gardener.
**www.twelvelimited.com** – excellent range all made from
natural and recyclable materials.

## Garden design

### www.thegardenplanner.co.uk
UK

THE GARDENER'S DIRECTORY
Everything you need to plan your perfect garden, this excellent
directory is the place to start.

*See also:*
**http://gardendesign-uk.com** – a good directory of
garden designers.
**www.gardendesigner.com** – a serious American site with
in depth advice.
**www.sgd.org.uk** – Society of Garden Designers to find a
landscape gardener.

# Organic and environmentally friendly gardening

### www.hdra.org.uk UK

HENRY DOUBLEDAY RESEARCH ASSOCIATION
The leading authority on organic gardening, this site offers a superb resource if you're into gardening the natural way. It's particularly good if you're growing vegetables with fact sheets and details on why you should garden organically.

*See also:*
**www.greengardener.co.uk** – specialists in biological pest control and wormeries.
**www.organiccatalogue.com** – a comprehensive store related to the HDRA.
**www.pan-uk.org** – the Pesticide Action Network who are working to eliminate the hazards associated with pesticides.
**www.rethinkrubbish.com** – the best ways to recycle your rubbish.
**www.soilassociation.org** – for advice on growing organic food plus the latest news on their campaigns.

## British wildflowers and plants

### www.nhm.ac.uk/science/projects/fff UK

FLORA AND FAUNA
Using the postcode search, find out which plants are native to your area, where to get seeds and then how to look after them once they're in your garden. Sponsored by the Natural History Museum.

### www.british-trees.com UK

FORESTRY AND CONSERVATION
Comprehensive information on British trees plus a good set of links and a list of books and magazines. For more information on how to care for trees go to **www.trees.org.uk**

**www.wildflowers.co.uk**                                    UK

> BRITISH WILDFLOWERS
> An online store specialising in British wildflowers with advice
> on how to grow them; there's also a search engine where you
> can find the plants you need using common or Latin names.
> If you want a wildlife friendly garden try
> **www.wildlifegardening.co.uk** which is a basic but
> informative site.

## Specific plants, societies and specialists

**www.alpinegardensociety.org**                             UK

> ALPINES
> An informative site on alpines with articles from the society
> magazine, seed exchange, newsletter and shop. You can also
> find out about their tours to the best alpines territories.

**www.discoveringannuals.com**                             UK

> ANNUALS GALORE
> Based on the successful book, this site offers information on
> hardy annuals, half-hardy annuals, biennials and seed-raised
> bedding plants of all kinds. There's an A–Z listing on the plants
> and it tells you where you can buy them.

**www.thecgs.org.uk**                                       UK

> COTTAGE GARDEN SOCIETY
> The place to go if you want the picture perfect cottage garden.
> The site is quite basic but there's plenty of information to get
> you started plus a seed exchange service via their magazine.

**www.hardy-plant.org.uk**                                  UK

> HARDY-PLANT SOCIETY
> A society devoted to conserving the older, rare or unusual
> garden plants. There's information about how you can get
> involved, their fairs, plus a seed list and limited plant
> information.

## www.herbnet.com                                                US

GROWING AND COOKING HERBS

An American network specialising in herbs, with links to
specialists, trade and information sites. It can be hard work to
negotiate, but there's no doubting the quality of the content
– although the quality of the music is up for debate. See also
**www.herbsociety.co.uk** which isn't a great site but does
contain some useful info.

## www.nccpg.com                                                  UK

CONSERVING PLANTS AND GARDENS

The National Council for the Conservation of Plants and
Gardens is responsible for maintaining the national collections
of which there are over 600. Here you can find out about
NCCPG's conservation work and plant database and how you
can get involved.

## www.rareplants.co.uk                                           UK

RARE PLANT NURSERY

A site developed by a specialist nursery, which is well illustrated,
and pretty comprehensive, it offers information on the plants and
can supply plants world-wide. Delivery costs vary.

## www.rosarian.com                                               UK

ROSES

As this is a generalist guide we wouldn't normally review such a
specialist site, but it's so well-designed in terms of how an
online magazine should look for its audience, that we couldn't
resist including it. If you love roses or just need information on
them, drop in here for a good, long browse. See also
**www.davidaustinroses.com** the outstanding rose specialist and
also the Royal National Rose Society at **www.rnrs.org**

## www.windowbox.com                                              US

CONTAINER GARDENING

A really good American site that is well worth a look if you're
into container gardening in any form. It's well laid out and very
well written with great ideas for unusual plant combinations.
Worth a long browse.

*Other specialists worth a look:*

**http://lockyerfuchsias.co.uk** – good mail order service from this Bristol based company, supplying fuchsias.

**http://www.orchids.uk.com** – attractive site and home of specialist grower Burham Nurseries and you can buy orchids online.

**www.brogdale.org.uk** – basically all you need to know about fruit grown in the UK.

**www.citruscentre.co.uk** – the place to go for your lemons, limes and more.

**www.oaklandnurseries.co.uk** – a specialist in showy but tender plants.

**www.topiaryart.com** – an online course with background on the subject.

## Seed specialists

**www.chilternseeds.co.uk**                                     UK

SEED SPECIALIST
Choose from over 5,000 different types of seeds with many unusual plants, including organically grown seeds. Very easy to find the right plant, excellent.

*See also:*
**www.suttons-seeds.co.uk** – comprehensive offering with a money-back guarantee and an easy-to-use site.
**www.thompson-morgan.com** – huge range, good advice and good value too.

## Gardening peripherals and equipment

**www.lawnmowersdirect.co.uk**                                  UK

BUY A LAWNMOWER ONLINE
A retailer specialising in mowers and other power tools, you can browse by make and it's quick and easy to use, if a little basic. Delivery within the UK is free if you spend more than £50.

**www.lightingforgardens.co.uk**                                UK

LIGHT UP YOUR GARDEN
A specialist that offers advice, ideas and a wide range of products to light up your garden, all on a nicely designed site.

## www.agriframes.co.uk                                    UK

### GARDEN STRUCTURES

A wide range of non-plant garden products from pergolas to watering cans from probably the UK's leading supplier; it could be a much more user-friendly site.

## www.simplygardeningtools.co.uk                          UK

### GARDEN TOOLS

A messy, bright site offering a wide range of tools and equipment and free delivery in the UK, plus a money back guarantee. For a more high class approach to garden tools try **www.hortus-ornamenti.com** but they do charge for delivery.

## www.garden-sheds-online.co.uk                           UK

### SHEDS!

A company that is passionate about sheds. There is information to help you pick the right one and a good selection to choose from. See also **www.fredshed.co.uk** For the lighter side of life in garden sheds you should check out the bizarre but excellent **www.readersheds.co.uk**

## www.watergardening-direct.co.uk                         UK

### WATER GARDENING PRODUCTS

Not a great web site, but it all works, there is a good range, you can order online and ask for advice too.

# TV tie-ins and celebrities

## www.bbc.co.uk/gardening                                 UK

### GARDENING AT THE BEEB

A set of web pages from the BBC site which offer a great gardening magazine, featuring celebrities but mixed with helpful advice and sections such as design inspiration, plant profiles, ask the expert and today in your garden. You can sign up for their free newsletter.

## www.barnsdalegardens.co.uk                              UK

### GEOFF HAMILTON'S GARDEN

To many people the real home of Gardener's World, this site tells you all about Barnsdale and has features about the garden, Geoff and his work. There's also an online store selling a limited range of products and a good set of gardening site links.

**www.alantitchmarsh.com**                                    UK
ALAN TITCHMARSH
Part of the Expert Gardener site with competitions, biographical details, sponsored events and some gardening details.

*Other important gardeners*
**www.bethchatto.co.uk** – find out about her garden and shop for plants too.
**www.gertrudejekyll.co.uk** – devoted to the work of this amazing woman.

# Visiting gardens and garden history

**www.gardenvisit.com**                                    UK
GARDENS TO VISIT AND ENJOY
With over 1,000 gardens listed world-wide, this site offers information on all of them and each is rated for design, planting and scenic interest with Sissinghurst scoring top marks. There's also information on the history of gardening, tours and hotels with good gardens.

*See also:*
**http://hcs.osu.edu/history** – from Ohio State University, the history of horticulture through biographies of the most famous gardeners.
**www.edenproject.com** – for the grandest garden scheme of them all.
**www.gardenhistorysociety.org** – an overview of what the society is about and information on what they're up to, but little in the way of history bar a few articles.
**www.greatbritishgardens.co.uk** – good regional reference and guide that includes biographies of great British garden designers.
**www.museumgardenhistory.org** – based in Lambeth, this site offers details of the museum and the famous Tradescant family.
**www.nationaltrust.org.uk** – offering information on their gardens and places of interest.

**www.ngs.org.uk** UK

NATIONAL GARDEN SCHEME

This is basically the famous yellow book converted into a
website with details on over 3,500 gardens to visit for charity
and the work they undertake with the money they earn from
your support. See also **www.gardensofscotland.org** who
operate a similar scheme.

## Gardeners with special needs

**www.thrive.org.uk** UK

NATIONAL HORTICULTURAL CHARITY

This charity exists to provide expert advice on gardening for
people with disabilities and older people who want to continue
gardening with restricted mobility. The site gives information on
how the charity works and links to related sites. See also
**www.gardenforever.com** who offer lots in the way of
horticultural therapy.

# *Gay and Lesbian*

**www.rainbownetwork.com** UK

LESBIAN & GAY LIFESTYLE

A very well thought out magazine-style web site catering for
all aspects of gay and lesbian life. It primarily covers news,
fashion, entertainment and health, but there's a travel agency
as well. There are also forums and chat sections, classified ads
as well as profiles on well-known personalities.

**www.gayscape.com** US

GAY SEARCH ENGINE

This isn't going to win design awards, but it is a useful and
well-categorised directory of over 89,000 sites. See also
**www.queery.com** and for the UK only try the well put together
**www.gayindex.co.uk**

*For other good gay/lesbian sites try:*
**www.aegis.com** – an excellent site giving the latest information
on combating AIDS and HIV.
**www.gaybritain.co.uk** – excellent graphics, a gay portal site.
**www.gaylifeuk.com** – well rounded magazine site with support
and advice sections.

**www.gaysports.com** – wide ranging sports site.
**www.gaytravel.co.uk** – gay travel guide, UK-oriented but with some good world-wide information.
**www.glinn.com** – the gay gateway to the web.
**www.lesbianuk.co.uk** – a good information site.
**www.navigaytion.com** – a travel specialist.
**www.planetout.com** – a good all-round magazine site.
**www.proudparenting.com** – interesting site aimed at helping gay and lesbian parents and their children.
**www.stonewall.org.uk** – campaigning for justice and equality for gay and lesbian people.
**www.uk.gay.com** – British page from the big American magazine site.

G

# Genealogy

### www.sog.org.uk                                              UK

THE SOCIETY OF GENEALOGISTS
This is the first place to go when you're thinking about researching your family tree. It won't win awards for web design, but it contains basic information and there is an excellent set of links you can use to start you off. See also the excellent **www.cyndislist.com** where you'll find over 213,000 links in 150 categories to help with your family research.

### www.pro.gov.uk                                              UK

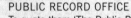

PUBLIC RECORD OFFICE
To quote them 'The Public Record Office is the national archive of England, Wales and the United Kingdom. It brings together and preserves the records of central government and the courts of law, and makes them available to all who wish to consult them. The records span an unbroken period from the 11th century to the present day'. The site is easy to use, the information is concisely presented and easy to access. See also **www.familyrecords.gov.uk** which can help enormously with tracing your family tree, the links selection is excellent.

### www.census.pro.gov.uk                                       UK

1901 CENSUS
You can search the database for free but for detailed information you have to pay using a rather odd system. Mapping is also available from the site to help with place names or boundary changes.

## www.accessgenealogy.com

US

GENEALOGY WEB PORTAL

A massive number of links and access to web rings from a
number of different countries give this site 'must check out'
status. It is biased towards an American audience but it's very
useful none-the-less. See also another portal site
**www.genealogyportal.com** which is less cluttered.

## www.familyhistorynetwork.net

US

GENEALOGICAL HELPER

Formerly **www.everton.com**, one of the best magazines devoted
to genealogy has become more commercial and very American
since the last edition. You can get their online magazine for
$2.50 and you have to pay to get full access to other sections.

G

## www.origins.net

UK

DEFINITIVE DATABASES

This site has information provided from the Society of
Genealogists' records from Scotland going back to 1553 and
from England going back to 1568, and unlike many other sites
in this area, it's also well designed and easy to use. There are
also search tips, access to discussion groups and a new section
devoted to Ireland.

## www.brit-a-r.demon.co.uk

UK

THE OFFICIAL BRITISH ANCESTRAL RESEARCH SITE

For £495 they will research one surname or line, for £895 two
or a minimum of 7 hours work for £195. They guarantee
results to four generations. Not as much fun as doing it
yourself though.

## www.genuki.org.uk

UK

VIRTUAL LIBRARY OF GENEALOGICAL INFORMATION

An excellent British-oriented site with a huge range of links to
help you find your ancestors. There is help for those starting
out, news, bulletin boards, FAQs on genealogy and a regional
search map of the UK and Ireland.

## www.ancestry.com                                            US

NO 1 SOURCE FOR FAMILY HISTORY
Find out about your ancestors for a subscription beginning at
$29.95 per month or take advantage of the 2-week free trial.
This US-oriented site has 1 billion names and access to 3,000
databases. It offers some information for free, but for real detail
you have to join. It's especially good if you're searching for
someone in the US or Canada. Linked to this is the chat site
**www.familyhistory.com** where you can visit surname
discussion groups.

## www.surnameweb.org                                         US

ORIGINS OF SURNAMES
A great place to start your search for your family origins. On top
of the information about your name, there are thousands of
links and they claim 2 billion searchable records.

*Other useful sites that may help in your family research:*
**www.achievements.co.uk** – a research outfit who have a track
record working with TV companies, but who will also give you
a quote to research your family tree.
**www.bbc.co.uk/education/beyond/factsheets/surnames/
surnames_intro.shtml** – a BBC factsheet on how to trace your
ancestors.
**www.englishorigins.com** – information for people tracking their
relatives from an excellent database, it costs though.
**www.familysearch.org** – the Church of Jesus Christ and the
Latter-day Saints excellent research site with good step-by-step
information.
**www.genealogypro.com** – a very comprehensive genealogists
and genealogy services directory.
**www.genfair.com** – a bookshop specialising in family history
books.
**www.genforum.com** – a huge number of forums devoted to
specific family names, US-oriented.
**www.gengateway.com** – claims to have the number one family
tree making software.
**www.ihgs.ac.uk** – the Institute of Heraldic and Genealogical
Studies offer information and help to research your family –
a good place to start.
**www.landsearch.me.uk** – find out who owned what property
for a price.
**www.morrigan.com** – specialist in Irish genealogy.

**www.rootsweb.com** – free genealogy site supported by
Ancestry.com with interactive guides and research tools.
**www.tartans.com** – resources for Scottish genealogists.

# Government

**www.ukonline.gov.uk**                                                      UK

THE ENTRY POINT FOR GOVERNMENT INFORMATION
A massive web site devoted to the workings of our government,
it is a superb resource if you want to know anything official
both at a national and a local level. Use the index or the search
facility to navigate, as it's easy to get side-tracked. There are
several major sections – in 'Citizenspace' you can have your say
and take part in decision making, there's life stage support and
advice in 'Yourlife', in 'Do It Online' there's information on
achieving things online from booking a driving test to help with
debt recovery. There's also a newsroom and a quick
search facility.

**http://parliament.uk**                                                     UK

UK PARLIAMENT
A good site giving information on how parliament works, what's
on in the House of Commons, Hansard and a directory of MPs
and Peers should you want to write, as well as links and
a glossary.

*Other key links:*
**http://europa.eu.int** – the European Union.
**http://www.scottish.parliament.uk** – for Scottish issues; to see
live broadcasts of the parliament in action go to
**www.scottishparliamentlive.com**
**http://younggov.ukonline.gov.uk** – a good site aimed at
explaining the workings of government to 11–18 year olds.
**www.bopcas.soton.ac.uk** – a service that announces when
government documents are published.
**www.cabinet-office.gov.uk** – how the Civil Service supports the
government.
**www.clicktso.com** – the Stationery Office bookstore.
**www.congress.org** – an excellent overview of the US Congress
and how it works.
**www.conservatives.com** – Conservative party.
**www.electoralcommission.org.uk** – managing and modernising
the electoral process in the UK.

**www.europarl.eu.int** – how the European Parliament works.
**www.hrw.org** – Human Rights Watch identifies corrupt governments and provides information on where they are going wrong.
**www.labour.org.uk** – Labour party.
**www.libdems.org.uk** – Liberal Democrats.
**www.parliamentlive.tv** – the workings of Parliament broadcast live. Comes with a calendar of events too.
**www.politicsonline.com** – a messy and dense site with an overview of US politics.
**www.royal.gov.uk** – for the monarchy.
**www.ukmeps.info** – information on Members Of European Parliament.
**www.ukmps.info** – a definitive non-political portal for United Kingdom Members of Parliament.
**www.un.org** – the United Nations.
**www.wales.gov.uk** – the National Assembly for Wales.

# Greetings Cards

## www.bluemountain.com                                           US

E-CARDS
Blue Mountain has thousands of cards for every occasion; it's easy to use but you have to subscribe to get the best designs. There are all sorts of extras you can build in like photos, music, cartoons and even voice messages.

## http://cards.webshots.com                                      US

YOUR PHOTOS INTO CARDS
Part of the Corbis site, there's a great deal to choose from in the form of photographic and general cards and you can also create your own cards although you need to sign up for free membership to take for this service.

*See also:*
**www.egreetings.com** – big range, busy design that gets on your nerves after a while.
**www.greeting-cards.com** – massive range and geared to the American market, not all free, masses of adverts.

**www.regards.com** – nice design and the best bit is that it's free!
**www.web-greeting-cards.com** – massive selection and well
categorised too.

## www.nextcard.co.uk                                              UK

3-D CARDS
Send free three-dimensional cards using this site, there are
great pictures of animals, sunsets and mountain scenery to
choose from.

## www.cybercard.co.uk                                            UK

REAL CARDS TO REAL PEOPLE
Create your card and message and they'll send it for you, all for
£2.95. For a similar service go to **www.moonpig.com** who
have personalised humorous cards to create and buy.

## www.charitycards.co.uk                                         UK

CONTRIBUTIONS TO CHARITY
Buy your cards here and give money to charity, this is
traditionally a Christmas thing but Charitycards have turned it
into an all year round possibility. They will also design and
personalise Christmas cards. There are also discounts available
and free postage if you buy in quantity and they also
sell stamps.

# Health Advice

*Here are some of the key sites for getting good health advice, featuring online doctors, fitness centres, nutrition and sites that try to combine all three. As with all health sites, there is no substitute for the real thing and if you are ill, your main port of call must be your doctor. Dietary advice sites are listed on page 148, specialist sites aimed at men, on page 256 and for women, on page 484. The advice for parents, page 300, and teens, page 406, may also be useful.*

## General health

**www.nhsdirect.nhs.uk**                                                        UK

### NHS ADVICE ONLINE
NHS Direct is a telephone advice service and this is the Internet spin-off, it comprises of an excellent guide to common ailments with the emphasis on treating them at home and a superb selection of NHS-approved links covering specific illnesses or parts of the body. There's also health information and an A–Z guide to the NHS.

**www.nelh.nhs.uk**                                                             UK

NATIONAL ELECTRONIC LIBRARY FOR HEALTH
This programme is working with NHS Libraries to develop a digital library for NHS staff, patients and the public; it is an outstanding resource already and can only get better. It should be the first port of call when researching.

*See also:*
**www.avma.org.uk** – an organisation working for better safety for patients. If something goes wrong then this site is worth a visit.
**www.doh.gov.uk** – for the Department of Health's informative site.
**www.helpthehospices.org.uk** – information on how you can support hospices and where to find one.
**www.npsa.nhs.uk** – the NHS Patient Safety Agency.

## www.bupa.co.uk
UK

BUPA HOMEPAGE

Health fact-sheets, special offers on health cover, health tips
and competitions are all on offer at this well-designed site.
You can also find your nearest BUPA hospital and instructions
on referral. See also **www.ppphealthcare.co.uk** who have over
150 fact-sheets available on a wide range of health conditions
located in the 'Health' section found in 'You and Your Family'.
See also **www.privatehealth.co.uk** a portal site devoted to all
things related to private health.

## www.healthfinder.com
US

A GREAT PLACE TO START FOR HEALTH ADVICE

Run by the US Department of Health, this provides a link to
more or less every health organisation, medical and fitness site
you can think of. In several sections you can learn about hot
medical topics, catch the medical news, make smart health
choices, discover what's best for you and your lifestyle and use
the medical dictionary in the research section. The site is well
designed, fast once it's fully downloaded and very easy to use.

## www.patient.co.uk
UK

FINDING INFORMATION FROM UK SOURCES

This excellent site has been put together by two GPs. It's
essentially a collection of links to other health sites, but from
here you can find a web site on health-related topics with a UK
bias. You can search alphabetically or browse within the site.
All the recommended sites are reviewed by a GP for suitability
and quality before being placed on the list. For a second
opinion you could visit **www.surgerydoor.co.uk** which is more
magazine-like in style with up to the minute news stories.
It's comprehensive and has an online shop. Also try the well-
designed **www.netdoctor.co.uk** who describe themselves as the
'UK's independent health web site' and offer a similar service.

## www.embarrassingproblems.co.uk
UK

FIRST STEP

An award-winning and much-recommended site that works
well; it's what the Internet should be about really. The site helps
you deal with health problems that are difficult to discuss with
anyone; it's easy to use and comprehensive. Younger people
and teenagers should also check out **www.coolnurse.com**
which is an excellent American site with similar attributes.

## www.drkoop.com US

THE BEST PRESCRIPTION IS KNOWLEDGE
Don't let the silly name put you off, Dr C. Everett Koop is a
former US Surgeon General and is acknowledged as one of the
best online doctors. The goal is to empower you to take care of
your own health through better knowledge. The site is very
comprehensive covering every major health topic and is aimed
at all, including both young and old.

## www.mayohealth.org US

RELIABLE INFORMATION FOR A HEALTHY LIFE
Mayo has a similar ethic to Dr Koop but is less fussy and very
easy to use. However, the amount of information can be
overwhelming, as they claim the combined knowledge of some
2,000 doctors in the 21 'centers'. Essentially it's a massive
collection of articles that combine to give you a large amount of
data on specific medical topics. There are also guides on how
to live a healthy life, first aid and a newsletter, plus information
on specific medical conditions and diseases.

## www.cellscience.com UK

MEDICAL DICTIONARY
The dictionary covers Aids, HIV, cancer, cystic fibrosis and
diabetes. It's easy to use and contains listings for links,
hospitals and charities as well as other essential information.

## www.quackwatch.com US

HEALTH FRAUD, QUACKERY AND INTELLIGENT DECISIONS
Exposes fraudulent cures and old wives tales, then provides
information on where to get the right treatment. It makes
fascinating reading and includes exposés on everything from
acupuncture to weight loss. Use the search engine or just
browse through it; many of the articles leave you amazed at
the fraudulent nature of some medical claims.

*For more health information:*
**http://medlineplus.gov** – a health information centre from the
US National Library of Medicine.
**www.24dr.com** – a site from a UK doctor, lots of help with self
diagnosis and what appears to be a good medical encyclopaedia.
**www.bbc.co.uk/health** – good all rounder covering lots of
topics, good links.

**www.dr-ali.co.uk** – a popular all round health advisory site run by the high profile Dr Ali. You have to register to get the best out of it.

**www.e-med.co.uk** – your own private doctor everywhere you go is the strap line for this site, it costs £20 to join then £15 per consultation.

**www.gmc-uk.org** – home of the General Medical Council, the place to go if you have a problem with a doctor.

**www.healthcyclopedia.com** – a straightforward health portal with comprehensive coverage.

**www.medterms.com** – a straightforward glossary of medical terms.

**www.nice.org.uk** – the National Institute of Clinical Excellence provides 'robust and reliable guidance on current health best practise'.

**www.studenthealth.co.uk** – written by doctors, sensible and funny with some good competitions.

## Medicine and pharmacy

### www.allcures.com                                                    UK

UK'S FIRST ONLINE PHARMACY

After a fairly lengthy but secure registration process you can shop from this site which has all the big brands and a wide range of products. There are also sections on toiletries, beauty, alternative medicine and a photo-shop. You can arrange to have your prescriptions made up and sent to you with no delivery charge.

*See also:*

**www.academyhealth.com** – who deliver free in the UK.

**www.mhra.gov.uk** – the government department that deals with safety in medicines.

**www.mypharmacy.co.uk** – good basic health site from a real pharmacist, with a shop stocking a relatively wide range of products.

**www.pharmacy2u.co.uk** – who have lots of offers and cover lots of health areas, even a section on embarrassing problems.

**www.postoptics.co.uk** – eye care products and contact lenses by post.

# Fitness and exercise

### www.netfit.co.uk                                              UK

DEFINITIVE GUIDE TO HEALTH AND FITNESS
Devoted to promoting the benefits of regular exercise with a
dedicated team who put a great deal of effort into the site.
You can gauge your fitness, there's information on some 200
exercises, tips on eating and dieting, nutrition and links to
useful (mainly sport) sites. For those hooked on the idea,
they've introduced a membership scheme which promises to
sculpt your body into shape – for $10 per month.

### www.hfonline.co.uk                                            UK

HEALTH & FITNESS MAGAZINE
A spin-off site from the magazine, which offers the latest health
news and advice, it's attractive and it's quite comprehensive.

### www.fitnessonline.com                                         US

PROVIDING PERSONAL SUPPORT
This good-looking site is from an American magazine group.
It takes a holistic view of health offering advice on exercise,
nutrition and health products. In reality what you get is a
succession of articles from their magazines, all are very
informative but getting the right information can be time-
consuming.

*The following sites also offer good advice and information:*
**www.exercise.co.uk** – a good health equipment store.
**www.exercise.co.uk** – information on exercise and the right
equipment to use and buy.
**www.exercisegroup.com** – natural body building.
**www.fitnesspeak.co.uk** – the best prices for gym equipment.
**www.thefitmap.com** – a portal site for the UK's health and
fitness clubs, find your nearest one.
**www.workout.com** – over 500 exercises, lots of ihformation
too. You've got to join to get the most out of it.

# Alternative medicine and therapies

## www.altmedicine.com    US

ALTERNATIVE HEALTH NEWS
Keep up-to-date with the latest therapies and trends with articles
and features from some of the key figures in the world of
alternative medicine. The site is supplemented by an excellent
medical search engine, an overview of the major philosophies and
associated healing techniques plus a good set of related links.

## www.therapy-world.co.uk    UK

THERAPY WORLD MAGAZINE
A well put together magazine covering many different types of
therapies with a good overview of all of them and some
interesting articles.

## www.medical-acupuncture.co.uk    UK

ACUPUNCTURE
A good-looking site with information from the British Medical
Acupuncture Society on the nature of acupuncture and where to
find a practitioner in your area. There are also good links and
information on courses. See also **www.acupuncture.org.uk**

## www.drlockie.com    US

HOMEOPATHY MADE EASY
An interesting, clear and simple site that offers sensible advice
at all levels. Click on any of the medicine jars to get to the
relevant sections on everything from basic information, products
and links.

*See also:*
**www.alternativemedicines.co.uk** – use the ailment search to
find the right alternative products.
**www.drweil.com** – the vitamin guru has a site that offers much
in advice and his own brand of balanced living.
**www.homeopath.co.uk** – attractive site but only partly
functional when we visited, good directory of homeopaths though.
**www.homeopathyhome.com** – slightly confusing but
comprehensive.
**www.homeopathy-soh.org** – home of the Society of
Homeopaths.
**www.ukselfhelp.info** – a listing of almost 800 self-help groups
and nearly 700 links to self-help sites.

**www.thinknatural.com**                                                    UK

> THINK NATURALLY
> A nicely designed site with a mass of information on every
> aspect of natural health including a comprehensive shop with
> loads of special offers and a very wide range of products.

**www.yogauk.com**                                                          UK

> YOGA
> Welcome to the yoga village where you can get information on
> yoga in the UK, subscribe to their magazine, or browse the
> links section, which has a comprehensive list of stores.
>
> *See also:*
> **www.bwy.org.uk** – the British Wheel of Yoga.
> **www.calmcentre.com** – calming experiences from Paul Wilson
> and take the stress test.
> **www.interconnections.co.uk** – up to date information on living
> holistically.
> **www.iyengaryoga.org.uk** – all about Iyengar yoga techniques.
> **www.mydailyyoga.com** – simple yoga exercises.
> **www.yogaplus.co.uk** – who offer courses and workshops.
> **www.yogatherapy.org** – using yoga to cure.

# Sites catering for a specific condition or disease

*Here is a list of the key sites relating to specific diseases, addictions
and ailments, we have not attempted to review them, but if you know
of a site we've missed and would like it included in the next edition of
this book please e-mail us at* **goodwebsiteguide@hotmail.com**

# Acne

> **www.m2w3.com/acne**

# Alcohol and drug abuse

> **www.al-anon-alateen.org**
> **www.alcoholconcern.org.uk**
> **www.alcoholics-anonymous.org**
> **www.wrecked.co.uk**

## Allergies
www.allergy.co.uk
www.allergy-info.com (sponsored by Zyrtec)

## Alzheimers and dementia
www.alzheimers.org.uk
www.dementia.ion.ucl.ac.uk

## Aids and HIV
www.avert.org
www.hiv-development.org
www.hivstopswithme.org
www.tht.org.uk

## Anxiety
www.anxieties.com
www.healthanxiety.com

## Arthritis
www.aboutarthritis.com
www.arc.org.uk

## Asthma
www.asthma.org.uk

## Autism
www.nas.org.uk

## Back and spinal problems
www.backpain.org
www.spinalnet.co.uk

## Blindness
www.rnib.org.uk
www.sense.org.uk

## Bowels and bladder
www.continence-foundation.org.uk
www.digestivedisorders.org.uk
www.ibsnetwork.org.uk
www.incontact.org

H

H

## Brain disease and injury
www.bbsf.org.uk
www.headway.org.uk

## Breast Cancer Campaign
www.bcc-uk.org

## Bullying
www.bullying.co.uk

## Cancer
www.bowelcancer.org
www.breastcancercare.org.uk
www.cancer.gov
www.cancerhelp.org.uk
www.cancerresearchuk.org
www.dipex.org (prostate cancer)
www.goingfora.com (oncology)
www.imperialcancer.co.uk

## Cerebral palsy
www.scope.org.uk

## Chiropody
www.drfoot.co.uk
www.feetforlife.org

## Crohns disease and colitis
www.crohns.org.uk
www.naccorg.uk

## Deafness
www.britishdeafassociation.org.uk

## Dental
www.bda-dentistry.org.uk
www.dentalwisdom.com
www.gdc-uk.org

## Depression
http://www.depressionalliance.org

## Dermatology
www.skinhealth.co.uk

## Diabetics
**www.diabetes.org.uk**
**www.diabetes-insight.info** formerly **www.diabetic.org.uk**

## Digestion
**www.digestivecare.co.uk**

## Disabled
**www.disability.gov.uk**
**www.radar.org.uk**

## Drugs
**www.acde.org**
**www.release.org.uk**

## Epilepsy
**www.epilepsy.org.uk**
**www.epilepsynse.org.uk**

## Eczema
**www.eczema.org**

## Eyes
**www.moorfields.org.uk**

## Fertility
**www.ifconline.org**

## Fibromyalgia
**www.ukfibromyalgia.com**

## Gambling
**www.gamblersanonymous.org.uk**

## Heart
**www.heartuk.org.uk** formerly **www.familyheart.org**
**www.bhf.org.uk**
**www.riskscore.org.uk**

## High blood pressure
**www.hbpf.org.uk**

## Kidney problems
**www.kidney.org.uk**

H

## Liver problems
www.britishlivertrust.org.uk

## Lupus
www.lupusuk.com

## Meningitis
www.meningitis-trust.org

## Mental health
www.mentalhealth.com
www.mind.org.uk
www.rcpsych.ac.uk
www.youngminds.org.uk

## Migraine
www.migraine.org.uk
www.migrainetrust.org

## Multiple sclerosis
www.mssociety.org.uk

## Older people
www.elderabuse.org.uk

## Osteopathy
www.osteopathy.org.uk

## Plastic surgery
www.baaps.org.uk

## Psoriasis
www.psoriasis-association.org.uk

## Repetitive Strain Injury
www.rsi.org.uk

## Sexually Transmitted Diseases (STDs)
www.playingsafely.co.uk

## Smoking
www.ash.org.uk
www.givingupsmoking.co.uk

## Social, personal and emotional support
www.samaritans.co.uk
www.shyness.com

## Spina bifida
www.asbah.org

## Stress
www.isma.org.uk
www.stressrelease.com

## Stroke
www.differentstrokes.co.uk
www.stroke.org.uk

**www.self-help.org.uk**

UK    THE SELF-HELP DATABASE

A portal site devoted to providing a searchable database of self help and patient organisations in the UK. There are currently over 1,000 on file.

# *History and Biography*

*The Internet is proving to be a great storehouse, not only for the latest news but also for cataloguing historical events in an entertaining and informative way, here are some of the best sites.*

## General history sites

**www.thehistorychannel.com**                                    US

THE BEST SEARCH IN HISTORY
Excellent for history buffs, revision or just a good read, the History Channel provides a site that is packed with information. Search by key word or timeline, by date and by subject, get biographical information or speeches. It's fast and easy to get carried away once you start your search.

## www.historyworld.net                                    UK

### HISTORY WORLD
An outstanding site containing timelines, articles, quizzes and tours all designed to educate and bring history to life in an engaging and stimulating way, and it's successful. The OCEAN historical index that was once part of this site has gone it alone and now contains more than 35,000 precise links to external sites. It can be found at **www.oceanindex.net**

## www.historytoday.com                                    UK

### WORLD'S LEADING HISTORY MAGAZINE
Contains some excellent articles from the magazine, but probably the most useful bit is the related links section, which offers many links to other history sites.

## www.newsplayer.com                                      UK

### RELIVE THE LAST CENTURY
Relive the events of the past hundred years, witness them at first hand as they happened. A truly superb site with real newsreel footage worth the £4 annual subscription fee. See also the BBC's excellent site **www.bbc.co.uk/onthisday** where you can see what happened on a particular day in history. Strongly biased to the 20th century with film clips and eye witness reports.

## www.ukans.edu/history/VL                                 US

### HISTORY LINKS
The folks at the University of Kansas love their history and have put together a huge library, organised by country and historical period. It's got an easy to use search engine too. For modern history go to **www.fordham.edu/halsall/mod/modsbook.html**

## http://history.about.com                                 US

### HISTORY AT ABOUT.COM
A massive archive notably bringing history to life the use of eyewitness accounts of people who were actually there. This site is excellent for most periods of history.

**www.bl.uk**                                                                    UK

THE BRITISH LIBRARY

An overview of who they are and what they provide, on the site you can get information about the library and see some of their key treasures such as the Magna Carta in close up.

**www.documentsonline.pro.gov.uk**                                               UK

DOWNLOAD YOUR HISTORY

From the Public Record Office, this site gives you the chance to see digitised versions of over 800,000 wills, ancient documents and other important academic papers.

**www.pbs.org/commandingheights**                                                US

GLOBAL ECONOMY

An outstanding site devoted to the explanation of how the global economy works, great for students of politics and history alike.

*For more general history sites try these:*

**www.eyewitnesstohistory.com** – containing a large catalogue historical recollections both ancient and modern, takes the 'history through the eyes of those who lived it' approach.

**www.historyhouse.com** – excellent for history trivia and odd facts.

**www.historylearningsite.co.uk** – great for school, it covers Key Stage 3 and upwards.

**www.historyplace.com** – biased towards the US but has some great historic photos.

**www.hmc.gov.uk** – home of the Historical Manuscripts Commission who are responsible for looking after and advising on the upkeep and use of historical documents.

**www.sbrowning.com/whowhatwhen/index.php3** – create your own history timelines at this innovative site.

**www.spartacus.schoolnet.co.uk** – a useful history encyclopaedia.

**www.thehistorynet.com** – a good resource from a US magazine site.

*Listed here are a selection of specific sites or pages from larger university sites that cover specific periods in time, events or regions, they may not win design awards but the information they contain is usually comprehensive or sufficient to enable you to access more from elsewhere.*

## UK History

**www.bbc.co.uk/history**                                           UK

HISTORY INTERACTIVE
Part of the outstanding BBC site, here you can find sections covering all the important bits of British history, it uses technology well and there are some good articles too.
It also shows what's on TV and radio that's history related.

*See also:*
**www.britannia.com** – an American site devoted to British History that offers a good overview of the subject.
**www.britarch.ac.uk** – a portal for British Archaeology.
**www.british-history.com** – a site offering sections on Roman Britain, 100 Years War, Wars of the Roses, English Civil War, Napoleonic wars and the Second World War.
**www.britainunlimited.com** – biographies of 250 people who shaped Britain.
**www.enrichuk.net** – links to local and regional history projects throughout the UK.
**www.history.uk.com** – excellent directory and portal featuring some 28,000 sites.
**www.lib.byu.edu/~rdh/eurodocs/uk.html** – documents through history.
**www.livinghistory.co.uk** – effectively a portal site for those who love to re-enact history.

## Middle Ages and before

**www.angelcynn.org.uk**                                           UK

ANGLO SAXON LIFE
A comprehensive site on how the Anglo-Saxons lived, using a living history approach it's entertaining as well as educational.

*See also:*
**www.pastforward.co.uk/vikings** – a directory of all things Viking.
**www.regia.org** – Anglo-Saxons, Vikings and Normans.
**www.suttonhoo.org** – information on the ship burial.
**www.vikingsword.com** – a sword expert's view, not only of Viking weaponry but swords generally, good links section.

## www.netserf.org
US

MEDIAEVAL LIFE
Excellent and well-categorised portal site covering every conceivable aspect of life in the Middle Ages.

*See also:*
**www.darkagestrust.org.uk** – an attempt to recreate England as it was 1,000 years ago.
**www.learner.org/exhibits/middleages** – a good educational resource.
**www.postroman.info** – a good overview of early mediaeval Britain.
**www.the-orb.net** – who also cover European history in mediaeval times.

## www.essentialnormanconquest.com
UK

THE NORMANS
A good-looking site from Osprey Publishing, which features a 1066 timeline, and blow by blow account of the conquest. It's got some good maps and a quiz too.

*See also:*
**www.bayeuxtapestry.org.uk** – a scene by scene explanation of the Bayeux Tapestry.
**www.normanconquest.co.uk** – an old site being updated but still useful.
**www.wsu.edu:8080/~dee/MA/NORMANS.HTM** – a dry overview.

# The Tudors to the Georges

## www.warsoftheroses.com
UK

WARS OF THE ROSES
Excellent site covering the period 1450 to 1490 with all its turmoil and politics, it also has a good timeline and links.

## www.tudorhistory.org

TUDOR FAMILY TREE
A basic but informative site with a who's who of Tudor times
and background on what it was like to live then.

*See also:*
**http://tudors.crispen.org** – a period by period overview, turn
the sound off if you don't like Tudor music.
**www.elizabethi.org** – a great biographical site with a good deal
of background on Elizabethan life as well.
**www.renaissance.dm.net** – the Renaissance was an amazing
time and, while this site doesn't cover it that well, it does have
a good links section; it's also very oriented towards England.
**www.tudorgroup.co.uk** – re-enacting Tudor and Elizabethan
times.

## www.pepysdiary.com                                             UK

DIARY OF SAMUEL PEPYS
Put together by an aficionado of Pepys, this is updated daily
with an entry from the diaries on the day he wrote them over
340 years ago. Apart from the fascinating social history there's
lots of annotation, explanation and cross referencing too, as
well as audio readings, which all help to picture the scene.

*See also:*
**www.cannylink.com/history17thcentury.htm** – a list of articles
on important 17th Century events.
**www.gunpowder-plot.org** – interesting site devoted to the
happenings that surround the Gun Powder Plot of 1605.

## www.olivercromwell.org                                         UK

OLIVER CROMWELL
A detailed biography of the man and his times. There's
background on the Civil Wars too and a guide to places linked
with him that you can visit.

*See also:*
**www.ecwsa.org** – the English Civil War Society of America with
a good site with lots of detail, articles and links.
**www.open2.net/civilwar** – detailed information on the English
Civil War.

## www.thegloriousrevolution.com UK

FROM CHARLES I TO WILLIAM III
A good encyclopedia charting one of the most turbulent times
in British and European history with biographies of the
monarchs and key individuals and events.

*See also:*
**http://dspace.dial.pipex.com/mbloy/c-eight/18chome.htm** –
a very detailed site on George III and what events took place
during his reign.
**http://regencygarderobe.com** – Regency fashion.
**www.elizabethpowell.net/history.htm** – a good overview of the
Regency Period.
**www.royal-stuarts.org** – the placing of the Stuart monarchy in
history with a strong Scottish bias.

# The Victorians and Empire

## www.victorianweb.org UK

VICTORIANS EXPLAINED
Background on events, social and political history, biographies
and even entertainment, it's all here.

*See also:*
**http://victorianresearch.org** – a scholarly site but with
excellent material.
**www.victorians.org.uk** – for information on the daily lives of
the Victorians.
**www.victorianstation.com** – everything from architecture
to shopping.

## www.britishempire.co.uk UK

THE BRITISH EMPIRE
A thorough walk through the Empire with articles, maps and
sections on science, arts and military power that round
everything off. It also has a useful timeline, just to put
everything in context.

*See also:*
**http://homepage.ntlworld.com/haywardlad** – a slow but pretty
comprehensive site on the rise and fall of the Empire.
**http://regiments.org** – an overview of the land forces who
served the Empire and Commonwealth.

# The 20th century

*There doesn't seem to be one really good site dedicated to the UK's 20th century history, although many of the larger history sites major on the 20th century anyway. Those listed below do a great job in bringing history to life whilst informing us about the historical details.*

**www.1940.co.uk** – remembering the 1940s, a nice site and shop.

**www.bbhq.com/sixties.htm** – a very ugly site but lots of info on the sixties.

**www.bergen.org/AAST/Projects/ColdWar/index2.html** – a chilling reminder of what it was like to live through the Cold War.

**www.britishpathe.com** – Pathe films covered most of the major events of the Century and you can buy and see clips here.

**www.fiftiesweb.com** – entertaining overview of the decade's events and culture.

**www.greatwar.co.uk** – a well laid out site on the 1914–18 war.

**www.holnet.org.uk** – the history of London.

**www.movinghere.org.uk** – a history of migration to England.

**www.sixties.net** – a bright and breezy stroll through the 1960s.

# World History

## General

### www.ancientsites.com

US

ANCIENT SITES

Seven key times and sites are featured and you must subscribe to get the best out of it. The whole thing is a little long winded although worth the pfaffing around as you get access to lots of background information and social history. You can also chat to few members.

### www.ancientcivilisations.co.uk

UK

INTERACTIVE HISTORY

An piece of outstanding site design from the British Museum. You choose a theme from the map: Cities, Religion, Buildings, Technology, Writing or Trade; this provides you with a short overview plus a timeline which you can stop at any point to get the information you need. If you want real detail then go to a specialist site; however, this site provides sufficient information to start you off.

# Africa

**www.thebanmappingproject.com**                                    US

THEBES AND THE VALLEY OF THE KINGS
A great and genuinely interesting site devoted to life in ancient
Thebes in what is now Egypt, with over 200 interactive maps,
narrative tours and 3D features. Excellent.

*See also:*
**www.fordham.edu/halsall/africa/africasbook.html** – excellent
database of sources and links covering African history from the
Ancient Egyptians to Nelson Mandela.

# Asia

**http://coombs.anu.edu.au/WWWVL-AsianStudies.html**

ASIAN STUDIES                                        AUSTRALIA
Basically a selection of links that cover the whole of Asia by
country, region and centre.

*See also:*
**http://sun.sino.uni-heidelberg.de/igcs** – more links on China
than you'll ever need.
**http://web.uccs.edu/~history/index/japan.html** – Japanese
history covered.
**http://www.asianinfo.org/asianinfo/korea/history.htm** –
an outline of Korean history.
**www.asterius.com/china** – a good basic overview of Chinese
history.
**www.fordham.edu/halsall/india/indiasbook.html** – excellent
overview of India's history.

# Australasia

**www.academicinfo.net/histaus.html**                    AUSTRALIA

AUSTRALIA
A pretty good directory of sites relating to Australian history
ancient and modern. There's an explanation and review of each
site featured.

*See also:*
**http://www.pvs-hawaii.com/history.htm** – A history of
Polynesia from the Polynesian Voyaging Society.

**www.awm.gov.au** – Australian war memorials.
**www.enzed.com/hist.html** – useful overview of
New Zealand's past.

# Europe

**http://www.hartford-hwp.com/archives/60**                    UK

EUROPE AS A WHOLE
A directory of links and articles covering the whole of Europe
and its history, the selection can be a bit disparate, but there
is a search facility on the main site.

*See also:*

FRANCE
**http://chnm.gmu.edu/revolution** – the French Revolution
explored, this site offers a huge amount of information.
**www.napoleonic-literature.com** – a very good site about
Napoleon and the effect he had on Europe, with background
on the battles and his writing.

GERMANY
**www.tau.ac.il/GermanHistory/links.html** – a chronological
set of links and articles covering German history from
ancient times.

GREECE
**www.ancientgreece.com** – an excellent site devoted to all
aspects of Ancient Greece.
**www.mythweb.com** – all the Greek Myths illustrated in a fun
and entertaining way.

ICELAND
**http://icelandic-history.hypermart.net/main.html** – a good run
through Icelandic history.

IRELAND
**www.ucc.ie/celt/** – excellent resource on Irish historical events,
literature and politics too.
**www.ireland.org/irl_hist/default.htm** – a good chronology of
Irish history.

### ITALY
**www.arcaini.com/italy/italyhistory/ItalyHistory.html** – a good chronological history of Italy from pre-history to the 20th century.
**www.roman-empire.net** – excellent site covering all aspects of the Roman Empire with a good kids' section.

### RUSSIA
**www.departments.bucknell.edu/russian/history.html** – complete overview and chronology of Russian History, and they've taken the trouble to make the site look good too.
**www.barnsdle.demon.co.uk/russ/rusrev.html** – an interesting site covering the events surrounding the Russian Revolution.

### SPAIN
**www.sispain.org/english/history** – a chronology of Spanish History with links.
**www.users.dircon.co.uk/~warden/scw/scwindex.htm** – the Spanish Civil War.

### TURKEY
**www.friesian.com/turkia.htm** – a dense, text heavy overview of the Ottoman Empire.

## Latin America

**http://users.snowcrest.net/jmike/latin.html**                    US

LATIN AMERICAN LINKS
An outstanding collection of links, categorised by country and region covering Latin and South America and also the Caribbean.

**www.ancientmexico.com**                    US

ANCIENT MEXICO
A beautifully illustrated site covering ancient Mexico and the Mayan and Aztec empires; there are also similar sister sites on Chile and Peru.

## Middle East

**www.albany.edu/history/middle-east/**                    US

HISTORY IN THE NEWS
A very good resource site with lots of documents, articles and links plus a chronology and social background on the Middle East and its tormented past.

*See also:*
**www.al-bab.com/arab/history.htm** – a good overview of Arab history with links and articles.
**www.fordham.edu/halsall/ancient/asbook05.html** – all you need on ancient Persia.
**www.prc.org.uk/palestine%2048/history.html** – an account of Palestinian history.

**www.hum.huji.ac.il/dinur/**                                         US
JEWISH HISTORY RESEARCH CENTRE
This site is a little difficult to navigate and use but it does offer some 6,000 links which are well categorised; it covers Biblical history too.

*See also:*
**www.cjh.org/** – Center for Jewish History, well illustrated and with a US bias.

## North America

**http://americanhistory.about.com/**                                 US
ABOUT AMERICA
Just about all you'll be needing on American history from the ever excellent About.com; it's well categorised with links and related articles too.

*See also:*
**http://earlyamerica.com/** – the chronicling of the early history of America.
**www.historyplace.com** – good for articles, features and links.

## Other history related sites

**www.biography.com**                                                 US

FIND OUT ABOUT ANYONE WHO WAS ANYONE
Over 25,000 biographical references and some 4,000 videos make this site a great option if you need to find out about someone in a hurry. There are special features such as a book club and a magazine. There is a shop but at time of going to press they don't ship to the UK.

*See also:*

**http://almaz.com/nobel/nobel.html** – a fascinating site about the people who have won the Nobel prize.

**www.fordham.edu/halsall** – a messy site, presenting copies of history source books that are freely available for use.

**www.royalty.nu** – the world of royalty, historical and recent.

**www.rulers.org** – an amazing database providing a list of the rulers of every country going back to 1700.

**www.s9.com/biography** – a biographical dictionary covering the lives of over 28,000 people!

## www.francisfrith.co.uk                                     UK

HISTORY IN PHOTOGRAPHS

This remarkable archive was started in 1860 and there are over 365,000 photographs featuring some 7,000 cities, towns and villages. The site is very well designed with a good search facility. You can buy from a growing selection of shots, different sizes are available and it's good value too. See also **www.photolondon.org.uk** where you'll find an excellent photo archive of the capital.

## www.old-maps.co.uk                                        UK

FREE OLD MAPS

Access to mapping as it was between 1846 and 1899, just type in your town and you get a view of what it looked like in those times. The quality is variable but it's fun to try and spot the changes. See also **www.alangodfreymaps.co.uk**

## www.museumofcostume.co.uk                                 UK

COSTUME THROUGH THE AGES

Excellent site showing how the design of costume has changed through the ages. There's a virtual tour and links to other museums based in Bath.

## www.blackhistorymap.com                                   UK

BLACK AND ASIAN HISTORY

Hosted by Channel 4, a beautifully designed and important site, which graphically describes how Black people and Asians, have contributed to British history. Search by region, use the timeline or category headings. It's well written and very informative with a wide range of contributions, there's also a selection of videos. For American Black history go to **www.brightmoments.com/blackhistory**

## www.findagrave.com                                           US

FIND A GRAVE!
Find graves of the rich and famous or a long lost relative, either
way there's a database of over 3 million to search. It really only
covers the US.

## www.the-reenactor.co.uk                                      UK

TAKE PART IN A BATTLE
Ok so you feel the urge to play at being a Viking for the day,
well here's where to start, the site lists some 90 societies to
join and play a part in. It is divided into sections according to
time period and you can find out where re-enactments are
taking place, plus the latest news.

## www.uchronia.net                                             US

ALTERNATIVE HISTORIES
A bibliography and review site featuring almost 2,500 books
that in some way or another scope out alternative histories,
it makes interesting reading, the 'what if' scenario fascinates
most historians after all.

# Hobbies

## www.yahoo.co.uk/recreation/hobbies                           UK

IF YOU CAN'T FIND YOUR HOBBY THEN LOOK HERE
Hundreds of links for almost every conceivable pastime from
amateur radio to urban exploration, it's part of the Yahoo
service (see page 351); also try **www.about.com/hobbies** who
have a similarly large list but with an American bias.

*See also:*
**www.allcrafts.net** – a wide-ranging directory covering all the
major crafts and many minor ones. Very good links pages.
**www.ehobbies.com** – they don't ship outside the US, but are
worth a visit anyway for information and links.
**www.hobbyseek.net/cgi-search/Great_Britain** – a German site
with good links to modelling sites.
**www.hobbywebguide.com** – a modest list with some good
hobby sites.

## www.save-on-crafts.com US

### SAVINGS EVERYWHERE YOU LOOK

An excellent craft supply and interiors store covering an
extensive range of crafts and merchandise. It's well worth a
browse and good for the unusual but shipping is expensive.

## www.cass-arts.co.uk UK

### ONE STOP SHOP FOR ART MATERIALS

A huge range of art and craft products available to buy online,
also hints and tips and step-by-step guides for the novice.
There is an online gallery and a section of art trivia and games.
The shop has a decent search engine which copes with over
20,000 items, delivery is charged according to what you spend.

*See also:*
**www.artdiscount.co.uk** – good value and a wide range on offer.
**www.pictureframes.co.uk** – show off your masterpiece to
best effect.

## www.hobbycraft.co.uk UK

### ARTS AND CRAFTS SUPERSTORE

A nice retro feel to this site with a wide selection of inspirational
ideas and information on what they sell and where their shops
are, sadly you can't buy online.

## www.sewandso.co.uk UK

### SHOP AT THE SPECIALISTS

This site offers a huge range of kits and patterns for cross-
stitch, needlepoint and embroidery. In addition, there's an
equally large range of needles and threads, some 15,000
products in all. There are some good offers and delivery starts
at £1 for the UK, but the cost is calculated by weight. It's also
worth checking out the specialist pages at About.com
**http://knitting.about.com** and **http://sewing.about.com**

## www.whaleys-bradford.ltd.uk UK

### FANTASTIC FABRICS

Whether you're looking for a simple cotton lawn, a shot taffeta,
or fabrics for the theatre, Whaley's have it all – and they will
send you up to 10 samples free of charge. There is a useful
A–Z of fabrics and a good search facility. There is a choice of
delivery options.

H

### www.horology.com                                                US

THE INDEX
The complete exploration of time, this is essentially a set of
links for the committed horologist. It's pretty comprehensive,
so if your hobby is tinkering about with clocks and watches,
then this is a must.

### www.jigboxx.com                                              CANADA

JIGSAWS
Excellent for jigsaw enthusiasts, there's a wide range, a search
facility, plus loyalty scheme and you can be kept abreast of the
latest designs too. Delivery charges vary.

### www.royalmint.com                                               UK

H

THE VALUE OF MONEY
The Royal Mint's web site is informative, providing a history of
the Mint, the coins themselves, plus details on the coins they've
issued. You can buy from the site and delivery is free.

*See also:*
**http://coins.to** – US coins and much more from the Austin Coin
Collecting Society.
**www.coinclub.com** – good for information and links.
**www.coinlink.com** – a good directory devoted to all
things numismatic.
**www.tclayton.demon.co.uk/coins.html** – Tony Clayton's
informative home page on coins.
**www.telesphere.com/ts/coins/faq.html** – commonly asked
questions about coin collecting.
**www.tokenpublishing.com** – owners of Coin News.

### www.stanleygibbons.com                                          UK

STAMPS ETC.
The best prices and a user-friendly site for philatelists, you can
buy a whole collection or sell them your own. Their catalogue is
available online and you can take part in auctions.

*See also:*
**www.corbitts.com** – auctioneers for stamps, coins, notes and
medals.
**www.duncannon.co.uk** – for accessories and albums.
**www.postcard.co.uk** – home of the Postcard Traders
Association.

**www.robinhood-stamp.co.uk** – for good prices and range.
**www.stampsatauction.com** – a good auction site devoted to stamps.
**www.ukphilately.org.uk/abps** – information on exhibitions and events at the Association of British Philatelic Societies.

## www.themodelmakersresource.co.uk                UK

MODEL-MAKING MATERIALS
A wide range of tools, materials, kits and other modelling essentials here, plus lots of information and links, some good prices too.

## www.towerhobbies.com                             US

EXCITING WORLD OF RADIO-CONTROLLED MODELLING
An excellent, clearly laid out site offering a vast range of radio-controlled models along with thousands of accessories and parts. The delivery charge depends on the size of the order.

*See also:*
**www.fusionhobbies.com** – for cars and tanks.
**www.otherlandtoys.co.uk** – radio-controlled gifts and gadgets too.
**www.rchobby.co.uk** – British-based shop with plenty of choice to buy by mail order.

## www.brmodelling.com                              UK

BRITISH RAILWAY MODELLING
A high quality magazine site devoted to model railways, it includes a virtual model set for you to play with and articles on specific types of trains and railways. There's also a forum where you to can chat to fellow enthusiasts.

*See also:*
**www.corgi.co.uk** – home of the leading model car maker.
**www.modelboats.co.uk** – a model boats magazine.
**www.toysoldier.freeuk.com** – informative site devoted to toy soldiers.
**www.ukmodelshops.co.uk** – a mainly railways-oriented directory.
**www.wingsandwheels.co.uk** – model aircraft specialists.

### www.ontracks.co.uk

MODEL AND HOBBY SUPERSTORE
They sell over 35,000 models and hobby items, but it's tricky to find what you want as the site is a bit messy with lots of annoying graphics. Having said that there are some good special offers and delivery prices are reasonable.

### www.woodworking.co.uk

WORKING WITH WOOD
A good amateur site offering loads of information about all aspects of woodworking. There's a gallery of work from featured craftsmen plus advice for beginners. See also www.toolpost.co.uk where you can get all your tools.

# Home and Do-it-yourself

*The web doesn't seem a natural home for do-it-yourself, but there are some really useful sites, some great offers on tools and equipment and plenty of sensible advice.*

## Superstores

### www.diy.com

THE DIY SUPERSTORE
B&Q has a bright and busy site with lots of advice, inspiration, tips and information on projects for the home and garden. It also has an excellent searchable product database. There are also plenty of offers and the store has a good selection of products covering all the major DIY areas. Delivery costs vary according to how much you buy and how fast you want it. Returns can be made to the stores. You need to be able to accept cookies before the site can operate effectively or you want to place an order.

### www.wickes.co.uk

DIY SPECIALISTS
Good ideas, inspiration and help are the key themes for this site, it's easy to use and genuinely helpful with well laid out project details. You can visit their showrooms for product information and download leaflets on a wide variety of domestic jobs. There's a handy calculator section where you can work out how many tiles or rolls of wallpaper you may need.

## www.focusdoitall.co.uk UK

FOCUS DO-IT-ALL

A functional site, which attempts to put over lots of ideas and inspiration, it also carries a wide range of products at good prices. Delivery is £4.99 minimum and you can return unwanted goods to your nearest store.

*Other DIY stores worth checking out are:*

**www.buildbase.co.uk** – good site but really one for the professional.

**www.decoratingdirect.co.uk** – functional and easy-to-use site that concentrates on home décor products at excellent prices.

**www.homebase.co.uk** – the site was being redeveloped at time of writing, but there was plenty of information on their product ranges.

**www.jewson.co.uk** – Jewson's site is more corporate than anything but it does have a small section on each part of the house and how they can help.

# Buying tools and equipment

## www.screwfix.com UK

PRODUCTS FOR ALL DIY NEEDS

Rightly considered to be one of the best online stores, Screwfix offer excellent value for money with free delivery on orders over £45 and wholesale prices on a massive range of DIY products.

## www.cooksons.com UK

TOOLS A-PLENTY

An award-winning site from this Stockport firm, it has a huge number of tools and related products available, with free delivery on orders over £38.29 ex VAT. There are plenty of special offers and a loyalty scheme for regulars.

## www.draper.co.uk UK

QUALITY SINCE 1919

A real turnaround from a site that used to have a life of its own to one that is attractive and easy to use, the only downside being that you have to have the latest downloads for it to work effectively. If you're a regular visitor and know the stock number of the item you want there's a good fast-track service too. It probably is the most improved site in the book.

## www.diytools.co.uk                                                   UK

MORE TOOLS
Another well-designed and extensive tool store with a huge
range of products, there's also free delivery for orders over £50.
Also check out **www.blackanddecker.co.uk** who have lots of
advice on how to use power tools correctly, and also the slow
but thorough **www.worldofpower.co.uk** who also supply garden
equipment, plus quad bikes and other motorised toys.

# Tool hire

## www.hss.co.uk                                                       UK

WHERE YOU CAN HIRE ALMOST ANYTHING
A useful site where you can organise the rental of a huge range
of tools and equipment, it's great for those one-off jobs.

# Trade information

## www.fmb.org.uk/consumers                                            UK

THE FEDERATION OF MASTER BUILDERS
Get help to avoid cowboys and advice on getting the best out of
a builder. There's information and articles on most aspects of
home maintenance, plus hints on finding reputable help.

*See also:*
**www.buildersguild.co.uk** – who also offer much in the way
of information.
**www.qualitymark.org.uk** – covering the government's scheme
to ensure the reliability of tradesmen and search for those
willing to work in your area.

# Advice and DIY encyclopaedias

## www.hometips.com                                                    US

EXPERT ADVICE FOR YOUR HOME
American the advice may be, but there is plenty here for every
homeowner. The site is well laid out and the advice good.
Alternatives are **www.naturalhandyman.com** which is fun or
the extensive **www.doityourself.com** which is very detailed.

## www.diyfixit.co.uk

ONLINE DIY ENCYCLOPAEDIA
Get help with most DIY jobs using the search engine or browse by room or job type. The information is good especially now they've added more illustrations.

*See also:*
**www.diyfaq.org.uk** – practical information from this UK-based forum site.
**www.diynot.com** – a good all-rounder, encyclopaedia, forums and DIY help.
**www.diystickit.co.uk** – from a glue manufacturer using glues to solve problems.
**www.finddiy.co.uk** – a list of DIY sites.
**www.fourwalls.co.uk** – DIY sites listed and reviewed.
**www.freddyfixit.co.za** – DIY help from South Africa.
**www.homedoctor.net** – an American site with lots of homey tips.
**www.ukdiyguide.co.uk** – a useful DIY portal site, could do with a search engine.

## www.howtocleananything.com

STAIN REMOVAL PAR EXCELLENCE
A group of cleaners have got together to produce a site that contains over 1,000 cleaning tips for outside or inside the house, the car – except curry!

# Building and improving on your home

*For further information and advice on finding and using an architect, refer to the section on Architecture, page 22.*

## www.ebuild.co.uk

BUILD YOUR OWN HOUSE
All the information and contacts you need if you're thinking of buying that plot of land and getting stuck in. There's also a continually updated list of what plots of land are available and where.

*The following sites will also prove useful if you're out to build your own:*
**www.bricksandbrass.co.uk** – the place to go if you have a period home to renovate.
**www.builditthisway.co.uk** – a good overview on what it takes to build your own house from a retired builder.

**www.homebuilding.co.uk** – a spin off from a magazine, lots of resources and information.

**www.planning.odpm.gov.uk** – the Office of the Deputy Prime Minister has information on the latest government initiatives on planning.

**www.plotfinder.net** – find a spot to build your dream home but you have to subscribe.

**www.selfbuildcentre.com** – pretty annoying design but lots of links and advice make it worth a visit.

**www.selfbuildit.co.uk** – help for first timers.

# Salvage

**www.salvo.co.uk**        UK

SALVAGE AND RECLAMATION
Salvo provides information on where to get salvaged and reclaimed architectural and garden antiques. The site is comprehensive and easy-to-use with interesting information such as what buildings are due to be demolished and when, so you can be ready and waiting.

# Conservatories

**www.conservatoriesonline.co.uk**        UK

ALL YOU NEED TO KNOW ABOUT CONSERVATORIES
A good portal site which offers links and advice on conservatories, sunrooms, garden rooms and solariums. There's a buyer's guide plus information on materials, styles, even on pools and orangeries.

*See also:*
**www.conservatories-direct.co.uk** – a good, comprehensive site from this specialist.
**www.diy-conservatories-uk.co.uk** – all you need if you want to erect your own.

# Plumbing, bathroom and kitchen

**www.plumbworld.co.uk**        UK

AN ONLINE PLUMBING SHOP
Good selection of plumbing tools at competitive prices. Not exactly the most informative site as you have to assume much, for example, there's very little information about shipping which, incidentally, is free to most of the UK when you spend £50 or more.

*See also:*
**www.plumbers.co.uk** – if you need to find a plumber try the
directory of plumbers.
**www.plumbnet.com** – for information on how to do work
yourself.
**www.registeredplumber.com** – home of the Institute of
Plumbing with a member directory and their code of practise.

## www.bathroomexpress.co.uk                                    UK
### BETTER BATHROOMS
A wide range of bathrooms and accessories are available at
decent prices, with some interesting luxury items such as
après-shower driers and some unique toilet seats. Delivery is
based on how much you spend. See also **www.bathroom-
association.org** and **www.thebathroomaccessoryshop.com**

## www.alarisavenue.co.uk                                       UK
### KITCHENS AND CANE
A beautifully designed store that offers much in the way of
inspiration and quality products for the kitchen.

## www.toppstiles.co.uk                                         UK
### TILES
You can't get tiles delivered but there's a shop finder service
and details of available ranges including floor tiles. See also
**www.tiles.org.uk** which is home to the Tile Association and full
of good advice. At **www.digitile.co.uk** you can find out about
how to get custom made tiles.

# Doors

## www.handlesdirect.co.uk                                      UK
### HANDLES GALORE
A functional site where you can buy, well, handles. It's also got
a selection of locks, switches and sockets that match certain
handles. The emphasis is on contemporary style, and there's a
good advice section which shows you how to fit them. See also
**www.knobsandknockers.co.uk** who offer a wide range
including security products.

**www.doorsdirect.co.uk**                                      UK

DOORS AND HANDLES
Features replacement doors for kitchens and bathrooms, you
can order made-to-measure or standard and there's a selection
of fittings as well.

## Paint and wallpaper

**www.decoratingdirect.co.uk**                                 UK

DECORATING MATERIALS
A really well designed store offering a very wide range of
decorating products, it's simple to use and fast. Orders are free
when you spend more than £50 and it will save a trip to one
of those huge DIY stores, or is it just me that hates them?
Check out the refund policy before you buy though.

H

**www.dulux.co.uk**                                            UK

DULUX
A good-looking, interesting but slow site from Dulux, with a
'mouse painter' that you can use to redecorate a number of
pre-selected rooms, there's also product information, and top
tips on painting techniques. You can't buy from the site
although there is a list of stockists. Crown has a similar but less
interactive site that can be found at **www.crownpaint.co.uk**

**www.farrow-ball.co.uk**                                      UK

TRADITIONAL PAINT AND PAPER
Excellently designed web site featuring details on how their
paint and paper is manufactured – something they obviously
take pride in. You can also order from the site or request
samples. For that traditional Mediterranean look try
**www.casa.co.uk** who have a good selection and a nice site.

**www.paintquality.co.uk**                                     US

PAINT QUALITY INSTITUTE
A very attractive site from a company that specialises in testing
paints. There's information on choosing the right type of paint
with decorating tips, a calculator and glossary.

## www.sanderson-online.co.uk                                    UK

WILLIAM MORRIS AMONGST OTHER WALLPAPER
oFind out about the company, its heritage and what designs
they have - new and old. You can also order a brochure and
visit the Morris & Co pages where they have all the favourite
designs. For more information on William Morris try visiting
**www.morrissociety.org**

## www.thedesignstudio.co.uk                                      UK

GET THE RIGHT DESIGN
This is an excellent database of wallpaper and fabric samples,
which is easy-to-use and good fun. Once you've selected your
swatch you can then find the nearest supplier. You need some
patience, as it can be quite slow and you have to register to use
the service.

## www.communityrepaint.org.uk                                    UK

REUSING OLD PAINT
Not a great web site but a very useful service. The site
highlights a number of schemes across the country that take
reusable paint and redistribute it to those who can't afford to
buy their own.

## www.photo-furnishings.com                                      UK

YOUR PHOTOS ON YOUR FURNISHINGS
Outstanding use of web design to sell a novel service, here they
will put your photos onto soft furnishings or wallpapers.
You have to apply for prices.

# Lighting

## www.lightsaver.co.uk                                           UK

SAVE ON LIGHTING
With lots of savings and a wide range to choose from this site
is worth a visit, it's not the epitome of great web design but
it's effective nonetheless. You should also check out
**www.thelightingsuperstore.co.uk** and **www.lighting-
direct.co.uk** who both offer good alternatives.

# Inspiration, design and interiors

### www.design-gap.co.uk                                      UK

DESIGNER DIRECTORY
A directory of UK-based designers and manufacturers with
some 300 pages to browse through. They are arranged
alphabetically by first name or company name as well as
by category. The illustrations are excellent. See also
**www.designdirectory.co.uk** which is a listing of design
consultants.

### www.design-online.co.uk                                   UK

NEED A DESIGNER?
Design Online's mission is to put buyers and suppliers in touch
with each other and to use the Internet to promote the use of
well-designed products and services. You just search for the
service you want and a list of suitable suppliers with contact
details quickly appears. Could do with some illustrations and
examples of the work that they are trying to promote. See also
**www.bida.org** home of the newly formed British Interior Design
Association and **www.britishdesign.co.uk** which is a showcase
site for British talent.

### www.geomancy.net                                          UK

FENG SHUI
What a mess of a site! Considering that it's supposed to
promote the principles of light and harmony, it isn't very well
designed. However, there's an excellent set of links and you
can learn all you need to know about Feng Shui. See also
**www.rising-dragon.co.uk** which is slow but better designed.

## Stores for design

### www.habitat.net                                           UK

HABITAT STORES
A clever information-only site with lots of details about their
product range all wrapped up in a funky design which is a little
jerky with a normal modem, and needs the latest version of
Flash to work. You can't order online although you can check
store availability.

### www.ikea.com  UK

IKEA STYLE

You can't buy from the site but you can check whether a store has the item you want to buy in stock before you go, it would be great if more stores did this. Otherwise the site is more the usual store fare with plenty of ideas, articles and product lists.

### www.maelstrom.co.uk UK

CONTEMPORARY SELECTION

A wide selection of contemporary gifts, accessories, gadgets and furniture on a good-looking site. Delivery is 10% of the value of order with a flat charge of £10 if you spend more than £100. For more designer furniture see **www.interiorinternet.co.uk**

### www.next.co.uk UK

NEXT HOME WARE

A good selection of Next homeware as well as the usual products on a fairly impractical site.

### www.bhglive.com UK

BETTER HOMES AND GARDENS

There's more to this than DIY, but superb graphics and videos give this site the edge. It's American, so some information isn't applicable to the UK. The 'How-to Encyclopaedia' is excellent. Beware of the audio advert for the magazine!

### www.bluedeco.com UK

DESIGN ONLINE

This site offers a selection of designer products for the home, from furniture to ceramics, with free delivery to the UK. Unfortunately, returns have to go to Luxembourg.

### www.pier.co.uk UK

THE PIER

A very good offering from the Pier, eclectic and always interesting there's a wide range to choose from. Delivery charges vary according to the type of product you buy.

### www.pussyhomeboutique.co.uk UK

DESIGNER BOUTIQUE

An eccentric and slightly kitsch range of products, furniture, home accessories and wall panels, delivery charges vary.

H

**www.simplyfurnishings.com**                                       UK

SOFT FURNISHING
All you need to know about making and buying soft furnishing
with plenty of advice for all levels and a good store directory.
See also **www.crowsonfabrics.com** and **www.monkwell.com**
who both offer quality selections.

## TV and celebrity designers

**www.llb.co.uk**                                                   UK

LAURENCE LLEWELYN-BOWEN
Join the fan club, view Laurence's designs from greeting cards
to cutlery to wallpaper, then find out how to buy them.
There's lots here, even competitions. See also
**www.bbc.co.uk/homes/changingrooms** which has top tips,
articles, biographies and links to related shows.

**www.mccloud.co.uk/kevin/kevin.htm**                               UK

KEVIN MCCLOUD
A straightforward site from the presenter of Grand Designs
showing his work and how you can commission his team to
create something for you; principally it's about his specialist
area, contemporary lighting.

**www.ukstyle.tv/homesandproperty**                                 UK

UK STYLE TV
A bright and breezy site packed with ideas from the TV shows
and features on the various projects and aspects of the home.
There's an 'ask the expert' section and a guide full of practical
ideas and tips too.

## Furniture

**www.mfi.co.uk**                                                   UK

MFI HOMEWORKS
MFI offer a nicely designed site with all the best aspects of
online shopping and a wide range of surprisingly good furniture
for home and office available for order online or via a hotline.
Delivery is included in the price.

## www.furniture123.co.uk                                      UK

SMART PLACE TO BUY FURNITURE

This company has a well laid out web site offering a good range of furniture, many offers, tips and free delivery.

## www.heals.co.uk                                             UK

STYLISH CONTEMPORARY DESIGN

Heals has a beautifully designed web site which gives information about the store and inspiration for the home. There's an online store which stocks primarily gifts and home accessories, but there's a special services section where you can get information on furniture and interior design.

## www.conran.com                                              UK

TERENCE CONRAN STYLE

As well as information on all his restaurants, this site has an online shopping facility that allows you to buy Conran-designed accessories as well as stuff for the home including a good range of furniture and kitchen products.

## www.ancestralcollections.co.uk                              UK

REPRODUCTIONS FROM THE BEST HOMES

If you've ever fancied a Regency stool or any decent piece of antique furniture but couldn't run to the expense, then this company will supply you with a reproduction. They have a wide range of products not just furniture and are great for unusual gifts too.

*See also:*

**www.furniturebusters.com** – a wide range and masses of offers too.

**www.sofaweb.co.uk** – good value sofa and sofa bed shop.

## www.amazingemporium.com                                     UK

REPRODUCTIONS FROM THE BEST HOMES

A web site that has developed well with a wide range of high quality beds and furniture on an attractive site with good pictures and descriptions of the products. They've expanded into gifts too and offer good value for money.

*Other furniture retailers that may be worth a virtual visit are:*
**www.bedbathandhome.co.uk** – excellent for soft furnishings.
**www.bfm.org.uk** – a useful directory of British furniture makers.
**www.cjfurniture.com** – contemporary furniture.
**www.courts.co.uk** – lots of good prices here as well as payment options and range selection.
**www.davidlinley.com** – posh contemporary classics.
**www.mufti.co.uk** – more posh beautifully designed furniture.
**www.new-heights.co.uk** – simple, stylish solid wood.
**www.pinesolutions.co.uk** – a very well-designed furniture store, they also sell sofas and oak furniture.
**www.sofaworkshopdirect.co.uk** – well designed with quality photos of the sofas and what looks like a good online service.

**www.furniturewizard.com**                                      US

LOOKING AFTER YOUR FURNITURE
Tips and information on how to keep your furniture in pristine condition and what to do if you have an accident, all from someone with 30 years experience in the trade.

**http://maltwood.finearts.uvic.ca/hoft/**                       US

THE HISTORY OF FURNITURE TIMELINE
An odd site but one that catalogues the development of furniture from the 16th century to the 1980s, for more information go to **www.cwru.edu/UL/preserve/stack/Furniture.html** where you can download a complete book on the subject. See also **www.tribu-design.com/en** which is devoted to the last 100 years or so, while the design of the site is great, it seems to be a little temperamental.

# Humour

*The Internet has become home to an amazing array of funny sites,
here's just a few of the best. You should be aware that most aren't
suitable for children.*

## Jokes, links and directories

### www.comedy-zone.net                                          UK

COMPLETE COMEDY GUIDE
Excellent and wide-ranging comedy site with lots of links and
competitions, alongside quotes, jokes and chat.

*For other comedy portals and loads of jokes go to:*
**http://uk.dir.yahoo.com/entertainment/humour** – Yahoo's
excellent listing devoted to humour and bizarre sites.
**www.bored.com** – a great directory of humour sites.
**www.funnybone.com** – huge database with lots of rude jokes.
**www.funnymail.com** – lots of jokes well categorised with good
features such as tests, top ten jokes of all time, newest jokes
and so on.
**www.humorlinks.com** – massive portal for all things funny.
**www.humournet.co.uk** – categorised jokes, links and funny
pictures.
**www.jokecenter.com** – hundreds of jokes, vote for your
favourites.
**www.jokepost.com** – hundreds, all well categorised.
**www.jokes2000.com** – e-mail you the latest jokes.
**www.jokes.com** – typical jokes directory but these are rated,
tame, racy etc...
**www.kidsjokes.co.uk** – 12,000+ jokes, great for the family.
**www.weirdwebbed.com** – a directory of the weirdest web sites.

### www.uebersetzung.at/twister                            AUSTRIA

TONGUE TWISTERS
An international collection of tongue twisters, over 2,000 in 87
languages when we last visited, nearly 400 in English –
'Can you can a can as a canner can can a can?' as they say.

## Multi-media

### www.funny-downloads.com                               US

THE BEST IN MULTI-MEDIA HUMOUR
What used to be Olley's Place has transformed into a
subscription only site costing 10 Euros per annum. For that you
get access to a superb selection of funny video clips and
comedy downloads, there is some free content though and you
should be aware the most of it is adult oriented. There's also
**www.cyberparodies.com** which is fun and
**www.ebaumsworld.com** who offer a huge amount of adult
humour and currently it's free. Another directory of fun clips is
the wonderfully named **www.spongi.com**

## British humour

### www.britcoms.com                                      UK

BRITISH COMEDY LINKS
If you want to find a link to a British comedy show or
comedian, then start here. The sites are selected for quality
and there's also a broader selection of links for you to browse.
You can also sign up for their newsletter. For traditional humour
check out **www.britishcomedy.org.uk**

### www.comedybutchers.com                                UK

SURREAL BRITISH COMEDY
A really good attempt at creating a web site that shows off
surreal adult comedy in the traditional British style, you click on
various rooms within a floating town to get clips and sketches.

## Stand-up comedy

### www.chortle.co.uk                                      UK

GUIDE TO LIVE COMEDY IN THE UK
Chortle provides a complete service, listing who's on, where
and when – also whether they're any good or not. There's also
a comic's A–Z so that you can find your favourites and get
reviews on how they're performing, or not, as the case may be.
See also **www.jongleurs.co.uk** whose entertaining site has
audio clips and details of what's on and when at their clubs.

# Comedy magazine and satirical sites

### www.theonion.com                                              US

AMERICA'S FINEST NEWS SOURCE

A great send-up of American tabloid newspapers, this is one of
the most visited sites on the Internet and easily one of the
funniest. See also the equally good *Framley Examiner* at
**www.framleyexaminer.com**

### www.private-eye.co.uk                                         UK

*PRIVATE EYE*

A pretty average effort really considering the wealth of material
that must be available, there are a few of the best cartoons and
features, but it's only updated every couple of weeks or so.

### www.punch.co.uk                                               UK

*PUNCH MAGAZINE*

A new look and more commercial approach from *Punch* with
plenty of cartoons and some of the best of *Punch* available to
browse and buy.

### www.viz.co.uk                                                 UK

NOT FOR CHILDREN

A very good reflection of what you get in the real thing with lots
of games and downloads, you can even contribute to Roger's
Profanisaurus.

### www.thespark.com                                              UK

TAKE THE SPARK TESTS

The Spark consists of a humorous news magazine and a few
other jokey bits and bobs plus lots of annoying adverts, but its
main feature, and the reason why millions visit, is for the tests.
From the popular personality test, through bitch and bastard
tests to the wealth test, all are good for a laugh and of course
very accurate. Dare you take the 'Death test' or the new 'Cut-
throat' test though?

### www.b3ta.com                                                  UK

WE LOVE THE WE

A messy site that catalogues all that is unusual and fun, they'll
e-mail you with their latest finds and it's a great place for the
unashamedly silly. Warning – contains adult material.

### www.bizarremag.com                                    US
BIZARRE MAGAZINE
The magazine is devoted to 'life in the extreme' and the site reflects this with a selection of pictures and stories. It's all geared to getting you to subscribe. Be aware that the content is adult oriented.

### www.whitehouse.org                                    US
THE WHITE HOUSE
A great micky-take on the US presidency, very clever and vicious too.

### www.nicecupofteaandasitdown.com                       UK
TAKE A BREAK
Put your feet up and while away some time here, review your favourite biscuit or not… take your time… make tea… lovely

### www.lazystuff.co.uk                                   UK
HOW TO WASTE TIME
Lots of pointless and time wasting things to do, but it's all so interesting and there's the top 50 lazy gifts to choose from.

## TV comedy

### www.comedycentral.com                                 US
THE HOME OF SOUTH PARK AND MORE
Great for South Park and selected American TV shows, but also with clips and background information and stand up comedy too.

### www.thesimpsons.com                                   US
HOME OF THE SIMPSONS
The official site with biographies, background, quizzes and more, plus the ever-present merchandise store. If you are a real fan then go to the Simpsons archive at **www.snpp.com**

## Urban legends, the unlikely and the unloved

### www.snopes2.com                                       US
URBAN LEGENDS
An outstanding collection of all those stories and myths that have that edge of unlikely truth about them. Well categorised and with a good search facility it's easy to find your favourites. See also **www.urbanlegends.com** another catalogue of unlikely stories from urban folklore as is the boringly laid out **www.snopes.com**

### www.darwinawards.com                                      US

FATAL MISADVENTURES

The Darwin Awards have been going several years now and
their site is packed with stories, urban legends and personal
accounts of those who have 'improved our gene pool by
removing themselves from it in really stupid ways'.

### www.halfbakery.com                                        US

INVENTIONS OR NOT

A fun catalogue of useless inventions and ideas, some real,
most not; very silly really, it's also a shame that there are not
more illustrations.

### www.craptowns.com                                         UK

OUR CRAP TOWNS

The site that spawned a best-selling book. Here's an eclectic
collection of towns in the UK and US that have been awarded
the status of being crap, most for no apparent reason. Irreverent
and pretty funny, there are some very angry people out there.

## Cartoons

### www.joecartoon.com                                        US

FREAKY CARTOONS

Follow the gruesome, messy adventures of Joe, download the
cartoons and send them to your friends and buy the T-shirt –
he's a legend after all. Superb animation and very funny, but
you need patience for the downloads.

### www.emilystrange.com                                      US

ENTER THE WORLD OF EMILY STRANGE

Another animated site with outstanding illustrations that's worth
a visit just to look at the design, if nothing else. Emily is a
popular icon with teenagers and here you can participate in her
freaky adventures.

*See also:*
**www.cartoonbank.com** – outstanding *New Yorker* cartoons for
sale in various formats and guises.
**www.cartoonstock.com** – a database of over 40,000 cartoons.
**www.justfunnycartoons.com** – an odd site with lots of
animated adverts but there are some funny cartoons to
be found.

**www.marsdencartoons.com/directory.htm** – a comprehensive directory of cartoonists with links.
**www.unitedmedia.com/comics/peanuts** – home of Charlie Brown and Peanuts.

# Miscellaneous

### www.losers.org                                  US

THE WEB'S LOSERS
A site that catalogues and rates the saddest sites and sights on the web, note that some of the content is strictly adults only. Still, it's one of the most fascinating giggles available, all web site designers should see this.

### www.strangereports.com                   US

PRANKS ONLINE
Play pranks on your friends using the service available here, with trick web sites and fake news reports it's almost irresistible but beware their revenge…

### www.freakydreams.com                     US

DREAM INTERPRETED
You just type in the description of your dream and an 'accurate' interpretation pops up in seconds.

### www.user-error.co.uk                       UK

EXCUSE GENERATOR
Apart from the excellent excuse generator which is very handy, there's also a virtual makeover section, articles on the unusual universe we live in and, if you're in a disagreement with someone over some fact or other, they'll help you settle your bet.

### www.museumofhoaxes.com                 US

HOAXES
The world's greatest hoaxes and April Fools are catalogued here, makes entertaining browsing and is sometimes unbelievable.

### www.smalltime.com/dictator                 UK

GUESS THE DICTATOR
You think of dictator or TV sit-com character, answer the questions put to you and the site will guess who you are thinking of…it's spookily accurate.

## www.optillusions.com US

OPTICAL ILLUSIONS

A good selection of optical illusions to download, plus links to other similar and funny sites. The visit is completely spoiled by the large amount of adverts, both pop-ups and banners.

## www.emotioneric.com US

EMOTIONAL ERIC

A cult site in the US. Eric will act out any emotion in any situation, you just have to place your request.

## www.snapbubbles.com US

VIRTUAL BUBBLE WRAP

How comforting, just when you have the urge to pop and there's no bubble wrap to hand, just come here for the nearest substitute.

## www.pickthehottie.com US

PICK THE HOTTIE!

Probably the best of many sites where people post photos of themselves and their friends (or enemies) the idea being that you vote for the hottest-looking people and the ugliest too. While we're on the subject of the unattractive check out these sites listed below…

**www.mulletmadness.com** – in celebration of the haircut and culture.

**www.uglydress.com** – Bridesmaids dresses from Hell, dare you to look at this without putting your hand over your mouth…

**www.uglyfootballers.com** – yes we well remember them…

# Internet Service Provision

*There are so many Internet Service Providers (ISPs) that it would be impossible to review them all and it's moving so fast that any information soon becomes outdated. However, help is at hand and here are some sites that will help you chose the right one for you. See also the section on broadband on page 51.*

### www.net4nowt.com
UK

THE PLACE TO START LOOKING FOR THE BEST ISP
This is a directory of Internet Service Providers offering news and advice on the best ones. There is an up-to-date critique on each ISP with comments on costs and reliability. There is also a good summary table featuring all the ISPs, which proves useful for comparisons.

### www.ispreview.co.uk
UK

INTERNET NEWS
Find out what's really going on at this impressive site – they are especially good at exposing the worst performers. There's plenty in the way of news, offers and a top ten ISP list. Also check out **www.thelist.com** which is international.

# Jobs and Careers

*There are several hundred sites offering jobs or career advice but it's largely a matter of luck if you come across a job you like. Still, it enables you to cover plenty of ground in a short space of time without trawling the newspapers. These sites offer the most options and best advice.*

## Career guidance

### www.careerguide.net
UK

ONLINE CAREER ADVICE RESOURCE
This is a comprehensive service with many sections on job hunting, vacancies, CVs, careers advice and professional institutions that can help.

### www.careers-portal.co.uk
UK

AWARD-WINNING CAREERS SERVICE
An excellent portal site that is part of the National Grid for
Learning, with lots of advice on universities, jobs and how to
apply. There's a very useful careers directory and it's all geared
to helping you choose the right career.

### www.careers-gateway.co.uk
UK

THE CAREER GATEWAY
Great advice and lots of information. For example, how to
launch a proper career, evaluate your options and read articles
to help you decide what you can do with your life. There's a
virtual career show, quizzes designed to help and advice for
HR professionals too.

### www.reachforthesky.co.uk
UK

CAREER ADVICE FROM SKY TV
Sky has put together a great web site that doesn't just look
good. However, it's developed into more of a teen magazine,
but there is a good deal of advice here plus some fun too.

### www.careersolutions.co.uk
UK

HELP TO GO FORWARD
A good place to start if you're not sure what you want to do
next with your career, don't know where to start or you've been
made redundant. Using the site enables you to narrow your
options and clarify things. The list of links is logically laid out
and very helpful.

## Job finders

### www.transdata-inter.co.uk/jobs-agencies
UK

DIRECTORY OF JOB SITES
Don't let the long URL put you off, this is an excellent place to
start on your search. The Directory lists all the major online
employment agencies and ranks them by the average number
of vacancies, the regions they cover, whether they help create
and store CVs and what industries they represent. Clicking on
the name takes you right to the site you need.

## www.jobs.co.uk                                          UK
### JOB SEARCH ENGINE
With this facility you can search all the major jobs sites in one
go, it's easy to use and quite accurate providing you have a
defined job title. They also offer all the usual features such
as CV help and advice. See also **www.jobsearch.co.uk**

## www.gisajob.co.uk                                       UK
### SEARCH FOR YOUR NEXT JOB HERE
The largest of the UK online job sites with over 64,000
vacancies. You can search by description or sector or get advice
on your career. It's good for non-senior executive types.

## www.workthing.com                                       UK
### IT'S A WORK THING
One of the best-looking job sites with a reputation to match,
this site must be one of the first to visit when job hunting
across a wide range of industries. Registered users can set
up an e-mail alert when a job matching their search criteria
appears. They also work with businesses to develop their
people skills and recruitment; you can also get advice on
training and personal development too.

## www.monster.co.uk                                       UK
### GLOBAL JOBS
With over one million jobs available world-wide there are plenty
to chose from. The site is well-designed and easy to use with
the usual help features. At time of writing there were over
26,000 UK jobs listed in over 20 categories.

## www.stepstone.co.uk                                     UK
### EUROPEAN INTERNET RECRUITMENT
Regarded as one of the best, Stepstone has a huge number of
European and international vacancies. It's quick, easy to use
and offers lots of timesaving cross-referencing features. You can
also register your CV. For other overseas jobs see
**www.overseasjobs.com**

*Other job finder and career sites worth checking out:*
**www.deskdemon.com** – jobs and resources for secretarial and
support staff.
**www.doctorjob.com** – only graduates need apply.

**www.jobpilot.co.uk** – good for European jobs, over 45,000 listed.
**www.jobserve.co.uk** – a well-categorised job search engine covering the major industries, good design.
**www.reed.co.uk** – some 153,000 vacancies from a wide range of categories.
**www.thegumtree.com** – jobs in London.
**www.totaljobs.co.uk** – 55,000 jobs listed in a wide range of sectors.

*These government run sites might also be useful:*
**www.aimhigher.gov.uk** – how to get the qualifications to get the job you really want.
**www.connexions.gov.uk** – an advice service aimed at 13–19 year olds.
**www.dfes.gov.uk** – the Dept of Education has lots of helpful advice.
**www.jobcentreplus.gov.uk** – information about job centres and how to go about finding a job.
**www.worktrain.gov.uk** – jobs, training, voluntary work, it's all here.

# Other careers and related sites

## www.i-resign.com/uk                                                    UK
THE INS AND OUTS OF RESIGNATION
Pay a visit before you send the letter, it offers a great deal of advice both legal and sensible. The best section contains the funniest selection of resignation letters anywhere. There are also jobs on offer, links to job finder sites and a career guide service.

## www.freelancecentre.com                                                UK
SELF-EMPLOYED
Great for anyone thinking of going it alone, or are looking for help if you're already working for yourself. There's plenty of advice here – a good deal of it is absolutely free.

## www.homeworking.com                                                     UK
WORKING FROM HOME
A site full of advice and information for anyone considering or actually working from home. There are links and directories as well as forum pages where you can share experiences with other home workers.

**www.eoc.org.uk**                                                            UK

> EQUAL OPPORTUNITIES COMMISSION
> A very informative site and it's where to go if you think you are
> being discriminated against.

## Online practise tests

**www.queendom.com**                                                          UK

> SERIOUSLY ENTERTAINING
> Apart from the fun tests there's a serious side to this site that
> allows you to take the sort of tests you're likely to face when
> applying for a job. See also **www.emode.com**

# *Legal Advice and the Law*

*We all need help with certain key events in life: marriages, moving
house, making a will or getting a divorce. Maybe you need advice
on lesser issues like boundary disputes or problems with services
or property? Here are several good sites that could really make
a difference.*

**www.advicenow.org.uk**                                                      UK

> INDEPENDENT LAW AND RIGHTS ADVICE
> An great site designed to keep up with and explain the law in
> layman's terms. It's well designed and information is easy to find;
> it also offers links to the relevant site if required. Excellent.

**www.compactlaw.co.uk**                                                      UK

> LEGAL INFORMATION FOR ENGLAND AND WALES
> An extremely informative and useful site that covers many
> aspects of the law in a clear and concise style, there are usable
> documents – you can download some free, others to buy,
> case histories, news, tips and plenty of fact-sheets.
> Formally **www.lawrights.co.uk**

**www.uklegal.com**                                                           UK

> LEGAL RESOURCES AT YOUR FINGERTIPS
> This site offers a superb selection of links to everything from
> private investigators to barristers to legal equipment suppliers.

## www.family-solicitors.co.uk

FAMILY LAW REFERENCE
Excellent resource for everyday legal issues covering everything
from wills to neighbourhood disputes. Great for links too with
an excellent search facility for finding a family law solicitor near
you. See also **www.solicitors-online.com** If you need to find a
lawyer then go to the well put together
**www.lawyerlocator.co.uk**

## www.desktoplawyer.net

THE UK'S FIRST ONLINE LAWYER
This site is quite straightforward if you know what you need
and have read through the instructions carefully. First you
register, then download the software (Rapidocs) enabling you to
compile the document you need. The legal documents you
create will cost from £2.99 upwards depending on complexity.
The range of documents available is huge and there are more
being added. See also **www.everyform.net** who have some
900 free forms to download.

## www.legalservices.gov.uk

GOVERNMENT ADVICE
The replacement for legal aid, this is the official line on legal
matters with guidance on how to access legal assistance,
where to get information and news on latest changes to the
Community Legal Service and Criminal Defence Service.
It could be a lot more user-friendly. For Scottish legal aid go
to **www.slab.org.uk**

*See also:*
**www.divorce-online.co.uk** – fast track divorces and
good advice.
**www.emplaw.co.uk** – the low down on British
employment law.
**www.lawassure.co.uk** – subscribe to excellent personal legal
advice and related services.
**www.lawpack.co.uk** – legal book specialist.
**www.lawscot.org.uk** – the Law Society of Scotland.
**www.legaladvicefree.co.uk** – excellent all rounder that provides
the answer to many legal questions.

**www.legalpulse.com** – well-designed site along the lines of Desktop Lawyer although not as comprehensive.
**www.legalshop.co.uk** – affordable solutions to your legal problems; a good site, with a business section too.
**www.oldbaileyonline.org** – interesting site offering up the proceedings of the Old Bailey from 1674 to 1834.

## www.dumblaws.com      US

THE DAFTEST, STUPIDEST LAWS
Did you realise that in England placing a postage stamp that bears the Queen's head upside down is considered treasonable, or that in Kentucky it's illegal to fish with a bow and arrow? These are just a couple of the many dumb laws that you can find on this very entertaining site. It's now been expanded to include dumbest criminals, dumbest warnings and place names.

# *Linux*

*Linux is a free operating system that competes with Windows; it has a reputation for stability and is gaining popularity. Here are some informative sites to help you.*

## www.linuxlinks.com      US

LINUX DIRECTORY
A Yahoo style directory with over 20,000 links, forums and articles. It's well categorised and a good place to start.

*See also:*
**http://beginnerslinux.org** – a personal guide for beginners.
**www.linux.com** – authoritative site with good tutorials.
**www.linux.org** – a Linux community site, good once you've learnt a bit.
**www.redhat.com** – a company with its own version of Linux, lots of support.

# Magazines

*Where to buy and subscribe to your favourite magazines.*

### www.newsstand.co.uk                                                    UK
A GIFT THAT LASTS ALL YEAR
A wide range of titles that are available by subscription, on a
well categorised site which has been upgraded. It has a strong
British bias although you can get overseas titles too.

### www.magazinecity.co.uk                                                 US
THE WEB'S LARGEST SUBSCRIPTION SOURCE
A site dedicated to magazine subscriptions, it's fairly slow but
easy to use; however, it is annoying that most prices are quoted
in dollars. See also the very similar and equally slow
**www.subscription.co.uk** who at least quote prices in pounds
and who have turned into a subscription-only retailer.

*See also:*
**www.actualidad.com** – newspapers of the world and links to
their sites.
**www.whsmith.co.uk** – some good offers on subscriptions
which are available to UK addresses only.

# Men

*Maybe not what you think, these are just a few sites especially for
blokes, lads and real men.*

## Magazines

### www.fhm.co.uk                                                          UK
*FHM* MAGAZINE
A good reflection of the real thing, with sections on everything
from serious news to the lighter side, with the usual blokey
features, it suffers from lots of advertising though.

### www.gqmagazine.co.uk                                                   UK
*GENTLEMEN'S QUARTERLY*
A stylish site that gives a flavour of the real magazine, it contains a
few stories, competitions, fashion tips and the odd feature.

## www.sharpman.com                                          UK

SHARP!
While a little odd, it's good fun and there's some useful advice.
Split into six key sections: dating, with tips on conversation and
repartee; toys, from fitness gadgets to snowboards; work,
getting the best out of the Internet; travel, staying sharp
abroad; grooming, looking the part; toys – the best advice
on windsurfing.

## www.fathersdirect.com                                     UK

A MAGAZINE FOR FATHERS
Written by fathers for fathers, this entertaining e-zine has all the
advice and support you need if you're a new dad or you're
trying to fit in both work and kids. There are competitions, a
rant section where you can let off steam and a games room.
Rather twee graphics let it down somewhat.

*See also:*
**www.askmen.com** – a very good American men's magazine
covering almost every topic you're likely to need.
**www.dullmen.com** – the dullest website from the National
Council for Dull Men, very funny too.
**www.modernman.com** – nicely designed men's magazine site
from the US with loads of interesting articles and features.

# Health

## www.menshealth.co.uk                                      UK

*MEN'S HEALTH* MAGAZINE
Lots of advice on keeping fit, healthy and fashionable too.
There's also an excellent section on the number one topic –
sex, plus others on wealth, health, sport and a shop that sells
subscriptions and recommends the latest gear.

## www.menshealthforum.org.uk                                UK

STOP MOANING!
An excellent all-rounder revealing the truth behind the state of
men's health and lots of discussion about specific and general
health issues facing men today – good for links too.

*Other men's health sites:*
**www.impotence.org.uk** – the Impotence Association.
**www.malehealth.co.uk** – comprehensive site where you can
check the state of your health and your health knowledge;
excellent links and advice make up the picture.
**www.orchid-cancer.org.uk** – promotes the awareness of
testicular and prostate cancer.
**www.vasectomy-clinic.co.uk** – no scalpel vasectomy – honest!

# Shopping

**www.firebox.com**                                                    UK

WHERE MEN BUY STUFF
An online shop aimed totally at boy's toys, with its own
bachelor pad containing all you need for the lifestyle. There are
masses of games, videos, toys and, of course, the latest
gadgets. Delivery costs vary. See also **www.big-boys-toys.net**
and **www.boysstuff.co.uk** both are worth a visit if you can't find
what you want at Firebox.

**www.condomsdirect.co.uk**                                            UK

CONDOMS UK
Many different types of condoms are available to buy, and you
get free delivery if you spend more than £10 – there's even a
price promise and the assurance of a fast and discreet service.
It's also worth checking out **www.condomania.com**

M

# *Motorcycles*

**www.bmf.co.uk**                                                      UK

BRITISH MOTORCYCLISTS FEDERATION
At this site you can join the BMF, get involved with their
activities or just use the site for information. You can also get
club information and e-mail them on any issues. For the
international governing body go to **www.fim.ch/en**

**www.motorcycle.co.uk**                                               UK

THE UK'S MOTORCYCLE DIRECTORY
Essentially a list of links by brand, dealer, importer, classics,
gear, books and auctions.

## www.moto-directory.com                                    US

THE WORLD MOTORCYCLE DIRECTORY
US-oriented, but links to hundreds of sites in 24 categories to
ensure that you'll know what's going on in motorcycling and
find the information you need.

## www.motorworld.com                                        US

ALL YOU NEED TO KNOW ABOUT MOTORCYCLES
Good coverage of both machines and events with multimedia
features. Although the site is American there's good British
coverage.

## www.fowlers.co.uk                                         UK

WHERE TO GET YOUR GEAR
A smart new look to this site which houses a good shop and
information site dedicated to motorcycles, clothing and
accessories, they seem intent on providing good customer
service too. Also worth a visit is **www.customlids.co.uk** who
offer a wide range of clothing.

*See also:*
**www.autotrader.co.uk/BIKES** – Bike Trader from *Auto Trader*
magazine has a huge number of bikes for sale and a good
place to put your bike up for sale too.
**www.hondahornet.co.uk** – a good-looking specialist site.
**www.mag-uk.org** – home of the Motorcycle Action Group
dedicated to campaigning on behalf of motorcyclists in the UK.
**www.motorcycleshow.co.uk** – details of the motor cycle show.
**www.scootermania.co.uk** – if you love scooters here's
where to go.
**www.umgweb.com** – owned by the auctioneer E-bay, here you
can find used motorcycles for sale.

# Movies

*All you need to know about films and film stars including where to go
to get the best deals on DVDs and videos. For information on the
stars also check out the Celebrities section on page 65.*

# News and information

**http://uk.imdb.com**

INTERNET MOVIE DATABASE
The best and most organised movie database on the Internet.
It's very easy to use and every film buff's dream with lots of
features and recommendations, plus games, quizzes, chat and
movie news. Another good database site is **www.allmovie.com**
which has a really good search engine.

**www.aintitcoolnews.com** US

AIN'T IT JUST COOL
A renowned review site that can make or break a movie in the
US, it's very entertaining and likeable, albeit a bit messy.
Harry Knowles' movie reviews are by far the best bit of the site,
although they can go on a bit. You can search the archive for a
particular review or contribute a bit of juicy gossip by e-mailing
Harry direct.

*See also:*
**www.metacritic.com** – a site that compiles reviews from
around the world, and gives the reviewed movies a score based
on them. Also covers games and music.
**www.mrqe.com** – the Movie Review Query Engine, just enter
the film title and reviews from magazines from all round the
world pop.
**www.rottentomatoes.com** – a comprehensive review site
and store.

# Film magazine sites

**www.empireonline.co.uk** UK

THE UK'S NUMBER ONE
The site has had an overhaul but remains an epic of a site with
masses of information and background on the latest movies and
the stars. There are two main review sections, one dedicated to
the cinema and one entitled At Home, for DVD and soundtrack
and book reviews. You can also see trailers of new films, see
pictures of the stars and production stills in the gallery and
subscribe to the magazine.

M

## www.insidefilm.com                                          US

US   FILM FESTIVAL DIRECTORY
Comprehensive news on the film festival with a calendar and
features on awards.

## www.eonline.com                                             US

E IS FOR ENTERTAINMENT
This is one of the most visited entertainment news sites and it
has a reputation for being first with the latest gossip and movie
news. It's vibrant, well designed and has a tongue in cheek
style which is endearing; sadly some of the reporters prattle
on though.

## www.variety.com                                             US

*VARIETY* MAGAZINE
The online version of the show business stalwart magazine has
an excellent and entertaining site with all the hot topics, news
and background information you'd expect plus biographies and
international film news. You have to subscribe to get access to
many of the sections.

*For more gossip see:*
**www.ew.com** – *Entertainments Weekly* has a really attractive
site with lots of features.
**www.hollywood.com** – over one million pages of gossip, news,
trailers and multi-media library.
**www.hollywoodreporter.com** – all the latest gossip and you can
subscribe to the magazine.

# Bollywood

## www.bollywoodworld.com                                   INDIA

If it's Bollywood, then it's covered on this site. There are the
movie reviews you'd expect plus lots of news, what's hot and
what's not, pictures of the stars and much more. There is a
music channel, radio and chat, but the Bollywoodshop only
ships within India.

*See also:*
**www.bollywhat.com** – here you can find a good beginners guide.
**www.planetbollywood.com** – odd design but loads of
information, gossip and awards.

# Awards and industry

## www.oscars.com US

### THE ACADEMY AWARDS
Stylish and as glitzy as you'd imagine it should be, this is the
official tie-in site for the Oscars. There's an archive and even
some games to play. For the Golden Globes go to
**www.thegoldenglobes.com**

## www.bafta.org UK

### BRITISH ACADEMY OF FILM & TELEVISION ARTS
A site giving all the information you need on the BAFTAs,
their history and how it all works.

## www.bfi.org.uk UK

### BRITISH FILM INSTITUTE
A top site from the BFI packed with information on how the
film industry works with archive material, links and how to
make movies. Refreshing that there's not much mention of
Hollywood! For the American Film Institute go to **www.afi.com**
where you'll find an excellent site.

# British and independent film making

## www.britmovie.co.uk UK

### DEDICATED TO BRITISH CINEMA
A site devoted to the history of British cinema and its wider
contribution to film-making in general. There's a great deal of
information, links and background and it's all well cross-
referenced, although it could do with a search facility.

*See also:*
**www.britishfilm.org.uk** – excellent set of articles on the history
of British cinema.
**www.britishhorrorfilms.co.uk** – a very entertaining romp
through the history of British Horror films, with lots of detail!
**www.cinerhama.com/britpage.html** – this site has a good
database of movies and actors, although it's not that up to date.

M

**www.indiewire.com** UK

> INDEPENDENT CINEMA
> An enthralling site covering independent cinema, the films, people and gossip. It stands out as a site that genuinely feels like it's contributing positively to an industry. See also **www.exposure.co.uk** who cover the low budget end of filmmaking.

**www.kamera.co.uk** UK

> ART HOUSE & INDEPENDENT REVIEWS
> A well written review site covering the world of Art House and Independent cinema. It also has a good book review section and interviews with important actors and directors. There's also a directory and forums where you can put your views.

## Specialist film sites

**www.bmonster.com** US

> COOLEST CULT MOVIES
> A highly entertaining site devoted to B movies, oddities and actors that aren't quite top drawer. It's well categorised and obviously a labour of love for its contributors.

**www.moderntimes.com** US

> HOLLYWOOD CLASSICS
> A great site devoted to classic Hollywood movies, when it really was the silver screen. It offers up lots of background, interviews and clips too.

> *See also:*
> **http://romanticmovies.about.com** – excellent section on romantic films from About.com.
> **www.americanwest.com/films/films.htm** – good for links to all things Western.
> **www.classichorrorfilms.com/** – not a great site but it's got all you need on the subject.
> **www.classicmoviemusicals.com** – a well-categorised but slightly dull site covering musicals.
> **www.earlycinema.com** – excellent site on the first decade of cinema with timeline, biographical details and information on the technology they used.
> **www.hardboiledflicks.com** – go here if you think your 'ard enough.

**www.horror.net** – a database of some 1,000 horror related sites.

**www.mysterynet.com/movies** – the top movies reviewed with links to other related genres.

**www.scifispace.com** – excellent fan site with lots of detail and links.

**www.sciflicks.com** – a comprehensive site covering the Sci Fi genre.

**www.silentsaregolden.com** – a great place to start if you want to find out about silent movies.

# Cinemas

*Listed below are the major cinema companies and their sites:*
**www.cineworld.co.uk** – straightforward and easy-to-use guide.
**www.odeon.co.uk** – book online at this attractive site.
**www.showcasecinemas.co.uk** – lots here to see and do.
**www.uci-cinemas.co.uk** – good-looking site with all the usual information and previews.
**www.warnervillage.co.uk** – excellent site with online booking. Going to change to **www.myvue.com** in coming months when the cinema changes its name to Vue.

# Movie humour

## www.moviesounds.com                                              US

LISTEN TO YOUR FAVOURITE MOVIES
Download extracts from over 50 movies, it's a little confusing at first but once you've got the technology sorted out it's good fun.

## http://rinkworks.com/movieaminute                                US

DON'T HAVE TIME TO WATCH IT ALL?
Summaries of the top movies for those who either can't be bothered to watch them or just want to pretend they did, either way it's really funny.

## www.moviecliches.com                                             US

THE MOVIE CLICHÉ LIST
Clichés listed by topic from aeroplanes to wood, there's something for everyone here...

M

### www.moviebloopers.com

#### BLOOPERS GALORE
A catalogue of mistakes and continuity errors from many of the world's greatest films – rather than be funny though, it just makes you wonder how long some people study films to spot such small errors! There are also reviews and quizzes.

## Film companies

*Some of the best web sites are those that promote a particular film. Here is a list of the major film producers and their web sites, all of which are good and have links to the latest releases. Most have clips, downloads, screensavers and lots of advertising.*

> **www.disney.com**
> **www.foxmovies.com**
> **www.miramax.com**
> **www.paramount.com**
> **www.spe.sony.com**
> **www.uip.com**
> **www.universalpictures.com**
> **www.warnerbros.com**

## Buying movies

M

*It's probably best to start with visiting a price checker site first such as* **www.kelkoo.com** *(see page 321) but these are the best of the movie online stores.*

### www.blackstar.co.uk

#### THE UK'S BIGGEST VIDEO STORE
The biggest online video and DVD retailer, it claims to be able to get around 50,000 titles. Blackstar is very good value, boasts free delivery and has a reputation for excellent customer service. If you want to shop around try **www.blockbuster.com** who have a less packed site and offers on a wide variety of films.

### www.dvdstreet.infront.co.uk

#### FOR DVD ONLY
Part of the Streets Online group, this is a great value and easy-to-use site that only sells DVD's. There are lots of other movie-related features too, such as the latest news and gossip or reviews. Delivery is free on orders over £19 for the UK.

## www.movietrak.com                                             UK

RENT A DVD MOVIE
Rent as many DVDs as you want for £13.95 per month. Pick
the title of your choice and it's dispatched the same day, you
then return it seven days later in the pre-paid envelope and
they immediately dispatch the next DVD on your list. The range
offered is excellent covering eleven major categories plus the
latest releases, coming soon and a good search facility too.

## www.reel.com                                                  US

OVER 50,000 MOVIES
Here is a mixture of news, gossip, interviews, event listings and
US-style outright selling. The content is good and you can get
carried away browsing. The search facility is very efficient but
shipping to the UK is expensive.

*See also:*
**www.discshop.com** – a wide-ranging DVD shop that sells
hardware too.
**www.dvdoptions.com** – rent your favourite DVDs from £3.25
for 7 nights.
**www.dvdpopcorn.com** – a good-looking UK-based DVD shop
with some good offers and prices include postage and packing.
**www.dvdreview.com** – great for news and reviews.
**www.mymovies.net** – a good review and film store with a
movie club.
**www.play.com** – a very strong selection of DVDs and CDs too
with some good offers.
**www.zoovies.com** – a good rental store with lots of choice,
you can either pay by movie or subscribe.

# Memorabilia

## www.vinmag.com                                               UK

POSTERS, CARDS AND T-SHIRTS
Vintage magazines, stand-up cut-outs, posters, T-shirts and
magazine covers complete the picture from this established
dealer. Shipping to the UK starts at around $2, but it depends
on how much you spend.

**www.asseenonscreen.com**                                    UK

AS SEEN ON SCREEN
At this site you can buy what you see on the screen, your
favourite star's shirt or dress can be replicated just for you.
You can also search by star, film and TV show.

**www.propstore.co.uk**                                       UK

PROPS FOR SALE
An extensive selection of props and replicas await you here with
everything from snow globes to clothing. Each piece is unique
and has been bought from the relevant film company and a
provenance is provided.

*See also:*
**www.efilmposters.com** – who sell posters from a good site.
**www.memomine.com** – for Hollywood memorabilia.
**www.moviemarket.co.uk** – posters, framed prints and
memorabilia delivered to your door.
**www.ricksmovie.com** – some 11,000 posters and related
items for sale.
**www.vinylandfilmposters.co.uk** – film and music
related posters.

# Music

*Before spending your hard earned cash on CDs it's worth
investigating MP3. MP3 technology allows the compression of a
music track into a file, which can be stored and played back.*

*An MP3 player can be downloaded free onto your PC from several
sites. It takes minutes to download the player and if you play CDs on
your PC it will also record them. You'll then be able to listen to
samples available on music stores. Once you've joined the MP3
revolution, there's an amazing amount of free music available.*

*Good MP3 players can be found at:*
**http://sonique.lycos.com** – the Sonique Player is good looking
with lots of options.
**www.liquidaudio.com** – the Liquid player is great and works
well with Windows XP.
**www.listen.com** – the Rhapsody player is adequate but there's
probably more music choice on the site.

**www.musicmatch.com** – a good all rounder with lots of functions and good looks.

**www.winamp.com** – the Winamp play is versatile and easy to use.

*Other sites with lots of MP3 downloads to buy that are worth checking out are listed below. Also have a look at* **www.100topmp3sites.com** *who list all the good MP3 sites including specialist ones.*

**http://magnatune.com** – great idea, try before you buy.

**www.apple.com/itunes** – if you have an i-Pod here's where to start.

**www.artistdirect.com** – great design, with the latest music news and tunes from over 500,000 artists.

**www.eatsleepmusic.com** – free karaoke!

**www.eclassical.com** – many free classical greats and many more to buy.

**www.emusic.com** – offers exclusive DJ mixes, live performances and prides itself on quality alternative music, 275,000 MP3s to choose from.

**www.listen.com** – good for previewing a wide variety of music from 15,000 artists.

**www.mp3-mac.com** – MP3 for Mac users.

**www.mperia.com** – downloads using the BitPass system which means you don't need to be at your own computer to buy them. Some free material too and a wide range of music styles covered.

**www.musicnet.com** – the might of AOL, providing top name downloads from three of the five major labels.

**www.real.com** – quality and range but you have to subscribe.

**www.weblisten.com** – subscription based service with over 140,000 songs to choose from, great that there are lots of subscription options.

**www.wippit.com** – good looking, wide range of downloads and only $6.50 a month.

## Downloading free music

*Much has been written about the effect that downloading free music has had on the music industry mainly at the expense of copyright. Some suggest that it's damaging the industry by taking away musicians' livelihoods, while others say it stimulates sales by enabling potential customers to sample music they wouldn't have heard otherwise.*

*The following sites are basically different file-sharing programs that allow users to exchange files easily whether it is music or not. It's best to read up on the subject before downloading any of the programs, but once you're up to speed it couldn't be easier.*

*Please be aware that some may contain adult material including pornography (music files aren't the only things traded) and most carry some sort of spyware so that they can adapt to your tastes and advertise accordingly. See our security section on page 351 if you want to get rid of spyware.*

*Some of these sites are also prone to change often, as regulations are introduced to block their activities, it's also quite difficult to establish their origin in some cases. The legal aspects that surround music file sharing are unclear so if you're not sure about using them I suggest you go to the pay sites.*

## www.zeropaid.com     US

### FILE SHARING PORTAL
A site that lists all the many file-sharing sites. It seems comprehensive but is not that easy to navigate as the text is quite dense. See also the even more confusing **www.pro-music.org** who also have a good listing.

## http://opennap.sourceforge.net     US

### CONNECTING PEOPLE
A variant of the original Napster program, this is freeware and you can select some of the many specialist and general servers that hold music (see **www.napigator.com** for a server list), then use the program to search them for the music you like.

## www.gnutella.com     US

### THE GNUTELLA NETWORK
Sounds like something you spread on toast, but is basically a mini search engine and file sharing system on one site. It consists of a network of thousands of computer users, all of whom use Gnutella software 'clones' that link them directly to other users to find music, movies and other files. Also check out **http://gnucleus.sourceforge.net**

## www.imesh.com
ISRAEL

OVER 40 MILLION USERS...
The latest version of iMesh is really a Napster clone; you type in an artist and song, and then a list of available matches from a centralised server appears. Since it's an Israeli site, it's likely to be immune from US copyright lawsuits, so it'll probably be around for a while yet. Supposed to be spyware free.

## www.kazaa.com
US

NUMBER 1
Kazaa rapidly became probably the most popular music download site last year. It has lots of features, it's easy to use and, unlike some of its competitors, attractive to look at. It comes with virus protection too, although some files we downloaded came with spyware attached.

## www.madster.com
US

IT'S MAD...
This used to be Aimster, though not affiliated, it combines AOL's instant message service with the ability to search for files and trade them with other users of the network, of Gnutella or even of Napster. It includes encryption software, so nobody can monitor your files while they're in transit and will even tell you which other AOL messenger buddies use it. Again it claims to have no spyware attached.

*See also:*
**www.musiccity.com** – uses the FastTrack file sharing system, their version is called Morpheus, it's quite secure, but lots of ads. Good design, lots of unsigned bands.
**www.rootnode.org** – this file-sharing network gets around legal shenanigans by concentrating on live recordings that are made available with the permission of the original artists. It's a good music magazine too.
**www.winmx.com** – a very flexible file-sharing program that does not contain spyware.

## www.riaa.org
US

RECORDING INDUSTRY ASSOCIATION OF AMERICA
Get the latest information of their attempts to stop music piracy, the legal issues plus their awards and industry statistics.
See also the site for Electronic Frontier Foundation **www.eff.org** who campaign on legal issues surrounding digital media.

# Buying music

*It's as well to start by checking prices of CDs through price comparison sites such as those listed on page 321. These will take you to the store offering the best combination of price and postage. All the stores listed below offer good value plus a bit extra.*

## www.hmv.co.uk                                                    UK

HIS MASTERS VOICE ONLINE
Excellent features and offers on the latest CDs and videos. There are sections on most aspects of music as well as video, DVD and games with a good search facility. You can listen to selections from albums before buying if you have RealPlayer. Spoken word or books on tape are available as well.

## www.cd-wow.com                                                   UK

OUTSTANDING VALUE
A very easy site to use with some great offers on CDs and there's free delivery too. Probably the best site for value at time of writing, let's hope they can keep it going.

## www.cduniverse.com                                               US

WIDE RANGE AND GREAT OFFERS
There is a massive range to choose from and some good discounts; delivery normally takes only five days. You can also buy games, DVDs and videos. Excellent, but can be quite slow, and delivery is very expensive.

## www.minidisco.com                                                US

HOME OF THE MINIDISC
The minidisc is alive and well here with some good offers on the players and information on the latest developments. Delivery to Europe takes about a week, costs vary. See also **www.minidisc.org** which is a messy site but contains everything you need to know about minidiscs.

*For more great offers on music try these sites:*
**www.101cd.com** – renowned for offering good value. (US)
**www.amazon.co.uk** – as good as you'd expect from Amazon. (UK)
**www.audiostreet.co.uk** – some good prices, free delivery in UK when you spend over £19. (UK)

**www.cdnow.com** – one of the originals but now part of Amazon. (US)

**www.recordstore.co.uk** – choose from thousands of vinyl records, CDs, T-shirts, record bags and assorted DJ gear. (UK)

**www.timelesstracks.com** – devoted to the music of the 50s, 60s, 70s and 80s with some excellent prices on CDs. (UK)

**www.towerrecords.co.uk** – wide variety and some good offers – better service than you get from the real store. (UK)

**www.virgin.net/music** – average music store with reviews. (UK)

## www.secondsounds.com

UK

THE USED CD STORE

With a huge range to choose from, prices from as low as £1.99 and free delivery you can't really go wrong, they guarantee mint condition or your money back. You can browse by artist or through the bargain bins, and of course they are interested in buying from you too.

## www.htfr.co.uk

UK

HARD TO FIND RECORDS

Although they specialise in new and deleted house, garage, techno, electro, disco, funk, soul and hip-hop vinyl, they will try and find any record previously released. They also offer a complete service to all budding and serious DJs.

M

*See also:*

**www.eil.com** – who specialise in rare and collectible CDs and vinyl.

**www.popetc.com** – who offer a wide range of memorabilia, vinyl and rare CD singles

**www.raregrooves.co.uk** – lots of choice and lots of offers too, strong in funk, soul and jazz.

# Bands, groups and stars

## http://ubl.artistdirect.com

US

THE ULTIMATE BAND LIST

It is the place for mountains of information on groups or singers. It has a totally brilliant search facility, and you can buy and download from the site as well, although the prices are not as good as elsewhere. For a similar, but better organised site try **www.allmusic.com** where you can also get excellent information and videos.

### www.onehitwondercentral.com                                    US

A CATALOGUE OF ONE HIT WONDERS
US-oriented information site on those who only triumphed
once, never to be seen again. It's arranged by decade and you
get some interesting titbits in the artist profiles.

### www.musicbrigade.com                                          US

WATCH YOUR FAVOURITE ARTIST
An excellent site where you can download your favourite music
videos; when we visited they had nearly 5,000. In the UK
subscription starts at £4.99 a month or £39.99 per annum.

## Music TV, awards and magazine sites

### www.bbc.co.uk/totp                                            UK

TOP OF THE POPS
The Top of the Pops sites are different, the principle site is a great
magazine featuring the current charts with loads of good features
and articles as well as competitions, trivia and lots of information.
For those with longer memories try **www.bbc.co.uk/totp2** for
golden oldies, 12,000 artists biogs, and half a million soundclips
and loads of general interest content.

### www.cdukweb.com                                               UK

UK'S NUMBER ONE MUSIC SHOW
Considering their boast, the web site is a bit of a
disappointment with not much in the way of information or
interaction. There are some quizzes, competitions and you can
download a few things but it has none of the buzz of the show.

### www.grammy.com                                                US

THE GRAMMY AWARDS
An overview of the awards, who won what and when, and
then where to buy their music. For the Brit awards go to
**www.brits.co.uk** where you'll find a similar site. The MOBO
awards are celebrated at **www.mobo.net**

### www.mtv.co.uk                                                 UK

MUSIC TELEVISION
MTV offers loads of info on events, shows and the artists as
well as background on the presenters and creative bits like
movie and music video clips. Great design.

## www.nme.com

*NEW MUSICAL EXPRESS*
If you're a rock fan then this is where it's at. There's all the usual information, it's well laid out and easy to access. The archived articles are its greatest asset, featuring 150,000 artists and every article, feature and review they've ever published plus full UK discographies, pictures, e-cards, ring-tones and links to the best web sites.

## www.q4music.com

*Q* MAGAZINE
A music magazine site that reflects its parent magazine extremely well, with many of the features and all the authority that goes with it.

## www.popworld.com

WHERE POP COMES FIRST
Brilliant site that concentrates on pop, it's fun and has great graphics. You have to register to join but once you're in you get access to their new shop, competitions, features on your favourite bands, clips from Popworld TV, fashion tips and much more. You need the latest Flash download from Macromedia to get the best out of it. For a view of pop in the swinging Sixties go to **www.sixtiespop.com** which is great fun.

M

## www.rollingstone.com

*ROLLING STONE* MAGAZINE
The archetypal music magazine has an excellent site with all the features you'd expect to see including reviews, photos, articles on the bands, downloads, links and games.

## www.thebox.co.uk

SMASH HITS YOU CONTROL
Similar to *Q* but with added features such as the ability for you to select a tune to be played on their TV channel and you can influence their overall selection by voting for your favourite songs.

# Sites for specific types of music

## Blues

### www.darkerthanblue.com                                      UK

HOME OF BLACK MUSIC
Very well-designed site dedicated to black-influenced music and
musicians, it has all the latest news, gig guides, artist features
and downloads as well as sections on reggae, garage, soul and
hip-hop.

### www.bluesworld.com                                          US

HOMAGE TO THE BLUES
If you're into the blues then this is your kind of site. There are
interviews, memorabilia, 78 auctions, bibliographies,
discographies and lists of links to other blues sites. You can
order CDs via affiliated retailers and if the mood takes you,
order a guitar too.

## Classical and opera

### www.gramophone.co.uk                                        UK

*GRAMOPHONE* MAGAZINE
An outstanding site with features, reviews, competitions, shop
and concert listings; there's also an awards section plus the
editor's choice with the top recommendations.

### www.classicalmusic.co.uk                                    UK

CLASSICAL MUSIC REVEALED
Excellent for lovers of classical music, with articles, guides,
reviews and concert listings, you can play in a fantasy concert
or just browse the excellent links section.

### www.operabase.com/en                                        US

OPERA BASE
This site offers opera listings, information on festivals and
provides background to the history of opera. For the *Opera*
magazine site go to **www.opera.co.uk** which offers articles
and links.

M

*Other key classical music sites:*
**www.aria-database.com** – information on over 1,000 arias.
**www.choralnet.org** – excellent site devoted to choral music.
**www.classical.net** – great for information and links.
**www.classicallink.com** – a very good portal site.
**www.eclassical.com** – download MP3s, many are free.
**www.eno.org** – the English National Opera.
**www.mdcmusic.co.uk** – good offers on CDs.
**www.orchestranet.co.uk** – excellent selection of links.
**www.royaloperahouse.org** – book online, see where your seat is and get the latest news.

# Country

## www.thatscountry.com                                    CANADA
COUNTRY MUSIC SCENE
A good overview of country music with offers and links as well as information on the artists and bands.

*See also:*
**www.cmdn.net** – country music dance.
**www.countrymusic.org.uk** – a very naff site that covers the UK scene.
**www.countrystars.com** – good all rounder with a messy design but the shop does supply the UK.
**www.roughstock.com** – all round magazine site, live radio and recommended for its excellent history of country.

# Dance and beat

## www.anthems.com                                         UK

DANCE, HOUSE AND GARAGE
Great design combined with brilliant content, there's everything here for dance fans – news, information and samples of the latest mixes, or if you're feeling rich, you can buy them too although you'll probably find cheaper elsewhere.

*See also:*
**www.garagemusic.co.uk** – reviews and samples plus the latest on the UK scene, annoying adverts though.
**www.fly.co.uk** – what was a good e-zine is now being revamped, watch this space.
**www.juno.co.uk** – good dance music store with a wide range.

## Folk

### www.folkmusic.net                                    UK

FOLK ON THE WEB
A straightforward site from *Living Traditions* magazine,
a collection of articles, features, reviews and news.

*See also:*
**www.folking.com** – a good all round site with news, downloads
and shopping.
**www.frootsmag.com** – a magazine site with news, information
and reviews.
**www.thetraditionbearers.com** – a project aimed at keeping
alive our traditional songs.

## Hip hop and rap

### www.sohh.com                                         US

SITE OF HIP HOP
Voted the best of its kind by *Rolling Stone*, this site offers all
you'd expect in terms of news, reviews, forums, interviews and
samples. It also has links to shops and other related sites.

*See also:*
**www.britishhiphop.co.uk** – the story of British Hip Hop and
artist listing and discography.
**www.hiphopville.com** – where to go for all the gear.
**www.rapsheet.com** – wide ranging and well put together site
offering much of what SOHH does.

## Indie

### www.playlouder.com                                   UK

INDIE MUSIC
Great graphics and excellent design make Playlouder stand out
from the crowd, it covers the Indie music scene in depth with
all the usual features, but with a bit more style. Another really
well designed web site covering Indie music in great depth is
Channel Fly **www.channelfly.com** – take your pick! See also
**www.drownedinsound.com** which is a very good e-zine
devoted to the scene.

# Jazz

## www.jazzonln.com US

JAZZ ONLINE

Whether you need help in working your way through the minefield that is jazz music, or you know what you want, Jazz Online can provide it. Its easy format covers all styles and it has a brilliant search facility. There is a good chat section and you can ask 'Jazz Messenger' just about anything. You can't buy from the site but there are links to Amazon's music section.

*See also:*
**www.allaboutjazz.com** – well organised, slightly dull but very comprehensive.
**www.jazzcorner.com** – a beautifully designed jazz magazine site and directory.
**www.jazzimprov.com** – a messy but thorough offering.
**www.jazzreview.com** – lots of reviews and discussion plus a photography section and downloads.

# Karaoke

## www.streamkaraoke.com US

SING ALONG

Over 20,000 tunes to download but you have to subscribe which costs from $8 a month depending on which package you take. See also **www.singtotheworld.com**

# Reggae

## www.reggaetrain.com US

REGGAE TRAIN A COME

An excellent and comprehensive portal site devoted to all things reggae, with several hundred links.

*See also:*
**www.reggaefusion.com** – a huge site devoted to Jamaican music.
**www.reggaereview.com** – a monthly web magazine from California.
**www.reggaetimes.com** – a good site connected with *Reggae Times*, lots of reviews and links.

M

## Rock music

**www.rocksite.com**                                                    US

INFORMATION THAT ROCKS
Devoted to rock music, there are band listings, tour news,
reviews plus links and a musicians directory. All this wrapped
up in an appropriately designed site.

*For more try:*
**www.eartothesound.fsnet.co.uk** – rock bands reviewed.
**www.history-of-rock.com** – a good overview of the roots of
rock and roll.
**www.rockhall.com** – the Rock and Roll Hall of Fame has an
outstanding site dedicated to celebrating only the best.
**www.rockhaven.co.uk** – a UK-oriented rock portal site.
**www.rocknrollzone.com** – a good, colourful portal and
news site.

## Music information

**www.clickmusic.co.uk**                                                UK

EVERYTHING YOU NEED TO KNOW ABOUT MUSIC
This is great for all music fans. It has quick access to details on
any particular band, with tickets, downloads, gigs and gossip.
Shopping is straightforward: just click on the store or use
the search engine to find something specific. See also
**www.musites.com** where you can find a rather variable but
improving music search engine.

**www.musicsearch.com**                                                 US

THE INTERNET'S MUSIC SEARCH ENGINE
Musicsearch is a directory site with over 20,000 links to
reviewed music sites, the search facility has improved and you
can offer up sites to be included.

**www.bl.uk/collections/sound-archive/cat.html**                        UK

BRITISH LIBRARY SOUND ARCHIVE
This catalogue contains over two and a half million entries,
there are only a few sounds you can listen to online, but more
are being put on the site. You can find out how to get a
listening appointment and order copies of the sounds, music or
oral recordings.

*See also:*
**www.hitsquad.com** – a well-categorised portal site aimed primarily at musicians.
**www.thisdayinmusic.com** – what happened on a particular day plus quizzes and competitions.
**www.sixtiespop.com** – the sound of the Sixties brought to life.
**www.vitaminic.co.uk** – a music club, excellent portal and host to many specialist music sites. You have to join to get the best out of it.

# Learning music

*Long-winded though the site URL is, it's worth visiting*
**www.si.umich.edu/chico/mhn/enclpdia.html** *where you can find a music encyclopaedia in which you can sample the sound of many instruments.*

**www.happynote.com/music/learn.html**                               US
LEARN MUSIC WITH A GAME
You download the game, which helps you learn the basics, but the more you learn and the better you get the higher the score. See also **www.abachamusic.com.au**

# Sites for specific instruments
## General
**www.backstreet.co.uk** – equipment hire and shop from this London based studio.
**www.harmony-central.com** – all sorts of instruments reviewed and rated.
**www.music4worship.co.uk** – a music store covering a wide range of musical instruments.
**www.musiciansfriend.com** – wide range but delivery charges are expensive from this US retailer.
**www.musicianshop.com** – another musical instrument store, especially good for guitarists.
**www.starland.co.uk** – musical instruments by mail order, some good offers too.

## Strings
**www.accessrock.com** – free interactive web site for aspiring rock guitarists, great range of lessons.
**www.basslobster.com** – playing the bass.

www.guitar.com – good all rounder, all you need to know.
www.guitarsite.com – masses of information.
www.guitarstrings.co.uk – a guitar specialist shop.
www.violin-world.com – complete resource for all string instruments.

## Percussion

www.drummersweb.com – drummer's delight.
www.drumweb.com – for all things drumming, good links to info on famous drummers.
www.giggear.co.uk – a well stocked shop.
www.rhythmweb.com – the place to go for all things percussive.

## Wind

http://kristin.newdream.net/flute – the flute resource.
www.saxophone.org – great for info and links.
www.wfg.sneezy.org – woodwind.

## Electronic

http://nmc.uoregon.edu/emi – great introduction to electronic music and instruments.
www.etcetera.co.uk – download all the latest sampling and music creation software here.
www.kvr-vst.com – technical site with downloads and reviews of the latest hardware and software.
www.synthzone.com – excellent source for articles, links and reviews for all things to do with electronic music making.

## Keyboard

www.pianonanny.com – complete piano course.
www.pianoshop.co.uk – masses of links, pianos for sale and information on learning.

## For aspiring bands

### www.taxi.com                                            US

FOR UNSIGNED BANDS
Looking to get a music contract for your band? You should start here, there's loads of information, contacts and links that will help you on the rocky road to success and stardom – well that's the theory anyway!

*For more places to find something new and get help if you're in a band, see also:*

**www.audiogalaxy.com** – for sampling new and some existing bands.

**www.bpi.co.uk** – the British Phonographic Industry and what they do.

**www.burbs.co.uk** – British Underground Rock Bands, home of the UK's real music scene.

**www.iuma.com** – massive selection of unsigned groups all well categorised.

## www.joescafe.com/bands

BAND NAMES                                                    UK

So you can't think of a name for your band? Here is the 'Band-o-matic' which will offer all sorts of never before used band names in seconds. This time we got 'Errant Spittle'. They've branched into song titles too, but can't imagine 'Mr Jerk Pioneer' making the top 20!

# Sheet music

## www.sunhawk.com                                            US

DOWNLOAD SHEET MUSIC

Well-designed site where you can download music from a wide variety of styles including pop, Christian, country, Broadway, jazz and classical, you have to pay but there are some freebies.

*See also:*

**www.musicroom.com** – a huge range and free postage in the UK.
**www.sheetmusicplus.com** – US-oriented but a wide range and some new stuff.

# Lyrics

## www.lyrics.com                                             US

THE WORDS TO HUNDREDS OF SONGS

There are songs from hundreds of bands and artists including Oasis, Madonna, Britney Spears and Queen, you'll have to ignore the directory section that makes up most of the page, there's an A–Z listing at the bottom. Hopefully they'll redesign soon.

*Other good lyric sites:*
**http://home.iae.nl/users/kdv/en/ring.htm** – a web ring for lyrics.
**www.britishacademy.com** – support an advice for songwriters.
**www.execpc.com/~suden** – songs from the 50s, 60s and 70s.
**www.letssingit.com** – big archive plus karaoke!

## www.kissthisguy.com          US

MISHEARD LYRICS
Mr Misheard lists all those lyrics that you thought were being
sung but in reality you were just not quite listening properly.
This time we liked 'Something in the way she boos, attracts me
to her mother's lover' but there are hundreds more.

# Concerts and tickets

## www.bigmouth.co.uk          UK

UK'S MOST COMPREHENSIVE GIG GUIDE
UK-based, with lots of links to band sites, news, events listing
and information on what's up and coming. Great search facilities
and the ability to buy tickets make this a really useful site for gig
lovers everywhere. It's geared to rock and pop though.

## www.ticketmaster.co.uk          UK

TICKETS FOR EVERYTHING
Book tickets for just about anything and you can run searches
by venue, city or date. The site is split into five key sections:
Theatre – theatre, drama and musical
Performing arts – comedy, classical and opera
Music – gigs, jazz, clubs, rock and pop.
Attraction – shows, anything from Disney on Ice to air shows
to museums
Sports – tickets for virtually every sporting occasion.

## www.concertphoto.co.uk          UK

PHOTOS OF YOUR FAVOURITE BANDS
OK so you've been to the gig and you didn't take a camera, well
the chances are that Pete Still has a photo available for you to
buy from this great web site. There are hundreds of bands to
choose from both old and new and he's covered the major
festivals too. Costs vary according to size and quantity.

M

# Nature and the Environment

*The Internet offers charities and organisations a chance to highlight their work in a way that is much more creative than ever before, it also offers the chance for us to get in-depth information on those species and issues that interest us.*

## Wildlife and environmental organisations

### www.panda.org                                           UK

THE WORLD WIDE FUND FOR NATURE
The official site for The World Wide Fund For Nature with information on projects designed to save the world's endangered species by protecting their environment. You can find out about how to support their work, how to get involved, the latest news, information on the key projects and some great photos. There is also some good kids' and educational material embedded in the news section. An American organisation called the National Wildlife Fund has a similar excellent site at **www.nwf.org**

### www.foe.co.uk                                           UK

FRIENDS OF THE EARTH
Not as worthy as you might imagine, this site offers a stack of information on food, pollution, green power, protecting wildlife in your area and the latest campaign news.

### www.envirolink.org                                      US

THE ONLINE ENVIRONMENTAL COMMUNITY
A huge site focused on personal involvement in environment issues. There are several sections including: organisations, educational resources, jobs, governmental resources, actions you can take to help and environment links. There is also a good search facility on environment-related topics.

### www.environment-agency.gov.uk                           UK

WHAT THE GOVERNMENT IS UP TO
The Environment Agency's site offers information on the latest initiatives and news of the latest research. It also helps with recycling and gives out information on how to improve the environment plus contact details regarding any issues you have.

## www.planetdiary.com                                    US

### WHAT'S REALLY HAPPENING ON THE PLANET
Every week Planetdiary monitors and records world events in
geological, astronomical, meteorological, biological and
environmental terms and relays them back via this web site.
It's done by showing an icon on a map of the world, which you
then click on to find out more. Although very informative,
a visit can leave you a little depressed.

## www.projectearth.com                                    US

### NAVIGATING TOWARDS A BETTER ENVIRONMENT
Outstanding site devoted to recognising the damaging effect
man has on the environment and pointing the way towards
a better future.

*See also:*

**http://wcs.org** – home of New York's Wildlife Conservation
Society who have a very informative site.

**www.cat.org.uk** – a messy site from the Centre for Alternative
Technology, but contains good information.

**www.defra.gov.uk** – the Department for Environment, Food and
Rural Affairs has a newsy site that offers lots of information and
does it pretty well when you consider the size of their brief.

**www.environmentwebsites.co.uk** – a portal for environmental
sites.

**www.ewg.org** – an excellent and detailed site from the
Environmental Working Group, dedicated to the fight against
pollution; warning – contains some scary information.

**www.forestry.gov.uk** – Forestry Commission has details of its
work and how you can help sustain our woods and forests.

**www.greenpeace.org** – find out about their latest activities and
how to get involved.

**www.ifaw.org** – home of the excellent International Fund for
Animal Welfare.

**www.scorecard.org** – the facts on local pollution from this
US-oriented but informative site.

**www.traffic.org** – a campaigning site working against the illegal
and sometimes appalling trade in animals throughout the world.

**www.ufaw.org.uk** – improving animal welfare using
scientific knowledge.

**www.wri.org** – World Resources Institute promoting effective
campaigning for a far better world.

# Eco help

## www.coralcay.org
UK

HOW YOU CAN JOIN IN
In Coral Cay's words its aim is 'providing resources to help
sustain livelihoods and alleviate poverty through the protection,
restoration and management of coral reefs and tropical forests'.
Sign up for an expedition or a science project in Malaysia or
the Philippines.

*See also:*

**www.ecoclub.com** – a network providing a wealth of
information about all aspects of ecotourism.
**www.ecotourism.org** – American site with useful links.
**www.ecovolunteer.com** – if you want to give your services to a
specific animal benefit project.

# Information and media

## www.nhm.ac.uk
UK

THE NATURAL HISTORY MUSEUM
A superb user-friendly web site that covers everything from ants
to eclipses. You can get the latest news, check out exhibitions,
take a tour, browse the Dinosaur database or explore the
wildlife garden. There are details on the collections, galleries,
educational resources and contacts for answers to specific
questions. See also the Smithsonian National Museum of
Natural History who also has a great site at **www.mnh.si.edu**

## http://earthobservatory.nasa.gov
US

THE EARTH FROM ABOVE
Really outstanding photography and detailed information on the
environment presented in an interesting and thought provoking
way. Owned by NASA, the site offers sections on the
atmosphere, land and air as well as the latest news stories.

## www.bbc.co.uk/nature
UK

WILDLIFE EXPOSED
A brilliant nature offering from the BBC with sections on key
wildlife programmes and animal groups. The information is
good and enhanced by video clips.

N

*Other nature sites worth checking out are...*

**www.enature.com** – an American magazine site with a huge amount of information and features on all aspects of nature.

**www.kalama.com/~mariner/qserwild.htm** – basically just a list of good sites devoted to nature; it has a US bias.

**www.naturephotographers.net** – a magazine devoted to wildlife photography with a great selection on shots and advice.

**www.virtualparks.org** – just stunning photography from the parks of Canada and the US.

# British nature

## www.naturenet.net                                              UK

### UK COUNTRYSIDE, NATURE AND CONSERVATION

Ignore the rather twee graphics and you'll find a great deal of information about nature in the UK. Their interests include: countryside law, upkeep of nature reserves, voluntary work, education and environmental news. You can also search the site for specifics and there is a good set of links to related sites.

## www.uksafari.com                                               UK

### BRITAIN'S WILDLIFE

A good overview of the UK's wild animals with a section on each and tips on wildlife gardening, a photo gallery and lots of additional stuff like film clips, facts and figures and information on nature sites.

*See also:*

**www.englishnature.org.uk** – supply maps, photos and information on all our nature reserves and explains why reserves are so important – all on an excellent site.

**www.phenology.org.uk** – how to help with this 'study of the times of recurring natural phenomena especially in relation to climate change' going on a woodland near you.

**www.treecouncil.org.uk** – inspiring a love of trees, it comes with a section on some of our favourite trees.

**www.wildlifebritain.com** – an attractive site devoted to preserving and nurturing interest in British wildlife, with lots of interesting features and articles; it's a pleasure to visit.

**www.wildlifetrust.org.uk** – who care for over 2,000 of Britain's nature reserves.

# Endangered and general animal sites

## www.arkive.org

RAISING AWARENESS OF ENDANGERED SPECIES
Sponsored by the Wildscreen Trust this site's aim is to catalogue
and picture all the world's endangered species with a separate
section for the UK. Each animal and plant has a page devoted
to it giving details on how and where it lives, including pictures
and movie clips. You can help by donating pictures and film.

*See also:*
**http://digimorph.org** – a collection of x-ray and computer
generated photos of many animals including dinosaurs,
fascinating stuff.
**http://netvet.wustl.edu/e-zoo.htm** – a fun portal site devoted to
the animal kingdom, good for research and homework.
**www.animalworlddirectory.com** – a massive site with a large
collection of articles on many aspects of nature and wildlife,
from care to tourism.
**www.endangeredspecie.com** – American site with lots of good
photography and background on the causes of species decline.
**www.iucnredlist.org** – the Red List of critically endangered and
threatened species.
**www.naturecom.de/eng/index.html** – a good nature site aimed
at children.
**www.umich.edu/~esupdate/** – for the endangered species
update, which has detailed information on species in danger,
albeit on a cluttered site.
**www.wildlifesearch.com** – links to sites on almost every
animal.

# Zoos and safari parks

## www.safaripark.co.uk

SAFARI ONLINE
A detailed site on the UK's safari parks including opening times,
animal information and facts on endangered species.
At **www.zoo-keeper.co.uk** you get information on the most
common zoo animals and some background about what it's like
to work with them.

## www.sandiegozoo.org

US

DAN DIEGO ZOO

Probably the best zoo site. You can get conservation information, check out the latest arrivals and browse their excellent photo gallery. The highlight is definitely the Panda Cam.

*Other good zoo sites:*

**www.bristolzoo.co.uk** – good looking and fun for kids.
**www.dublinzoo.ie** – slow but good content.
**www.londonzoo.co.uk** – excellent and comprehensive zoo site, also covers Whipsnade Wildlife Park.
**www.marwell.org.uk** – masses to see and do.
**www.mbayaq.org** – beautiful site from Monterey Bay Aquarium with web cams, online field guide and info on ocean research projects.
**www.seaworld.com** – information on holidays and the attractions at their three zoos.

## www.bornfree.co.uk

UK

ZOO CHECK

Zoo Check is a charity whose mission is to promote Born Free's core belief that wildlife belongs in the wild. They expose the suffering of captive wild animals and investigate neglect and cruelty. They want tighter legislation and the phasing out of all traditional zoos. If you want to know more then this is where to go.

# African wildlife and the big cats

## www.africam.com

SOUTH AFRICA

ALWAYS LIVE, ALWAYS WILD

Web cameras have come a long way and this is one of the best uses of them. There are strategically placed cameras at water holes and parks around Africa and other of the world's wildlife areas, and you can tap in for a look at any time. You have to register to get the best out of it, but even a quick visit is rewarding.

*See also:*

**http://elephant.elehost.com** – an excellent elephant only portal site.
**www.5tigers.org** – excellent site on Tigers and how we can help to save the remaining five species.

**www.cheetahspot.com** – all you need to know about
the cheetah.
**www.greatcatsoftheworld.com** – an overview of the big cats
from a US nature centre.
**www.lioncrusher.com** – all large carnivores and a good
picture archive.
**www.wildnetafrica.com** – the wild life portal has lots of all
aspects of provides information onAfrican animals and how to
see them.

# Rain forest

### www.rainforestlive.org.uk                                    UK
THE RAINFOREST – LIVE
A largely educational site about rainforests and their
importance. It gives a good illustrated overview of the subject
plus chat, links, competitions and colouring pages for the
very young.

*See also:*
**http://ths.sps.lane.edu/biomes/rain3/rain3.html** – a long URL
but worth a visit for the information it contains. It also offers
possibly the worst combination of background and text colours
we've seen, so be prepared!
**www.rainforest.org** – home of the Tropical Rainforest Coalition
with up-to-date information on rainforest destruction and how
you can help.
**www.rainforest-alliance.org** – excellent for information and
links to related sites.
**www.rainforestconcern.org** – home of a charity which aims
to protect the world's rain forests. The site gives an
overview of the problems faced and details on how you
can help.
**www.ran.org** – Rainforest Action Network, another group
devoted to saving the rainforest, this one is American. You can't
help asking why these charities don't get together?
**www.saveordelete.com** – a campaigning site from Greenpeace
aimed at exposing the tragic loss of rain forests throughout
the globe.

N

# Insects

### www.bugbios.com                                                    US

BUGS AND INSECTS
A beautifully designed site exposing insects as miracles of
nature, with amazing macro-photography, information and
links. See also **www.virtualinsectary.com** which contains some
great photography.

### http://butterflywebsite.com                                       US

BUTTERFLYING
Not that great design-wise but an interesting site on butterflies.
Although it's biased towards the US, it does have sections that
cover Britain and also has a very good links section. For
another excellent site devoted to British butterflies go to
**www.butterfly-conservation.org** who hold information on all
resident and migrating butterflies and moths found in the UK.

# Birds

### www.birds.com                                                     US

ALL ABOUT BIRDS
An online directory and guide to birds covering both wild and
pets, biased to America but excellent except that it's a bit
too commercial.

*See also:*
**www.birdsofbritain.co.uk** – a strong monthly web magazine for
British bird watchers.
**www.ornithology.com** – a good, if serious site dedicated to
wild birds.
**www.rspb.org.uk** – the Royal Society for the Protection of Birds
have a nice site detailing what they do, and how you can help.

# Dinosaurs and geology

### www.prehistoricplanet.com                                         US

PREHISTORIC PLANET
A great site put together by some dinosaur enthusiasts. It's got
information on what the planet looked like in prehistoric times,
you can ask a palaeontologist a question or just browse the
many articles.

*See also:*
**www.bbc.co.uk/dinosaurs** – excellent Walking with Dinosaurs site with lots of features.
**www.dinodata.net** – easy to use and information packed.
**www.dinosaur.org** – a messy and unstructured site, but packed with dino facts and links.
**www.geology.com** – an American site covering the whole subject.
**www.geologylink.com** – an educational bias to this site from a specialist publisher.
**www.rockwatch.org.uk** – an ebullient site aimed at bringing geology to life for young people.
**www.strangescience.net** – an interesting site showing how scientists have developed the latest theories about dinosaurs and mistakes made along the way.
**www.ucmp.berkeley.edu/diapsids/dinolinks.html** – horrid URL but phenomenal list of dino-related web links.
**www.ukfossils.co.uk** – excellent and informative site on where to find fossils in the UK, includes information on geology too.

# Apes and early humans

**www.becominghuman.org**                                       US
  HUMAN ORIGINS
  A superb site detailing the progress of human evolution, showing our development in an interactive and enthralling way. Beautifully illustrated throughout, however it can be a little slow, so best seen by broadband users.

*For other sites that feature our evolution and our nearest relatives try:*
**www.archaeologyinfo.com/evolution.htm** – good site on human evolution, the Hall of Skulls is great for showing our development through time.
**www.chimps-inc.com** – a non-profit organisation devoted to chimpanzees.
**www.gorilla.org** – home of the Gorilla Foundation and Koko
**www.greatapeproject.org** – campaigning on rights for apes.
**www.janegoodall.org** – very well put together site featuring the work of this pioneer with biographical details and information on chimpanzees and how you can help preserve them.
**www.unep.org/grasp** – the Great Apes Survival Project aims to help preserve the species, specifically Oranutangs, Bonobos, Gorillas and Chimpanzees.

# Bears

**www.bears.org**                                                              US

BEAR BELIEFS
An overview of the major species of bears with lots of
background, photos, myths and also detailed information on
their habits and lifestyles.

*See also:*
**http://nationalzoo.si.edu/Animals/GiantPandas/** – excellent site
on Pandas from the Smithsonian.
**www.polarbearsalive.org** – the web's largest Polar bear site!
Lots of info and photos too.

# Marine mammals

**www.wdcs.org**                                                              UK

WHALE AND DOLPHIN SOCIETY
All the latest news and developments in the fight to save
whales and dolphins. There's also information on them, how
and where they live, a 'Sightings and Strandings' section and
details of how to book a whale-watching holiday.

*See also:*
**www.cetacea.org** – an excellent site where you can get
background info on every species of dolphin, whale and
porpoise.
**www.flmnh.ufl.edu/fish** – the University of Florida's
Department of Ichthyology has a good site where you can find
an overview of all things fishy plus links and a good selection
of photographs.
**www.seawatchfoundation.org.uk** – here you can learn more
about cetaceans, and their sightings around the UK.

# Natural phenomena

**http://library.thinkquest.org/C003603/**                                    US

FORCES OF NATURE
An amazing site that covers all the known natural disasters,
giving background information, simulations and multimedia
explanations with experiments for you to try at home.

*See also:*
**www.earthquake.com** – check out the most recent seismic activity and even buy earthquake insurance!
**www.fema.gov/kids** – Federal Emergency Management Association site aimed at young kids.
**www.geographyiq.com** – comprehensive geography site.
**www.naturalhazards.org** – interesting site with basic information on natural phenomena and links.

# News and the Media

*The standard of web sites in this sector is usually very high making it difficult to pick out one or two winners, just find one that appeals to you and you won't go far wrong.*

## World news

**www.sky.com/skynews**                                      UK

WITNESS THE EVENT
Sky News has fast developed a reputation for excellence and that is reflected in their web site. It has a well rounded news service with good coverage across the world as well as the UK. You can view news clips, listen to news items or just browse the site. There are special sections on sport, business, technology and even a few games.

**www.bbc.co.uk/news**                                       UK

FROM THE BBC
As you'd expect the BBC site is excellent – similar to Sky but without the adverts. You can also get the news in several languages and tune into the World Service or any of their radio stations.

**www.channel4.com/news**                                    UK

AWARD-WINNING NEWS
High quality journalism reflects the independent and serious nature of their news coverage. There are some interesting links and a forum – you can even register to receive 'Snowmail' from John Snow himself.

### www.itn.co.uk    UK
INDEPENDENT TELEVISION NEWS
A corporate site where you get information on what they do
plus links to their news sites, which are clear and to the point.

### www.teletext.com    UK
TELETEXT NEWS
Excellent and clear layout makes Teletext's site stand out, it has
lots of added features and links too.

### www.cnn.com    US
THE AMERICAN VIEW
CNN is superb on detail and breaking news with masses of
background information on each story. It has plenty of feature
pieces too. However, it is biased towards the American
audience, for a similar service try **www.abcnews.com**

### www.newsnow.co.uk

NEWS NOW!    UK
A superb news gathering and information service that you can
tailor to your needs and interests. The layout is confusing at
first but it allows you to flick between latest headlines from
3,000 leading news sources without visiting each site
separately, you can then read their choice of stories in full on
the publishers' web sites. It's updated every five minutes!

### www.ananova.co.uk    UK
NEWS ON THE MOVE
Ananova has been changed a few times and in the latest guise
you get a well put together site that is much clearer than some.
They've also teamed up with Orange to produce a mobile text
messaging news service.

### www.moreover.com    US
DYNAMIC CONTENT
With real time news and rumour reporting, Moreover has
become the news site of choice for many business people and
journalists as it enables them to target the type of news and
information they are looking for, saving time and effort all
round. You need to subscribe to gain access.

**http://english.aljazeera.net/HomePage**                    UAE

AL JAZEERA
The English version of the well known Arab news agency.
It's very good for world events and as you'd expect outstanding
when it comes to gaining an insight into the Arab world.

*Other news sites worth a visit are...*
**www.anorak.co.uk** – humorous newspaper reviews.
**www.copydesk.co.uk** – a very good blog site devoted to news
and popular culture, it's great for news links too.
**www.economist.co.uk** – business, world events and in
depth reports.
**www.nuzgeeks.com** – excellent links.
**www.positivenews.org.uk** – for a positive spin on the news.
**www.private-eye.co.uk** – some of the best features from the
mag, but not much news if true be told.
**www.reuters.co.uk** – strong site from this world renowned
news agency.
**www.theregister.co.uk** – for technology news.
**www.time.com** – an excellent site from *Time* magazine.
**www.topix.net** – a news collation site which is exceptional for
American news.

# Events and future news

**www.drudgereport.com**                    US

NOW FOR THE REAL NEWS
One of the most visited sites on the web. It's a pain to use,
but the gossip and tips about upcoming features in the papers
make it worthwhile. One of its best features is its superb set of
links to other news sources.

**www.foreignreport.com**                    UK

PREDICT THE FUTURE
Owned by Janes, the Foreign Report team attempt to pick out
trends and happenings that might lead to bigger international
news events. Browsing through their track record shows they're
pretty good at it too.

**www.wwevents.com**                                                    UK

WORLD EVENTS
Details of events that are happening in the world today,
tomorrow and this weekend all available at the touch of a
button, it really is that simple. You can search by country or
even region and county.

# Newspapers online

**www.telegraph.co.uk**                                                 UK

*DAILY TELEGRAPH*
The *Telegraph* has the best site for news and layout with all its
sections mirrored very effectively on the site.

*Other major newspapers with sites worth a visit include:*
**www.dailymail.co.uk** – not so much the paper as a portal for
Associated Newspapers, which is disappointing, but there are
some good articles and features.
**www.guardian.co.uk** – clean site with lots of added features
and guides.
**www.independent.co.uk** – good online debate as well as news.
**www.thesun.co.uk** – very good representation of the paper with
all you'd expect.
**www.timesonline.co.uk** – no surprises here.

**www.fish4news.co.uk**                                                 UK

LOCAL NEWS MADE EASY
An outstanding web site, just type in your postcode and back
will come a collated local 'newspaper' with regional news
headlines, sport and links to the source papers sites and small
ads. Also see **www.newspapersoc.org.uk** and go to 'newspaper
links' to find your local paper.

**www.whatthepaperssay.co.uk**                                          UK

WHEN YOU'VE NOT GOT TIME
Can't be bothered to sift through the papers? At this site you
can quickly take in the key stories and be linked through to the
relevant newspaper site too. You can also sign up to its daily
e-mail bulletin so you need never buy a paper again. See also
**www.thepaperboy.com** which is a bit more colourful and has a
good search facility.

# Organiser and Diary

**www.opendiary.com**                                                    UK

THE ONLINE DIARY FOR THE WORLD
Your own personal organiser and diary, easy to use, genuinely
helpful and totally anonymous. Simply register and away you go
but follow the rules faithfully or you get deleted. Use it as you
would any diary, go public or just browse other entries.

*See also:*
**www.filofax.co.uk** – if you can't live without the real thing.
**www.livejournal.com** – download your own journal and
customise it to suit.
**www.yourorganiser.com.au** – good-looking site, easy to use
with a group organiser facility.

# Over-50s

*If you're over 50 then you're part of the fastest growing group of
Internet users, and some sites have cottoned on to the fact with
specific content just for you.*

## Magazines, fun and advice

**www.saga.co.uk**                                                      UK

THE SAGA GROUP
While this is a commercial organisation aimed at the over-50's
it offers much in the way of advice, help and information in key
areas such as health, travel and money plus the magazine
is excellent.

**www.idf50.co.uk**                                                     UK

I DON'T FEEL FIFTY
Graham Andrews is retired and this is his irreverent and
opinionated magazine site. It's very positive about the power of
being over fifty and it has a great deal of motivational advice on
how to get the best out of life combined with a superb set of
links to useful sites.

*See also:*
**www.theoldie.co.uk** – *The Oldie* magazine, which is great fun.
**www.togs.org** – where devoted fans of Terry Wogan meet.
**www.over50s.com** – a magazine style site, good information and design.

# Links

**www.50connect.co.uk**                                                   UK

LIVE LIFE TO THE FULL
A very strong portal site with masses of information and links covering a wide range of topics. It's incredibly useful, however, there are plenty of annoying adverts to go with it.

*See also:*
**www.age-net.co.uk** – another portal site but one that takes a magazine-style approach.
**www.laterlife.com** – a comprehensive site with lots of links and advice in many categories.
**www.lifes4living.co.uk** – an upbeat site dedicated to chat and links, some good offers too.
**www.seniority.co.uk** – a very comprehensive offering covering all you are likely to need with advice and links. Not exactly the most inspiring design though.
**www.silversurfers.net** – not the easiest site to get to grips with but it has a huge number of links in over 50 different categories.

# Information and help

**www.ageconcern.co.uk**                                                  UK
WORKING FOR ALL OLDER PEOPLE
Learn how to get involved with helping older people, get information and practical advice on all aspects of getting old. You can also make a donation. There are also over 100 links to related and special interest sites.

**www.arp.org.uk**                                                         UK
ASSOCIATION OF RETIRED PERSONS
ARP's mission is to change the attitude of society and individuals towards age in order to enhance the quality of life for people over 50 – and this site goes a long way to achieving that. It has great design and plenty of features aimed at helping you get the most out of life. It's excellent for a place to chat if nothing else.

## www.helptheaged.org.uk

### HELP THE AGED

Find out how you can get involved in their work, what they do plus the latest news. You can also go to 'home shopping' and buy all sorts of useful gadgets to make life easier.

## www.hairnet.org

### TECHNOLOGY EXPLAINED

So you've bought the PC and now you need to know how to work it properly? Hairnet explains all through a series of forums and specific courses designed to help you get the most from technology. See also **www.seniornet.org** which is a pretty boring but comprehensive guide.

## www.u3a.org.uk

### LIFELONG LEARNING

An organisation working to improve the lives of older people through the concept of life long learning, learning for the pleasure of it. The site offers details of the subjects covered and how contact the relevant groups.

## www.age-exchange.org.uk

### MAKE YOUR MEMORIES MATTER

Share your experiences and pass them on, Age Exchange aims to 'improve the quality of life for older people by emphasising the value of their memories to old and young, through pioneering artistic, educational, and welfare activities' they are also active in improving care for older people. This site gives details of how you can join in.

# Travel

## www.saga.co.uk/travel

### HOLIDAYS FOR THE OVER-50S

A superbly illustrated and rich site from Saga who've been specialising in holidays for older people for many years. Here you'll find everything from top quality cruises to weekend breaks.

*See also:*
**www.takeaholiday.co.uk** – Direct Reader holidays specialise in the over-50s.
**www.travel55.co.uk** – a great database of travel sites specialising in travel for older people.

# Parenting

*As a source of advice the Internet has proved its worth and especially so for parents. As well as information, there are great shops and useful sites that filter out the worst of the web and give advice on specific problems. Some of the education web sites, page 99, also have useful resources for parents as do the health sites, page 200. In addition, there is loads of useful stuff for parents about taking children on holiday and activities to do with the children in the UK in the travel section, page 463.*

## Advice and information

### www.babyworld.co.uk                                        UK

BE PART OF IT
Babyworld is an online magazine that covers all aspects of parenthood. There's excellent advice on how to choose the right products for your baby and for the pregnancy itself. The layout is much improved and it's easier to find information.

### www.babycentre.co.uk                                       UK

A HANDS-ON GUIDE
A superb site with a massive amount of information and links to all aspects of pregnancy, childbirth and early parenthood. The content is provided by experts and you can tailor-make your profile so that you get the right information for you. There's also a series of buying guides to help you make the right decision on baby shopping.

### http://england.babyzone.com                               US

PARENTAL ADVICE
These are the UK pages from the massive American site on parenting. It gives a week-by-week account of pregnancy, information on birth and early childhood, links are very good and there's plenty of information on offers to parents, although some are for the US only. See also the similarly well-put-together **www.parentsoup.com**

## www.raisingkids.co.uk
UK

FROM BIRTH TO...
An excellent and information laden site devoted to helping
parents get through the minefield of child raising with sections
on every life stage. You can also ask an expert, and amongst
many sections, there's advice on travel, education and safety.
Excellent.

## www.ukparents.co.uk
UK

YOUR PARENTING LIFELINE
Chat, experiences, stories and straightforward advice make this
site worth a visit – there are competitions, links and plenty of
opportunities for interaction.

## www.all4kidsuk.com
UK

IF YOU'RE LOOKING FOR SOMETHING TO DO
This aims to be a comprehensive directory covering all your
parental needs from activities to schools. It's got an easy-to-use
search engine, where you can search by county if you need to.

## www.miriamstoppard.com
UK

MIRIAM STOPPARD LIFETIME
An excellent web site from the best selling author with lots of
advice on being a parent, how to cope with pregnancy and
keeping yourself and your family healthy. New information is
continually being added, so it's very up-to-date and will become
a great resource for parents.

## www.parentalk.co.uk
UK

THE SENSIBLE APPROACH
Interesting articles and sensible advice characterise this site.
There is a helpful section for working parents and one for
employers plus a good links section for expert advice on a wide
range of topics. If the advice here isn't enough, you can buy
their books or take the course.

## www.parentcentre.gov.uk
UK

THE LOW-DOWN ON EDUCATION
The Parent Centre is for all parents and carers who want to help
their child or children to learn. It really covers everything from
choosing a school or nursery to detailed information on what a
child should learn. It also provides information about the rights
and responsibilities of parents in a wider sense, advice and links.

## www.babydirectory.com                                        UK

A–Z OF BEING A PARENT
The Baby Directory catalogue is relevant to most parts of the
UK. It lists local facilities plus amenities that care for and
occupy your child. The quality of information varies by
area though.

## www.gingerbread.org.uk                                       UK

SUPPORT FOR LONE PARENT FAMILIES
Gingerbread is an established charity run by lone parents with
the aim of providing support to lone parents. The site is fun to
use and well designed, and is one of the few websites that is
available in several languages.

## www.tommys.org                                               UK

PREMATURE BIRTH, MISCARRIAGE AND STILLBIRTH
RESEARCH
Information on getting through some of the tragedies that occur
in pregnancy plus details on how you can help.

*Other useful sites:*
**www.allkids.co.uk** – a well-categorised portal site covering all
things for children including good shopping directory.
**www.babyandkids.co.uk** – an American style advice site aimed
at the UK.
**www.babynames.com** – over 6,500 names to choose from
plus other services and lots of adverts!
**www.fnf.org.uk** – support for dads at Families Need Fathers.
**www.mumsnet.com** – a rather advert laden site devoted to
product reviews with advice and tips thrown in. You have to
subscribe to get the best of it.
**www.ncb.org.uk** – home of the National Children's Bureau
who provide support for children's charities and support
organisations.
**www.nctpregnancyandbabycare.com** – a well-designed and
informative site from the NCT covering the first year or so.
**www.oneparentfamilies.org.uk** – advice for single parents.
**www.parenthood.com** – lots of advice from this
US-oriented site.

# Childcare

**www.bestbear.co.uk**                                            UK

> MARY POPPINS ONLINE
> Select your postcode and they will provide you with a list of
> reputable childcare agencies or nurseries in your area. There
> are also homepages for parents, childcarers and agencies all
> with information and ideas. There is also a parents' forum.
> See also **www.sitters.co.uk**

**www.daycaretrust.org.uk**                                       UK

> CHILDCARE ADVICE
> Daycare Trust is a national childcare charity which works to
> promote high quality, affordable childcare for all. This site is
> designed to give you all the information you need on arranging
> care for your child; there are sections on finance, news and you
> can become a member.

# Shopping

**www.bloomingmarvellous.co.uk**                                  UK

> MATERNITY, NURSERY AND BABY WEAR
> Excellent online store with a selection of maternity, baby and
> nurseryware available to buy, or you can order their catalogue.
> Delivery in the UK is £3.95.

**www.mothercare.com**                                            UK

> MOTHERCARE
> An attractive site with a good selection of baby and toddler
> products, also clothing, entertainment and equipment. It's good
> value and there are some excellent offers, delivery is £3.95 for
> the UK. It's not all about shopping though, there are advice
> sections on baby care, finance, tips on how to keep
> kids occupied and chat rooms where you can share
> your experiences.

**www.ethosbaby.com**                                             UK

> FOR GREEN BABIES
> A good store where all products are environmentally friendly,
> there's not a huge selection but you can order a catalogue.
> Delivery charges vary according to spend. For similar site go to
> **www.greenbabyco.com**

*See also:*
**www.babyhut.net** – natural products for baby's and parents.
**www.bibsandstuff.co.uk** – great for all those hard to get things and equipment generally.
**www.cheekyrascals.co.uk** – a very good baby equipment store.
**www.mamasandpapas.co.uk** – good-looking site, you can't buy online but you can order a catalogue.

# Dealing with areas of parental concern

## General

**www.childline.org.uk**           UK
### A CHILD'S EYE VIEW
There's a huge amount of advice on a wide range of issues from bullying, domestic violence, dealing with death, racism and exam stress. The advice is aimed at youngsters, but it is worth parents looking at that advice too.

**www.nchafc.org.uk**           UK
### NATIONAL CHILD HELP
A charity aimed at helping children and parents across a wide range of subjects, issues and problems. A good place to start getting help.

## Alcohol

*See Drugs and alcohol on page 307.*

## Allergies

**www.anaphylaxis.org.uk**           US
### ALLERGY AND ANAPHYLAXIS
A useful site with information and links on food allergies and their reactions, it's very much oriented to the US so also try **www.anaphylaxis.org.uk** which is also very helpful and UK-based. For info on e-numbers go to **www.foodag.com**

# Bereavement

**www.childbereavement.org.uk**                                    UK

> CHILD BEREAVEMENT TRUST
> Support for those who have suffered the loss of a loved one.
> There is a section dedicated to families and one for young
> people. The Cruse Bereavement Centre also has a site aimed
> at young people at **www.rd4u.org.uk**

# Bullying

**www.bullying.co.uk**                                             UK

> HOW TO COPE WITH BULLYING
> Advice for everyone on how to deal with a bully; there are
> sections on tips for dealing with them, school projects, problem
> pages and links to related sites. See also
> **www.successunlimited.co.uk**

# Child protection

**www.teachernet.gov.uk/wholeschool/familyandcommunity/
childprotection**                                                  UK

> KEEP THEM SAFE
> Although primarily aimed at teachers, this site gives the low
> down on child protection law and policy. The 'Advice and
> Guidance' is particularly useful as it addresses the wider
> community and parents and provides further links.

# Computers and the internet

**www.cyberpatrol.com**                                            US

> INTERNET FILTERING SOFTWARE
> The best for filtering out unwanted web sites, images and
> words. As with all similar programs, it quickly becomes
> outdated but will continue to weed out the worst. You can
> download the very commercial free trial from the site. See also
> **www.netnanny.com** whose site offers more advice and seems
> to be updated more regularly.

**www.pin.org.uk**                                                      US

PARENTS' INFORMATION NETWORK
Provides good advice for parents worried about children using
computers. It has links to support sites, guidance on how to
surf the Net, evaluations of software and buyer's guides to PCs.

*See also:*
**www.iwf.org.uk** – the Internet Watch Foundation who combat
child online abuse.
**www.giggleweb.com** – a place where you can set up your own
family website.
**www.kidsmart.org.uk** – aimed at schools, this is a good course
on how to stay safe on the net.
**www.parentsonline.gov.uk** – a government site used to
promote the benefits of the Internet as an educational tool to
parents. Excellent for links.
**www.safekids.com** – a basic site that is a useful place to go for
links and resources if you're worried about your children coming
across something unsuitable on the Net.

## Disability and rare disorders

**www.cafamily.org.uk**                                                 UK

SUPPORT FOR FAMILIES
A charity that provides support and advice to parents of
children with a medical problem or disability. They have
information on over 1,000 rare syndromes and can often put
families in touch with others facing similar problems. See also
the Council for Disabled Children at **www.ncb.org.uk**

## Divorce

**www.itsnotyourfault.org**                                             UK

DIVORCE AND SEPARATION
A useful site with sections for parents, teens and children that
attempts to take some of the anguish and guilt out of divorce
and separation.

# Drugs and alcohol

### www.theantidrug.com US

TRUTH. THE ANTIDRUG
An outstanding site devoted to the fight against drugs with help
for parents and children alike. There's plenty of advice, articles
and general information and it's all written in an accessible
style, and in several languages.

### www.trashed.co.uk UK

TALK TO FRANK
The NHS's drug site has non-judgemental, factual information
on all the major recreational drugs with useful information on
what to do in an emergency. See also **www.ndh.org.uk** –
The National Drugs Helpline 0800 776600, and
**www.hit.org.uk** or **www.drugscope.org.uk**

## Dyslexia/dyspraxia

### www.bda-dyslexia.org.uk UK

BRITISH DYSLEXIA ASSOCIATION
A good starting point for anyone who thinks that their child
might be dyslexic. There is masses of information on dyslexia,
choosing a school, a list of local Dyslexia Associations where
you can get assessment and teaching, articles on the latest
research and educational materials for sale. There is also
information on adult dyslexia. For similar material visit
**www.dyslexia-inst.org.uk** who also offer testing and teaching
through their centres. If you're thinking of opting out and taking
the home education route go to **www.dyslexics.org.uk**

### www.dyspraxiafoundation.org.uk UK

DYSPRAXIA EXPLAINED
Information and practical help aimed at anyone who is coping
with a dyspraxic child including how to find your local support
group and up-to-date research news.

# Eating disorders

### www.edauk.com
UK

EATING DISORDERS ASSOCIATION
If you think you have a problem with eating then at this site you can get advice and information. It doesn't replace going to the doctor but it's a place to start. There are help lines – youth is 01603 765 050, others 01603 621 414.

## Health

### www.iemily.com
US

GIRL'S HEALTH
A massive A–Z listing of all the issues and problems you might face, it's easy to use and the information is straight to the point and often accompanied by articles relating to the subject. If you can't find what you need here try **www.prematuree.com** which is especially useful for older teenage girls. See also section on Health Advice page 200 and Women's Health on page 484.

## Law

### www.childrenslegalcentre.com
UK

FREE LEGAL HELP
A charity that provides free and confidential legal advice and an information service, covering all aspects of the law affecting children and young people. They can help provide advocates in disputes with the Local Education Authority and campaigns for children's rights in the UK and overseas. To keep in touch with policy changes relating to children and young people go to **www.childpolicy.org.uk3**

## Missing children

### www.missingkids.co.uk
UK

UK'S MISSING CHILDREN
This site is dedicated to reuniting children with their families, the details of those missing are based on police and home office data. You can search by town or date and there's also a section on those who've got back together.

*Also try:*
**www.missingpersons.org** – the missing persons helpline –
0500 700 700.
**www.salvationarmy.org.uk** – for their family tracing service.

# Racism

**www.britkid.org**                                           UK
### DEALING WITH RACISM
A game that shows how different ethnic groups live in the
Britain of today, full of interesting facts and information.
There's a serious side, which has background information on
dealing with racism, information on different races and their
religious beliefs.

# Safety

**www.childalert.co.uk**                                      UK

### CHILD SAFETY
This is about bringing up children in a safe environment;
there are tips, product reviews and a shop, stories, links and
masses of advice and information. Except for the shop,
the site is well-designed and it's easy to find things. See also
**www.yoursafechild.com**

**www.childcarseats.org.uk**                                  UK
### CAR SAFETY
All you need to know about buying, fitting and using child
car seats.

# Sex

P

*The following sites provide accessible, factual information. The sections
on Health, page 200, Men, page 256, Teens, page 406 and Women,
page 484, may also provide relevant information.*

**www.lovelife.uk.com** now **www.playingsafely.co.uk**       UK
### HERE TO ANSWER YOUR QUESTIONS
Great site that has lots of information on sex as well as games
and links to related sites. The emphasis is on safe sex and
AIDS prevention. See also the Terence Higgins Trust at
**www.tht.org.uk** this is the leading AIDS charity.

**www.likeitis.org.uk**                                    UK

TELLING IT LIKE IT IS
A really outstanding site from the Marie Stopes Institute giving good, straight information on all the major issues around sex and puberty that face teenagers today. The 'Cool or Fool' quiz is excellent and there's a 'Dear Doctor…' facility too.

**www.fpa.org.uk**                                         UK

FAMILY PLANNING ASSOCIATION
Straightforward and informative, you can find out where to get help and there's a good list of web links too. See also the British Pregnancy Advisory service at **www.bpas.org**

## Speech

**www.speechteach.co.uk**                                  UK

SPEECH THERAPY
Information, help and advice on what to do if your child has speech problems or communication difficulties. The site aims to provide a learning resource for parents and teachers alike.

## Stress and mental health

**www.rethink.org/at-ease**                                UK

YOUR MENTAL HEALTH
At-ease offers loads of good advice on how to deal with stress and is aimed specifically at young people. Go to the A–Z section which covers a large range of subjects from dealing with aggression to exam stress to how to become a volunteer to help others.

**www.isma.org.uk/exams.htm**                              UK

EXAM STRESS
Top tips on coping with exams from the International Stress Management Association.

# Party Organising

*In this new section you'll find all you need to organise the perfect party.*

## www.partydomain.co.uk

PARTY PARTY!!                                           UK

Probably the best of the party shop sites with a wide range of
fancy dress gear, lots of themed party ideas and options plus a
party calendar. Shopping is secure with lots of delivery options.

*See also:*
**www.charliecrow.co.uk** – a wide range of fancy dress costumes
primarily for kids parties.
**www.evite.com** – a US site where you can create your own
party invitations.
**www.justforfun.co.uk** – a good selection of party
products here.
**www.kids-party.com** – a great resource, find out all you need
to hold a kid's party in your area.
**www.partypieces.co.uk** – very experienced party suppliers with
a wide range of products and 48-hour delivery.
**www.partyzone.co.uk** – specialises in supplying gear and
goods for children's parties.
**www.printed4u.co.uk** – party invitations printed.

# Pets

*Here's a selection of web sites devoted to pets, shop and information
sites and specialists too.*

## www.mypetstop.com                                    UK

MULTINATIONAL PETS
Apparently the only multilingual web site about pets. It's superb
for information and health advice as well as links too. It has
sections devoted to each pet and animal and each is pretty
comprehensive.

*For other good online pet information, services and stores visit:*
**www.allaboutpets.org.uk** – excellent advice and care site from
the Blue Cross charity.
**www.bluepet.co.uk** – specialists in organic food for pets.
**www.lostpets.co.uk** – an informative site on what to do if you
lose your pet with a lost pet finder service.
**www.naturallypaws.com** – complementary medicine for pets.
**www.petpack.co.uk** – an attractive store, advice and care site
with a wide range of products.
**www.petpals.com** – at home pet care services.

**www.petplanet.co.uk** – good for the shop and up-to-the-minute news.
**www.petsathome.com** – a fairly basic site from this pet retailer.
**www.petsmiles.com** – a good directory site featuring some 35,000 companies.
**www.ukpets.co.uk** – a directory of pet shops and suppliers, plus advice and a magazine devoted to pets.

# Pet insurance

## www.pethealthcare.co.uk                                UK

PET INSURANCE
This is a good place to start looking for insurance to cover your vet's bill. It also has lots of good advice on how to look after pets and what to do when you first get a pet.

*See also:*
**www.animalfriends.co.uk** – an insurance company that devoted all profits to animal charities.
**www.petloversinsurance.co.uk** – cat and dog insurance.
**www.petplan.co.uk** – one of the largest pet insurers.

# Travel

## www.pets-on-holiday.com                                UK

UK HOLIDAYS WITH PETS
This site is devoted to finding holiday accommodation where your pets are always welcome simply arranged by region, easy. There's also a bookshop and a good set of links.

*See also:*
**www.defra.gov.uk/animalh/quarantine/index.htm** – animal quarantine and advice on overseas travel.
**www.preferredplaces.co.uk** – a holiday specialist with a good pets welcome section.

# Animal charities

## www.rspca.org                                          UK

THE RSPCA
News (some of which can be quite disturbing) and information on the work of the charity plus animal facts and details on how you can help. There's also a good kids' section. It's a good site but a bit tightly packed.

*Other charity sites:*

**www.aht.org.uk** – applying clinical and research techniques to help animals.

**www.animalrescue.org.uk** – fight animal pain and suffering.

**www.animalrescuers.co.uk** – a directory of centres and people who will help distressed animals.

**www.animalsanctuaries.co.uk** – index of charities and animal rescue centres.

**www.bluecross.org.uk** – excellent site with information, help and advice.

**www.pdsa.org.uk** – Peoples Dispensary for Sick Animals has a good looking site with details on how to look after pets and how you can help.

**www.petrescue.com** – home of the pet action league.

**www.giveusahome.co.uk**                                          UK

RE-HOMING A PET

A nice idea, a web site devoted to helping you save animals that need to be re-homed, it's got a large amount of information by region on shelters, vets and the animals themselves as well as entertainment for kids.

## TV-related

**www.channel4.com/petrescue**                                    UK

PET RESCUE

Details of the program plus information and links on animal charities and sites, there are also stories, games and chat. See also the excellent BBC web pages on pets which can be found at **www.bbc.co.uk/nature/animals/pets**

## Sites for different species

## Birds

**www.avianweb.com**                                              US

FOR BIRD ENTHUSIASTS

A massive site devoted to birds, it's especially good for information on parrots. There are sections on species, health and equipment as well as advice on looking after birds.

*See also:*
**www.birdcare.co.uk** – lots of articles and advice on avian health.
**www.parrot-rescue.co.uk** – excellent site devoted to rescuing and looking after birds that have out-grown their owners or need help.
**www.rspb.org.uk** – mainly wild birds but some good advice.

# Cats

**www.cats.org.uk**                                                          UK
HOME OF CAT PROTECTION
A well-designed and informative site, with advice on caring, re-homing, news and general advice, an archive of cat photos and competitions for the best. The online shop offers delivery in the UK but charges vary.

*See also:*
**www.catoutofthebag.com** – a wide range of cat-related products from a good-looking site, it also includes things like homewares and gifts.
**www.crazyforkitties.com** – nice site devoted to all things cat and kitty.
**www.fabcats.org** – a charity devoted to cat care.
**www.freddie-street.com** – fantastic and funny the story of the Freddie Street cats, there's some good information in there too.
**www.i-love-cats.com** – a directory of cat sites.
**www.moggies.co.uk** – home of the Online Cat Guide, not an easy site to use, but has exceptional links to pet sites.

# Dogs

**www.the-kennel-club.org.uk**                                           UK
DOGS OFFICIAL
The place to go for the official line on dogs and breeding with information on Crufts and links to related web sites, plus shop and tips on looking after your pooch.

*See also:*
**www.bugsie.co.uk** – yes, it's a mobile dog-washing service!
**www.canineworld.com** – an average site with some good links.
**www.canismajor.com/dog** – an American magazine site.
**www.dogmadshop.com** – good-looking doggie-oriented shop with lots of interesting products for you and your pooch.

**www.dogs-and-diets.com** – comprehensive nutritional
information for dogs.

**www.dogster.com** – yes, you can set up a website devoted to
your dog alone…

**www.howtoloveyourdog.com** – a children's guide to caring
for dogs.

**www.i-love-dogs.com** – a directory of web sites devoted
to dogs.

**www.woofwoofdirect.com** – daft sounding title but a very good
dog-related gift and accessory shop.

## www.ncdl.org.uk                                    UK

### THE DOG'S TRUST

Excellent web site featuring the charitable works of the Dog's
Trust (formerly the National Canine Defence League) the largest
charity of its type. Get advice on how to adopt a dog, tips on
looking after one and download doggie wallpaper. For Battersea
Dogs Home go to **www.dogshome.org** who have a well-
designed site.

# Fish

## www.ornamentalfish.org                              UK

### ORNAMENTAL AQUATIC TRADE ASSOCIATION

An excellent site beautifully designed and well executed.
Although much of it is aimed at the trade and commercial side,
there is a great deal of information for the hobbyist about
looking after and buying fish.

*See also:*

**www.aquariacentral.com** – a huge site with masses of
information on every aspect of looking after fish.

**www.fishlinkcentral.com** – a good directory site for information
on fish.

# Horses

## www.equiworld.net                                   UK

### GLOBAL EQUINE INFORMATION

Not the most helpful design but a directory, magazine and
advice centre in one, with incredible detail plus some fun stuff
too including video and audio interviews and footage, holidays
and the latest news. The shop consists of links to
specialist traders.

*See also:*

**www.equine-world.co.uk** – lots here too including classified ads, shopping and links.

**www.horseadvice.com** – a health-oriented site that supplies a huge amount of information.

## Rabbits and rodents

### http://www.rabbit.org                                                US

HOUSE RABBIT SOCIETY
It's all here, from feeding, breeding, behaviour, health advice and even info on house-training your rabbit. Has a nice kids' section and plenty of cute pictures.

*See also:*

**www.rabbitwelfare.co.uk** – lots of chat, advice and links from the Rabbit Welfare Association.

**www.rabbitworld.com** – a personal tribute to rabbits, which also has information on caring for your fluffy friend.

**www.caviesgalore.com** – information, forums, games and names.

**www.cavycapers.com** – a guinea pig haven on the web! A nice site too.

**www.gerbils.co.uk** – home of the National Gerbil Society.

**www.rodentfancy.com** – good all round site about the small creatures.

## Other pets

**http://exotic.pets.about.com** – comprehensive information and news stories.

**www.ameyzoo.co.uk** – a specialist exotic pet shop with fact sheets on how to look after them properly.

**www.animalsexoticandsmall.com** – an odd site and e-zine devoted to animal exotica.

**www.easyexotics.co.uk** – Attractive site covering exotic plants as well as pets, it aims to take the mystery out of looking after them, sections on tarantulas and arrow frogs.

**www.petreptiles.com** – comprehensive pet reptile information.

**www.ukreptiles.com** – an OK directory site for reptile enthusiasts, good for links.

# Photography

**www.photographyworld.co.uk**                                    UK

COMMUNITY OF PHOTOGRAPHERS
A very good portal site with links to all aspects of photography,
there's information on everything from models to lessons.

**www.rps.org**                                                   UK

THE ROYAL PHOTOGRAPHIC SOCIETY
Slowish site dedicated to the works of the RPS. There are
details on the latest exhibitions and the collection, you can
become a member and get the latest news about the world of
photography. Good for photographic history and links, while the
shop has some related merchandise.

**www.nmpft.org.uk**                                              UK

NATIONAL MUSEUM OF PHOTOGRAPHY, FILM AND
TELEVISION
Details of this Bradford museum via a high tech web site,
opening times and directions, what's on, education resources
and a very good museum guide.

**www.eastman.org**                                               US

THE INTERNATIONAL MUSEUM OF PHOTOGRAPHY
George Eastman founded Kodak and this New York-based
museum too. This site is comprehensive and amongst other
things, you can learn about the history of photography, visit the
photographic and film galleries, or obtain technical information.
Become a member and you're entitled to benefits such as free
admission and copies of their *Image* magazine.

P

**www.nationalgeographic.com/photography**                        US

*NATIONAL GEOGRAPHIC* MAGAZINE
Synonymous with great photography, this excellent site offers
much more. There are sections on travel, exhibitions, maps,
news, education, and for kids. In the photography section pick
up tips and techniques, follow their photographers' various
locations, read superb articles and accompanying shots in the
'Visions Galleries'. Good links to other photographic sites.

### www.life.com/Life                                    US

*LIFE* MAGAZINE
*Life* magazine, it's wonderfully nostalgic and still going strong.
There are several sections, features with great photos, excellent
articles, and an option to subscribe; however they could do
much more and it's a little frustrating to use.

### www.panoramas.dk                                DENMARK

PANORAMIC PHOTOGRAPHY
A great use of the Quicktime program, thousands of sites and
movies all devoted to or celebrating panoramic photography.

*See also:*
**www.photographymuseum.com** – odd site from the American
Museum of Photography.
**www.iphotocentral.com** – a dealer in old photographs.
**www.rleggat.com/photohistory** – the history of early
photography.

## Great photographers

### www.masters-of-photography.com                        US

ONLINE GALLERIES
A simple site with a superb array of galleries devoted to the real
masters of the art of photography – you can spend hours
browsing here.

*See also:*
**www.adamsgallery.com** – a great place to buy Ansel
Adams photos.
**www.davidbaileyphotography.com** – the official site with some
great shots to view.
**www.davidde.com/beaton.html** – a good celebration of Cecil
Beaton's work.

## Photo Libraries

### www.corbis.com                                        US

THE PLACE FOR PICTURES ON THE INTERNET
Another Microsoft product, this is probably the world's largest
online picture library. Use the pictures to enhance
presentations, web sites, screensavers, or to make e-cards
for friends.

*See also:*
**www.freefoto.com** – who offer the largest free image database.
**www.freeimages.co.uk** – 2,500 free quality pictures.
**www.webshots.com** – which is great for wallpaper and
screensavers.

# Photographic advice

### www.bjphoto.co.uk UK

THE BRITISH JOURNAL OF PHOTOGRAPHY
An online magazine with loads of material on photography.
Access their archive or visit picture galleries that contain work
from contemporary photographers, find out about careers in
photography and where to buy the best photographic gear.

### www.betterphoto.com UK

TAKE BETTER PICTURES
A very well laid out and comprehensive advice site for new and
experienced photographers with a buyer's guide and introductions
to and overviews of traditional and digital photography.

### www.photomentor.co.uk UK

SHARE YOUR KNOWLEDGE
A community site devoted to photography, here you can share
advice and photos, and also access information and reviews;
good for links too.

*See also:*
**www.photo.net** – an American site with lots of advice
and reviews.
**www.photobuzz.com** – the place to discuss digital photography.
**www.shortcourses.com** – all you need to know about
digital photography.

# Photography stores

### www.jessops.com UK

TAKE ADVICE TAKE GREAT PICTURES
Jessops are the largest photographic retailer in the UK and they
offer advice on most aspects of photography plus courses and
free software for their digital printing service. They do give you
an opportunity to go shopping for your camera and accessories,
of course.

*See also:*

**www.bestcameras.co.uk** – good range and a clutter free site. Recommended, delivery charges vary though.

**www.camerasdirect.co.uk** – well-designed store, delivery starts at £7.99.

**www.digitaltruth.com** – unusual design and but very comprehensive equipment shop and portal site.

**www.ffordes.com** – a good site offering used equipment along side the new.

**www.internetcamerasdirect.co.uk** – a good value independent store with reviews and a digital dictionary. Delivery costs vary according to weight.

**www.photoglossy.com** – specialists in paper, material and printing accessories.

**www.photographicdirect.co.uk** – more than just a shop, this site has been redesigned and is now much more interactive with forums chat and galleries.

# Equipment reviews

### www.whichcamera.co.uk                                    UK

FIND THE RIGHT CAMERA
Get advice on the best camera for you then use links to find your local dealer or to the manufacturer direct. The information is very good, there's a good search engine and camera finder service too.

*See also:*

**www.camerareview.com** – hundreds of cameras reviewed.
**www.dpreview.com** – digital photography cameras and equipment reviewed.

# Photo storage and development

### http://photos.fotango.com                                UK

ONLINE DEVELOPERS
Fotango will take your film and digitise it, then place your pictures on a secure site for you to view and select for printing the ones you like. The service is quick and easy to use; costs don't seem much different from the high street although single prints can be expensive.

*Other sites offering a similar service are:*
**www.ofoto.com** – another online photo album service.
Printing costs are low but delivery to UK starts at about £3.
**www.photobox.co.uk** – great design, probably the best for
digital photo storage.
**www.photoscrapbook.com** – an American site offering
good value.

## Miscellaneous photography sites

**www.getmapping.com**                                    UK
AERIAL PHOTOGRAPHS
Just type in your postcode and get a picture of your home taken
from above on a sunny day last year. There are lots of cost
options and you can also get a map to go with it.

**www.playingwithtime.org**                               US
TIME LAPSE PHOTOGRAPHY
This site is part of a larger photographic project, here you can
see incredible movies filmed with time lapse photography.
Excellent.

# *Price Checkers*

*Here's a good place to start any online shopping trip – a price
comparison site. There are many price checker sites, however, the sites
listed here allow you to check the prices for online stores across a much
wider range of merchandise than the usual books, music and film.*

**www.kelkoo.co.uk**                                  EUROPE

P

COMPARE PRICES BEFORE YOU BUY
Kelkoo is probably the best price-checking site with 20
categories in their shop directory including books, wine, white
goods, even cars and utility bills – they have links with eBay.
There are plenty of bargains to be had, in fact they keep
popping up on every page.

**www.checkaprice.com**                                        UK

CONSTANTLY CHECKING PRICES
Compare prices across nearly a huge range of products, from the
usual books to cars, holidays, mortgages and electrical goods.
If it can't do it for you, it patches you through to a site that can.

*Other good sites:*
**www.buy.co.uk** – excellent for the utilities – gas, water and
electrical as well as credit cards and mobile phones.
**www.dealtime.co.uk** – easy-to-use directory and price checker
covering a wide range of goods.
**www.pricechecker.co.uk** – straightforward site, also covers
flights and telephone tariffs.
**www.price-guide.co.uk** – a comprehensive offering including,
unusually food and wines.
**www.pricerunner.com** – a good all-rounder with a news section
giving the latest information on deals and technology updates.
**www.pricescan.com** – all the usual, plus watches, jewellery,
sports goods and office equipment – good store finder.
**www.price-search.net** – mainly computers and gadgets.
**www.pricewatch.co.uk** – good for computers and
personal finance.
**www.unravelit.com** – unravel your troubles and get the best
deal here. Good for utilities and finances.

# *Property*

*Every estate agent worth their salt has got a web site, and in theory
finding the house of your dreams has never been easier. These sites
have been designed to help you through the real life minefield.
For advice on building your own house got to page 231 in the
Home section.*

**www.upmystreet.com**                                        UK

FIND OUT ABOUT WHERE YOU WANT TO GO
Type in the postcode and up pops almost every statistic you
need to know about the area in question. Spooky, but
fascinating, it's a good guide featuring not only house prices,
but also schools, the local MP, local authority information, crime
and links to services. It also has a classified section and puts
you in touch with the nearest items to your area. See also
**www.hometrack.co.uk** which is a subscription service but
offers a huge amount of data about house prices and the area.

## www.landreg.gov.uk
UK

LAND REGISTRY

An OK site for information on house prices by region, you can also make inquiries about property and land values. Could be loads better.

## www.conveyancing-cms.co.uk
UK

CONVEYANCING MARKETING SERVICE

Conveyancing is a bit of a minefield if you're new to it, this site aims to help with advice and competitive quotes. See also **www.easier2move.com** which is nicely designed and very informative.

## www.reallymoving.com
UK

MAKING MOVING EASIER

A directory of sites and help for home buyers including mortgages, removal firms, surveyors, solicitors, van hire and home improvements. You can get online quotes on some services and there's good regional information. The property search is fast and has plenty to choose from.

*For more properties try these sites:*

**www.arla.co.uk** – home of the Association of Residential Letting Agents with lots of useful information.

**www.assertahome.com** – great all-rounder, excellent site with lots of advice, information, houses and associated services.

**www.beach-huts.co.uk** – great site, providing you want to buy or rent a beach hut.

**www.easier.co.uk** – free, no hassle advertising, also has a finance section.

**www.findaproperty.com** – over 86,000 properties listed, biased to the South East.

**www.flatmate.com** – find a flatmate from anywhere in the world.

**www.helpiammoving.com** – helpful directory of removal and storage companies with information and advice.

**www.heritage.co.uk** – covers listed buildings for sale only plus information on their upkeep.

**www.hol365.com** – really good site design and a massive range of services and properties from 6,000 estate agents.

**www.homelet.co.uk** – claim to take the risk out of renting by offering sound advice and insurances for both tenants and landlords – good design.

**www.houseweb.co.uk** – highly rated with comprehensive advice and thousands of properties for sale.

**www.itlhomesearch.com** – independent home search and advice site that also covers Spain and Ireland – rent or buy.

**www.knightfrank.com** – world-wide service, easy-to-use site.

**www.naea.co.uk** – National Association of Estate Agents with their code of conduct, links and the latest property news.

**www.propertyfinder.co.uk** – Britain's biggest house database.

**www.rightmove.com** – very clear information site with a good property search engine.

**www.smartnewhomes.com** – search engine dedicated to new homes.

**www.themovechannel.co.uk** – an okay portal site, each agent or property site gets a review and a link. Better than it looks at first glance.

**www.ukpad.com** – details of property auctions in the UK.

**www.ukpropertyshop.com** – claims to be the most comprehensive covering 3,000 towns in the UK.

**www.vebra.com** – above average property search engine, much faster than most.

## www.home-repo.org                                                    UK

HOME REPOSSESSION

A very useful and informative site that blows the lid off the goings on behind what happens when a house is repossessed and what you should do if you find yourself in arrears. It's assertive and entertaining too.

## www.landlordzone.co.uk                                              UK

RENTAL PROPERTY KNOWLEDGE

Very useful for landlords and tenants alike with the latest news available and lots of advice too, it's great for links though a bit advert heavy; it's easy to navigate.

# Property abroad

### www.french-property.com                                    UK

NO.1 FOR FRANCE
If you are fed up with the UK and want to move to France this
is the first port of call. They offer properties for rent or for sale
in all regions and can link you with other estate agents.

### www.spanish-property-online.com                            UK

MOVING TO SPAIN
Avoid all the pitfalls by stopping off for a browse at this
informative site that covers all you need to know about buying
property in Spain.

*See also:*
**www.fopdac.com** – home to the Federation of Overseas
Property Developers, a trade association site that has some
useful advice and contact information.
**www.french-property-news.com** – a poorly designed site,
but good advice and links.
**www.prestigeproperty.co.uk** – links with over 100 estate
agents in 20 countries.
**www.worldclasshomes.co.uk** – properties in Spain, Portugal,
France and Arizona...

P

# Radio

*You need a decent downloadable player such as RealPlayer or Windows Media Player before you start listening. The downside is that quality is sometimes affected by Net congestion although that's becoming less of a problem these days.*

**www.mediauk.com/directory**                                     UK

DIRECTORY OF RADIO STATIONS
Excellent site. You can search by station, presenter or by type, there's also background on the history of radio and articles on topics such as digital radio. The site also offers similar information on television and magazines.

*See also:*
**http://dir.yahoo.com/News_and_Media/Radio/** – Yahoo's list of over 900 stations and related sites.
**http://windowsmedia.com** – home to Microsoft's media listings, which is very comprehensive.
**www.comfm.com** – a French site with access to over 11,000 stations.
**www.live365.com** – good-looking site with thousands of radio stations to choose from and it's easy to customise to your tastes too.
**www.publicradiofan.com** – ugly site with thousands of stations listed but they are listed by time-zone so you should be able to find something you like playing at any one time.
**www.radio-locator.com** – a huge directory of radio, US oriented.
**www.shoutcast.com** – another huge selection using the Winamp player.
**www.spinner.com** – a virtual radio which comes with over 175 stations.
**www.virtualtuner.com** – tune in to a vast number of stations at this good looking site, the top 500 is interesting in itself.

R

## www.radioacademy.org UK

UK'S GATEWAY TO RADIO
Radio Academy is a charity that covers all things to do with radio including news, events and its advancement in education and information. It has a list of all UK stations including those that offer web casts. You get more from the site if you become a member.

## www.bbc.co.uk/radio UK

THE BEST OF THE BBC
Listen to the news and the latest hits while you work, just select the station you want. There's also information on each major station, as well as a comprehensive listing service. Some features such as football commentary on certain matches will be missing due to rights issues. Most of the stations have some level of interactivity, with Radio 1 being the best and most lively, you can also tap into their local stations and of course the World Service.

## www.virginradio.co.uk UK

VIRGIN ON AIR
Excellent, if slightly messy site, with lots of ads plus plenty of stuff about the station, its schedule and stars, there's also a good magazine with the latest music news. You can listen if you have Quicktime, Windows Media Player or RealPlayer.

*Other independent radio stations online are:*
**www.capitalfm.com** – Capital Radio.
**www.classicfm.com** – classical music and background information.
**www.coolfm.co.uk** – Northern Ireland's number one.
**www.galaxyfm.co.uk** – good range of dance music.
**www.heart1062.co.uk** – London's heart.
**www.jazzfm.com** – live broadcasts, cool site too.
**www.koko.com** – independent local radio stations from the Wirral south.
**www.lbc.co.uk** – the voice of London.
**www.resonancefm.com** – London-oriented arts station.
**www.studentradio.co.uk** – Internet Student Radio.
**www.wwfm.co.uk** – international, pop all-rounder.

R

# Railways

*These are sites aimed at the railway enthusiast. For information on trains and timetables see page 469.*

**www.nrm.org.uk**                                                    UK
> NATIONAL RAILWAY MUSEUM
> An excellent museum site packed with information and details on their collection, you can even take a virtual tour.
> See also Great Western's very informative museum site at
> **www.steam-museum.org.uk**

**http://ukhrail.uel.ac.uk**                                          UK
> HERITAGE RAILWAY ASSOCIATION
> This site offers an online guide to the entire heritage railway scene in the UK, including details of special events and operating days for all heritage railways with lots of links world-wide.

**www.narrow-gauge.co.uk**                                            UK
> NARROW GAUGE
> The new and improved Narrow Gauge Heaven (formerly Narrow Gauge on the web) steams in with latest news and a better photo gallery plus all the narrow gauge information you'll need. You can also contribute your own articles or just browse.

> *See also:*
> **www.drcm.org.uk** – good site on the Darlington Railway Museum.
> **www.gensheet.co.uk** – keep up to date with timetable changes and diversions.
> **www.heritagerailway.co.uk** – geared to selling the mag but plenty of links and some archive material.
> **www.pcrail.co.uk** – a rail enthusiast's dream, simulations of railway operations and journeys. The site is well designed and simulations cost around £33.
> **www.railcentre.co.uk** – the Stockton and Darlington railway.
> **www.railway-technology.com** – the latest industry news.
> **www.rpsi-online.org** – Ireland's Railway Preservation Society.
> **www.trainspotters.de** – a good site from a German rail fan.
> **www.trainweb.org** – a directory of train and railway related sites.
> **www.vintagetrains.co.uk** – home of the Birmingham Railway Museum.

R

# Reference and Encyclopaedia Sites

*If you are stuck with your homework or want an answer to any question, then this is where the Internet really comes into its own. With these sites you are bound to find what you are looking for. For schoolwork also refer to the Education section, page 99.*

## www.refdesk.com
US

### THE BEST SINGLE SOURCE FOR FACTS

Singled out for its sheer size and scope, this site offers information and links to just about anything. Its mission is 'only about indexing quality Internet sites and assisting visitors in navigating these sites'. It's won numerous awards and it never fails to impress.

## www.knowuk.co.uk
UK

### ALL ABOUT BRITAIN

A subscription service which offers a massive amount of data about the UK from the arts to the civil service, education, government, law, travel and sport. Although most of the information can be accessed through separate sites, the advantage here is that you only need the one. Prices aren't listed on the site but you can contact them for a free trial.

## www.about.com
US

### IT'S ABOUT INFORMATION

A superb resource, easy to navigate and great for beginners learning to search for information, experts help you to find what you need every step of the way. It offers information on a wide range of topics from the arts and sciences to shopping.

## www.ipl.org
US

R

### THE INTERNET PUBLIC LIBRARY

Another excellent resource, there are articles on a vast range of subjects, its particularly good on literary criticism. Almost every country and its literature is covered. If there isn't anything at the library, there is invariably a link to take you to an alternative web site. It also has sections for young people.

*See also:*
**www.ibiblio.org** – which holds a huge collection of textual, audio and software resources.
**www.libraryspot.com** – which is similar in scope to IPL but has a more literary emphasis and has an entertaining trivia section for those obsessed by top tens and useless facts.
**www.questia.com** – claims to be the biggest online library with over 48,000 books and almost 400,000 articles. Excellent search facility.

## www.theanswerbank.co.uk                                UK

### QUESTIONS ANSWERED
Just go to any one of the listed categories and type in your question, you'll get a list of results; articles and links relating to your query. Often some results returned are quite odd so you have to be quite specific, it may be better to use a search engine such as **www.ask.co.uk**

## www.homeworkelephant.co.uk                             UK

### LET THE ELEPHANT HELP WITH HOMEWORK
A resource with some 5,000 links and resources aimed at helping students achieve great results. There's help with specific subjects, hints and tips, help for parents and teachers. It's constantly being updated, so worth checking regularly.

*See also:*
**www.homeworkhigh.co.uk** – Channel 4's excellent homework help site.
**www.kidsclick.org** – more than 600 topics and subjects covered.

# Encyclopaedias

## http://encarta.msn.com                                 US

### THE ENCARTA ENCYCLOPAEDIA
Even though the complete thing is only available to buy, there is access to thousands of articles, maps and reference notes via the concise version. It's fast and easy to use, though navigating it is a bit of a pain.

*Other useful encyclopaedias:*
**http://encyclozine.com** – wide range of topics covered plus good use of games, quizzes and trivia.

**http://i-cias.com/e.o/index.htm** – Encyclopaedia of the Orient – for North Africa and the Middle East.

**http://plato.stanford.edu** – Stanford Encyclopaedia of philosophy.

**www.babloo.com** – interactive encyclopaedia aimed at kids.

**www.bartleby.com** – one of the best. It offers access to a huge amount of reference work, but also fiction, verse and narrative non-fiction, largely with an American bias.

**www.eb.com** – Encyclopaedia Britannica for $9.95 per month.

**www.encyberpedia.com** – some 500 links to reference sites.

**www.encyclopedia.com** – the most comprehensive free encyclopaedia on the net, nice design too.

**www.highbeam.com** – outstanding site with access to huge amounts of data, from newswires to books, maps and images. You have to subscribe though ($19.95 per month) to get full access to the information although you can preview texts for free.

**www.infoplease.com** – the biggest collection of almanacs, plus an encyclopædia and an atlas.

**www.si.edu/resource** – encyclopaedia and links to the massive resources of the Smithsonian.

**www.spartacus.schoolnet.co.uk** – Spartacus Encyclopaedia is excellent for history homework.

**www.utm.edu/research/iep** – the Internet Encyclopaedia of Philosophy.

**www.wsu.edu/DrUniverse** – ask Dr Universe a question, any question…

# Specialist reference sites

## Classics and Literature

**www.eserver.org**                                                         US

THE ENGLISH SERVER
A much-improved humanities site, which provides a vast amount of resource data about almost every cultural topic, there are some 32,000 texts, articles and essays available on subjects from the arts, fiction through to web design.

**http://classics.mit.edu**                                                 US

THE INTERNET CLASSICS ARCHIVE
An excellent site for researching into the classics, it's easy to use and fast, with more than enough information for homework whatever the level. See also the excellent **www.bibliomania.com** for a wider range of resource materials.

### www.perseus.tufts.edu
US

PERSEUS DIGITAL LIBRARY
An excellent source of data for ancient Classics and Mythology,
history and early science. It also offers most of Shakespeare
and Marlowe and, although it concentrates largely on pre-
1600, it's ever expanding.

*See also:*
**www.archive.org** – An excellent resource in the making,
the 'Wayback Machine' is fun though it has a serious side
– it catalogues old sites so that they may never be lost.
**www.mythweb.com** – an enjoyable and informative site
devoted to Greek Mythology.
**www.pantheon.org** – which contains over 6,000 definitions
covering mythology, legends and folklore.

## Dictionaries and words

*For information on grammer pronounciation, plain English and
learning English, see the English Usage section on page 111.*

### www.askoxford.com
UK

ASK OXFORD UNIVERSITY
A pretty decent effort at making a dry subject interesting, you
can ask an expert, get advice on how to improve your writing
and, of course, use the famous dictionary and thesaurus.
See also **www.oed.com** where you can find the Oxford English
Dictionary, which is available by subscription.

### www.cup.cam.ac.uk/elt/dictionary
UK

CAMBRIDGE UNIVERSITY
This site has five dictionaries including English, American English,
Idioms, Phrasal Verbs and a Learner's dictionary – all free.

### www.onelook.com
US

DICTIONARY HEAVEN
Onelook claim to offer access to 966 dictionaries and over 6
million words, at a fast, user-friendly site, it also offers a price
checking service for online shopping.

*See also:*
**www.allwords.com** – a well categorised portal site on
everything to do with words, whether you want help with
crosswords or translation.

**www.dictionary.com** – here you can play word games as an added feature.

**www.quinion.com/words** – International English from a British point of view, new words and phrases analysed.

**www.wordorigins.org** – the origins explained to some 400 words and phrases.

**www.wordspy.com** – the latest on how words are being used and new words.

**www.yourdictionary.com** – very comprehensive, the last word in words, apparently.

## www.thesaurus.com
UK

### IF YOU CAN'T FIND THE WORD
Based on Roget's Thesaurus, this site will enable you to find alternative words, useful but not worth turning your PC on for in place of the book. The site is related to **www.dictionary.com** and has several other facilities including translation into eleven languages.

## www.visualthesaurus.com
US

### THE VISUAL THESAURUS
If you get bored looking up words or looking for alternative meanings for words in the usual way, then check out the Visual Thesaurus. It's fun to use if a bit weird, unfortunately, it now requires a subscription after the free trial.

*Other word related sites:*
**http://phrases.shu.ac.uk** – check out the meanings of over 2,000 phrases and sayings.

**www.identifont.com** – identify any font and find one that you like, also has information on the many different types available.

**www.rhymezone.com** – type in a word, up pops all those that rhyme with it.

**www.word-detective.com** – a magazine devoted to words and wordplay.

# Languages

## http://dictionaries.travlang.com
US

### FOREIGN LANGUAGE DICTIONARIES
After scrolling through the adverts, you'll find 16 language dictionaries on this site, just select the dictionary you want, and then type in the word or sentence to be translated – it couldn't be simpler. Originally aimed at the traveller, but it's very useful in this context.

*See also:*
**http://babelfish.altavista.com/tr** – excellent site where you can convert sentences of up to 150 words into many languages.
**www.ilovelanguages.com** – a directory and portal site devoted to languages.
**www.langtolang.com** – you can translate words in up to seven languages, you can even download on to your mobile, and there are quizzes to play too.

## www.peevish.co.uk/slang UK

DICTIONARY OF SLANG
A comprehensive dictionary of English slang as used in the UK, with good articles and search facility.

## www.acronymfinder.com US

WHAT DO THOSE INITIALS STAND FOR?
If you don't know your MP from your MP3 here's where to go, with over 150,000 acronyms you should find what you're looking for.

## www.symbols.com US

WHAT DOES THAT SYMBOL MEAN?
Here you can find the meaning of over 4,500 symbols, with articles on their history.

## www.techweb.com US

THE TECHNOLOGY DICTIONARY
Get the latest business and technology news plus an excellent technology encyclopaedia. For a dictionary that specialises in jargon and Internet terms only go to either **www.jargon.net** or **www.netdictionary.com** for enlightenment.

## Maths, numbers and statistics

## www.maths-help.co.uk UK

E-MAIL YOUR MATHS PROBLEMS
Send your queries to maths-help and they'll e-mail you back the answers in a couple of days. You can also visit the knowledge bank to see past queries and answers. See also www.mathacademy.com for a more bizarre view of maths and also the well put together **www.easymaths.com** which is much more conventional.

**http://www.tractorz.com/Zimmer/Other/metriccalc.htm**   US
>    CONVERSION CHART
>    Simply a very useful conversion device for the metric and
>    imperial systems, covering length, temperature, weight, volume,
>    distance and speed.

**www.ntu.edu.sg/Library/Collections/Databases/**   SINGAPORE
>    STATISTICS AND MORE STATISTICS
>    Free information and statistics about national economies,
>    not that easy to use at first, but it's all there.

>    *See also:*
>    **www.ameristat.org** – all you need on the US from the
>    Population Reference Bureau. Try their main site too at
>    **www.prb.org** which holds masses of data on the world as well
>    as the US.
>    **www.cia.gov/cia/publications/factbook** – the CIA's famous
>    fact book.
>    **www.citypopulation.de** – a really impressive site with a world
>    population database including maps and flags.
>    **www.geohive.com/index.html** – population statistics combined
>    with information on other key economic factors.
>    **www.google.com/help/features.html#calculator** – this link
>    takes you to Google's very useful calculator function.
>    **www.population.com** – which has a huge amount of data
>    and information.
>    **www.statistics.gov.uk** – great for statistics on the UK.

## Atlases and geography

**www.nationmaster.com**   US
>    WORLD STATS
>    A well-designed site excellent for comparative statistics on
>    countries and people, the great benefit to this one is that it also
>    includes access to a good encyclopedia too.

**www.atlapedia.com**   US
>    THE WORLD IN BOTH PICTURES AND NUMBERS
>    Contains full colour political and physical maps of the world
>    with statistics and very detailed information on each country.
>    It can be very slow, so you need patience, but the end results
>    are worth it.

**www.geographyiq.com**                                         US

> THE WORLD LISTED
> A great site covering all the information you'd expect. List freaks
> will love the rankings pages, they cover everything from largest
> to oldest to richest. Great for homework.
>
> *See also:*
> **http://plasma.nationalgeographic.com/mapmachine** – home of
> the National Geographic's Map Machine where you can zoom
> in to any part of the world.
> **www.plcmc.org/forkids/mow** – where you can find depicted all
> the flags of the world.
> **www.worldatlas.com** – a pretty comprehensive world atlas
> and gazetteer.

# Religion

*In this section we've attempted to list sites that are of interest and try
to explain the philosophy of the religions rather than the opinions of
those who preach.*

**www.omsakthi.org/religions.html**                             US

> RELIGION WORLD-WIDE
> This site provides a clear description of each world religion
> including values and basic beliefs with links to books on
> each one. See also the World Religion Gateway at
> **www.academicinfo.net/religindex.html** and
> **www.adherents.com** who offer statistics on some 4,000
> religions and religious bodies.
>
> *Key religious sites in alphabetical order:*
> **http://buddhanet.net** – the world-wide Buddhist information
> and education network. A huge site with, one would guess,
> everything you need to know.
> **http://shamash.org/trb/judaism.html** – a good overview of
> Judaism plus lots of links.
> **www.al-islam.org** – informative site with good information
> and links.
> **www.anglicancommunion.org** – the world-wide Anglican
> communion.
> **www.anglicansonline.org** – a huge resource site devoted to
> Anglicanism with over 10,000 links.

**www.buddhanet.net** – useful links from this non-profit organisation.

**www.catholic.net** – a slick site devoted to the Catholic religion, here you'll find everything on the religion, and it seems very comprehensive.

**www.chiefrabbi.org** – the official site of the Chief Rabbi.

**www.ciolek.com/wwwvl-Buddhism.html** – the Buddhist studies virtual library.

**www.cofe.anglican.org** – home of the Church of England.

**www.druidnetwork.org** – an overview of the Druid religion with links and database.

**www.hindu.org** – a good overview of this complex religion with excellent directory.

**www.islamicity.com** – a newsy site aimed at explaining Islam and to create more awareness of the religion.

**www.islamonline.net** – very comprehensive and interesting news and Islamic information site.

**www.islamworld.net** – a good overview of Islam.

**www.jewfaq.org** – an encyclopaedia devoted to Judaism.

**www.methodist.org.uk** – the official line in Methodism.

**www.newadvent.org/cathen** – the Catholic encyclopaedia.

**www.panthkhalsa.org** – information on the Sikh nation.

**www.pres-outlook.com** – a magazine site covering all forms of Presbyterianism US-orientated.

**www.quaker.org.uk** – information on what it is to be a Quaker.

**www.ritualwell.org** – ceremonies for Jewish living.

**www.russian-orthodox-church.org.ru/en.htm** – the home site with the latest news.

**www.salaam.co.uk** – wide ranging site covering all aspects of Islamic culture.

**www.salvationarmy.org.uk** – excellent site with lots of background information.

**www.scientology.org.uk** – comprehensive site on Scientology and what it is.

**www.ship-of-fools.com** – excellent radical Christian magazine.

**www.singhsabha.com** – understanding the religious and philosophical teachings of Sikhism.

**www.thetablet.co.uk** – a well-designed Catholic news site.

**www.usc.edu/dept/msa/reference/glossary.html** – a glossary of Islamic terms and concepts.

**www.vatican.va** – the official site of the Vatican, slow but informative.

R

*More general information sites about religion:*

**http://about.com/religion** – About has an excellent overview of the major religions and some minor ones, it also offers a newsletter and covers areas such as spirituality too.

**http://religion.rutgers.edu/vri/index.html** – Rutgers University has made available a library of information on the world's religions.

**www.bbc.co.uk/religion** – the BBC's excellent site on religion and ethics.

**www.beliefnet.com** – a wide ranging and multi-faith approach to spirituality.

**www.divinedigest.com** – a good overview of the major religions.

**www.religioustolerance.org** – an organisation devoted to religions co-operating with each other, it has good information on all major faiths.

R

# Science

*The Internet was originally created by a group of scientists who wanted faster, more efficient communication. Today, scientists around the world use the Net to compare data and collaborate. In addition, the non-scientist has access to the wonders of science in a way that's never been possible before, and as for homework – well now it's a doddle.*

## Pure science

**www.scirus.com**                                                        US

> SCIENCE SEARCH
> A straightforward and easy to use search engine devoted to scientific information only.

**www.royalsoc.ac.uk**                                                    UK

> THE ROYAL SOCIETY
> An attractive site where you can learn all about the workings of the society, how to get grants and what events they are running. They've improved the content to include more links and more interactivity.

**www.scicentral.com**                                                    US

> LATEST SCIENCE NEWS
> Apart from being a very good portal, this site offers the latest news in the major categories of science, plus a searchable database of articles gleaned from papers and magazines around the world.

**http://scienceworld.wolfram.com**                                       US

> PURE SCIENCE EXPLAINED
> Eric Weisstein's World of Science contains encyclopaedias and detailed information written in accessible language on astronomy, scientific biography, chemistry, maths and physics. The design is easy on the eye and the site is logical to use. The site isn't finished yet so it can only get better. Can also be accessed on **www.treasure-troves.com**

S

*See also:*

**www.bottomquark.com** – a messy site with the latest news and discussion.

**www.firstscience.com** – which is slightly more accessible and colourful.

**www.treasure-troves.com** – an eccentric site on various aspects of science, quite fun in places too

# Magazines

### www.newscientist.com                                                    US

*NEW SCIENTIST* MAGAZINE

Much better than the usual online magazines because of its creative use of archive material which is simultaneously fun and serious. It's easy to search the site or browse through back features – the 'Even More Bizarre' bit is particularly entertaining. Unfortunately, you now need to be a member to get access to the archive. For a more traditional science magazine site go to Popular Science at **www.popsci.com** which is great for information on the latest gadgets.

### www.sciencemag.org                                                      US

*SCIENCE* MAGAZINE

A serious overview of the current science scene with articles covering everything from global warming to how owls find their prey. The tone isn't so heavy that a non-scientist can't follow it and there are plenty of links too. You need to register to get the best out of it.

# Chemistry

### www.webelements.com                                                     US

THE PERIODIC TABLE

So you don't know your halides from your fluorides, with this interactive depiction you can find out. Just click on the element and you get basic details plus an audio description, all in all a great teaching aid.

### www.chemsoc.org                                                         UK

CHEMICAL SOCIETY

A really creative site that covers not only industry issues, but also educational ones too, all in a very entertaining fashion. The timeline is especially well done and there is a very useful links page too.

# Innovation, invention and technology

## www.innovations.co.uk                                           UK

GADGETS GALORE
Impress your friends with your knowledge of the newest
gadgets, innovations or what's likely to be the next big thing.
Innovations is well established and has one of the best online
stores with a wide range. There's a reward scheme with
delivery costs being a flat £3.95, free over £75. See also
**www.streettech.com** who specialise in the latest hardware
and also **www.firebox.com** who have a good selection.

## www.21stcentury.co.uk                                          UK

YOUR PORTAL TO THE FUTURE
A stylish site that gives an overview of the latest technology
put over in an entertaining way. Whether you're using it for
homework or just for a browse, it's useful and interesting, they
have 12 categories from cars through to humour, people and
technology, they even cover fashion.

## www.nesta.org.uk                                                UK

THE CREATIVE INVENTOR'S HANDBOOK
The National Endowment for Science Technology not only helps
inventors get their ideas off the ground with support and
guidance, but also encourages creativity and innovation.
They'll also inspire you, as a visit to this well-designed site will
show. See also the creatively designed **www.inventorlink.co.uk**

## www.invent.org                                                  US

THE INVENTOR HALL OF FAME
This outstanding and beautifully designed site is sponsored
by Hewlett Packard and features advice on how to patent
inventions and details of those who have been inducted into the
Hall of Fame. If for no other reason, just go to appreciate the
web site design.

S

# Popular science

### www.sciencemuseum.org.uk UK

THE SCIENCE MUSEUM

An excellent site detailing the major attractions at the museum with 3-D graphics and features on exhibitions and forthcoming attractions, you can also shop and browse the galleries.

You can't help feeling they could do more though. See also **www.exploratorium.edu** a similar but more child friendly site by an American museum.

### www.discovery.com US

THE DISCOVERY CHANNEL

A superb site for science and nature lovers, it's inspiring as well as educational. Order the weekly newsletter, get information on the latest discoveries as well as features on pets, space, travel, lifestyle and school. The 'Discovery Kids' section is very good with lots going on.

### www.madsci.org US

THE LAB THAT NEVER SLEEPS

A site that successfully combines science with fun, you can ask a question of a mad scientist, browse the links list or check out the archives in the library.

### www.howstuffworks.com US

HOW STUFF REALLY WORKS

An outstanding and popular site, it's easy to use and truly fascinating, there are sections ranging from the obvious like engines and technology, through to food and the weather. The current top ten section features the latest answers to the questions of the day. It's written in a very concise, clear style with lots of cross-referencing. See also the less accessible **http://howthingswork.virginia.edu**

### www.si.edu/science_and_technology US

SMITHSONIAN SCIENCE AND TECHNOLOGY

Another excellent set of pages from the outstanding Smithsonian site, these cover everything from biology to flight and there are some really well-written and interesting articles and sections too.

## www.extremescience.com

ULTIMATE SCIENCE EXPERIENCE

Not sure that it really lives up to its billing, but it is a really entertaining site with lots of useful and useless facts to bamboozle your brain. Features include a time portal where you can learn the effects of relativity, and other sections on weather, maps, technology, nature and the Earth. It uses the word 'cool' a lot.

## www.dangerouslaboratories.org

DON'T DO IT YOURSELF

Science with a smile, here you get details of various 'experiments' in a range of scientific fields. It all looks very amateur and fun as well as educational too.

## www.voltnet.com

DON'T TRY THIS AT HOME!

This is literally a high voltage site devoted to electricity and how it works. While there is a serious side, by far the best bit is where they 'stress test' all sorts of objects by sending 20,000 volts through them.

## www.science-frontiers.com

SCIENTIFIC ANOMALIES

*Science Frontiers* is a bimonthly newsletter providing digests of reports that describe scientific anomalies – 'those observations and facts that challenge prevailing scientific paradigms'. There's a massive archive of the weird and wonderful, it takes patience but there are some real gems.

## www.world-mysteries.com

WEIRD SCIENCE

All the mysteries and unexplained phenomena are here, explained and illustrated in a fairly unbiased way. It makes for an interesting browse.

## www.improbable.com

THE IG NOBLE AWARDS

These awards are for those inventors whose project initially makes others laugh, then makes them think about the science behind it. To quote the site, they 'celebrate the unusual and honour the imaginative'. The site also offers much in the way of unusual scientific gems.

US

US

US

US

US

UK

S

**http://whyfiles.org**                                             US
> SCIENCE BEHIND THE NEWS
> If you've ever wondered why things happen and what's the real
> story behind what they tell you in the papers, then a visit here
> will be rewarding. With in-depth studies and brief overviews,
> Why Files is easy to follow and you'll get the latest news too.

## Practical science and science for children

**www.doscience.com**                                              US
> EXPERIMENTS FUN AND SERIOUS
> A slightly messy but entertaining site that has a number of
> experiments to try both at home and outside. It's informative
> and most of the experiments seem easy to do.

**www.planet-science.com**                                         US
> FAST FORWARD TO THE FUTURE
> A visually gratifying site with lots to offer by way of helping
> children (and adults for that matter) to learn about science in
> an interactive and entertaining way.

> *See also:*
> **http://insideout.rigb.org** – a good, if a little dull, educational
> e-zine from the Royal Institute.
> **www.amasci.com** – for the science hobbyist.
> **www.funsci.com** – a serious site with many experiments to try,
> both hard and easy.
> **www.tryscience.org** – aimed at children, with a few
> experiments.

# *Science Fiction and Fantasy*

*A new section and probably a belated one, SF deserves a section to
itself, many top films and books are SF-based or related in some way,
so here's a few of the massive number of sites that are around. A big
vote of thanks should go to George Walkley from Ottakars for his help
with this section.*

S

# Directories and reviews

## www.thealienonline.net                                        UK

THE ALIEN ONLINE
Great for SF news, reviews and information, with opinionated
comments on books, films, television, comics and games from
some of SF's biggest names, and links to a host of websites.

*See also:*
**www.feministsf.org** – comprehensive offering on the role of
women in SF.
**www.locusmag.com** – the online version of US SF magazine
*Locus*. Dull but authoritative.
**www.scifisource.com** – a directory of all things SF, not pretty or
easy to navigate but it seems comprehensive.
**www.sfrt.com** – good for reviews, links and forums.
**www.sfsite.com** – the dated design doesn't detract from the fact
that this is one of the most comprehensive review sites you can
find; it's quite dense so needs time to digest.

# Awards and organisations

## www.sfwa.org                                                  US

SCIENCE FICTION WRITERS OF AMERICA
A helpful and informative site from the SFWA including details
of their prestigious Nebula awards. If truth were told it's not a
great site but the links and writing advice are good.

*See also:*
**www.appomattox.demon.co.uk/acca** – home of the UK's
Arthur C. Clarke Awards.
**www.asfa-art.org** – the Association of Sci Fi and Fantasy Artists
with an index of artists and gallery.
**www.bsfa.co.uk** – this chatty site represents the British Science
Fiction Association.
**www.wsfs.org** – the World Science Fiction Society, home of the
Hugo awards and with details of the World Science Fiction
Convention.

S

# TV and film

### www.sciflicks.com                                                      US

SF FILM REVIEW
A comprehensive listing of SF films with reviews, links,
descriptions, cast listing and so on. There's plenty of detail and
there is also information on forthcoming movies.

### www.scifi.com                                                          US

SCIFI.COM
An excellent site from the Sci Fi Channel with a very strong
emphasis on film and television, although it also includes
books, games and other products. It's beautifully designed,
easy to navigate, and there is a wealth of extra features,
including weekly newsletters.

### www.sfon.tv                                                            UK

SF ON TV
A very good site featuring everything SF on television from the
famous and obscure, Dr Sci Fi will even attempt to answer your
SF questions. There's also a good movie review section.

*See also:*
**www.bbc.co.uk/cult** – the BBC's cult television page includes
all the favourites.
**www.greatlink.org** – a UK-oriented site devoted to all
things Trek.
**www.sadgeezer.com** – great for fans of Sci Fi cult TV, though
pretty difficult to navigate, it has plenty of other SF resources
too; you should be aware that it is possible to access some
adult-oriented content.
**www.startrek.com** – everything you need to know about Star
Trek and its spin-off series.
**www.starwars.com** – outstanding official Star Wars site.

# SF writing

### http://isfdb.tamu.edu/sfdbase.html                                     US

INTERNET SPECULATIVE FICTION DATABASE
This excellent resource is an encyclopaedic guide to authors of
'speculative fiction', which includes every SF writer you could
think of. The trouble is that it looks more like a library catalogue
than a modern web site.

*See also:*
**www.fantasticmetropolis.com** – this good-looking and acclaimed site is dedicated to 'new wave' SF authors, it includes fiction, essays, interviews, reviews and more. It also has an excellent links section.
**www.infinityplus.co.uk** – original fiction and non-fiction by many top names in SF.
**www.sfwa.org** – Science Fiction Writers of America.
**www.sfnovelist.com** – a writing group who believe in SF based on hard science, some good short stories, but you need to be a member really.
**www.sff.net** – somewhere amongst the commercial bits there's a really good SF web site, you just have to be patient and sign up.

# SF writers

### www.lordoftherings.net                                         US

LORD OF THE RINGS
Slick on the movie trilogy, including information on the films, interviews, picture galleries, trailers and other downloads. Best accessed on broadband. See also **www.tolkien.co.uk** which is home to the official UK website from Tolkien's publishers, including a biography, his books, artwork, downloads and other information. Ordering facility through Amazon.

*Other key authors:*
Clive Barker – **www.clivebarker.com**
Terry Brooks – **www.terrybrooks.net**
Katherine Kerr – **www.deverry.com**
Stephen King – **www.stephenking.com**
George R.R. Martin – **www.georgerrmartin.com**
Philip Pullman – **www.philip-pullman.com**
Tad Williams – **www.tadwilliams.com**

*Below is a list of key SF publishers:*
**www.2000adonline.com** – home to the venerable British comic, featuring Judge Dredd.
**www.marvel.com** – great interactive site from Marvel Comics with all their major characters suitably involved.
**www.orbitbooks.co.uk** – home of authors such as Robert Jordan and Iain Banks, it's an attractive, frequently updated site with author pages, new releases, sample chapters, a monthly e-mail newsletter and exclusive offers.

S

**www.titanbooks.com** – the UK's largest publisher of graphic novels – also features information on their range of film and TV tie-ins.

**www.voyager-books.com** – home of HarperCollins's SF publishing. It's a classy-looking site, with author profiles, news, new titles, sample chapters, interactive features and extras such as downloadable screensavers.

# Search Engines

*The best way to find what you want from the Internet is to use a search engine. Even the best don't cover anywhere near the of available web sites; so if you can't find what you want from one, try another. These are the best and most user friendly. For children's search engines see page 82.*

### www.searchenginewatch.com                         US

A GUIDE TO SEARCHING

This site rates and assesses all the search engines and it's a useful starting point if you're looking for a good or specific search facility. There's a newsletter and statistical analysis plus strategies on how to make the perfect search. See also **www.searchengineshowdown.com** who do much the same thing but it's less comprehensive.

### www.google.co.uk                                   US

BRINGING ORDER TO THE WEB

Google is a massive success story and is one of the most useful sites around. Apart from the simple search facility it also has a host of other features including a directory, image search, calculator, translation tools and many specialist research facilities; you can even access it via a mobile. If you want to get the best out of Google then pay a visit to the non-affiliated but very helpful **www.googleguide.com** You may also want to try one of our favourites, **www.teoma.co.uk** for general searches, it's more focused and you can refine more easily.

S

## www.ask.co.uk                                            US

### ASK JEEVES
Just type in your question and the famous old butler will come
back with the answer. It may be a bit gimmicky but works very
well, it's great for beginners and reliable for old hands too.
See also **www.ajkids.com** which is the child-oriented version.

## www.mamma.com                                            US

### THE MOTHER OF ALL SEARCH ENGINES
Mamma claim to have technology enabling them to search the
major search engines thoroughly and get the most pertinent
results to your query – it's fast too, your query comes back
with the answer and the search engine it came from.

*See also:*
**http://turbo10.com** – claims to search the bits of the Internet
where the major search engines don't go, this is one of the
most impressive results wise. A star of the future?
**www.37.com** – a bit of a mess but can search 37 other search
engines in one go.
**www.ungoogle.com** – searches many of the major search
engines and is good for when 'Google lets you down'.
**www.clusteredhits.com** – clutter free and easy to use, US
oriented in its results.
**www.metacrawler.com** – uses similar technology to Mamma
and is a popular choice.

## www.vivisimo.com                                         US

### CLUSTERING TECHNOLOGY
With Vivisimo instead of the usual list, you get your search
results back categorised by subject, or clustered. It makes for
easy researching and is one of the three search engines I most
use. I can't wait for a UK-oriented version.

## http://eurekster.com                                     US

### SEARCHING WITH FRIENDS
Here you get the usual search facility with clustered results but
you can also sign up with a group of friends, then when one of
them does the same search your preferred result will appear
higher up their list of results. It's excellent if you share a
particular hobby or interest.

**www.lii.org**                                                              US

THE LIBRARIANS INDEX TO THE INTERNET
This is a search engine with a difference in that all the source material has been selected and evaluated by librarians specifically for their use in public libraries. This doesn't stop you using it though, and it is very good for obscure searches and research – like putting together a web site guide, for example.

**www.dmoz.org**                                                    WORLD-WIDE

THE OPEN DIRECTORY PROJECT
The goal is to produce the most comprehensive directory of the web by relying on an army (some 62,000) of volunteer editors, and if you want to get involved it's easy to sign yourself up. If it can't help with your query it puts you through to one of the mainstream search engines.

*Finding the search engine that suits you is a matter of personal requirements and taste, here are some other very good, tried and trusted ones:*

**http://uk.altavista.com** – limited but very efficient.
**http://whittlebit.com** – the idea is that you whittle down your search until you find the site you want; cumbersome in practise.
**www.alltheweb.com** – no frills, similar to Google, becoming very popular.
**www.bbc.co.uk** – a heavily advertised and new search engine that is simple to use.
**www.completeplanet.com** – chooses from over 100,000 searchable databases.
**www.copernic.com** – download a free search program.
**www.dogpile.com** – straightforward and no mess.
**www.hotbot.com** – good for shopping and entertainment.
**www.infoplease.com** – good for homework.
**www.invisibleweb.com** – a pretty OK directory and search engine.
**www.iwon.com** – US site that's great for prizes and shopping.
**www.kidtastic.com** – safe search for kids.
**www.lifestyle.co.uk** – a massive directory of specially selected sites.
**www.looksmart.com** – good business-oriented site.
**www.lycos.co.uk** – easy to use and popular, good for highlighting offers.
**www.msn.co.uk** – searching is just one of the many things you can do here.

**www.overture.com** – straightforward, easy to use, it used to be goto.com.
**www.profusion.com** – an excellent and fast, advanced search tool.
**www.ranks.com** – a search engine and directory that ranks sites in each category.
**www.yahoo.com** – one of the most used and comprehensive.

# UK-oriented searching

### http://uk.yahoo.com                                                        US

FOR THE UK AND IRELAND
The UK arm of Yahoo! is the biggest and one of the most established search engines. It's now much more than just a search facility as it offers a huge array of other services: from news to finance to shopping to sport to travel to games. You can restrict your search to just UK or Irish sites. It's the place to start, but it can be a little overwhelming at first.

### www.mirago.co.uk                                                          UK

THE UK SEARCH ENGINE
Mirago searches the whole web but prioritises the search for UK families and businesses. It's very quick, easy to use and offers many of the services you get from Yahoo! You can tailor your search very easily to exclude stuff you won't need.

*For other UK-oriented search sites try:*
**http://UK20.co.uk** – a good-looking site, it's OK as a search engine too.
**www.britishinformation.com** – well designed and comprehensive.
**www.clickclick2.net** – odd design and more of a directory.
**www.scotland.org** – small Scotland-oriented site.
**www.searchsaint.com** – good-looking and easy to use.

S

# *Security*

*Keeping your computer, its contents and those who use it safe is one of the biggest priorities for any user; albeit unlikely you'll have any problems. Here's a list of sites that will help you keep secure and some protection software that's available for nothing.*

### www.isr.net                                                           US

INTERNET SECURITY REVIEW
An exhaustive overview of Internet security with explanations
and sections on all the major aspects of the subject. See also
**www.uksecurityonline.com** which is an informative site and
gives guidance on what's the right security set up for your PC
and operating system.

### www.grc.com                                                          US

SHIELDS UP!
Click on the 'Shields Up' logo and follow the instructions.
You can then leave the program to run a security revue of your
PC – it probably won't make happy reading, it depends on how
anxious you are about security. For their check up Mac users
can go to **www.symantec.com/mac/security**

### www.firewallguide.com                                                US

HOME PC FIREWALL GUIDE
According to my DK Internet Dictionary, a firewall is a piece of
filtering software that protects your PC and prevents unknown
users from sending material to it. But which is the best one?
Find out here. For a good and well-regarded firewall program
that has a free version available go to **www.zonelabs.com**

### www.software-antivirus.com                                           US

THE INDEPENDENT ANTI-VIRUS RESOURCE
All the anti-virus programs reviewed and rated. This site sets
out to blow the myth that once you have virus technology
installed you're safe, or that the best selling products are
actually the best at the job. An authoritative site written by
several experienced computer experts.

*See also:*
**http://housecall.antivirus.com** – a free virus scanner.
**www.grisoft.com** – for the free AVG anti-virus scanner.
**www.kaspersky.com** – home of the top rated
anti-virus program.
**www.macafee.com** – security specialists.
**www.norton.com** – where to go for the well-known
Norton products.
**www.pandasecurity.com** – another top rated program.
**www.viruslist.com** – if you're really interested in viruses the go
here where you'll find a virus encyclopaedia.

## www.anti-trojan-software-reviews.com                    US

### THE ANTI-TROJAN RESOURCE

OK so you thought you were protected, but not entirely. Trojans
are programs that pretend to be other programs and usually
hitch a ride into your PC on the back of e-mail attachments.
Go here to find the best anti-Trojan programs or just ensure that
your anti-virus software does the job on Trojans too.

## www.spybot.com                                          US

### SPYWARE DETECTED

As if viruses and Trojans weren't enough, the chances are that
you've got some spyware on your PC sending information on
your surfing activities to one of many companies who provide
marketing data to retailers for example. This little program will
search and destroy the little so and sos. It's also worth checking
out the excellent ad-aware program, which is available at
**www.lavasoftusa.com** For an overview go to
**www.spyware.co.uk**

## www.cookiecentral.com                                   US

### COOKIES EXPLAINED

An excellent site dedicated to explaining the workings of that
mysterious animal the 'cookie' and how you can deal with them.

## http://nclnet.org/essentials                            UK

### PRIVACY

An informative site giving an overview of security and privacy
issues on the Internet, it has plenty of helpful advice and links
to related sites.

# Ships and Boats

*For shipping and boating enthusiasts here are a few sites that may
interest you. Sailing is listed under Sport, page 395 and water-borne
holidays can be found in the Travel section, page 466.*

S

# Boats

## www.boatlinks.com                                        US
### BOATING DIRECTORY
A well-categorised directory and the place to start if you're
looking for any information on shipping or boating.

## http://boatbuilding.com                                  UK
### THE BOAT BUILDING COMMUNITY
If you want to repair or build a boat then here's where to go,
with features and discussion forums to help you on your way.
There's also a very good directory of links to suppliers and
resource sites.

## www.buyaboat.co.uk                                       UK
*BUY A BOAT* MAGAZINE
Primarily a vehicle to get you to subscribe to the magazine,
the site offers information on brokers and the details of over
14,000 boats for sale. See also the well designed
**www.boats.com** and **www.boats-for-sale.com**

*See also:*
**www.boatingnews.com** – news and classifieds.
**www.boatingontheweb.com** – an American boating directory.
**www.boatlaunch.co.uk** – a mapping service showing all the
places in the UK where you can launch your boat.
**www.uscgboating.org** – a good site for advice and information
on safe boating.

# Ships and Navy

## www.royal-navy.mod.uk                                    UK

### THE ROYAL NAVY
An excellent site from the Royal Navy giving details of the
ships, submarines and aircraft and what it's like to be a part of
it all. There's a video gallery featuring highlights from the fleet
and details of all the Royal Navy ships. Apart from all the
information, you can have a go on the interactive frigate.

## www.hazegray.org                                    US

NAVAL HISTORY AND PHOTOGRAPHY
A well-categorised and comprehensive site featuring naval
histories, background on the world's ships and navies and also
shipbuilding. It's oriented to the US.

*More naval and historical sites:*
**www.cronab.demon.co.uk** – poor site but with some good
articles and links.
**www.naval-history.net** – a messy site, good for 20th century
and links.
**www.navalhistory.plus.com** – an unofficial and patchy history
of the Royal Navy.
**www.navsource.org** – a thorough unofficial overview of the
US navy.
**www.nmm.ac.uk** – a good site from the National Maritime
Museum in Greenwich.

## www.red-duster.co.uk                                UK

*RED DUSTER* MAGAZINE
Red Duster is a merchant navy enthusiasts' site offering lots in
the way of history covering sail, stream and shipping lines.
There's also a section on the history of customs. To find out
what the current merchant navy are up to go to
**www.merchantnavyofficers.com** where you find information
and links.

## www.maritimematters.com                             UK

OCEAN LINERS AND CRUISE SHIPS
An informative site with data on over 100 ships from the
earliest liners to the most modern, each has its own page with
quality pictures and some virtual tours. It is also good for news
and links to related sites.

# Other watercraft

S

## www.hovercraft.org.uk                               UK

HOVERCRAFT
If you're into hovercrafts or are just interested, here's the place
to look with three sections – Britain, Europe and the world,
which just about covers it all.

**www.jetskier.co.uk**                                                    UK
>    JET SKI
>    Home of *Jetskier* magazine and while it's geared to sell the
>    mag, the site does offer much in the way of links and advice.
>    For more tips, forums and chat go to the US-oriented
>    **www.jetskinews.com**

**www.rontini.com**                                                       UK
>    SUBMARINE WORLD NETWORK
>    A directory site with over 1,000 links all devoted to the world
>    of submarines, it covers everything from navies to models.
>
>    *See also:*
>    **http://ws1.lr.org/** – Lloyd's register.
>    **www.nao.rl.ac.uk** – home of the Nautical Almanac Office.
>    **www.paddling.net** – for buying canoes and kayaks.
>    **www.tpl.lib.wa.us/v2/nwroom/ships.htm** – the Tacoma public
>    library has a searchable database of some 13,000 ships.

# Shopping

*To many people shopping is what the Internet is all about, and it does
offer an opportunity to get some tremendous bargains. Watch out for
hidden costs such as delivery charges, import duties or finance deals
that seem attractive until you compare them with what's available
elsewhere. For help on finding comparative prices, see the price
comparison sites on page 321, in fact, starting your shopping trip at
a site like* **www.kelkoo.com** *may prove to be a wise move. There is
also the new section on Consumer Information on page 88 for the
low-down on your rights and what to do when things go wrong.*

**www.tradingstandards.gov.uk**                                           UK
>    TRADING STANDARDS CENTRAL
>    Find out where you stand and what to do if you think you're
>    being ripped off or someone is not trading fairly – you can even
>    take a quiz about it. There are advice guides to print off or
>    download and there is help and advice to businesses and
>    schools as well as consumers.

*Two other consumer-oriented sites worth checking out are:*
**www.consumer.gov.uk** – Rights advice from the Department of Trade and Industry.
**www.howtocomplain.com** – advice on how to go above airing your grievances and getting a result.

## www.which.net                                                    UK

*WHICH?* MAGAZINE
A good place to start your shopping experience but you have to be a member to get the best out of it. There's a good shopping directory plus their product picks section which highlights the 'best in class' on a wide variety of products. There are also the useful sections that you associate with the magazine such as legal advice and personal finance.

## www.dooyoo.co.uk                                                 UK

MAKE YOUR OPINION COUNT
Media darling Doo Yoo is a site where you the consumer can give your opinion or a review on any product that's available to buy, this way you get unbiased opinions about them – in theory. They cover a wide range of 'products' from books to TV shows and it's easy to contribute. See also **www.ciao.co.uk** where you can actually get paid a small amount of money for your opinion.

## www.recallannouncements.co.uk                                    UK

CONSUMER SAFETY
An informative site listing all the latest product recalls covering the US, UK and Australia, it also offers a consumer guide, an 'Ask the Experts' facility and statistics on recalls. Some of the site can only be accessed if you register.

# The virtual high street

## www.marks-and-spencer.co.uk                                      UK

CLOTHES AND GIFTS
A clear, attractive site that has a good selection of products from clothes to gifts for all, as well as fashion advice and a quick order facility. There's not much emphasis on offers, more on quality. Delivery costs start at £3.50.

S

## www.boots.com                                          UK

BOOTS

All that nice 'wellbeing' stuff has gone and been replaced by an
online shop that reflects what you see when you visit the real
store. There's lots of choice and it's well categorised, functional
too. You can get points with your purchase and delivery starts
at £4.50, although at time of writing was free if you spend £40
or more.

## www.whsmith.co.uk                                      UK

W.H.SMITH

The Smiths site has a clean, easy-to-navigate format, with the
emphasis on offers and best-sellers. There is a great deal here
though including the usual books, music, mags, games,
stationery and DVDs. Delivery is £2.99 whatever the size of
your order, free if you collect the goods from your nearest store,
you can also claim loyalty points with online purchases.

## www.woolworths.co.uk                                   UK

WELL WORTH IT

A bright and breezy site from Woolworths with all you'd expect
in terms of range and prices. They are particularly good on kids'
stuff with strong prices on movies, chart music, clothes and
games, delivery is a bargain at £1.50 per order.

## www.argos.co.uk                                        UK

ARGOS CATALOGUE

Argos offers an excellent range of products (some 8,000) across
thirteen different categories as per their catalogue. There are
some good bargains to be had. You can now reserve an item at
your local store, once you've checked that they have it in stock.
There's a good search facility and you can find a product via
its catalogue number if you've a catalogue handy that is.
Delivery is £3.95 unless you spend more than £125 in which
case it's free. Returns can be made to your local store. It's no
wonder that's it's the UK's most popular shopping site.

## www.debenhams.com                                      UK

AWARD-WINNING FAMILY SERVICE

Not a common sight on the high street but Debenhams have a
very good site aimed at their retailing strengths: gifts, weddings
and fashion. Delivery costs vary.

### www.johnlewis.co.uk

NEVER KNOWINGLY UNDERSOLD
A really attractive and usable site with a wide range of products and some good offers too. Delivery costs start at £3.95. Especially good if you haven't got one of their excellent stores near by. For more upmarket gear check out **www.liberty.co.uk** and also **www.selfridges.com** both have interesting site designs and products to match.

## General retailers, directories and online department stores

### www.2020shops.com
UK

THE SHOPPER'S FRIEND
A really likeable site with a great ethic – they don't do cosy deals with other retailers for exposure so the shops they select and rate are there on merit. They are one of the few that give extra information on the shops such as delivery costs, plus some shopping advice. It's fast too.

### www.goldfish.com/guides/guide.html
UK

GOLDFISH GUIDES
Another good place for consumer advice and an easy approach to selecting the right store. The Goldfish guides cover a wide range of shopping categories all written by independent journalists. Essentially the idea is that you read up on it, compare prices on it then buy it – simple really. The site is well designed and easy to use.

### www.shopperuk.com
UK

UK SHOPPING DIRECTORY
An excellent directory of UK shops both specialist and general. It's well categorised both by type and alphabetical, a genuinely useful site.

S

### www.edirectory.co.uk
UK

IF IT'S OUT THERE, BUY IT HERE
A nice-looking directory with a wide variety of shops and goods to choose from, it has a good reputation for service as well as being topical.

## www.shopspy.co.uk
UK

### THE GUIDE THAT SHOPS BEFORE IT RATES
A great idea, the shop spy team actually use the shops on their listing and then report back on things like value, quality of the goods and service then rate them accordingly. The list of more than 500 stores is fairly eclectic and you can easily see the best rated ones. The site could be organised much better though and it's not always that up-to-date.

## www.virgin.net/shopping
UK

### LIFESTYLE AND SHOPPING GUIDE
Virgin's shopping guide is comprehensive covering all major categories while allowing retailers to feature some of their best offers. It also attempts to be a complete service for entertainment and leisure needs with excellent sections on music, travel and cinema in particular.

## www.shoppingunlimited.co.uk
UK

### INDEPENDENT RECOMMENDATION
Owned by the *Guardian* newspaper, this site offers hundreds of links to stores that they've reviewed. It also offers help to inexperienced shoppers and guidance on using credit cards online. There are also links to other Guardian sites such as news and sport.

## www.thevirtualmall.co.uk
UK

### THE VIRTUAL SHOPPING CENTRE
Literally browse by floor then click on the shop you want to go into. There's no real advantage in using it other than having all the best stores represented graphically in one place and now you can create your own virtual floor composed entirely of all your favourite stores. There are some good offers to be found here too.

## www.screenshop.co.uk
UK

### SHOP VIA TV, WEB OR CATALOGUE
As a shopping channel on Sky, Screenshop was already successful; this well-put-together site shows off the breadth of their range and has some good offers. See also the wide-ranging QVC shop at **www.qvcuk.com** which offers some 10,000 products.

**www.streetsonline.co.uk**                                    UK

STREETS AHEAD
One of Britain's most successful online retailers, Streets Online
not only offers excellent books, music and movie shops but an
entertainment magazine too, you can also download trailers,
audio clips and e-books.

# Ethical shopping

**www.crueltyfreeshop.com**                                    UK

CRUELTY-FREE SHOP
A wide range of products on sale all of which are guaranteed
not to have had any animal cruelty or exploitation in their
production. The range is wide and the prices aren't bad either.
It can only improve, a good idea that deserves some success.

*See also:*
**www.afrigoods.org** – quality gifts from Africa with profits going
to the artists who made them.
**www.fairtrade.org.uk** – home of the Fair Trade Foundation,
which exists to enable poor artists and workers to get a
better deal.
**www.getethical.com** – who have shopping, advice, links,
holidays and a magazine.
**www.onevillage.org** – A shop specialising in ethnic products
and using the Fair Trade system.
**www.traidcraftshop.co.uk** – good selection of crafts, foods and
other goods from around the world.

# Value for money

**www.onlinediscount.com**                                     US

THE VERY BEST DISCOUNTS
Online Discount specialise in monitoring Internet stores and
highlighting those giving the best discounts in any one of
sixteen major categories. You are quickly put through to a list
of the key shops and their bargains.

**www.thesimplesaver.com**                                     UK

WHERE TO GET THE BEST DEAL
What started off as a simple e-mail conversation about where to
go for savings has snowballed into a web site and newsletter
that lets the whole world know where the best shopping
bargains are to be had.

S

**www.gooddealdirectory.co.uk**                                UK
>  THE BARGAIN HUNTERS BIBLE
>  Based on the book of the same name, this is basically a
>  searchable directory of discount shops and sales. It's easy to
>  use and the information seems comprehensive.

# Gift finding

*The following sites should help you find the perfect gift, but if you're
shopping for the women in your life, there are more gift sites
recommended in the Men's section on page 257.*

**www.hard2buy4.co.uk**                                        UK
>  GIFT IDEAS
>  Excellent gift shop with a wide range of unusual products
>  including celebrity items, activities and gifts for men, women
>  and children in separate sections, some good offers too.

>  *See also:*
>  **www.blissonline.com** – lifestyle enhancing gifts and upmarket
>  presents in a hurry.
>  **www.buyagift.co.uk** – activities and experiences for those who
>  have everything.
>  **www.find-me-a-gift.co.uk** – gifts, both products and special
>  experiences can be found here, loyalty scheme and wishlists
>  thrown in too.
>  **www.hawkin.com** – odd design but good for range, children
>  and the unusual.
>  **www.iwantoneofthose.com** – for more unusual gifts and stuff
>  you don't need but would really like, it also has a great
>  gift finder.
>  **www.jun-gifts.com** – Japanese gifts and other products,
>  excellent for the unusual.
>  **www.needapresent.com** – very good site with some out of the
>  ordinary gifts including the best-selling Orgasmatron!
>  **www.powderedwater.co.uk** – great design and excellent for
>  designer gifts.
>  **www.rebirth.co.za** – authentic African art and gifts.
>  **www.thesharperedge.co.uk** – some good stuff in amongst
>  the tat.

S

# British shopping

## www.british-shopping.com                                    UK

UK SHOPPING LINKS AND DIRECTORY
An excellent comprehensive portal site specialising in British
shops, it also has plenty of related links and information.
**www.shops247.com**, **www.somucheasier.co.uk** and
**www.cataloguecity.co.uk** also offer a comprehensive UK
oriented shop listing.

*For more quintessentially British shops check out these sites:*
**www.brooksandbentley.com** – classy British gifts.
**www.classicengland.co.uk** – the best British products on a
fun-looking and easy to use site.
**www.distinctlybritish.com** – a British shop directory with a
wide range of food, clothing, gift and children's retailers on offer.
**www.harrods.com** – a selection of their products available to
buy from an attractive-looking site.

## www.scotsmart.com                                           UK

SCOTSMART
A Scottish directory of sites, not just for shopping but covering
most areas, you can search by theme or category and the
shopping section is split into books, clothing, food, gifts and
highland wear. See also **www.scotch-corner.co.uk** which is
Scottish through and through.

# The rest

*There are hundreds, possibly thousands of online stores and shopping
malls, it would be impossible to include them all, but here is a list of
some of this year's best reviewed sites and what they do.*

# The best

**http://theukhighstreet.com** – a good UK directory, with the
shops rated by you the customer.
**www.abound.co.uk** – an excellent site offering a wide range of
clothes, leisure and electrical products; well executed and with
some good offers too.
**www.bobsshopwindow.com** – Bob's Shop Window is a
comprehensive directory of shops, well categorised but not
rated in any way, the site descriptions are provided by
the retailers.

S

**www.buy4now.ie** – an Irish shopping portal with a massive selection of goods.

**www.eshopone.co.uk** – posh products and cheap prices.

**www.eshops.co.uk** – great design, loads of shops listed in the directory with some excellent offers and a good search engine.

**www.l-stores.com** – a very good store search engine and directory.

**www.mailorderexpress.co.uk** – excellent for toys and kids' stuff.

**www.shoptour.co.uk** – links to over 1,000 secure shops in 14 categories, much improved now with a price comparison tool.

**www.somucheasier.co.uk** – a good-looking directory site with each shopping site reviewed, icons are used to show what each shop offers in the way of service etc.

**www.ukshopsearch.com** – above average search engine and quality design make this stand out from the crowd, you can also vent your frustrations out on the shopping experience in the shoppers forum.

**www.ukshopsnet.com** – well-designed and well-categorised store directory site and search engine.

**www.worthaglance.com** – great-looking shop with some outstanding bargains.

## Could be useful

**www.1shop.org** – mall supporting small or medium sized UK businesses.

**www.oneshopforall.co.uk** – odd looking shop, good for unusual gifts though

**www.shopq.co.uk** – massive set of shopping links, well categorised on a messy site

**www.shoppingtrolley.net** – lots of shops and categories, boring design.

**www.theukmall.co.uk** – minimalist design, odd ratings and shop selection.

## So you can't be bothered to shop…

### www.webswappers.com                                    UK

SWAP IT!

An interesting angle, at this site you can swap almost anything from the smallest item to a car or house! It's all backed by a confidential e-mail service and it looks quite good fun too.

**www.anythingforhire.co.uk**                                    UK
> HIRE IT!
> A comprehensive directory of goods and services for hire across
> the UK, well laid out and easy to use.

# Skiing and Snowboarding

*These sites tend to include information on both skiing and related
travel, so we've moved it from Sports to create a combined section
devoted to all things snowy.*

**www.fis-ski.com**                                              US

> INTERNATIONAL SKI FEDERATION
> Catch up on the news, the fastest times, the rankings in all
> forms of skiing at this site. Very good background information
> and a live on line section enabling events to be monitored as
> they happen.

**www.ski.co.uk**                                                UK
> THE PLACE TO START – A SKI DIRECTORY
> Straightforward site, the information in the directory is useful
> and the recommended sites are rated. The sections include
> holidays, travel, weather, resorts, snowboarding, gear, fanatics
> and specialist services.

**www.1ski.com**                                                 UK
> COMPLETE ONLINE SKIING SERVICE
> With a huge number of holidays, live snow reports, tips on
> technique and equipment and the ultimate guide featuring over
> 750 resorts, it's difficult to go wrong. The site is well laid out
> and easy to use. There's a good events calendar too.

> *Other good ski and snowboarding sites:*
> **www.descent.co.uk** – specialists in luxury alpine holidays.
> **www.ifyouski.com** – comprehensive skiing site that has a very
> good holiday booking service with lots of deals.
> **www.iglu.com** – holiday specialists with lots of variety and offers.
> **www.mountainzone.com** – great for features, articles and ski
> adventurers.
> **www.natives.co.uk** – aimed at ski workers, there's info on
> conditions, ski resorts, a good job section, where to stay and
> links to other cool sites all wrapped up on a very nicely
> designed site.

S

**www.skiclub.co.uk** – Ski Club of Great Britain with lots of offers and information too.
**www.skidream.com** – skiing and snowboarding in America and Canada.
**www.skisolutions.com** – one of the oldest travel companies specialising in skiing holidays, with a huge range of holidays and expertise.
**www.snow-forecast.com** – weather forecasts for snow areas.
**www.snowrental.net** – online equipment rental, all seems very easy.

## www.boardtheworld.com                                           UK

SNOWBOARDING
Masses of information and links covering the world of snowboarding, the site is well designed and doesn't seem to miss out any aspect of the sport.

*See also:*
**www.boardz.com/snowboard/snowboardcentral.html**
– the snowboarding e-zine from Boardz.
**www.goneboarding.co.uk** – the UK boarding community with lots of information and chat.
**www.snowboardinguk.co.uk** – forums and snowboarding chat.

# Social Networking

*One of the latest trends on the Internet is to start up a social network with your friends and consequently with their friends. It's a great way to share experiences, data or photos and particularly good for clubs or if you're fed up with the traditional dating sites. Here are some of the best and most useful sites.*

## www.friendster.com                                              US

COMMUNITY
A very easy to use set-up with clear instructions and design; it's oriented towards dating but it's really adaptable.

*See also:*
**www.orkut.com** – affiliated to Google, it has the air of an exclusive club but it's very popular and the design is excellent.
**www.flickr.com** – fantastic if you want to share lots of photos.
**www.notfriendster.com** – a dull site but offers links to sites that are good alternatives to Friendster.

**www.dudecheckthisout.com** – here you can get together online with people who share your interests basically by sharing the contents of your favourites box.

# Software, Upgrades and Debugging

*If you need to upgrade your software, then these are the sites to go to. Shareware is where you get a program to use for a short period of time before you have to buy it, freeware is exactly what you'd think – free. Debugging programs fix problems in established programs that weren't previously identified.*

### www.softwareparadise.co.uk UK

THE SMART WAY TO SHOP FOR SOFTWARE
With over 250,000 products and excellent offers make this site the first stop. It's a bit messy but easy to use, there's a good search facility and plenty of products for Mac users.

### www.download.com US

CNET
A superb site covering all types of software and available downloads. There are masses of reviews as well as buying tips and price comparison tools; it also covers handheld PCs, Linux and Macs.

### www.softseek.com US

ZDNET
Another excellent site with a huge amount of resources to download, it's all a little overwhelming at first but the download directory is easy to use and there's lots of free software available.

### www.tucows.com US

TUCOWS
Probably less irritating to use than ZDNet and CNet, the software reviews are also entertaining in their own right, the best thing about it though is that it's quick.

*If you feel like shopping around a bit more see also:*

**http://freshmeat.net** – lots of shareware, also good for Linux fans.

**http://home.netscape.com/plugins** – if you're a Netscape fan then you can improve its performance with 'plug-ins' from this site.

**www.completelyfreesoftware.com** – hundreds of free programs for you to download, from games to useful desktop accessories; if it's available free, then its here. Membership is essential, but free.

**www.cooltool.com** – some of the best and 'coolest' software specially selected by this team of toolsters…

**www.freewarehome.com** – a great selection of free programs including a specialist site aimed at software for children, **www.kidsfreeware.com**

**www.handango.com** – a good site specialising in downloads for handheld PCs.

**www.neatnettricks.com** – an archive of useful tips and downloads with regular updates, you need to subscribe though.

**www.versiontracker.com** – a massive selection, particularly good for Mac software.

**www.vnunet.com** – UK-orientated review and download site.

**www.winplanet.com** – specialises in improving and discussing Windows applications.

**www.wired.com** – popular technology magazine with all the latest news and reviews.

## www.bugnet.com                                      US

FIX THAT BUG

Subscribe to the Bug Net and they alert you to software bugs, keep you up-to-date with reviews, analysis and the tests they carry out. You can then be sure to buy the right fixes. See also **www.annoyances.org** which is a good site devoted to fixing problems in Microsoft Windows

## www.winzip.com                                      US

MANAGE FILES

Winzip allows you to save space on your PC by compressing data, making it easier to e-mail files and unlock zipped files that have been sent to you. It takes a few minutes to download. For Macs go to **www.aladdinsys.com**

# Space

## E-zines and reference sites

### www.space.com                                              US

MAKING SPACE POPULAR
An education-oriented site dedicated to space; there's news,
mission reports, technology, history, personalities, a games
section and plenty of pictures. The science section explores
the planets and earth. See also Thinks Space at
**http://library.thinkquest.org/26220** which is great for
photos and links.

### www.spacedaily.com                                         US

YOUR PORTAL TO SPACE
A comprehensive newspaper-style site with a huge amount of
information and news about space and related subjects. It also
has links to similar sister sites covering subjects like Mars,
space war and space travel. See also the eccentric
**www.astspace.demon.co.uk** which is good portal, once you find it.

### www.astronomynow.com                                       UK

THE UK'S BEST SELLING ASTRONOMY MAG
Get the news and views from a British angle, plus reviews on
the latest books. The store has widened out to include patches,
T-shirts and videos as well as the magazine and posters.

### www.windows.ucar.edu                                       US

WINDOWS TO THE UNIVERSE
A well-designed site that provides information about the earth,
solar system and universe at three levels of detail making it
suitable for everyone from children to the most serious-minded.
There are interesting sections exploring the link between the
world's mythology and space, history and space, on geology,
space exploration and art.

### www.nauts.com                                              US

THE ASTRONAUT CONNECTION
In their words 'The Astronaut Connection has worked to create
an educational and entertaining resource for space enthusiasts,
young and old, to learn about astronauts and space exploration'
and that just about sums up this very informative site.

**www.heavens-above.com**                                      US

IT'S ABOVE YOUR HEAD
Type in your location and they'll give you the exact time and
precise location of the next visible pass of the International
Space Station or space shuttle. They also help you to observe
satellites and flares from Iridium satellites.

## Space organisations

**www.nasa.gov**                                              US

THE OFFICIAL NASA SITE
This huge site provides comprehensive information on the US
National Aeronautical and Space Administration. There are
details on each NASA site, launch timings, sections for news,
kids, project updates, and links to their specialist sites such
as the Hubble Space Telescope, Mars and Earth observation.
For Britain's place in space go to **www.bnsc.gov.uk** or
**www.ukspace.com** which is great for links.

*See also:*
**www.arianespace.com** – attractive site from the makers of the
Ariane rocket.
**www.isro.org/space_science** – the Indian space program.
**www.jpl.nasa.gov** – the goings on at the Jet Propulsion Lab
with excellent photography.
**www.russianspaceweb.com** – a good overview of the Russian
space program with a history and the latest news.
**www.sinodefence.com/space/facility/spaceagency.asp** –
information on China's national space program.

## The solar system

**www.seds.org/billa/tnp**                                    UK

THE NINE PLANETS
A multimedia tour of the nine planets, stunning photography,
interesting facts combined with good text. See also Bill Arnett's
site on Nebulae at **http://seds.lpl.arizona.edu/billa/twn** where
there are some beautiful pictures.

*For more excellent resources try:*
**www.solarviews.com**
**www.the-solar-system.net**

## www.redcolony.com

MARS US

A superb site all about the red planet. There is a synopsis of its history, plus details on past and future space missions with a focus on the colonisation of Mars. There's a great deal of information on things like terra forming and biogenesis, it's all taken very seriously too. See also the equally imaginative **www.exploremarsnow.org** where you can find a plausible manifestation of what a Mars mission could look like, backed up with outstanding graphics. At **http://marsrovers.jpl.nasa.gov** you can learn about the latest Mars missions.

# Is there life out there?

## www.setiathome.ssl.berkeley.edu UK

GET IN TOUCH WITH AN ALIEN

To borrow the official site description 'SETI@home is a scientific experiment that uses Internet-connected computers in the Search for Extraterrestrial Intelligence (SETI).' You can participate by running a free program that downloads and analyses radio telescope data. Millions have participated and 5 billion potential signals have been located; they're pointing their scopes at the most promising now. There's still time for you to be the first!

## www.ufosightingsuk.co.uk UK

UFOS IN THE UK

This is a great catalogue of 'eye witness' accounts of encounters with UFOs in the UK. Whether you believe in it or not makes for an interesting read.

# Miscellaneous

S

## www.spaceadventures.com US

SPACE TOURISM

OK so you want to be an astronaut? Well now you have a golden opportunity, so long as you have $2 million! Having said that there are actually some cheaper options including shuttle tours and a trip to the edge of space.

**www.badastronomy.com**                                    US
> DEBUNKING THE MYTHS
> A site devoted to exploring some of the myths and stories that
> surround astronomy and science fiction. It gives the facts in a
> straightforward and (because the site owner sometimes gets on
> his 'high horse') entertaining way.

# Sport

*One of the best uses of the Internet is to keep up-to-date with how
your team is performing, or if you're a member of a team or
association, keep each other updated.*

## General sport sites

**www.sporting-life.com**                                   UK
> *SPORTING LIFE*
> A very comprehensive sport site, with plenty of advice, tips,
> news and latest scores. It's considered to be one of the best,
> good for stories, in-depth analysis and overall coverage of the
> major sports.

**www.bbc.co.uk/sport**                                     UK

> BBC SPORT COVERAGE
> They may have lost the right to broadcast many sporting events
> but their coverage at this level is excellent – much broader than
> most and it's always up-to-date.

**www.skysports.com**                                       UK
> THE BEST OF SKY SPORT
> Excellent for the Premiership and football in general, but also
> covers other sports very well particularly cricket and both forms
> of rugby. Includes a section featuring video and audio clips,
> and there are interviews with stars. You can vote in their polls,
> e-mail programmes or try sports trivia quizzes. Lots of adverts
> spoil it.

## www.rivals.net                                    UK

### THE RIVALS NETWORK
Independent of any news organisations, Rivals is basically a
network of specialist sites covering the whole gamut of major
and some minor sports, each site has its own editor who is
passionate about the sport they cover. In general its promise is
better than the delivery but what there is, is excellent with good
quality content and pictures.

## www.sportonair.com                                UK

### HEAR ALL ABOUT IT...
If you can't see it then you can always come here to listen to it,
this site offers up lots of audio content including interviews and
commentary from most of the major sporting events. There's a
good archive and most major sports are covered.

## www.talksport.net                                 UK

### HOME OF TALK SPORT RADIO
A pretty down-market site where you can listen to sports news
and debate while you work. The information comes from
*Sporting Life* but it's up-to-date.

## http://sport.telegraph.co.uk                      UK

### *DAILY TELEGRAPH*
Very comprehensive and well written with lots of archive
material. All the major sports are covered and with contributors
like Mike Atherton, Henry Winter and Sebastian Coe, you know
it has authority.

## www.sportzine.co.uk                               UK

### SPORTS SITE DIRECTORY
Excellent links listing site with each site getting a review or
description, covering all the major sports and most of the minor
ones, plus news too.

*Other good all-rounders, and sites with good links:*
**http://dmoz.org/sports/** – links galore at the Open
Directory project.
**http://sport.independent.co.uk** – good all round coverage from
the *Independent* newspaper.
**http://sportsillustrated.cnn.com** – the latest in American sport
from CNN.

S

**www.EL.com/elinks/sports** – list of American-oriented sports links.
**www.eurosport.com** – the world of European sport.
**www.sportal.co.uk** – good, football-oriented magazine site.
**www.sportsline.com** – excellent coverage from CBS.

## www.sportspubs.co.uk                                    UK

WHERE TO WATCH SPORT
A building directory of pubs where you can watch sport. You can search it by sport or by region and there's a good links section too.

## www.culture.gov.uk/sport                                 UK

WHAT THE GOVERNMENT IS UP TO
Here's where to go to find the latest policies, what the minister for sport does and how they are helping sport develop in the community at large. Fairly dull site though.

# Sites on specific sports

## American football

## www.nfl.com                                              US

NATIONAL FOOTBALL LEAGUE
American football's online bible, it's a huge official site with details and statistics bursting from every page. It's got information on all the teams, players and likely draft picks; there's also information on NFL Europe and links to other key sites. All it really lacks is gossip!

*See also:*
**http://football.espn.go.com/nfl/index** – ESPN's site is authoritative and offers links to other sports.
**www.hot-iron.co.uk** – a very good Scottish gridiron e-zine.
**www.nfleurope.com** – thorough coverage of the European league.
**www.nflplayers.com** – for the latest news and background on all the key people in the game plus nostalgia from ex-players.
**www.ukgridiron.co.uk** – the UK-oriented view of the games.

# Archery

**www.archery.org**                                          UK
> INTERNATIONAL ARCHERY FEDERATION
> Get the official news, events listings, rankings and records
> information from this fairly mundane site.

> *See also:*
> **www.bownet.com** – *Bow International* magazine.
> **www.scottisharchery.org.uk** – the Scottish Archery Association.
> **www.theglade.co.uk** – an entertaining and chatty site, basically
> an e-zine, devoted to all forms of archery.

## Athletics and running

**www.iaaf.org**                                             UK
> INTERNATIONAL ASSOCIATION OF ATHLETICS
> FEDERATIONS
> The official site of the IAAF is a results-oriented affair with lots
> of rankings in addition to the latest news. There's also a
> multimedia section where you can see pictures, listen to
> commentary or watch video of the key events. There's a good
> links page and information on the organisation's activities.

**www.ukathletics.net**                                      UK

> THE GOVERNING BODY
> Many official 'governing body' sites are pretty boring affairs, not
> so UK Athletics which contains lots of features, is newsy and
> written with an obvious sense of enthusiasm. There are details
> on forthcoming events, reports on aspects of the sport, records,
> biographies of key athletes and advice on keeping fit. Somehow
> you get the impression the site is sponsored…

**www.athletix.org**                                         UK
> THE ATHLETICS SITE
> A statistics and results led site with coverage of all the major
> events and some minor ones. It covers international
> competitions as well as having a good gallery and biographical
> details of some of the major athletes, it's also good for links.

S

**www.runnersworld.com**                                    US

> *RUNNER'S WORLD* MAGAZINE
> A rather dry site with tips from getting started through to
> advanced level running. There's lots of information, news and
> records plus reviews on shoes and gear. See also the less
> visually exciting but comprehensive **www.runnersweb.com**

**www.realrunner.com**                                    UK

> A RUNNING COMMUNITY
> A very well put together site with lots of resources to help
> runners in terms of both equipment and advice. There's an
> online health check, details of events, marathons and profiles of
> the athletes. Good design ensures that the site is a pleasure to
> use. For equipment advice try Runnersworld
> **www.runnersworld.ltd.uk**

> *See also:*
> **www.athletics-online.co.uk** – *Athletics Weekly* magazine.
> **www.bal.org.uk** – results from the British Athletics League.
> **www.boja.org** – a great site for young athletes, not much to
> look at but contains lots of information
> **www.british-athletics.co.uk** – a boring site but it has a
> directory of clubs and regional events. It's good for links to
> newsgroups though.
> **www.gbrathletics.com** – great for statistics and rankings.
> **www.marathonguide.com** – all you need to know about
> marathons with news and advice.
> **www.nuff-respect.co.uk** – see what Linford Christie is up to
> these days.
> **www.runnersweb.co.uk** – a good site covering all aspects of
> running including marathon training.
> **www.runtrackdir.com** – details of all the UK's running tracks
> and their facilities.
> **www.trackandfieldnews.com** – all the latest from *Track & Field
> News*. US bias.

## Australian rules football

**www.afl.com.au**                                    AUSTRALIA

> AUSTRALIAN FOOTBALL LEAGUE
> A top quality site covering all aspects of the game including
> team news, player profiles and statistics as well as the latest
> gossip and speculation.

# Baseball

## www.mlb.com
US

### MAJOR LEAGUE BASEBALL
All you need to know about the top teams and the World
Series, it's not the best-designed site but there's good
information, statistics on the game and notes about the key
players as well as related articles and features.

*See also:*
**www.baseball1.com** – not that up to date but very detailed.
**www.baseball-links.com** – easy to use and has over
10,000 links.
**www.bigbadbaseball.com** – one for the real die-hard fans.
**www.gbbaseball.co.uk** – all about the game in the UK.

# Basketball

## www.nba.com
UK

### NATIONAL BASKETBALL ASSOCIATION
A comprehensive official site with features on the teams,
players and games; there's also an excellent photo gallery and
you can watch some of the most important points if you have
the right software.

*See also:*
**www.basketball.com** – really extensive coverage including the
women's game.
**www.basketball365.co.uk** – comprehensive overview of the
game with news of what's going in on both sides of
the Atlantic.
**www.bbl.org.uk** – the official site of the British
Basketball league.
**www.britball.com** – Newsy site taking in the British and
Irish games.

# Bowls

## www.bowlsengland.com
UK

### ENGLISH BOWLING ASSOCIATION
A straightforward design making it easy to find out all you need
to know about lawn bowls in England, including a good set of
links to associated sites and even tips on green maintenance.

**www.eiba.co.uk**                                                    UK

ENGLAND INDOOR BOWLING ASSOCIATION
A pretty basic site giving an overview of the game, links and
background information on competitions and rules.

*See also:*
**www.bowlsclub.info** – a portal site devoted to lawn bowls.
**www.bowlsinternational.com** – home of a bowls magazine,
good for links.
**www.bowlsnews.co.uk** – information on some local leagues.
**www.esmba.org.uk** – informative site from the English Short
Mat Bowling Association.
**www.short-mat-magazine.com** – aimed at selling the mag,
but has information on the Irish, English and Welsh games.

# Boxing

**www.boxing.com**                                                    US

BOXING NEWS
A comprehensive site covering world boxing in a pretty newsy
way with lots of exclusives and features, there are regular
columnists and it's authoritative. There's also chat, links and
the latest headlines.

*See also:*
**www.bbc.co.uk/boxing** – great for the latest news and
background information.
**www.boxinginsider.com** – really good-looking site with lots of
information on the sport plus it's good for chat and stats.
**www.boxingzone.co.uk** – a boxing equipment retailer.
**www.heavyweights.co.uk** – who cover the hype around
heavyweight boxing.
**www.ibhof.com** – the International Boxing Hall of Fame has
information on the best ever boxers, it's great but could do with
more photos.
**www.secondsout.com** – excellent magazine and portal site for
fight fans everywhere.

*For the different boxing authorities:*
**www.aiba.net** – the official site from the Amateur International
Boxing Association.
**www.wbaonline.com** – the WBA has an OK-looking and
functional site.

**www.wbcboxing.com** – a straightforward site from the WBC.
**www.wbu.cc** – the World Boxing Union covers the sport well
from an unusual site.
**www.womenboxing.com** – a very comprehensive site devoted
to women's boxing.

# Clay shooting

## www.clayshooting.co.uk
UK
*CLAY SHOOTING* MAGAZINE
A good introduction to the sport with a beginner's guide to start
you off and a good set of links to key suppliers and associated
sites. There's also an online shop where you can buy the odd
essential item such as global positioning systems and dog food.
Serious shooters can go to the comprehensive
**www.hotbarrels.com**

# Cricket

## www.cricinfo.com
UK
THE HOME OF CRICKET ON THE NET
The best all round cricket site on the Internet, with in-depth
analysis, match reports, player profiles, statistics, links to other
more specialised sites and live written commentary. There's also
a shop with lots of cricket goodies, delivery is included in the
price. It also looks after the official sites of Lords and the ECB
and is affiliated to Wisden.

## www.lords.org
UK
THE OFFICIAL LINE ON CRICKET
Here you'll find news with plenty of information about the game
and players and an excellent section on women's cricket.
Good links to governing bodies, associations, the MCC and
ECB. See also **www.play-cricket.com** which is home to the
English Cricket Board and a fine source of information and
statistics on the game.

S

## www.webbsoc.demon.co.uk
UK
WOMEN'S CRICKET ON THE WEB
There are not many sites about women's cricket, this is
probably the best, with features, news, fixture lists, match
reports and player profiles. Nothing fancy, but it works.

**www.theprideside.com**                                              UK

CRICKET TO THE ROOTS
A good attempt at encouraging young people to take an interest
in cricket with an overview of the game on a really interesting
and interactive site.

*See also:*
**http://sport.guardian.co.uk/cricket** – good-looking and up to
the minute site from the *Guardian* newspaper.
**www.cricketonly.com** – a comprehensive and news-oriented
cricket enthusiasts site.
**www.cricketrecords.com** – one for the statistics freaks, lots of
pop up adverts too.
**www.cricketsupplies.com** – a good-looking online store
specialising in cricket gear, delivery is £6 per order.
**www.cricnet.co.uk** – the Professional Cricketers' Association
official site.
**www.windiescricket.com** – keep up to date with the West
Indies team here, it also covers the game by island too.

## Cycling

*These are sites aimed at the more serious sportsman, for more*
*leisurely cycling see page 92 and for holidays turn to page 464.*

**www.bcf.uk.com**                                                   UK

BRITISH CYCLING FEDERATION
The governing body for cycling, the site has become more
comprehensive, you can get information on events, rules, clubs
and rankings, as well as contact names for coaching and
development, plus a news service.

**www.bikemagic.com**                                                UK

IT'S BIKETASTIC!
Whether you're a beginner or an old hand, the enthusiastic and
engaging tone of this site will convert you or enhance your
cycling experience. There's plenty of news and features, as well
as reviews on bike parts and gadgets, a classified ads section
and a selection of links to other biking web sites, all of which
are rated.

## www.letour.fr
FRANCE

TOUR DE FRANCE

Written in English and French this site covers the Tour in some
depth with details on the teams, riders and general background
information.

## www.mtbbritain.co.uk
UK

MOUNTAIN BIKING

Routes, tips, advice and gear; it's all here whether you're a real
enthusiast or just a weekender.

# Darts

## www.planetdarts.co.uk
UK

PROFESSIONAL DARTS CORPORATION

A messy site but one that has lots of league information,
statistics, news, articles and rules.

*See also:*

**www.bbc.co.uk/darts** – good for news and background,
good design.

**www.dartbase.com** – rules, techniques and equipment advice.

**www.cyberdarts.com** – Darts e-zine, one that contains lots of
information such as articles, chat, forums and rules too.

# Dog racing

## www.thedogs.co.uk
UK

BRITISH GREYHOUND RACING BOARD

A well-designed site offering an overview of the sport, the top
dogs and track information, also has help for owners and all
the results.

*See also:*

**www.retiredgreyhounds.co.uk** – how to adopt a retired
greyhound.

**www.ugo4u.co.uk** – the Union of Greyhound Owners.

**www.greyhoundmonthly.co.uk** – a magazine-derived site
with shop, also very good for links.

S

# Equestrian

**www.bhs.org.uk** UK

BRITISH HORSE SOCIETY
A charity that looks after the welfare of horses, here you can get information on insurance, links, riding schools, competitions, events and trials.

*For more information try:*
**http://horses.about.com** – About.com's excellent suite of pages devoted to all things equestrian.
**www.badminton-horse.co.uk** – background and information on the famous horse trials with lots of extra features and links.
**www.britishdressage.co.uk** – very good site covering this aspect of the sport.
**www.britisheventing.com** – an attractive text based site with details on the sport and links.
**www.equestria.net** – Equestrian ISP and news service.
**www.horseandhound.co.uk** – excellent magazine site from the leading authority.
**www.horseselect.co.uk** – buying and selling competition horses.

# Extreme sports

**www.extreme.com** US

EXTREME SPORTS CHANNEL
The official site of the Extreme Sports Channel is hi-tech but quite slow, however once downloaded it's got lots to offer in terms of information, shopping and the latest headlines.

*See also:*
**www.adrenalin-hit.com** – good-looking site with loads of information, good music too.
**www.adventuredirectory.com** – useful sport-by-sport portal site.
**www.awezome.com** – informative and wide ranging.
**www.expn.go.com** – excellent extreme sports magazine with a US bias.
**www.extremepie.com** – good extreme sports gear shop.
**www.extreme-sports-world.com** – very useful portal site.

# Fishing

**www.fishing.co.uk**

HOME OF UK FISHING ON THE NET
A huge site that offers information on where to fish, how to fish,
where's the best place to stay near fish, even fishing holidays.
There's also advice on equipment, a records section and links
to shops and shop locations. Shop on-site for fishing books
and magazines.

*See also:*
**www.anglersnet.co.uk** – good magazine site with lots of
information and chat.
**www.anglers-world.co.uk** – great for fishing holidays.
**www.bdaa.co.uk** – home of the British Disabled Anglers
Association and a comprehensive offering it is too.
**www.fishandfly.co.uk** – another good magazine site, this one
devoted to fly fishing.
**www.fisheries.co.uk** – excellent for coarse fishing and links.
**www.thefishfinder.com** – yes it's a fish search engine and a
pretty good one at that.
**www.nfsa.org.uk** – home of the National Federation of
Sea Anglers with lots of links and information.
**www.nimpopo.com** – basic site with over 3,000
tackle bargains.
**www.pacgb.com** – the Pike Anglers Club, a bit specialist
perhaps, but a good site nonetheless.
**www.specialist-tackle.co.uk** – excellent store for equipment
plus much more in the way of chat and information.
**www.tackledirectory.com** – a store 'run by anglers for anglers'.

# Football

**www.football365.co.uk**

FOOTBALL NEWS
Probably the best of the football e-zines in terms of the
combination of looks, quality writing and features, although it
can be a bit dense at times.

*It's worth having a look at the sites listed below; just pick the
one you like best.*
**http://pinkfootball.com** – a girls guide to football.
**www.e-soccer.com** – hundreds of links and the latest news.

S

**www.guardian.co.uk/football** – great writing and irreverent articles, uncluttered design.

**www.laughfc.co.uk** – a humourous look at the game, good for jokes and chants, some adult content.

**www.planetfootball.com** – news, information and OPTA statistics and the world game.

**www.pureworldcup.com** – a fun and informative look at the World Cup.

**www.soccerage.com** – excellent for world soccer, in 14 languages.

**www.soccerhighway.com** – a strange site but good for links.

**www.soccernet.com** – well put together from ESPN, comprehensive but a bit boring.

**www.wsc.co.uk** – home of the magazine *When Saturday Comes*.

## www.teamtalk.com    UK

CHECK OUT THE TEAMS!
The place to go if you want all the latest gossip and transfer information, it's opinionated but not often wrong. They have around 90 journalists on their books and they also cover rugby and racing too. See also **www.fansFC.com** which is great for the latest news and shenanigans.

## www.icons.com    UK

THE WORLD'S LEADING FOOTBALLERS
Keep up-to-date with transfer news, gossip and hear the word from the players themselves. Each has a page or site devoted to them with a biography and other important details like what they think of their team-mates, an interview, achievements to date and the all important gallery.

## www.soccerbase.com    UK

SOCCER STATISTICS
The site to end all pub rows, it's described as the most comprehensive and up-to-date source of British football data on the Internet. See also **www.footballfigures.co.uk**

## www.fifa.com    SWITZERLAND

FIFA
This is FIFA's magazine where you can get information on what they do, the World Cup and other FIFA competitions. For the UEFA go to **www.uefa.com** where you can see how everyone is faring in the Champions League and UEFA cup.

*See also:*

**www.irishfa.com** – the Irish Football Association with a pretty standard site.

**www.leaguemanagers.com** – home of the League Managers Association.

**www.ourweecountry.co.uk** – a good fanzine covering football in Northern Ireland.

**www.premierleague.com** – a top site covering the latest news and information.

**www.scotprem.co.uk** – a comprehensive offering with links too.

**www.welsh-football.net** – an independent magazine on the Welsh soccer scene.

## www.footballaid.com    UK

FOOTBALL CHARITY
Football aid is a charity that helps good causes by running football events, you can sign on to play for the team of your choice or just send a cheque.

## www.footballgroundguide.co.uk    UK

FOOTBALL GROUNDS
Details of all 92 league football club grounds, locations and facilities, incredibly useful for all away supporters. Excellent for team links too.

## Golf

## www.golftoday.co.uk    UK

THE PREMIER ONLINE GOLF MAGAZINE
An excellent site for golf news and tournaments with features, statistics, rankings and also a course directory. It's the best all-round site covering Europe. There are also links to sister sites about the amateur game, shops and where to stay. Golf Today also hosts a comprehensive site on the amateur game; you can find it at **www.amateur-golf.com**

## www.golfingguides.net    UK

UK GOLF COURSES
Detailed information on selected golf courses classed as 'gems', plus contact information on those lesser courses. A good search facility rounds it off, plus the fact it's pretty well designed.

S

## www.golfweb.com                                              US
### PGA TOUR
The best site for statistics on the PGA, and keeping up with
tournament scores, it also has audio and visual features with
RealPlayer. For the official word on the tour go to
**www.pga.com** while for the European tour go to
**www.europeantour.com**

## www.golf.com                                                 US
### THE AMERICAN VIEW
Part of NBC's suite of web sites, this offers a massive amount
of information and statistics on the game, the major tours and
players, both men and women.

## www.uk-golfguide.com                                         UK
### GOLF TOURISM
A useful directory of courses and hotels with courses, with links
to travel agents for the UK and abroad, you can also get
information on golf equipment suppliers and insurance.
See also **www.whatgolf.co.uk** and **www.grassrootsgolf.com**

## www.onlinegolf.co.uk                                         UK
### GOLF EQUIPMENT
A good-looking and comprehensive golf store with lots of offers
and a good range, it has a ladies section, a good search facility
and you can trial some clubs for 30 days. Delivery on orders
over £50 is free in the UK.

*See also:*
**http://golfbidder.co.uk** – store for second hand clubs and
equipment.
**http://golfwebcenter.fol.nl** – links to all things golf around
the world.
**www.fade-fashion.com** – golfing equipment and gear.
**www.golfingguides.net** – authoritative reviews of the best
golf courses.
**www.golflinks.co.uk** – a large, UK oriented site database.
**www.grassrootsgolf.com** – for summer camps for junior golfers,
corporate golf and golf tours.
**www.mygolfzone.com** – a good all-rounder.
**www.rydercup.com** – a good overview of the competition.

# Gymnastics

**www.gymmedia.com**                                    GERMANY
GYMNASTIC NEWS
A bilingual site giving all the latest news, it covers all forms of
the sport and offers lots of links to related sites.

*See also:*
**www.baga.co.uk** – for the official UK gymnastics site, which is
comprehensive.
**www.british-gymnastics.org** – an official site offering lots of
information and advice.
**www.intlgymnast.com** – the latest news from *International
Gymnast* magazine.
**www.scottishgymnastics.com** – comprehensive coverage but
tied to the magazine so it's not all it could be.
**www.trampoline.co.uk** – Jumpers trampoline club with
information and advice too.

# Hockey

**www.hockeyonline.co.uk**                                    UK

THE ENGLISH HOCKEY ASSOCIATION
A slick site covering the English game with information and
chat on the players, leagues and teams for both the men's
and the women's games. For the Welsh game go to
**www.welsh-hockey.co.uk** and for the Scottish
**www.scottish-hockey.org.uk** neither are great on design
but give all the relevant information.

*See also:*
**www.fieldhockey.com** – advert-laden and dull design but has
all the latest news.
**www.hockeyweb.co.uk** – chat, news and links.
**www.hockeydirect.co.uk** – good equipment store.

# Horse racing

*For sites that cover the gambling side of horse racing go to page 169.*

S

## www.racingpost.co.uk UK

*RACING POST*
Superb, informative site from the authority on the sport, every
event covered in-depth with tips and advice. To get the best out
of it you have to register, then you have access to the database
and more.

## www.bhb.co.uk UK

BRITISH HORSE RACING BOARD
A very well put together site offering up information and
background on the sport including interviews, details of the
latest meetings and horse ownership advice.

## www.racenews.co.uk UK

RACING, COURSES AND BETTING
A slightly different spin from Racenews, they have three main
sections: their news service, a course guide and a tipsters
column, there's also an excellent links section covering racing
world-wide.

## www.flatstats.co.uk UK

FLAT RACING STATISTICS
This site contains masses of detailed and unique statistics –
horse, trainer, jockey, sire and race statistics, favourites
analysis, systems analysis and much more. You have to be a
member to get the best out of it. See also **www.workrider.com**

## www.thejockeyclub.co.uk UK

THE JOCKEY CLUB
A campaigning site aimed at promoting confidence in racing.
It has news, details on the rules and how stewarding works,
as well as links and sporting guidelines. See also
**www.jockeysroom.com**, which has an A–Z of, jockeys with
biographies and pictures.

*Other sites work a visit are...*
**www.attheraces.co.uk** – live action, tips and the latest news
plus great design.
**www.bbc.co.uk/racing** – the BBC's excellent race pages.
**www.racecall.co.uk** – hear all the action on your phone.
**www.racecoursewhisper.com** – all the goings on at the
all-weather tracks.

S

**www.teletext.co.uk** – for a good summary of what's going on in the sport check out the racing pages at Teletext, also has a good search facility.

# Ice hockey

## www.nhl.com UK

NATIONAL HOCKEY LEAGUE
Catch up on the latest from the NHL including a chance to listen to and watch key moments from past and recent games.

## www.icehockeyuk.co.uk

ICE HOCKEY UK
The official site with bags of information and background on the game. It's well designed and great for beginners and those who want to find out more about the sport.

*See also:*
**www.azhockey.com** – home of the Encyclopaedia of Ice Hockey.
**www.britnatleague.co.uk** or **www.fbnl.co.uk** – now the Findus British National League information and news
**www.crazykennys.com** – ice hockey equipment suppliers.
**www.icehockeyhistory.co.uk** – a sparse site covering the history of the game in the UK.

# Ice skating

## www.bladesonice.com

FIGURE SKATING MAGAZINE
From the magazine *Blades on Ice*, this site features archive material, the latest news, details of events, advice and of course how to subscribe.

*See also:*
**www.iceskating.org.uk** – the official site of the National Ice Skating Association of the UK, a good-looking site covering all aspects of ice skating.
**www.iceskatingworld.com** – comprehensive US site with excellent links and the latest news.
**www.sisa.org.uk** – The Scottish Ice Skating Association.
**www.skating-shop.co.uk** – for all your skating gear.

## Martial arts

### www.martial-arts-network.com                                          US

PROMOTING MARTIAL ARTS
Possibly qualifies as the loudest introduction sequence,
but once you've cut the volume or skipped the intro, the site
offers a great deal in terms of resources and information about
the martial arts scene, including *Black Belts* magazine.
Its layout is a little confusing and the site is quite slow.

### www.britishjudo.org.uk                                                UK

JUDO
Judo has a proud tradition in the UK, and if you want to follow
that you can get all the information you need at the British
Judo Association site. It gives a brief history of judo,
a magazine and event information. For a broader view go
to **www.judoinfo.com**

### www.btkf.homestead.com                                                UK

BRITISH KARATE FEDERATION
Information on all forms of the discipline as well as events
listings, fun pages and an online martial arts club, which is
hosted by Yahoo.

*See also:*
**http://physical-arts.com** – a site in the making, more a way of
life than combat.
**http://uk.dir.yahoo.com/recreation/sport/martial_arts** – a huge
number of links.
**www.martialinfo.com** – slow but comprehensive site with an
online magazine.
**www.martialresource.com** – good-looking site which explains
the background to each type of martial art and gives hints and
tips to those just starting out.
**www.practical-martial-arts.co.uk** – useful advice on techniques
and an overview of key combat types, there are also forums
where you can have your say.
**www.ryoku.co.uk** – where to go for your gear.

# Motor sport

## www.crash.net UK

MOTORSPORT PORTAL
An excellent but very commercial news and directory site
covering the major motor sports and most of the minor ones
too. There's an online shop selling motor sport merchandise
amongst other things and there's a good photo library.

## www.ukmotorsport.com UK

INFORMATION OVERLOAD
This site covers every form of motor racing; it's got lots of links
to appropriate sites covering all aspects of motor sport. There
are also chat sections and forums plus links to product and
service suppliers.

## www.autosport.com UK

*AUTOSPORT* MAGAZINE
Excellent for news and features on motor sport plus links and
an affiliated online shopping experience for related products
such as team gear, books or models.

## www.linksheaven.com US

THE MOST COMPREHENSIVE LINKS DIRECTORY
Whatever, whoever, there's an appropriate link. It's bias towards
Formula 1, CART and Nascar though.

## www.MSport-UK.com UK

UK MOTOR SPORT
A good site covering all aspects of motor sport in Britain,
highlights include the 'must see' section (I wish more sites had
one) and the links page. As they've kept out clutter it's fast to use.

## www.itv-f1.com UK

F1 ON ITV
This web site is excellent, it doesn't miss much and there is
plenty of action. There's all the background information you'd
expect plus circuit profiles, schedules and a photo gallery.
For more news and links to everywhere in F1 go to
**www.f1-world.co.uk** or the eccentric **www.f1nutter.co.uk**
alternatively try **www.f1weekly.net**

**www.fota.co.uk**                                          UK

> FORMULA 3
> Formula 3 explained plus info on the teams, drivers and
> circuits. It's the breeding ground for F1 drivers of the future
> which adds to the excitement reflected in the energy of this site.

**www.rallysport.com**                                      UK

> COVERING THE WORLD RALLY CHAMPIONSHIP
> Good for results and news on rallying in the UK and across the
> world. See also **www.rallyzone.co.uk** which is a comprehensive
> international e-zine. You can follow a race stage by stage at
> **http://rally.racing-live.com/en** as well as get all the latest news.

**www.btccpages.com**                                       UK

> BRITISH TOURING CAR CHAMPIONSHIP
> This site offers a great deal of information and statistics on the
> championship, driver and team profiles, photos and links to
> other related sites. There are also a number of forums you can
> get involved with if you feel like chatting to fellow enthusiasts.

**www.karting.co.uk**                                       UK

> GO KARTING
> A well-laid out portal site to all things karting in the UK,
> with links and directories covering the tracks, manufacturers,
> events and a photo gallery plus the latest news. See also
> **www.gokartingforfun.co.uk**

## Motorcycling

**www.motorcyclenews.com**                                  UK

> NEWS AND VIEWS
> A very good magazine-style site giving all the latest news,
> gossip and event information, there are also sections on buying
> a bike, where to get parts and the latest gear, off-road biking
> and a links directory. There's also a chat room and a good
> classified section.

**www.acu.org.uk**                                          UK

> AUTO-CYCLE UNION
> The ACU is the governing body for motorcycle sports in the
> UK and this site gives information on its work and the benefits
> of being a member. There are also links and details of
> their magazine.

S

### www.motograndprix.com
UK

TRACK AND OFF-ROAD
A well-laid out magazine site, covering the world of Moto Grand
Prix with results, background and biographical details. See also
**www.motoGP.com** which is a busy and informative site.

### www.british-speedway.co.uk
UK

SPEEDWAY
A text-based site giving information on the leagues as well as
the latest news, there's also an events calendar and links to
related sites.

### www.motocross.com
US

MOTOCROSS
An authoritative site covering the sport but it's centred on the
US, although it has got some information on the European
scene. See also **www.motolinks.com**

## Mountaineering and outdoor sports

### www.mountainzone.com
US

FOR THE UPWARDLY MOBILE
Thoroughly covers all aspects of climbing, hiking, mountain
biking, skiing and snowboarding with a very good photography
section featuring galleries from major mountains and climbers.

### www.ukclimbing.com
UK

CLIMBING NEWS
Excellent and very informative site covering all aspects of
climbing, it has plenty of opportunities for chat along with the
latest news, there's also weather information and a very good
database of climbs with comments and essential information
for each one.

### www.rockrun.com
UK

ALL THE RIGHT EQUIPMENT
Excellent equipment shop covering climbing and walking gear,
which is also pretty comprehensive on the information front too,
delivery starts at £3.50 for the UK. See also
**www.gearzone.co.uk** who have a similar offering.

*Other good climbing sites:*
**www.blacks.co.uk** – good camping and equipment store.
**www.cruxed.com** – nice-looking site with advice on techniques and training, good links.
**www.onward-outward.co.uk** – a good outdoor clothing store with a wide range and the best brands.
**www.outdoorgear.co.uk** – everything you need for the outdoors.
**www.thebmc.co.uk** – good all-round climbing and hill-walking magazine-style site from the British Mountaineering Council with good links pages.
**www.upandunder.co.uk** – Welsh mountaineering store, good links section.

# Netball

**www.netball.org**                                                        UK

INTERNATIONAL FEDERATION OF NETBALL ASSOCIATIONS
Get information on the work of the federation and the rules of the game, plus rankings and the events calendar. See also **www.netballcoaching.com** which is good for advice and links.

# Olympics

**www.olympics.org**                                                       UK

BRITISH OLYMPIC ASSOCIATION
A new-look site with sections on the forthcoming winter and summer games, information for collectors and also the doping policy, for a history of the games there's the Olympic museum link and links to sports federations and committees.

*See also:*
**www.olympianartifacts.com** – good site featuring an Olympic memorabilia store.
**www.olympics.com** – the official site of the Olympic movement.

# Rowing

**www.ara-rowing.org**                                                     UK

AMATEUR ROWING ASSOCIATION
This site offers information on the history of the sport, plus the latest news, coaching tips and links.

See also:
**www.steveredgrave.com** – Sir Steve's official site offers
biographical information, training instruction and tips, links and
background on the sport.
**www.total.rowing.org.uk** – a good rowing portal site.

# Rugby

## www.scrum.com UK

RUGBY UNION
An excellent site about rugby union with impressively up-to-the-
minute coverage, for a similar but lighter and more fun site
go to **www.planet-rugby.com** which has a comprehensive
round-up of world rugby with instant reports, lots of detail and
information on both union and league. **www.rugbyheaven.com**
is also worth checking out.

## www.rfu.com UK

RUGBY FOOTBALL UNION
Masses of features, articles and news from the official RFU site,
it's got team news and information, links and a shop where you
can buy gear – delivery is free for the UK for orders under £5.

## www.rleague.com UK

WORLD OF RUGBY LEAGUE
Another very comprehensive site, featuring sections on
Australia, New Zealand and the UK, with plenty of chat,
articles, player profiles and enough statistics to keep the
most ardent fan happy. See also the magazine site
**www.totalrugbyleague.com** and also **www.ozleague.com**

## www.rugbyrelics.com UK

RUGBY MEMORABILIA
A good memorabilia store covering most countries and aspects
of the game, everything from autographs to ties and programs.

# Sailing

## www.madforsailing.com UK

THE DAILY SAIL
An informative and well-laid out site covering all aspects of
sailing both as a sport and as a hobby. There are some really
good and well written articles and features such as a crew
search facility and weather information.

## www.yachtmonster.com                                    US

### FOR ALL THINGS YACHTING
A combination of search engine, site directory and news round up all devoted to one subject – yachting. See also **www.yachtpeople.com** which has an American bias.

## www.ukdinghyracing.com                                  UK

### UK DINGHY RACING
Devoted mainly to this one aspect of sailing, it covers the sport comprehensively and gives advice on buying and hosts links to auctions and specialist shops.

## www.ellenmacarthur.com                                  UK

### ELLEN MACARTHUR
An interesting and well put together site where you can find out what Ellen is up to as well as biographical details.

*See also:*
**www.madforsailing.com** – the Daily Sail magazine has a better than average site.
**www.rya.org.uk** – a good advice laden site from the Royal Yachting Association, very informative at all levels.
**www.sailing-411.com** – excellent American sailing portal.
**www.smartguide.com** – a useful sailing site index.
**www.uksail.com** – a sailing portal site offering some 1,000 links.

*Skiing and snowboarding – see page 365.*

# Snooker

## www.embassysnooker.com                                  UK

### WORLD CHAMPIONSHIPS
An overview of the world championships from their sponsor, the site is comprehensive and there are good features such as a hall of fame, rankings and a look behind the scenes.

*See also:*
**www.snooker.net** – great for the latest news and gossip.
**www.snookersports.co.uk** – a snooker equipment shop.
**www.worldsnooker.com** – informative site which is run by the games governing body.

# Tennis and racquet sports

## Tennis

### www.lta.org.uk

LAWN TENNIS ASSOCIATION
An excellent and attractively designed all-year tennis
information site run by the Lawn Tennis Association, it has
information on the players, rankings and tournament news,
as well as details on clubs and coaching courses. There's also
an online tennis shop where you can buy merchandise and
equipment. See also **www.atptour.com** which gives
a less UK biased view of the game, with excellent sections on
the players, tournaments and rankings.

### www.wimbledon.org

THE OFFICIAL WIMBLEDON SITE
Very impressive, there's a great deal here and not just in June,
but you need to be patient. Apart from the information you'd
expect, you can download screensavers, visit the online
museum and eventually see videos of past matches.
The shop is expensive.

*Other tennis sites worth a look:*
**www.cliffrichardtennis.org** – excellent site aimed at
encouraging children to take up the game.
**www.pwp.com** – a comprehensive tennis and racquet sport
related store.
**www.racquet-zone.co.uk** – a good racquet shop with free
delivery to the UK.
**www.tennis.com** – good magazine, with gear guides, tips and
hot news.
**www.tennisnews.com** – the latest news updated daily and
e-mailed to you.

## Badminton

### www.badders.com

BADMINTON COMMUNITY NETWORK
A very good example of a site that pulls together an interest
group. It's excellent for news and chat as well as links and
information on the sport.

*See also:*

**www.badmintonplayer.com** – a good-looking site with results, tips, classifieds and links too.

**www.badzone.co.uk** – a pretty comprehensive offering, interesting design!

**www.baofe.co.uk** – the site of the Badminton Association of England with all the latest news.

**www.intbadfed.org** – home of the International Badminton Federation.

## Squash

**www.squashplayer.co.uk**                                            UK

WORLD OF SQUASH AT YOUR FINGERTIPS
A really comprehensive round up of the game, with links galore and a great news section, there's also a section for the UK, which has club details and the latest news. See also **www.worldsquash.org** for a good site on what's going on world-wide.

## Table tennis

**www.ettu.org**                                                      UK

EUROPEAN TABLE TENNIS UNION
Find out about the ETTU, its rankings, competition details and results plus a section devoted to world table tennis links. See also **www.ittf.com** which gives a worldview.

## Ten pin bowling

**www.btba.org.uk**                                                   UK

BRITISH TENPIN BOWLING ASSOCIATION
The home of the game in the UK with rules, information on clubs and background on what the governing body does.

*See also:*

**www.bowluk.co.uk** – a useful directory of bowling centres, shops, links and events.

**www.probowluk.co.uk** – a serious site with useful tips and links.

# Water sports and swimming

## Swimming

### www.swimnews.com                                                    US
SWIMMING NEWS
It's up-to-date and offers a wide coverage of news, with other
features such as rankings, events calendar, shopping and
competition analysis.

### www.pullbuoy.co.uk                                                  UK
UK SWIMMING
A good site that covers the UK scene, you can find unusual
features such as a job finder and time converter, it's great for
links too.

*Other good swimming sites:*
**www.learn-to-swim.co.uk** – learn to swim holidays.
**www.swiminfo.com** – US magazine site with articles,
information and results.
**www.swimmersworld.com** – pretty average site with news
and links.

## Surfing

### www.coldswell.co.uk                                                 UK
SURFING THE UK COAST
Includes forecasts for weather and surf, satellite images,
live surf web cams from around the world and a complete
directory of surfing web sites.

*See also:*
**www.coastalwatch.com** – great, if you're in Australia.
**www.surfline.com** – check out weather, sea conditions, the
latest gear – all you need before you go essentially.
**www.surflink.com** – good coverage of surfing world-wide.
**www.surfstation.co.uk** – for links, shopping and surf speak.

S

### www.2xs.co.uk                                                      UK
WINDSURFING IN THE UK
Where to go windsurfing, plus tips and the latest sports news,
shopping, weather information and advice.

## Water-ski

### www.waterski.com                                    US

WORLD OF WATER SKIING
An American site that features information about the sport,
how to compete, news, tips, equipment and where to ski.
See also **www.bwsf.co.uk** although not an attractive site,
it does have UK-based information on places to ski, clubs,
competitions and a message board. Another good site is
**www.planetwaterski.com** another American site with a
global guide to places to ski.

## Diving

### www.ukdiving.co.uk                                  UK

DIVING RESOURCE
A very good resource site with the latest news. It seems to
cover all aspects of the sport but you'd have to say the design
is odd. It has some good articles, useful advice and is good for
links too.

*See also:*
**www.bsac.com** – the British Sub Aqua Club, a basic site with
info on what they do.
**www.cmas2000.org** – the World Underwater Federation with
an odd but informative site.
**www.divegirl.com** – a magazine site about women and scuba.
**www.padi.com** – the place to start when you want to learn
to dive.
**www.saa.org.uk** – home of the Sub Aqua Association with links
and information.

## Wrestling

### www.wwe.com                                        US

WORLD WRESTLING ENTERTAINMENT
Whether you think it's sport or soap opera, here you can keep
up with the twists and turns plus all the action at this exciting
site, which has news, clips and of course a merchandise shop.

See also:

**www.amateurwrestlingnews.com** – amateur wrestling scene with US bias.

**www.prowrestling.com** – all the latest news and controversy.

**www.wrestlingusa.com** – a more serious and credible magazine site.

# Sports clothes and merchandise

## www.sweatband.com                                    UK

SHOP BY SPORT

A wide-ranging shop that supplies equipment for many sports, but it's especially good for tennis, rugby and cricket. Delivery costs depend on the weight of your parcel. See also **www.newitts.com** which is comprehensive.

## www.kitbag.com                                        UK

SPORTS FASHION

Football kits and gear galore from new to retro; covers cricket and rugby too. Costs on delivery vary according to order. Also offers shopping by brand and a news service.

## www.sportspages.co.uk                                 UK

TAKING SPORT SERIOUSLY

Book and video specialists, concentrating on sport, they offer a wide range at OK prices, even signed copies. Great for that one thing you've been unable to find.

## www.sportsworld.co.uk                                 UK

SPORT TRAVEL

Specialists in making travel arrangements to sporting events; at this site you can book tickets and find out about future events. It's also good for corporate hospitality; the site is a little temperamental though and not that easy to use.

## www.sportingheritage.co.uk                            UK

SPORTING GIFTS

A selection of prints, gifts and collectibles available to buy from this well laid out site and they cover all the major sports.

S

# Stationery

## www.stationerystore.co.uk                                           UK

STATIONERY STORE
A well-designed and easy-to-use stationery store supplying
everything from paperclips to office machinery. There are also
sections on green stationery, electronics and lots of offers.
Delivery is free for orders over £40, £2.99 if below that.

## www.staples.co.uk                                                   UK

NOT JUST STAPLES
A good all rounder with a wide range and some good offers;
next day delivery is available and free if you spend more
than £30.

*For other stationery stores try:*
**www.cardcorp.co.uk** – good place to go for your business cards
and other printing needs.
**www.office-world.co.uk** – Office World have at last introduced
an online shopping service delivery is next day and free if you
spend over £35.
**www.paperchase.co.uk** – you can't buy online but it
looks great.
**www.staples.co.uk** – still no online store except for business
customers, but you can order a catalogue and find your
nearest store.
**www.viking-direct.co.uk** – good, but business to business only.
**www.whsmith.co.uk/stationery** – another good W.H.Smith site
with some offers and multi-buys but a limited range which does
include some of their fashion stationery.

## www.katespaperie.com                                                US

POSH PAPER
To many people it's just 'paper with bits in' but for those who
pay regular homage to the New York stores, Kate's Paperie
represents the best in hand-made stationery and wrapping
paper. Here you can buy online, but shipping can be expensive.

S

**www.greenstat.co.uk**

UK    GREEN STATIONERY
Green as in environmentally friendly, they supply a wide
range of recycled paper products and desk accessories.
It's unsophisticated with delivery costs being well hidden and
you have to go through an annoying process of making a note
of product code numbers for your order form. It's got good links
to other environmentally friendly businesses.

*See also:*
**www.reactivated.co.uk** – stationery amongst other recycled
products.
**www.remarkable.co.uk** – for pencils made from recycled
plastic cups.

# Student Sites

*There's masses of information for students on the Net. Here are some
sites worth checking out. The links are generally very good, so if the
topic isn't covered here, it should be easy to track down.*

## Universities and colleges

**www.ucas.co.uk**                                                    UK

THE UNIVERSITY STARTING BLOCK
A comprehensive site listing all the courses at British
universities with entry profiles. You can view the directory
online and order your UCAS handbook and application form.
If you've already applied, you can view your application online.
There are links to all the universities plus really good links to
related sites. There is good advice too. If you want to study
abroad you can try finding a course through **www.edunet.com**

**www.nusonline.co.uk**                                               UK

STUDENTS UNITE
Lots of relevant news and views for students on this really
good-looking site. You need to register to get assess to their
discounts directory and special offers. Once in, you can send
e-cards and use their mail and storage facilities too.

S

*See also these other useful sites:*

**www.braintrack.com** – a comprehensive directory of links to universities world-wide.

**www.britishcouncil.org/education** – the student section is full of options for further education and training.

**www.careers-portal.co.uk** – an excellent portal site that is part of the National Grid for Learning.

**www.hotcourses.com** – a very good database of courses for students at all levels, with career and money advice thrown in.

**www.slc.co.uk** – home of the Student Loan Company.

**www.unn.ac.uk/~iniw2/bestsite.htm** – a useful directory of sites for students.

# Working abroad and job finding

**www.gapyear.com**                                              UK

COMPLETE GUIDE TO TAKING A YEAR OUT
Whether you fancy helping out in the forests of Brazil or teaching in Europe you'll find information and opportunities here. There's loads of advice, past experiences to get you tempted, chat, a message board, competitions and you can subscribe to their magazine (an old-fashioned paper one).

**www.payaway.co.uk**                                            UK

FIND A JOB ABROAD OR WORKING HOLIDAY
A great starting place for anyone who wants to work abroad. There is a magazine, reports from travellers and you can register with their online jobs service. They've missed nothing out in their links section from embassies to travel health.

**www.anyworkanywhere.com**                                      UK

JOBS IN THE UK AND WORLDWIDE
A bright and breezy site with jobs and all the right advice, plus links.

*See also:*

**www.bunac.co.uk** – combine work and travel with these programmes from an experienced specialist.

**www.yearoutgroup.org** – a mass of information and help for both those taking a gap year and their parents too.

# Careers

**www.prospects.ac.uk** UK

CAREER OPTIONS
Home of the official graduates careers guide offering a huge
amount of information, which is all packed into a pretty dense site.

# Discount cards

**www.istc.org** UK

INTERNATIONAL STUDENT TRAVEL CONFEDERATION
Get your student and youth discount card as well as info on
working and studying abroad. Also help with such things
as railpasses, phonecards, ISTC registered travel agents
world-wide, plus e-mail, voice mail and fax messaging.
For a European youth card for discounts within the EU
go to the cool **www.euro26.org**

# Student life

**www.studentuk.com** UK

STUDENT LIFE
A good-looking, useful and generally well-written student's
magazine featuring news, music and film reviews, going out,
chat, even articles on science and politics. There's also some
excellent advice on subjects such as gap years, accommodation
and finance.

**www.good2bsecure.gov.uk** UK

FIGHT CRIME AGAINST STUDENTS
Students are more likely to be victims of crime than any part of
society, here you can get advice on security and keeping safe.

# Links

**www.lazystudent.co.uk** UK

SITE LISTING
The perfect site for those who can't be arsed to look things up
properly, it's well categorised and has listed virtually any site
that a student might need.

# *Teenagers*

*Here's a small selection of the best sites aimed at teenagers. Many of the most hyped sites are just heavily disguised marketing and sales operations, treat these with scepticism and enjoy the best, which are done for the love of it. We've also indicated the sort of age group that the magazines are aimed at. We should add our thanks to all those who keep writing in to us suggesting sites for this section. Don't forget your personal safety if you chat online, see page 70 for details or go to **www.thinkuknow.co.uk** for a cartoon-based interactive look at the issues.*

## Teenage magazines

**www.globalgang.org.uk**                                                    UK

> WORLD NEWS, GAMES, GOSSIP AND FUN
> See what the rest of the world gets up to at Global Gang.
> You can find out what kids in other countries like to eat, what
> toys they play with, chat to them or play games. Lastly you get
> to find out how you can help those kids less fortunate than
> yourself. *10 plus*

**www.girland.com**                                                          UK

> GIRL AND...
> An excellent, really attractive and well put together site aimed
> at teenage girls, it has chat forums, news and lots of features,
> but you do have to register. It has won loads of awards and the
> environment is safe. *11 plus*

**www.mykindaplace.com**                                                     UK

> IT'S MY KINDA PLACE
> Excellent site for teens, with the latest news, gossip and
> celebrity features, aimed squarely at girls it seems to have
> everything, including lots of adverts! *11 plus*

**www.teentoday.co.uk**                                                      UK

T

> FOR TEENAGERS BY TEENAGERS
> Get your free e-zine mailed to you daily or just visit the site
> which has much more; games, chat, news, entertainment,
> free downloads, ringtones and message boards. It's well
> designed and genuinely good with not too much advertising.
> *13 plus*

## http://www.bbc.co.uk/teens/ UK

### E-ZINES FOR BOTH SEXES

The BBC's teen magazine site addresses the loves and concerns of the two sexes. Boys get plenty of games, quizzes, cartoons and useless facts while the girls get a dose of celebs, beauty, horoscopes plus some fun and games too. There are excellent advice and information sections for both sexes and both are treated to some brilliant competitions, prizes and fun articles too. *13 plus*

## www.alloy.com US

### *ALLOY* MAGAZINE

On the face of it this is great, it's got loads of sections on everything from personal advice to shopping albeit a bit American. But with too many adverts, it all seems to be geared to getting your name for marketing purposes and selling stuff. *13 plus*

## www.cheekfreak.com US

### FOR THE FREAK IN ALL OF US

Best for stories, online diaries and free downloads. It's got chat sections, message boards and a search engine. *13 plus*

## www.cyberteens.com UK

### CONNECT TO CYBERTEENS

One of the most hyped sites aimed at teenagers, it contains a very good selection of games, news, links and a creativity section where you can send your art and poems. Don't bother with the shop, which was still being re-designed at time of writing, but on previous visits it was expensive, as is the credit card they offer. *13 plus*

## www.dubit.co.uk UK

### GAMES, ARTICLES – THE LOT

Dubit combines 3-D graphics with chat, games, video, music and animations in a fun and interactive way. It's a completely different approach to the normal teen magazine. It needs a little patience but it's worth it in the end. Registration required, which is a pity as it is a pain and very slow. *13 plus*

T

### www.spacegirl.org

FUN AND ANGST

Get it off your chest, check out the issues, read a good book recommendation, have fun, then dress space girl up. Good-looking site, lots to do. Shame about Kyle's haircut. *14 plus*

### www.mindbodysoul.gov.uk

GET THE LOW-DOWN ON HEALTH

A health site for teenagers. It covers all you'd expect, all wrapped up in good-looking graphics, it's also not too densely written or too patronising. *14 plus*

### www.thesite.org.uk

THE SITE

This site offers advice on a range of subjects: careers, relationships, drugs, sex, money, legal issues and so on. Aimed largely at 15 to 24 year olds, it's well laid out and very informative. *15 plus*

### www.4degreez.com

INTERACTIVE COMMUNITY

A friendly and entertaining site with reviews, poetry, jokes, polls and links to other related sites. You have to become a member to get the best out of it though. *15 plus*

### www.missminx.com

UK'S LEADING ALTERNATIVE GRRL SITE...

To quote them 'dedicated to shouting about all that is kick-ass and female, mainly in music, and rock-orientated'. *15 plus*

## Directories

### www.teensites.org

WEB DIRECTORY FOR TEENS

A huge directory of sites covering loads of subjects of interest to teenagers. It's biased to the US, but if you don't mind that, then it should have everything you need.

T

**www.ipl.org/div/teen/**                                        US

TEEN SPACE
Part of the Internet Public Library, these pages offer a directory
of links for help and information on everything from careers,
homework, issues, fashion and dating.

See also:
**http://directory.google.com/Top/Kids_and_Teens** – good
directory from Google.
**www.kidgrid.com** – well laid out and easy to use, with a
US bias.
**www.kidsclick.org** – massive database of sites put together by
a group of librarians.
**www.spike2000.com** – bright and breezy listing with an
educational bias.
**www.surfnetkids.com** – a comprehensive directory put together
by an American journalist.

## Advice

**www.worriedneed2talk.org.uk**                                 UK

CRUELTY TO CHILDREN MUST STOP!
A site from the NSPCC aimed at helping teenagers and children
cope and deal with violence, family problems and drug advice.

# Telecommunications

*In this ever changing section there's information on ADSL and
computer-related communications, where to go to buy mobiles, get
the best out of them and even have a little fun with them. For phone
numbers see the section entitled 'Finding Someone' on page 134.*

**www.oftel.gov.uk**                                            UK

OFFICE OF TELECOMMUNICATIONS
A useful site that shows the workings of Oftel with the latest
news and consumer information surrounding the complex world
of telecommunication. See also **www.icstis.org.uk** for the
Independent Committee for the Supervision of Standards of
Telephone Information Services.

T

# ADSL/broadband

*Asymmetric Digital Subscriber Line (ADSL) is a technology for transmitting digital information at a high bandwidth on existing phone lines to homes and businesses. It enables you to access the Internet many times faster than with conventional phone lines. Unfortunately, access to broadband is limited and its introduction slower than in other parts of the world. See also Broardband, page 51.*

### www.btopenworld.com UK

BRITISH TELECOM

Here you can establish whether you are in line to get access to broadband and more or less when. There are details of the various BT packages, other suppliers and also information for business users too.

*See also:*

**www.adslguide.org.uk** – a good guide to everything broadband.
**www.ispreview.co.uk/broadband.shtml** – informative pages from the excellent ISP review.
**www.ntlhome.com/broadband** – supplies most of the UK.
**www.satdrive.com** – broadband using satellite technology.
**www.telewest.co.uk** – supplies selected parts of the UK.
**www.theregister.co.uk** – the latest telecom and broadband news.

## Mobile phones

### www.carphonewarehouse.com UK

CHOOSING THE RIGHT MOBILE

You need to take your time to find the best tariff, then take advantage of the numerous offers. Excellent pictures, details of the phones and the information is unbiased. There's a shop that also sells handheld PCs and delivery is free too. You can download a wide range of new phone ring tones, from classical to the latest pop tunes.

### www.mobileedge.co.uk UK

MOBILE INFORMATION

A really well-designed site with help on buying the right mobile, it also offers information on health and mobiles, links and contact numbers, pre-pay deals, global networks, ring tones, shop and much more.

*See also:*
**www.b3k.net** – excellent site with a wide range of phones and accessories, good for the hard to get bits too.
**www.expansys.com** – dense site with masses of information and competitive prices.
**www.dialaphone.co.uk** – another phone shop. They'll match anyone else's prices though, usually this is a sure sign they'll disappear by the next edition but let's hope they survive.
**www.miahtelecom.co.uk** – another good site with a wide range of products and some excellent offers.
**www.mobilefun.co.uk** – a huge range of phones and accessories.
**www.mobileshop.com** – nice design and lots of offers.
**www.smartphones.org.uk** – free delivery on all orders.
**www.themobilerepublic.com** – one of the most complete offerings with lots of deals, also sells PDAs.

*Here's where to find the major phone operators:*
**www.motorola.co.uk**
**www.o2.co.uk**
**www.orange.co.uk**
**www.three.co.uk**
**www.t-mobile.co.uk**
**www.virginmobile.com**
**www.vodafone.co.uk**

# Recycling

**www.oxfam.org.uk/what_you_can_do/recycle/phones**          UK
### SEND YOUR OLD MOBILES HERE
If you have all your old mobiles hanging around the house then go here to find out how you can put them to good use. See also **www.nru.org.uk/mobilephones.htm**

# Text messaging

**www.yourmobile.com**                                        UK
### NEW RING TUNES FOR YOUR PHONE
There are several hundred tunes, icons and logos that you can download on to your mobile using text messaging and most are free.

T

**www.treasuremytext.com**    UK

SAVING YOUR TEXTS
Here you can store your text messages online, even create a
mobile blog and share your text conversations with your friends.

*See also:*
**www.onmymob.com** – offering hundreds of free ringtones
and logos.
**www.boltblue.com** – wide range including adult-oriented
wallpaper, pretty sad really.

**www.chatlist.com/faces.html**    UK

TEXT MESSAGING
Confused about your emoticons? %-) Here's a list of several
thousand for you to choose from.

## Accessorising your phone

**www.coverfrenzy.com**    UK

DESIGN YOUR OWN PHONE COVER
You can use one of their images or one of your own to create a
unique phone cover, however it costs £18.50. It's available for
a wide range of Nokia phones but their range of options is
expanding not only to phones but apparently to hairdryers too.

## Services

**www.buzzme.com**    UK

NEVER MISS A CALL
An online answering machine that gives you the option of
accepting, ignoring or sending voice messages, very useful if
you only have the one line.

**www.mediaring.com**    SINGAPORE

PC TO PHONE COMMUNICATION
Media Ring offer a PC to phone service through their My Voiz
technology. This enables users to communicate at a much
lower cost than phone to phone, it's especially useful if you use
the phone a lot.

**www.mapminder.co.uk**                                                    UK
>    MOBILE PHONE TRACKING
>    Map Minders phone tracking service is excellent if, for example,
>    you're a parent wanting to keep track of your kids or you're a
>    business wanting to co-ordinate sales teams, It combines their
>    mapping which is pretty clear with mobile technology. See also
>    **www.mapaphone.co.uk** and also **www.verilocation.com**

## Technology

**www.bluetooth.com**                                                      US
>    OFFICIAL BLUETOOTH
>    A superb official Microsoft site devoted to Bluetooth technology;
>    it's amazing how fast it's become so widespread.

**www.3g.co.uk**                                                           UK
>    3G
>    Excellent site devoted to bringing you the latest information and
>    developments in this technology.

## *Television*

*TV channels, listings and your favourite soap operas are all here
– some have great sites, others are pretty naff, especially when you
consider they're in the entertainment business.*

**www.ofcom.org.uk**                                                       UK
>    OFCOM
>    Ofcom have taken over from the ITC and is now the regulator
>    for the UK communications industries including television,
>    radio, telecommunications and wireless communications
>    services. If you've a complaint, here's the place to go – they've
>    made it quite easy.

**www.tvlicensing.co.uk**                                                  UK
>    TELEVISION LICENCE
>    All you need to know about your TV licence, how to pay and
>    how to deal with problems.

T

# Channels and digital

## www.bbc.co.uk

### THE UK'S MOST POPULAR WEB SITE

The BBC site deserves a special feature, it is huge with over 300 sections and it can be quite daunting. It has sections covering everything from business to the weather and there are also regional sections, a web guide, as well as tips on how to use the Internet and you can subscribe to a newsletter.
There are feature sites on all their major programs and most of the minor ones too, it's a fantastic site and resource.

## www.itv.co.uk

### ITV NETWORK

ITV has a pretty straightforward site with links to all the major programs, soaps, topics and categories, their related web sites and a 'what's on' guide, plus a few extras such as quizzes.

## www.citv.co.uk

### CHILDREN'S ITV

A bright and breezy site that features competitions, safe surfing, features on the programs including all the favourite characters and much more. You need to join to get the best out of it though, and because there's so much on the site, it can be a little slow.

## www.channel4.co.uk

### CHANNEL 4

A cool design with details of programmes and links to specific web pages on the best-known ones. There are also links to other initiatives such as Filmfour and the 4learning programme.

## www.channel5.co.uk

### CHANNEL 5

The usual programme information, scheduling details, news and competitions. There are also some useful programme-related factsheets and a bright-and-breezy children's section.

## www.sky.com

### SKY TV

Links to the main Sky sites – news, sport, etc, plus information on their digital packages.

## www.nick.com UK

NICKELODEON
Bright doesn't do this site justice, you need sunglasses!
It's got info on all the top programmes plus games and quizzes.

## www.freeview.co.uk UK

FREEVIEW
Details of the Freeview service and where it's available in the UK.

## www.wwitv.com US

WORLD WIDE INTERNET TV
Watch several international channels, the BBC and listen to
radio too. Probably best for broadband users. See also the
excellent **www.liketelevision.com** which is very much geared
to broadband.

# TV fans and nostalgia

## www.whowantstobeontv.co.uk UK

HOW TO GET ON TV
A listing of the TV shows that are looking for participants and
contributors whether it be game shows, reality TV or talent
shows, it's here. Contact details of the shows are supplied as
well as an overview of the program.

## www.standroom.com UK

TICKETS FOR TV SHOWS
If you want to watch a TV show being made or be in the
audience, then here's where to go for tickets. See also
**www.clappers-tickets.co.uk**

## www.sausagenet.co.uk UK

CULT AND CLASSIC TV
Having lost most of the material, this site is up again and is
once again an outstanding nostalgia site devoted to popular
children's TV programs from the last 40 years. You can
download theme tunes or buy related merchandise via the
excellent links directory. See also **www.sadgeezr.com** which
is Sci Fi-oriented.

T

## www.televisionheaven.co.uk UK

PRESERVING TV MEMORIES
An excellent site devoted to archiving reviews and memories of
as many TV favourites they can, a visit is very nostalgic and
very time consuming. Good for links too.

## www.transdiffusion.org/emc/ UK

MEDIA HISTORY
A selection of articles, sites and links which look back at
television history, it's pretty diverse and not easy to navigate
but there's some excellent stuff here especially in the Halcyon
Days section.

## www.tvhome.co.uk UK

TV LOGOS
This good-looking site is devoted to cataloguing all the TV logos,
presentations and 'idents', you may ask 'why?' but it's actually
quite nostalgic.

*See also:*
**www.625.uk.com** – a personal celebration and overview of the
rights and wrongs of British telly, with downloads of logos and
even public information films.
**www.advertsongs.co.uk** – find music used in adverts, pretty
out of date though.
**www.bigglethwaite.com** – great for TV-related links.
**www.petford.net/kaleidoscope** – the site of a voluntary
organisation devoted to the appreciation of classic TV, lots of
links and information to be found here.
**www.whirligig-tv.co.uk** – great site for 1950s TV nostalgia.

# TV review and listings sites

## www.digiguide.co.uk UK

THE DOWNLOADABLE GUIDE
If you have Sky digital you'll be familiar with this guide,
it follows a similar format, although you can customise it.
Simply download the program and you get 14 days forward
programming for up to 200 channels, masses of links and
background information. It costs £8.99 per annum.

**www.radiotimes.com**                                                          UK

THE RADIO TIMES
Excellent listings e-zine with a good search facility for looking
up programme details, plus competitions, links and a cinema
guide. There are also sections on the best-loved TV genres
– children's, sci-fi, soaps and so on.

*See also:*
**www.onthebox.com** – a simple and effective daily TV guide.
Lots of pop-up ads.
**www.teletext.co.uk/tvplus** – great site, a far cry from the
listings you get via your television.
**www.thecustard.tv** – a personal, fun and well put together TV
and listings guide, deserves to succeed.
**www.tvhome.co.uk** – a well-designed listings site that includes
clips too. You need to download Real Player though.

## Soaps

**www.thebill.com**                                                             UK

THE BILL
Police soap The Bill gets a good looking site with history,
news, character spotlights and episode downloads.

**www.brookside.com**                                                           UK

THE OFFICIAL BROOKSIDE WEB SITE
This site was being redeveloped at time of writing so we
suggest you check out these alternatives, though to be honest
none of them are very good.

*See also:*
**http://members.aol.com/edward2910/brookside.html** – for the
alternative Brookside scripts...
**www.brooksider.co.uk** – for messages and chat.
**www.btinternet.com/~brookside.oapbox** – lots here but the
site is a mess.

T

### www.corrie.net

UK

CORONATION STREET BY ITS FANS
Còrrie was formed in 1999 from several fans' sites and has no
connection with Granada, the site is written by volunteer fans
who have contributed articles, updates and biographies.
There are five key sections. One for Corrie newbies (are there
any?) with a history of the Street; a catch up with the story
section; what's up and coming; profiles on the key characters;
a chat section where you can gossip about the goings on.
For another fan's eye view try out **www.csvu.net**

### www.bbc.co.uk/eastenders

UK

THE OFFICIAL EASTENDERS PAGE
A page from the massive BBC site, it's split into several sections:
catch up on the latest stories and hints on future storylines; play
games and competitions; get pictures of the stars; vote in their
latest poll; reminisce and visit the 'classic clips' section; take a
virtual tour and view Albert Square with the Walford Cam.

### www.hollyoaks.com

UK

THE OFFICIAL HOLLYOAKS WEB SITE
A very cool site with lots on it, you can subscribe to the
fortnightly newsletter; peek behind the scenes; catch up on the
latest news; chat with fellow fans. There's also the expected
photos and downloads to be had.

### www.ramsay-street.co.uk

UK

NEIGHBOURS WORLD-WIDE FANPAGES
This is a labour of love by the fans of Neighbours, it has
everything you need: storylines past, present and future; info on
all the characters; clips from some episodes; complete
discographies of the singing stars; and access to all the related
web sites through the links page. Unfortunately, you can't
buy Neighbours merchandise from the site. See also
**www.perfectblend.net** which is an excellent fan site for the series.

### www.bbc.co.uk/radio4/archers

UK

THE ARCHERS
OK so it's not strictly TV but we couldn't think where else
this should go. It's a great site with all the information and
background you'd wish for including the ability to listen to
the last episode and catch up on previous ones.

# *Theatre*

*Here's a great selection of sites that will appeal to theatre goers everywhere.*

### www.whatsonstage.com                                    UK
HOME OF BRITISH THEATRE
A really strong site with masses of news and reviews to browse through plus a very good search facility and booking service (through a third party), a real theatre buff's delight.

### www.aloud.com                                           UK
ONLINE TICKET SEARCH
You can search by venue, location or by artist, it's fast and pretty comprehensive and there's a hot events section – it mainly covers music and festivals, nowadays though it's good for comedy. The review section is good and you can buy tickets.

### www.theatrenet.com                                      UK
THE ENTERTAINMENT CENTRE
Get the latest news, catch the new shows and, if you join the club, there are discounts on tickets for theatre, concerts, sporting events and holidays. You can also search their archives for information on past productions and learn how to become a theatre angel.

### www.uktheatre.net                                       UK
PASSIONATE ABOUT THEATRE
Whether you're a fan or an actor this site has much to offer both as a useful source of information and as a good site directory.

### www.uktw.co.uk                                          UK
UK THEATRE WEB
A cheerful site offering all the usual information on theatre plus amateur dramatics, jobs, chat, competitions and just gossip.

T

### www.rsc.org.uk                                          UK
THE ROYAL SHAKESPEARE COMPANY
Get all the news as well as information on performances and tours. You can book tickets online although it's via a third party site.

## www.reallyuseful.com                                      UK
ANDREW LLOYD WEBBER
At this attractive, hi-tech site you can watch video and listen to top audio clips, download screen savers and wallpaper, take part in competitions and chat. There's also a good kids' section plus details on the shows.

## www.nt-online.org                                         UK
THE NATIONAL
Excellent for details of their shows and forthcoming plays with tour information added. You can't buy tickets online, but you can e-mail or fax for them.

## www.officiallondontheatre.co.uk                           UK
SOCIETY OF LONDON THEATRES
The latest news, a show finder service and hot tickets are just a few of the services available at this great site. You can also get a theatreland map, half price tickets and they'll even fax you a seating plan. See also **www.thisislondon.co.uk** who have a good theatre section.

*To book online try the following sites:*
**www.lastminute.com**
**www.londontheatretickets.com**
**www.ticketmaster.co.uk**
**www.uktickets.co.uk**

# Travel and Holidays

*Travel is one of the biggest growth areas on the Internet, from holidays to insurance to local guides. If you're buying, then it definitely pays to shop around and try several sites, but be careful, it's amazing how fast the best deals are being snapped up. You may find that you still spend time on the phone, but the sites are constantly improving. The amount of information available is staggering and it's no wonder this is the biggest section in the book.*

T

# Starting out

### www.abtanet.com                                          UK

ABTA

Make sure that the travel agent you choose is a member of the
Association of British Travel Agents as then you're covered if
they go bust halfway through your holiday. All members are
listed and there's a great search facility with links for you to
start the ball rolling. See also the Air Travellers Licensing home
page **www.atol.org.uk** which is part of the Civil Aviation site.

### www.brochurebank.co.uk                                  UK

BROCHURES DELIVERED TO YOUR HOME

Holiday brochures from the major and specialist travel
companies can be selected then delivered to your home,
free of charge. The selection process is easy and the site is fast.
Delivery is by second class post.

### www.tourismconcern.org.uk                               UK

ETHICAL TOURISM

If you're concerned about the impact of your trip, then come
here for advice or help with one of their campaigns. It all goes
to ensuring that the poorest holiday workers are not exploited.

## Travel information, news and tips

### www.fco.gov.uk/travel                                    UK

ADVICE FROM THE FOREIGN OFFICE

Before you go, get general advice, safety or visa information.
Just select a country and you get a run-down of all the issues
that are likely to affect you when you go there, from terrorism
to health.

*For more travel safety information go to:*

**www.1000traveltips.org** – tips from the very well travelled
Koen De Boeck and friends.

**www.cdc.gv/travel** – official American site giving sensible
health information world-wide.

**www.etravel.org** – masses of tips for the independent traveller
to browse through from book reviews to flying advice and
weather updates.

**www.first48.com/guide/features/muslimcode.php** – clothing
advice for women travelling to Muslim countries.

**www.flyingwithkids.com** – sensible air travel advice for those travelling with babies and small children.

**www.tips4trips.com** – all the tips come from well-meaning travellers and are categorised under sections such as pre-planning, what and how to pack, travelling for the disabled, for women, for men or with children.

**www.tripprep.com** – country-by-country risk assessment covering health, safety and politics; it can be a little out of date so check with the foreign office as well.

## www.guardian.co.uk/travel                                    UK

FROM THE *GUARDIAN* NEWSPAPER
A good reflection of the excellent *Guardian* weekly travel section with guides, information and inspiration throughout, there's also the latest news and links to sites with offers plus extra features such as audio guides and articles on parts of the UK. The special offers are worth checking out.

## www.vtourist.com                                             UK

THE VIRTUAL TOURIST
Explore destinations in a unique and fun way. Travellers describe their experiences, share photos, make recommendations and give tips so others benefit from their experience. See also **www.travel-library.com** which is less entertaining but combines recommendation with hard facts very well, and also **http://picturesofplaces.com** where you can find a huge number of photos from around the world.

*See also:*
**www.citysearch.com** – US-oriented site with some excellent city guides.
**www.nytimes.com/pages/travel/index.html** – travel news and information from the *New York Times*.
**www.zyworld.com/brancatelli** – excellent site, albeit a little staid, devoted to tips for the business traveller.

# Travel services and information

## www.johnnyjet.com                                            US

TRAVEL PORTAL
Very detailed and comprehensive portal site devoted to all things travel, it's well categorised but has an American bias. See also **www.thetravelportal.com** who have an excellent set of links from a bigger web directory.

## www.whatsonwhen.com UK
WORLD-WIDE EVENTS GUIDE
An easy-to-use site with information on every type of event you can think of from major festivals to village fêtes.

## www.ukpa.gov.uk UK
UK PASSPORTS
Pre-apply for your passport online and get tips on how to get the best passport photo amongst other very useful information.

## www.hmce.gov.uk UK
HM CUSTOMS AND EXCISE
All you need to know about visiting the UK, exporting and importing and the regulations surrounding what you can bring in.

## www.visaservice.co.uk UK
QUICK VISA
This service will get you your visa in double quick time, for a price.

## www.travelhealth.co.uk UK
STAY HEALTHY
An authoritative site with sections on general health advice, disease prevention, a shop and links.

*See also:*
**www.bloodcare.org.uk** – the Blood Care Foundation offers a wide range of advice and tips for many illnesses and situations.
**www.flyana.com** – advice from an experienced traveller.
**www.travelhealthresources.com** – data on over 250 countries though US-oriented.

## www.worldtimezone.com US
TIME ZONE MAP
Useful time zone mapping, although it's heavily advert laden.

## www.kropla.com US
PHONE HELP
Here you can find out about where to plug in your modem, if your mobile will work, international dialling codes, even TV standards.

### www.bananabuzz.com    UK
GET BACK IN TOUCH
OK so you've had your holiday and lost touch with all those
friends you've made, here's where to go. It's a sort of Friends
Reunited for backpackers basically. There's also chat and
messaging services.

### www.goplaces.co.uk    UK
BUYING LUGGAGE
A wide range and with some good offers, this store is worth a
visit if you have to replace that tatty old case.

### www.excessluggage.co.uk    UK
EXCESS LUGGAGE
For problems concerning excess baggage here's the place to go,
there are lots of options and it's best to discuss your
requirements with them.

## Travel money and insurance

### www.xe.net/ucc    UK
ONLINE CURRENCY CONVERTER
The Universal Currency Converter could not be easier to use,
just select the currency you have, then the one you want
to convert it to, press the button and you have your
answer in seconds. See also **www.oanda.com** and
**www.x-rates.com/calculator.html**

### www.taxfree.se    US
GLOBAL REFUND
Find out how to make the most out of tax-free shopping at this
very useful web site.

### www.onlinefx.co.uk    UK
FOREIGN CURRENCY DELIVERED
A pretty straightforward and potentially hassle free way of
getting your currency, just order with you card and it gets
delivered the next working day. There are also other financial
services available such as international transfers.

## www.travelinsuranceclub.co.uk                                   UK

AWARD WINNING TRAVEL INSURANCE CLUB
Unfortunately there isn't one site for collating travel insurance
yet, it's a question of shopping around. These sites make a
good starting point offering a range of policies for backpackers,
family and business travel.

*All these companies offer flexibility and good value:*
**www.columbusdirect.co.uk** – good information, nice, but fiddly
web site and competitive prices.
**www.costout.co.uk** – well rated and good value.
**www.direct-travel.co.uk** – nice design and some good offers
too, online quotes.
**www.jameshampden.co.uk** – wide range of policies,
straightforward and hassle free.
**www.underthesun.co.uk** – good for annual and six monthly
policies.
**www.worldwideinsure.com** – good selection of policies, instant
online cover.

# Travel shops

## www.travel-lists.co.uk                                          UK

TRAVEL OPERATORS DIRECTORY
A largely subscription-based service but with free access to their
database of travel specialists and agents. Each entry has a link,
contact number and a short overview of what they do.

## www.expedia.co.uk                                            US/UK

THE COMPLETE SERVICE
This is the UK arm of Microsoft's very successful online travel
agency. It offers a huge array of holidays, flights and associated
services, for personal or business use, nearly all bookable
online. Its easy and quicker than most, and there are some
excellent offers too. Not the trendiest, but it's a good first stop.
As with all the big operators, you have to register. They've also
got sections on travel insurance, mapping, guides, ferries
and hotels.

T

### www.lastminute.com                                    UK

DO SOMETHING LAST MINUTE
Last Minute has an excellent reputation not just as a travel
agent, but as a good shopping site too. For travellers there are
comprehensive sections on hotels, holidays and flights, all with
really good prices. There is also a superb London restaurant
guide and a general entertainment section. Mostly, you can
book online, but a hotline is available.

### www.thomascook.com                                    UK

THE WIDEST RANGE OF PACKAGE HOLIDAYS
This site is easy to use and well laid out and, with over two
million package holidays to chose from, you should be able to
find something to your liking. You can also browse the online
guide for ideas or search for cheap flights or holiday deals.
Again you have to call the hotline to book.

### www.e-bookers.com                                     UK

FLIGHTBOOKERS
Acclaimed travel agents specialising in getting good flight deals,
but also good for holidays, special offers and insurance.

### www.travel.world.co.uk                                UK

FOR ALL YOUR TRAVEL REQUIREMENTS
A massive, comprehensive site, it basically includes most
available travel brochures with links to the relevant travel agent.
It concentrates on Europe, so there are very few American sites,
but provides links to hotels, specialist holidays, cruises,
self-catering and airlines.

### www.uk.mytravel.com                                   UK

SEARCH FOR THE RIGHT DEAL
This site has got an excellent search engine that enables you
to find a bargain or just the right holiday, there are also good
offers and the late escapes holiday auction site.

T

**www.priceline.co.uk**                                                    UK

LET SOMEONE ELSE DO THE WORK

You could leave it to someone else to do the travel searching for you, here you provide details of the trip you want and how much you're willing to pay, then they try to find a deal that will match your requirements. If you're flexible about timing then there are some great offers. They cover flights, hotels and car hire. Another site to try is **www.myownprice.com** both this site and Priceline want your credit card details before you agree to any transaction so you may feel more comfortable using a more traditional route.

## Online travel agents

*Here's a selection of well-proven and independent online travel agents sorted by type. For more specialist holiday information, look under the specialist topics such as Sports, Nature, Students, Cycling, etc.*

## Backpacking, ecotourism, activity and adventure

**www.backpackeurope.com** – aimed at the US but useful for Europeans too.

**www.changingworlds.co.uk** – outstanding site design and presentation from a company that helps people find worthwhile working holidays.

**www.exploreworld-wide.com** – adventure holidays from around the world.

**www.gvillage.co.uk** – specialising in independent travellers and students with some great deals and adventure holidays to the world's most interesting places, excellent round the world trip planner.

**www.igougo.com** – more of an information exchange for global travellers but you can book trips through them, there are plenty of features and the IgoUgo awards too.

**www.inntravel.co.uk** – specialists in walking and cycling holidays, excellent, informative site.

**www.international-academy.com** – life changing experiences through sport and travel.

**www.madadventurer.com** – excellent site design with loads of mad adventures to choose from while helping community development in 23 countries.

T

**www.spicemcr.com** – vibrant activity and social club with holidays to match.
**www.theleap.co.uk** – similar approach to Mad Adventurer but based in Africa.

## Bargain deals

### www.budgettravel.com                                    UK

BUDGET TRAVEL
Masses of links and information for the budget traveller plus advice on how to travel on the cheap. It can be difficult to navigate but the information is very good.

*See also:*
**www.bargainholidays.com** – probably the best for quick breaks, excellent for late availability offers.
**www.firstchoice.co.uk** – bargains from First Choice holidays.
**www.holiday.co.uk** – good deals on package holidays from a very well designed site.
**www.packageholidays.co.uk** – late bargain holidays and flights from over 130 tour operators including Thomson, Sunworld, Airtours and specialist agents.

## General travel agents

**www.aito.co.uk** – offers and information from the Association of Independent Tour Operators, excellent for the unusual.
**www.beachtowel.co.uk** – good all-round site from an independent travel agent who is ABTA and ATOL covered.
**www.firstresort.com** – a good general site with some good deals and a price promise, owned by Thomsons.
**www.lunn-poly.co.uk** – updating the site at time of writing.
**www.opodo.co.uk** – slick newcomer from some of the major airlines, worth checking out for flight offers.
**www.teletext.co.uk/holidays** – much better than browsing the TV, you can now get all those offers on one easy-to-use site. There is also lots of useful travel information to help you on your way.
**www.thisistravel.co.uk** – in association with the newspaper group that publishes the Daily Mail, this is a comprehensive offering with some good offers. Lots of pop-up ads too.
**www.travelagents.co.uk** – another all-rounder, nothing special but competent.

**www.travelbag.co.uk** – straightforward and easy to use flight and holiday finder.

**www.travelcareonline.com** – loads of deals and honest information from the UK's largest independent.

**www.travelfinder.co.uk** – lots of options and great bargains at this simple-to-use site.

**www.travelocity.com** – one of the oldest online travel agents; it's similar to Expedia and there's a reward scheme too. The trip expert facility is a fun planning tool.

**www.travelmood.com** – follows the standard site design for an all-rounder, has some good offers though.

**www.tripsworld-wide.co.uk** – despite the name it specialises in Latin America and the Caribbean. Some beautiful photography enhances the site.

## Luxury and tailor-made

**www.abercrombiekent.com** – one of the most experienced luxury travel operators with a very competent site.

**www.amanresorts.com** – exclusive hotels and villas in gorgeous locations.

**www.audleytravel.com** – tailor-made itineraries for escorted groups.

**www.balesworldwide.com** – for something special, tailor-made holidays to the exotic parts of the world; hi-tech site is excellent but no online booking.

**www.bridgetheworld.com** – a good site from this multi-award winning company.

**www.carrier.co.uk** – luxury holiday specialists, nice-looking site too.

**www.coxandkings.co.uk** – a slightly disappointing site from one of the oldest travel companies.

**www.essentialescapes.com** – exclusive luxury spa holidays.

**www.exsus.com** – tailor-made luxury adventures.

**www.hayesandjarvis.co.uk** – long-haul holiday specialists, lots to choose from.

**www.itcclassics.co.uk** – luxury everything basically.

**www.jewelholidays.com** – Goa, India, Turkey and Cambodia.

**www.originaltravel.co.uk** – holidays for activity and well-being, outstanding site design too.

**www.pura-aventura.com** – active holidays in comfort, mainly Latin America and Spain.

**www.rbrww.com** – opulence and fishing.

T

**www.seasonsinstyle.co.uk** – world-wide luxury in the world's finest hotels.
**www.tailor-made.co.uk** – basic site but the holiday options look good.
**www.world-widejourneys.co.uk** – tailor-made packages, especially experienced in wildlife holidays.

## Specialist agencies

**www.divechannel.co.uk** – excellent site specialising in diving holidays and travel.
**www.footprint-adventures.co.uk** – birding, trekking and wildlife all over the world.
**www.golfbreaks.com** – a travel agent specialising in holidays for golfing nuts.
**www.regaldive.co.uk** – learn to dive in the best diving locations.
**www.transitionsabroad.com** – excellent for long-term travelling and working holidays.
**www.wildlifeworld-wide.com** – world-wide wildlife holidays.

## Short breaks

**www.shortbreaks.com** – hotel breaks in the UK, Europe and US; arranges theatre breaks too.
**www.webweekends.co.uk** – specialists in weekend breaks both in the UK and abroad.

## Villas

**www.cvtravel.net** – passionate about villas, mainly in Europe.
**www.jamesvillas.co.uk** – over 500 villas in the Med.
**www.ownerssyndicate.com** – a wide choice with some good offers.
**www.villa-rentals.com** – from Abercrombie & Kent, villas world-wide, some look outstanding.

T

# Cruises

## www.cruiseinformationservice.co.uk

UK    CRUISE INFO
A trade site put together to encourage people to take cruise
holidays. There's an introduction to cruising, information on the
cruise lines, a magazine and links to useful sites. There's also
information on how to book and what sort of cruise is right
for you.

*See also:*
**www.cruisedeals.co.uk** – easy to use, a little sparse on info but
some good offers.
**www.cruise-direct.com** – information, advice and good prices.
**www.cruiseline.co.uk** – a great site from one the UK's leading
specialist cruise companies.
**www.cruisesandvoyages.com** – cruise specialist with a basic
site and some good deals.
**www.psa-psara.org** – useful information from the Passenger
Shipping Association.

# Sailing holidays

## www.sunsail.com                                                US

SAILING AND WATERSPORT HOLIDAYS
Wide-ranging and informative site with lots to offer whether
you're an enthusiast or a beginner, plenty of special offers too.

*See also:*
**www.allafloat.com** – lots of choice and online booking.
**www.compass24.com** – a good shop for sailing enthusiasts,
over 8,000 products.
**www.elitesailing.co.uk** – learn to sail.
**www.sailingholidays.com** – specialists in Greece and Croatia.
**www.sea-trek.co.uk** – specialist in Greece, learn to sail
holidays too.
**www.tenrag.com** – charter your own yacht.

T

# Airline and flight sites

### www.cheapflights.co.uk                                    UK
NOTHING BUT CHEAP FLIGHTS
You don't need to register here to explore the great offers
available from this site; you still need to phone some of the
travel agents or airlines listed to get your deal though and some
of the prices quoted seem magically to disappear once you've
clicked on the link. Having said that, there are obviously some
great deals to be had.

### www.netflights.com                                        UK
THE AIRLINE NETWORK
Discount deals on over 100 airlines world-wide make The
Airline Network worth checking out for their flight offers page
alone. It's good for flights from regional airports. They also do
all the traditional travel agent things and there are some good
holiday bargains too.

### www.deckchair.com                                         UK
RELAX WITH DECKCHAIR
A strong site where you can get some good flight bargains as
well as plan the rest of your holiday.

### www.openjet.com                                           UK

NO FRILLS MADE EASY
This site searches the low-cost carriers to find you the best
prices to European destinations and gives you the results for
adjacent days to enable you to fly at the lowest possible price.
See also **www.whichbudget.com**

*For more cheap flight deals try these sites:*
**www.attitudetravel.com/lowcostairlines** – Europe's low-cost
airlines and where they fly to. For world-wide coverage try the
ugly but comprehensive **www.etn.nl/lcostair**
**www.bargainflights.com** – good search facility and plenty of
offers, but you need to be patient.
**www.bmibaby.com** – the low-cost arm of British Midland.
**www.dreamticket.com** – the usual flight offers, but the site also
offers much in the way of information too.
**www.easyjet.co.uk** – great for a limited number of destinations,
particularly good for UK flights. See also **www.easyvalue.co.uk**

**www.flightcentre.com** – they guarantee to beat any genuine current quoted airfare!

**www.ryanair.com** – very good for Ireland, northern Europe, Italy and France. Clear and easy to use web site, massive discounts.

**www.travelselect.com** – good flight selection and lots of different options available at this very flexible site.

# Airport and airline information

**www.worldairportguide.com**                                    GERMANY

WHAT ARE THE WORLD'S AIRPORTS REALLY LIKE?
It seems that no matter how out of the way, this guide has details on every airport – how to get there, where to park, facilities, key phone numbers and a map. There are also guides on cities, resorts and even world weather.

**www.baa.co.uk**                                                UK

BRITISH AIRPORT AUTHORITY
Details on all the major UK airports that are run by the BAA, you get all the essential information plus flight data, weather and shopping information.

**www.a2bairports.com**                                          UK

UK AND IRISH AIRPORTS
This odd-looking site from A2B Travel offers all the relevant information on all the major airports and lots of the smaller ones too. Another site with information on UK airports is **www.airport-maps.co.uk** which also has flight route information along with the eponymous mapping, facility details and related links.

**www.airlinequality.com**                                       UK

RANKING THE AIRLINES
An independent ranking of all the world's airlines and their services, see who's the best and the worst and why.
Each airline is rated using a number of stars (up to five) on criteria such as seat quality, catering and staff. See also **www.flyaow.com**

T

## www.sleepinginairports.net                                    UK

### GUIDE TO SLEEPING IN AIRPORTS

Rated 'Good', 'Tolerable' or just 'Hell' here is a sleeper's guide for budget travellers on many of the world's airports, it's actually pretty funny too.

## www.airfraid.com

US   CONQUER YOUR FEAR OF FLYING

A good place to go if you're of the opinion that getting on a plane is the last thing you'll ever do. There's advice gleaned from various reputable sources and details on how you can go on courses to help you overcome your fears.

*The key airlines:*

**www.aa.com** – American Airlines, standard airline site.
**www.aerlingus.ie** – good easy to use site.
**www.airfrance.co.uk** – plenty of offers.
**www.airindia.com** – good offers and travel information and destination guide.
**www.alitalia.it** – a no-nonsense site.
**www.britishairways.co.uk** or **www.ba.com** – easy to use, efficient site.
**www.cathaypacific.com** – comprehensive flight service and guide.
**www.emirates.com** – no-frills design and flight booking facilities.
**www.flybmi.com** – British Midland, good offers for European destinations.
**www.klm.com** – good design with lots of offers.
**www.lufthansa.co.uk** – masses of information and express booking.
**www.quantas.com** – straightforward booking facility.
**www.singaporeair.com** – follows the formula but with the added extra of a multi-city flight planner.
**www.united.com** – United Airlines offers a good all round service for this site.
**www.virgin-atlantic.com** – good online booking facility with some offers.

# UK regional airlines

*It's worth trying out regional airlines, not only because they may be cheaper, but also they might fly to your destination from a more convenient local airport. Here are the best of them.*

**www.air-scotland.com** – billed as Scotland's low-cost airline, this lot flies out of Glasgow and Edinburgh to Spanish resorts. The site follows the usual design and at time of writing, there's lots of offers even as low as £25.

**www.airsouthwest.com** – small airline offering great value flights from the South West of England to London.

**www.airwales.co.uk** – Awyr Cymru offer a wide variety of flights throughout the UK and Ireland from Swansea and Cardiff, again it looks good value. Better than average site too.

**www.excelairways.com** – an ambitious and service-oriented charter airline, they offer luxuries such as leather seating and fly to a wide range of European and Middle East destinations.

**www.flyglobespan.com** – this one is Scotland's newest low-cost airline offering much of what Air Scotland does on a no-frills site.

**www.jet2.com** – flying from Leeds-Bradford airport to a select number of European destinations Jet2 is offering seats at very low prices

# Airport parking

**www.uk-airport-car-parking.co.uk**                              UK

BOOK YOUR SPACE

Probably the best of the sites dedicated to helping you find somewhere to park your car while you're away. It offers more options and information than the others listed but it's always worth shopping around, so you should try these alternatives.

*See also:*

**www.bcponline.co.uk** – easy to use and with some good savings on airport car park rates.

**www.holidayextras.co.uk** – who are also good for parking, airport hotels, airport lounges and also has information on getting to airports by public transport.

**www.parking4less.co.uk** – high-quality secured parking assured.

**www.securedcarparks.com** – as the title suggests a useful guide to car parks with decent security.

# Hotels and places to stay

### www.hotelguide.com                                                   UK

COMPREHENSIVE
With services available in nine languages and specialist
sections such as golfing breaks, this site ranks among the best
for finding the right hotel. It lists around 85,000 at time
of writing.

### www.hiphotels.net                                                    UK

FOR THE HIPPEST HOTELS
Excellent for the unusual, it's a directory of the unique and
off-beat with good illustrations of each hotel, not much in the
way of deals, but then they are very special.

### www.from-a-z.com                                                     UK

A–Z OF HOTELS
A well-designed British site with over 20,000 hotels to choose
from in the UK, Eire and France and a further 40,000 world-
wide, it's quick and easy-to-use and there's online booking
available plus plenty of special discounts.

*Other good hotel directory and booking sites:*
**www.all-hotels.com** – 100,000 hotels listed with lots of
options, American bias.
**www.best-inn.co.uk** – another directory of 60,000 hotels,
very good for London and links to specialist accommodation.
**www.discount25.com** – great for hotel discounts, primarily in
Spain but also the major European cities.
**www.laterooms.co.uk** – easy to use directory featuring unsold
hotel rooms at great prices.
**www.openworld.co.uk** – a collection of links to hotel sites,
just use the interactive world map.
**www.placestostay.com** – another with an interactive map,
you drill down until you find the place you want to stay,
then you get a list of hotels, a description, price and online
reservation service.

T

# Travel guides

### www.mytravelguide.com                                                    US
ONLINE TRAVEL GUIDES
A general American travel site that offers a good overview of
most countries, with points of interest, a currency converter,
very good interactive mapping and live web cams too. You need
to become a member to get the best out of it though.

### www.lonelyplanet.com                                                     UK

LONELY PLANET GUIDES
A superb travel site, aimed at the independent traveller,
but with great information for everyone. Get a review on most
world destinations or pick a theme and go with that; leave a
message on the Thorn Tree; find out the latest news by country;
get health reports; read about the travel experiences of others –
what's the real story? They've revamped the site since we last
visited, now it's better organised and even easier to find your
way around.

### http://travel.roughguides.com                                           UK

ROUGH GUIDES
Lively reviews on a huge number of places – some 14,000.
In addition, there's general travel information, a place to share
your travel thoughts with other travellers, or you can buy a
guide. Excellent for links and you can get some good deals
via the site.

### www.fodors.com                                                          US
FODOR'S GUIDES
These guides give an American perspective, but there is a huge
amount of information on each destination. The site is well laid
out and easy to use.

### http://kasbah.com                                                        UK
WORLD'S LARGEST TRAVEL GUIDE
Clear information, stacks of links and a good search engine
should mean that you will find the low down on most
destinations. The highlights on each destination are useful and
the 'Global Travel Toolbox' provides info, telecommunications,
maps, currency and more. Unfortunately, some of the site's
links were not working when we visited.

T

### www.packback.com    UK

PACKBACK TRAVEL GUIDE
A good-looking and useful site with an independent travel guide, a growing membership and a reputation for quality reviews. It includes a discussion forum, travel tools and flight booking.

### www.gorp.com    US

FOR THE GREAT OUTDOORS
A great title, Gorp is dedicated to adventure, whether it be hiking, mountaineering, fishing, snow sports or riding the rapids. It has an American bias, but is full of relevant good advice, links and information.

### www.timeout.com    UK

TIME OUT GUIDE
A slick site with destination guides covering many European cites and some further afield such as New York and Sydney. Not surprisingly, it's outstanding for London and you can also book tickets and buy books via other retailers.

### www.bradmans.com    US

BRADMAN'S FOR BUSINESS TRAVELLERS
A really excellent city guide with none of your fancy graphics, just a straightforward listing of countries and sensible information on each one, includes tips on orienting yourself in the city and restaurant reviews.

*Other global guides and sites worth checking out are:*
**www.about.com/travel** – a comprehensive travel directory from About.com.
**www.citysearch.com** – a listing for mainly US cities with entertainment and orientation guides.
**www.officialtravelinfo.com** – a directory covering the world's official tourism sites.
**www.world-heritage-tour.org** – a list and tour of World Heritage sites around the globe with panoramic views.
**www.worldinformation.com** – not specifically a travel guide but there is a mountain of information on the world's countries, their culture and advice about how to deal with issues like corruption.

# Online maps and route finders

### www.mappy.co.uk    UK

START HERE
Mappy has a great-looking site that is easy to use and has lots of added features such as a personal mapping service where you can store the maps you use most. The route finder is OK, doesn't use postcodes but business users can fill in their mileage allowance and Mappy will calculate how much you should claim.

### www.multimap.com    UK

GREAT BRITAIN
Outstanding design, easy to use, excellent for the UK, you can search using postcodes, London street names, place names or Ordnance Survey grid references. Once you've found what you're looking for, you can also see an aerial view of the area.

*See also:*
**http://maps.expedia.co.uk** – limited to the US, France, Germany and the UK for detailed maps – modest route finder.
**http://maps.msn.com** – excellent mapping and route finding service from MSN, incorporating what used to be Map Blast.
**www.map24.co.uk** – easy to use site with functional design, covers UK and Europe.
**www.mapquest.com** – find out the best way to get from A to B in Europe or America, not always as detailed as you'd like, but easy to use and you can customise your map or route plan.
**www.mapsonus.com** – it's notoriously difficult to find your way around America, but using the route planner you should minimise your risk of getting lost.
**www.ordsvy.gov.uk** – a good site with mapping for sale but the interactive mapping was suspended at time of writing.
**www.stanfords.co.uk** – travel book and map specialists.
**www.viamichelin.com** – a good all-round travel site with an improved route finder service which is OK.

### www.theaa.co.uk    UK

AUTOMOBILE ASSOCIATION
A superb site that is divided into four key sections: breakdown cover, route planning and traffic information, hotel guide and booking, in addition, help with buying a car. There is also information on insurance and other financial help.

T

**www.rac.co.uk**                                                    UK

> GET AHEAD WITH THE RAC
> Great for UK traffic reports and has a very reliable route
> planner, which seems to be very busy and slow at peak times.
> There's also a good section on finding the right place to stay,
> and lots of help if you want to buy a car.

# Destinations

*Here's an alphabetical list of countries and regions to help you
research your chosen destination and plan your holiday.*

**www.antor.com**                                                    UK

> ASSOCIATION OF NATIONAL TOURIST OFFICES
> A useful starting point for information about the 90 or so
> countries that are members of the association. It also has very
> good links to key tourism sites.

**www.embassyworld.com**

> US EMBASSIES AROUND THE GLOBE
> Pick two countries one for 'whose embassy', one for 'in what
> location', press go and up pops the details on the embassy with
> contact and essential information.

## A

**www.africaonline.com**                                 SOUTH AFRICA

> AFRICA
> Exhaustive site covering news, information and travel in Africa,
> with very good features and articles.

**www.africatravelresource.com**

> EAST AFRICA                                                        UK
> An exceptional site that specifically covers Burundi, Kenya,
> Rwanda, Uganda and Tanzania plus the resorts of Lamu and
> Zanzibar. The level of detail is great but because the site is
> packaged so well, it doesn't overwhelm. A lesson in how a
> travel site should be set up.
>
> *See also:*
> **http://i-cias.com** – excellent information site covering North
> Africa and the Middle East.

**www.africaguide.com** – detailed country-by-country guides, discussion forums, shopping, culture and a travelogue feature make this site a good first stop.

**www.africanodyssey.co.uk** – African and Arabian specialist agents.

**www.africansafariclub.com** – cruises and safaris a speciality.

**www.backpackafrica.com** – excellent site for backpackers with over 400 links and advice on where to go and what to see.

**www.ecoafrica.com** – tailor-made safaris with the emphasis on eco-tourism.

**www.onsafari.com** – good advice on what sort of safari is right for you.

**www.phakawe.demon.co.uk** – safaris in Botswana.

**www.travelinafrica.co.za** – budget travel in Southern Africa.

**www.vintageafrica.com** – awesome safaris and destinations from this specialist travel agent, who will tailor-make holidays if requested.

**www.wilderness-safaris.com** – specialises in providing safaris that go to pristine wilderness.

**www.wildnetafrica.net** – an excellent travel and information portal for safaris to south and south-east Africa.

## www.arab.net                                      SAUDI ARABIA
RESOURCE FOR THE ARAB WORLD
A wide ranging site covering North Africa and the Middle East with excellent country guides. See also **http://l-cias.com** and **www.arabianodyssey.co.uk**

## www.turisme.ad                                         ANDORRA
ANDORRA
A nice little site extolling the many virtues of this tiny country.

## www.polartravel.co.uk                                         UK
ARCTIC AND ANTARTICA
How to get to the Poles in safety and even enjoy yourself when you get there! See also **www.arctic-experience.co.uk**

## www.argentour.com                                      ARGENTINA
ARGENTINA
Outstanding (but very slow loading) travel site with video clips, regional information, history and slide shows of the major cities, even a section on how to tango.

T

**www.asiatour.com**                                    PHILIPPINES
> ASIA
> Good travel information on all Asian countries. See also
> **www.accomasia.com** which concentrates mainly on the
> Far East.

**www.austria-tourism.at**                                AUSTRIA
> AUSTRIA
> An excellent site covering all you need to know about the
> country, with information on skiing and summer holidays too.

**www.australia.com**                                    AUSTRALIA
> DISCOVER AUSTRALIA
> The Australian Tourist Commission offer a good and informative
> site that gives lots of facts about the country, the people,
> lifestyle and what you can expect when you visit.
>
> *See also:*
> **www.travelaustralia.com.au** – informative site, good for
> regional information.
> **www.voyages.com.au** – stay in luxury at Ayers Rock or Uluru
> as it's officially known as now.
> **www.wilmap.com.au** – excellent for Australian maps and links.

# B
**www.indo.com**                                        INDONESIA
> BALI ONLINE
> Bali and its top hotels, but there's also plenty of information on
> the rest of Indonesia as well as links to other Asian sites.

**www.trabel.com**                                        BELGIUM
> BELGIUM
> The Belgium Travel Network offers a site packed with
> information about the country and its key towns and cities.
> You can get information on hotels, travelling, an airport guide,
> flight information and there's also a good links page. See also
> the well-designed **www.belgium-tourism.net** and
> **www.visitflanders.co.uk**

## www.brazil.com
BRAZIL

### BRAZIL
A straightforward, no-nonsense guide, travelogue and listing site for Brazil that also contains information on hotels and resorts. The Brazilian embassy in London sponsors an excellent sister site **www.brazil.org.uk**

*See also:*
**www.helisight.com.br** – book your over Rio helicopter tour.
**www.varig.co.uk** – the national airline, good site with online booking.

## C
## www.cambodia-travel.com
CAMBODIA

### HOME OF THE KHMER
Wide-ranging site with some interesting spelling! There are sections on Angkor Wat, the Khmer and the usual accommodation details. See also **www.eyeoncambodia.com**

## www.travelcanada.ca
CANADA

### EXPLORE CANADA
Did you know that the glass floor at the top of the world's tallest free-standing structure could support the weight of 14 large hippos? Find out much more at this wide-ranging and attractive site, from touring to city guides. See also **www.canadian-affair.com** who offer some excellent low cost flights and tours, and for the outdoor experience of the country go to **www.out-there.com**

## www.turq.com
US

### CARIBBEAN
All you need to organise a great holiday in the Caribbean. There's information on flights, hotels, cruises, a travel guide and trip reports to the islands, all on a well presented and easy-to-use site.

*See also:*
**www.caribbeandreams.co.uk** – UK travel agent specialising in the Caribbean.
**www.caribbeansupersite.com** – good information, over 4,000 links.
**www.doitcaribbean.com** – information, booking and an interactive map.

T

## www.chinatour.com
CHINA

INFORMATION CHINA

A comprehensive site stuffed with data on China: where to go and stay, how to get there and what to see, maps and visa application information. See also the China Travel System at **www.chinats.com** who have a good-looking and very polite site where you can book hotels and tours, get travel information and chat to others who've experienced China. For Hong Kong go to **www.discoverhongkong.com**

## www.croatia.hr
CROATIA

CROATIA

An excellent site covering the country and its virtues with sections on events, attractions, background, accommodation and an all round travel guide.

## www.cubanculture.com
US

CUBA

A fast, easy-to-use site with the basic information about Cuba and its heritage. There are lots of useful links too.

## www.cyprustourism.org
CYPRUS

CYPRUS

A pretty basic site about the country, well the Greek run bit anyway.

## www.czech-tourism.com
CZECH REPUBLIC

CZECH REPUBLIC

A good directory site providing information and links in 15 categories from business to the weather including tour operators and a country guide.

# D

## www.visitdenmark.com
DENMARK

DENMARK

The official Danish tourist board site where you can get links to book a holiday and all the advice and information you'd expect from a well-run and efficient-looking site. See also **www.woco.dk** for an excellent site on Copenhagen.

# E
## www.ecuadorexplorer.com

ECUADOR
Very well-put together directory site covering all you need for
a visit to one of the most beautiful countries on the planet.
For specific sites on the Galapagos go to the thorough
**www.galapagos-travel.com** and also the Galapagos
Conservation Trust at **www.gct.org** which is full of information
and good for links.

## http://touregypt.net
EGYPT

EGYPT
A pretty ugly but very comprehensive site covering the country
and in particular its history, it's really a very good portal site as
well as a travel guide.

*See also:*
**www.discoveregypt.co.uk** – a well-illustrated site from a UK
based specialist.
**www.peltours.com** – great site from this Egypt specialist agent.

## www.visitestonia.com
ESTONIA

ESTONIA
Gushing with enthusiasm for the charms of this small Baltic
state, this site gives you information on travel, accommodation,
history, climate and money. For another view try the no-
nonsense **www.estoniantravel.com**

## www.eurotrip.com
UK

BACKPACKING EUROPE
Student and independent European travel with in-depth
information, facts, reviews, articles, discussion, live reports,
links and travel advice on a good looking and well-designed
site. Also connects to a no frills airline booking service and a
section with information on finding low cost air fares.

## www.eurocamp.co.uk
UK

T

SELF-CATERING EUROPE
The leading self-catering company with over 160 holiday
parks in nine countries. Here you can find details of the
accommodation and book a holiday and there are some
bargains too. See also **www.eurocampindependent.co.uk** who
offer a European campsite reservation service.

**www.europeaninternet.com/centraleurope**                EUROPE
CENTRAL EUROPE ONLINE
A messy news-based site with comprehensive information on
the region. You can get travel information and airline tickets via
the links sections.

**www.visiteurope.com**                                        US

EUROPEAN TRAVEL COMMISSION
A site aimed at Americans to encourage them to visit Europe,
it's informative and there's a section for each country.

# F
**www.franceway.com**                                      FRANCE

VOILA LA FRANCE!
Excellent site giving an overview of French culture, history, facts
and figures, and of course, how to book a holiday. You can also
sign up for the newsletter.

*See also:*
**www.franceguide.com** – official French Government Tourist
Office portal site.
**www.francemag.com** – really informative and useful e-zine
devoted to France.
**www.francetourism.com** – the official French Government
Tourist Office site for the US; great information for the UK too.
**www.justparis.co.uk** – details on how to get there and hotels
when you've arrived.
**www.logis-de-france.fr** – reliable guide to 3,000 hotel-
restaurant throughout France.
**www.magicparis.com** – good Paris guide with some offers.
**www.vive-la-france.org** – very comprehensive and good fun.

**www.visitfinland.com**                                  FINLAND
FINLAND
Look under the 'Individual holiday planner' for good quality
information on travelling around, accommodation and outdoor
activities. There are also organised tours available for the British
traveller. Don't miss out on Santa's homepage and arrange a
Christmas visit.

# G
## www.visitthegambia.gm

GAMBIA

A good tourist site, which promotes Gambia's wildlife and
ecological sites with particular emphasis on the bird-life and
waterways.

## www.germany-tourism.de

GERMANY – WUNDERBAR

As much information as you can handle with good features on
the key destinations, excellent interactive mapping and links to
related sites. For further information try **www.germany-info.org**

## www.gibraltar.gi/tourism

GIBRALTAR – THE ROCK

A good site devoted to the area with sections on the sights plus
travel information.

## www.gnto.gr

GREEK NATIONAL TOURIST ORGANISATION

An attractive site with the official word on travelling in Greece,
with a good travel guide and information for business travellers
plus accommodation, advice and details on what you can
get up to.

*See also:*

**www.agn.gr** – holidays, information and travel on the Aegean,
the site has a good interactive map with lots of features.
Aimed at US audience.

**www.culture.gr** – excellent site covering Greek culture and
its legends.

**www.filoxenia.co.uk** – a specialist, good for unusual
accommodation in Greece.

**www.gogreece.com** – a search engine devoted to all
things Greek.

**www.greekisland.co.uk** – an entertaining and personal view of
the Greek islands with over 200 links.

**www.gtpnet.com** – the Greek Travel Pages with the latest ferry
schedules for island hoppers.

**www.islands-of-greece.com** – another specialist operator with
a good site and features on the better islands.

**www.travelalacarte.co.uk** – specialists in holidays in the best of the Greek islands.

**www.travel-greece.com** – masses of links to everything about holidaying in Greece.

# H

## www.holland.com
HOLLAND

HOLLAND IS FULL OF SURPRISES

Very professional site offering a mass of tourist information and advice on how to have a great time when you visit. There are sections on how to get there, what type of holiday will suit you and city guides.

## www.gotohungary.com
HUNGARY

HUNGARY

All the information here to enable you to plan your trip to Hungary including information on the wide range of cultural events taking place in Budapest. If it's restoration you're after, there's an interesting section on Hungary's curative spas.

# I

## www.iceland.org
ICELAND

ICELAND

Official site of the Icelandic Foreign Service with a wealth of information about the country, the people and its history. It's easy to navigate and there are good links to related sites. See also **www.iceland.com** and **www.icetourist.is** both of which are more tourism oriented.

## www.indiatouristoffice.org
UK

INDIAN TOURIST OFFICE UK

Essential tourist information and advice as well as cultural and historical background on the country and its diverse regions. It has a massive hotel database as well.

## www.indiamart.com
UK

INDIA TRAVEL PROMOTION NETWORK

Basically a shopping site with diverse information including travel, hotels, timetables, wildlife, worship, trekking, heritage and general tourism. It's well organised and easy to use.

*See also:*

**www.hindustantimes.com** – full of useful information, news and gossip.

**www.indianrail.gov.in** – passenger information and timetables of the largest rail network in the world.

**www.india-travel.com** – a really strong travel site with lots of information and guidance as well as essential links.

**www.indiatraveltimes.com** – great for links and the latest news.

**www.mapsofindia.com** – an excellent site with maps of the country and a rail timetable and route planner.

**www.partnershiptravel.co.uk** – specialist Indian travel agent.

**www.rrindia.com** – another good information site offering tour itineraries and hotel booking.

**www.taj-mahal.net** – explore the Taj Mahal.

## www.tourismindonesia.com                    INDONESIA

INDONESIA
A very good overview of the country and its people, with lots of useful information about travelling there and a good links section.

## www.shamrock.org                              IRELAND

IRELAND
Wide-ranging site giving you the best of Ireland. Aimed at the American market, it really sells the country well with good links to other related sites.

*See also:*

**www.12travel.co.uk** – Irish holiday specialists with lots of holiday options.

**www.camping-ireland.ie** – over 100 parks listed for caravanning and camping.

**www.heritageireland.ie** – exploring the history of Ireland.

**www.iol.ie/~discover** – a good travel guide plus lots of links.

**www.ireland.travel.ie** – the very good official Irish Tourist Board site.

## www.goisrael.com                              ISRAEL

ISRAEL
Excellent site with information on the country, its sights and sites, how to get there and how to organise a tour. See also **www.infotour.co.il** and **www.e-israel.com**

T

## www.italytour.com
ITALY

### VIRTUAL TOUR OF ITALY
Good looking, stylish and cool, this site is essentially a search engine and directory but a very good one.

*See also:*

**www.doge.it** – a basic but informative site on Venice.
**www.emmeti.it** – slightly eccentric site with bags of good information, although it takes a while to find it. Very good for hotels, regional info and museums.
**www.enit.it** – from the Italian State Tourist board, another wacky site but useful nonetheless.
**www.initaly.com** – another 'Italian' site but generally well organised, informative and useful.
**www.itwg.com** – Italian hotel reservations with online booking.
**www.travel.it** – a messy information site but you can book online.
**www.tuscanynow.com** – villas for rent in Tuscany.

## J

## www.jnto.go.jp
JAPAN

### JAPAN
This excellent site is the work of the Japanese Tourist Association. There's a guide to each region, the food, shopping and travel info with advice on how to get the best out of your visit.

*See also:*

**www.embjapan.org.uk** – Japanese Embassy site, useful but not that up-to-date.
**www.jaltour.co.uk** – travel agents specialising in Japan.
**www.japan-guide.com** – comprehensive information site about Japan with links, culture notes, shopping and a hotel finder.

## www.see-jordan.com
JORDAN

### JORDAN
An attractive and interesting site from the Jordanian tourist board, very cultural and informative with good links and a photo gallery. See also **www.jtehome.com** where you'll find the attractive site of the Jordan Travel Exchange.

# K

## www.visit-kenya.com                                        KENYA

KENYA

A slightly amateurish site with links and information on
travelling in Kenya. There are sections on Nairobi and the
coast as well as the expected safari information.

*See also:*
**www.kenya.com** – good-looking site with a safari deal finder
and information on the country too.
**www.kenyaweb.com** – a good portal site on all things Kenyan.

# L

## www.lata.org                                                UK

LATIN AMERICA

The Latin American Trade Association's text-based site has a
good country-by-country guide to the region plus links and
general information.

*See also the sites below and the sites listed under South
America:*
**www.journeylatinamerica.co.uk** – lots of tour and country
options from this specialist agent.
**www.lastfrontiers.com** – tailor-made itineraries for holidays
across the continent.
**www.latinamericatraveler.com** – great for links and information.
**www.steppeslatinamerica.co.uk** – from the Steppes Group
offering tailor-made packages.
**www.travellatinamerica.com** – really comprehensive travel,
directory and news site.

## www.nexteurope.com/tourism                                 LATVIA

LATVIA

A valiant effort with information on what to do when you get
there and a good selection of links. They will also arrange for a
translator/guide to show you around. For a second opinion go
to **www.latviatravel.info**

## www.lebanon.com                                            LEBANON

THE LEBANON

The Lebanon is going through a resurgence and is successfully
rebuilding itself. Here you can find all the resources you need to
organise a visit and see its many attractions. Also try the official
**www.lebanon-tourism.gov.lb**

### www.tourism.lt
LITHUANIA

LITHUANIA

A straightforward offering from the State Department with basic tourist information.

### www.luxembourg.co.uk
LUXEMBOURG

LUXEMBOURG

Comprehensive information on the Grand Duchy with good links to other sites. Could do with a few pictures to whet the appetite though.

## M

### www.malaysianet.net
MALAYSIA

MALAYSIA

Great for hotels in particular but you'll also find flight information and hidden away is a pretty good travel guide to the country. For air travel info see also **www.malaysiaair.com**

### www.visitmaldives.com
MALDIVES

MALDIVES

A good overview of the islands and all the options available to tourists with links and a section on the capital Male, plus resort information.

### www.visitmalta.com
UK

MALTA

A text-heavy but informative site about this beautiful island, with good details on accommodation and interactive mapping.

### www.tourbymexico.com
MEXICO

MEXICO

A basic site, but there is a travel guide to Mexico plus information on tours, hotels, health, tips, links and sights to see. See also the bright and breezy European gateway into Mexico **www.mexicanwave.com/travel**

### http://i-cias.com/morocco
MOROCCO

MOROCCO

A dense and detailed site about Morocco with over 650 articles and 900 photos covering cultural, musical and town by town information. See also **www.morocco.com** and **www.morocco-travel.com** both are pretty good or take the guided tour at **www.tourism-in-morocco.com**

**http://i-cias.com**                                    NORWAY

   THE MIDDLE EAST
   Very good for information on the Middle East, just click on the
   interactive map, there's travel information on selected countries.

# N

**www.nepal.com**                                        US

   NEPAL AND THE HIMALAYAS
   A beautifully presented site showing Nepal in its best light.
   Business, sport, culture and travel all have sections and it's a
   good browse too. The travel section is not that comprehensive,
   it has a basic guide, lots about Everest and access to the useful
   *Sherpa* magazine. See also the specialist tour company
   **www.trans-himalaya.ndirect.co.uk** and also
   **www.rrindia.com/nepal.html** plus **www.nepaltravelinfo.com**

**www.purenz.com**                                       NEW ZEALAND

   NEW ZEALAND
   A good-looking and informative site about the country with a
   section devoted to recollections and recommendations from
   people who've visited. See also the comprehensive
   **www.nz.com** and **www.newzealand.com**

**www.visitnorway.com**                                  NORWAY

   NORWAY
   The official site of the Norwegian Tourist Board offers a good
   overview of what you can get up to when you're there, from
   adventure holidays to lounging around in the midnight sun to
   cruising the coast. See also **www.norway.org** which is the
   Norwegian Embassy's site.

# P

**www.tourism.gov.pk**                                   PAKISTAN

   PAKISTAN
   A pretty lightweight site but it has all the basic information and
   a good set of links with a travel guide built in. See also
   **www.pak.org** which is a very comprehensive portal site.

**www.enjoyperu.com**                                    PERU

   PERU
   It's amazing how much there's to see in Peru and this site does
   a good job of reflecting the country's assets. Plenty of tourist
   information and deals. See also the basic but useful site of the
   Peruvian embassy **www.peruembassy-uk.com**

## www.polandtour.org                                          US

POLAND
Basic overview of the country and tourist facilities and travel
information.

## www.portugal-web.com                               PORTUGAL

PORTUGAL
A complete overview of the country including business as well
as tourism with good regional information, news and links to
other related sites.

*See also:*
**www.portugal.com** – a news and shopping site with a good
travel section.
**www.portugal.org** – well-designed information site with a good
travel section.
**www.thealgarve.net** – all you need to know about the Algarve.

# R

## www.russia-travel.com                                 RUSSIA

RUSSIA
The official guide to travel in Russia with good information on
excursions, accommodation, flights and trains, there's even
a slide show, plus historical facts and travel tips. See also
**www.themoscowtimes.com/travel** who offer a more
traditional approach.

## www.rotravel.com                                     ROMANIA

ROMANIA
Good historical information, maps and regional guides backed
up with tourist services both for the independent traveller and
those wanting a ready-made tour, make this site a good
starting point for the exploration of this central European gem.
The Romanian National Tourist Office has a good web site at
**www.romaniatourism.com**

T

# S

**www.sey.net** US

SEYCHELLES, PARADISE – PERIOD

A good all-round overview of the Seychelles with background
information on the major islands and activities, there are also
links to travel agents.

*See also:*

**www.seychelles.uk.com** – informative and geared to a
British audience.

**www.seychelleselite.co.uk** – specialists in the Seychelles.

**www.seychelles-travel.co.uk** – excellent site from another
specialist agent.

**www.sg** SINGAPORE

SINGAPORE

The shortest URL in the book brings up one of the most
detailed and comprehensive sites – all you need to know about
the country and its people. See also **www.satours.com**

**www.slovenia-tourism.si** SLOVENIA

SOLVENIA

A good introduction to the country which is trying to establish
a tourist industry. They boast that a visit here will regenerate
'lost psychophysical strength'.

**www.sacr.sk** SLOVAKIA

SLOVAKIA

The official word of the Slovak Republic on their tourist
attractions. For similar but more wordy information go to
**www.slovakia.org/tourism** who also have an audio guide to
common phrases in Slovak.

**www.southafrica.net** SOUTH AFRICA

SOUTH AFRICA

Official tourist site with masses of information about the country
and how you can set yourself up for the perfect visit with
suggested itineraries.

*See also:*

**www.gardenroute.org.za** – excellent site covering the Garden
Route and south coast.

T

**www.southafrica.com/travel** – very good portal site with
a comprehensive travel section.
**www.southafricanaffair.com** – tailor-made itineraries,
basic site though.

## www.southamericanexperience.co.uk                    UK

SOUTH AMERICA
Specialists on South America are hard to come by, but at this
site you can get tailor-made tours to suit you plus some scant
information on the countries and special offers. See also
**www.adventure-life.com** and **www.gosouthamerica.about.com**
both are very informative and are good for links. Check out the
listings under Latin America too.

## www.tourspain.es                                  SPAIN

TOURIST OFFICE OF SPAIN
A colourful and award-winning web site that really makes you
want to visit Spain. Very good for an overview.

*You could also try any of these listed below:*
**www.costaguide.com** – your Costa del Sol companion, lots
of information.
**www.iberia.com** – Iberian airlines site, with helpful advice
and offers.
**www.majorca.com** – great site about the island.
**www.okspain.org** – nice all round information and travel site.
**www.red2000.com** – a colourful travel guide, with a good
search instrument!

## www.lanka.net                                  SRI LANKA

SRI LANKA
An exhaustive site, which isn't easy to navigate, but it has loads
of information and news on the country, see also
**www.slmts.slt.lk** for the Ministry of Tourism.

## www.sverigeturism.se/smorgasbord                  SWEDEN

SWEDEN
The largest source of information in English on Sweden.
It's essentially a directory site but there are sections on culture,
history and a tourist guide. For more details of Sweden's
cities see the very good **http://cityguide.se** and
**www.visit-sweden.com** and also **www.sweden.com**

**www.switzerlandtourism.ch**                    SWITZERLAND

SWITZERLAND
An excellent overview of the country with the latest news, travel information, snow reports and links.

# T

**www.tanzania-web.com**                    TANZANIA

TANZANIA
Find your way round Tanzania with its wonderful scenery, Mount Kilimanjaro, safaris and resorts with this very good and comprehensive online guide from the official tourist board.

**www.allaboutzanzibar.com**                    TANZANIA

ZANZIBAR
An outstanding tourist site with concise (then very detailed if your need it) descriptions covering all the information you need, including accommodation and cultural stuff. Other tourism sites could learn a lot from this. See also **www.zanzibar.net**

**www.thailand.com/travel**                    THAILAND

THAILAND
Another excellent portal site, which acts as a gateway to a mass of travel and tourism resources. It covers some of South East Asia too and it has a good search facility. **www.tourismthailand.org** is the official tourist board site and is very informative, as is **www.nectec.or.th/thailand**

**www.tourismtunisia.com**                    TUNISIA

TUNISIA
A welcoming and easy-to-use site with lots of interactive links that gives you a good introduction to the country, its tourist sites and its people. There's information on hotels and restaurants – plus what to eat when you get there and links to travel agencies.

**www.allaboutturkey.com**                    TURKEY

TURKEY
The best-looking and most informative site on the country and its people, though some sections are pretty odd, it's the work of one professional tour guide.

*See also:*
**www.exploreturkey.com** – pretty boring but comprehensive.
**www.tourismturkey.org** – great for links and basic information from the Ministry of Culture and Tourism.
**www.turkey.org** – informative site from the Turkish Embassy in Washington DC.

# U

## www.uae.org.ae                                            UAE

UNITED ARAB EMIRATES
A useful guide to the seven states that make up the UAE, it carries historical and social information as well as the usual travel guide stuff. See also **www.godubai.com**

## www.visituganda.com                                    UGANDA

UGANDA
Great site and directory from the Ugandan Tourist Board with excellent quality pictures.

## www.usatourism.com                                          US

US
A state-by-state guide to the US, just click on the interactive map and you get put through to the relevant state site. See also **www.areaguides.net** which is very detailed.

## www.usembassy.org.uk                                        US

VISA INFO
For a dull look at the latest tourist entry requirements plus information on gripping topics such as driving requirements and some limited but useful links. For tourist information they send you to **www.visitusa.org.uk**

*See also:*
**www.americanadventures.com** – great site devoted to budget adventure tours. Now merged with **www.treckAmerica.com** what they offer an even broader range of holidays.
**www.amtrak.com** – rail schedules and fares across America.
**www.disneyworld.com** – all you need to know about the world's number one theme park.
**www.gohawaii.com** – great site for checking out Hawaii and it's many attractions.
**www.greyhound.com** – coach and bus schedules, but you can't buy tickets online from outside the US.

**www.seeamerica.org** – an excellent portal to American travel sites.

**www.usahotelguide.com** – reserve your room in any one of 50,000 hotels across the US.

# V

## www.vietnamtourism.com                                    US

VIETNAM

Vietnam is the hot destination apparently, here's the official tourism site, which is informative and good for links.

## www.zamnet.zm/tourism-travel.html              ZAMBIA

ZAMBIA

Basic tourist information and directory from the well-put together Zamnet portal site.

# Travel in Britain

## www.visitbritain.com                                      UK

HOME OF THE BRITISH TOURIST AUTHORITY

Selling Britain using a holiday ideas-led site with lots of help for the visitor, maps, background stories, images, entertainment, culture, activities and a planner. There's also a very helpful set of links.

## www.informationbritain.co.uk                             UK

HOLIDAY INFORMATION

Where to stay and where to go with an overview of all the UK's main tourist attractions, counties and regions; it has good cross-referencing and links to the major destinations.

## www.ukholidaybreaks.co.uk                                UK

FIND YOUR PERFECT HOTEL

A directory of hotels in the UK, you find the one you want by drilling down through a series of maps or select by category. It's easy although results are a bit hit and miss, but it claims to use the latest technology to find just the right break for you.

*See also:*

**www.aboutbritain.com** – attractive, well-laid out and comprehensive UK guide.

**www.atuk.co.uk** – billed as the UK travel search engine, unattractive design.

**www.enjoybritain.com** – useful links directory.
**www.travelbritain.com** – a modest directory site.
**www.ukguide.org** – well-organised directory with a UK and a London guide plus mapping.

**www.knowhere.co.uk**                                              UK
THE USER'S GUIDE TO BRITAIN
An unconventional 'tourist guide' that gives a warts-and-all account of over 1,000 places in Britain; it's very irreverent and if you are squeamish or a bit sensitive, then they have a good list of links to proper tourist sites.

*For separate countries and regions see also:*

# England
**www.londonhotelreservations.com** – some good deals on London hotels.
**www.londontown.com** – very comprehensive survival and holiday guide rolled into one, with sections on restaurants, hotels, attractions and offers. It is quite slow.
**www.timeout.com/london** – *Time Out* mag's excellent guide to the capital.
**www.travelengland.org.uk** – nice online guide to everything English, places to visit and accommodation.

# Northern Ireland
**www.discovernorthernireland.com** – Northern Ireland Tourist Board has an attractive site showing the best that the region has to offer. It has a virtual tour, holiday planner.
**www.guide-to-nireland.com** – a good directory site and guide.

# Scotland
**www.aboutscotland.com** – excellent site with information on a broad range of accommodation and sights to see, it's fast too.
**www.scotac.com** – accommodation by region.
**www.scotland.com** – nicely illustrated site with a good overview of the country.
**www.scotland-info.co.uk** – very good online guidebook, covering Scotland by area; it's quite slow but the information is very good.
**www.visithebrides.com** – a light and airy site with links and information relating to the islands. See also **www.hebrides.com** which offers beautiful photography.

**www.visitorkney.com** – from the Orkney Tourist Board a very informative and appealing site. See also **www.orknet.com**
**www.visitshetland.com** – a definite green theme to this site devoted to Shetland, highlighting its outdoor life and spirit of adventure.

## Wales

**www.cadw.wales.gov.uk** – historic monuments in Wales.
**www.data-wales.co.uk** – not so much a tourist site, but excellent for history and culture and quite funny too.
**www.holidays-in-wales.co.uk** – holidays in the Welsh countryside with limited online booking, a good overview of the country.
**www.valleyconnection.co.uk** – a useful directory devoted to all things Welsh.

## The UK's islands

**www.alderney.net** – a good-looking site devoted to the third largest Channel Island.
**www.guernseytouristboard.com** – all the information you need on Guernsey.
**www.jerseyhols.com** – good-looking site with lots of information and info on where to stay and what to do, see also **www.jersey.com** who have a very slick site.
**www.isle-of-man.com** – learn all about this unique island with help on where to stay and, of course, background on the famous TT races.
**www.sark.info** – a lively site with all the information you need plus online booking for ferries.
**www.simplyscilly.co.uk** – specialists in travel to the Scilly islands with info on how to get there and what to do.

## Things to do in Britain and Ireland

**www.sightseeing.co.uk**                                          UK

SIGHT-SEEING MADE EASY
A good-looking and very useful site if you're looking for something to do. Just type in what you want to see and where you are, then up pops a listing giving basic information on each attraction, how far it is to get there, entrance fee and a map. However, it would be better if there was more background information on each attraction or at least a link.

T

## www.daysoutuk.com                                         UK

GO TO A GARDEN
Excellent directory of venues and events with lots of search
options, easy to use and you can get discounts to many
attractions too.

*See also:*
**www.anothertravel.com** – a good-looking site, a bit light on
information though.
**www.daysout.co.uk** – similar to Days Out above but more
colourful, it includes a useful section for the disabled too.
**www.i-uk.com** – useful information on the UK, mainly aimed
at visitors.

## www.gardenvisit.com                                       UK

GO TO A GARDEN
A basic text-based site, which lists some 1,000 of the UK's
gardens open to the public, giving details of each, how to get
there and how they rate. It also covers the US and Europe and
there's also an excellent overview of garden history. See also
section on Gardening page 192.

## www.nationaltrust.org.uk                                  UK

PLACES OF HISTORIC INTEREST AND BEAUTY
The National Trust's site has an excellent overview of their
activities and the properties they own. There is a very good
search facility and up-to-date information to help with your
visit. See also **www.nts.org.uk** for the National Trust
for Scotland.

*See also:*
**www.castles-of-britain.com** – informative and lively site on the
UK's castles.
**www.english-heritage.org.uk** – excellent, high quality site with
information on their properties and an events calendar.
**www.hrp.org.uk** – pretty boring site devoted to five historic
royal palaces – the Tower, Hampton Court, Kensington,
Kew and the Banqueting House.
**www.statelyhomes.com** – comprehensive site devoted to our
stately homes, with links and an e-zine to keep you updated.

T

**www.goodbeachguide.co.uk**                                    UK

> THE BEST BEACHES
> From the Marine Conservation Society you can find out which
> are Britain's worst and best beaches. It's set out regionally and
> the site is updated regularly.

## What to do with the kids

**www.babygoes2.com**                                          UK

> ESSENTIAL TRAVEL GUIDE FOR PARENTS
> An excellent resource for parents who have children under 5,
> it covers a wide range of holiday options, plus plenty of advice,
> guides and information.
>
> *For more ideas try:*
> **www.ate.org.uk** – Active, Training and Education and by the
> looks of it lots of fun.
> **www.barracudas.co.uk** – activity camp holidays.
> **www.campbeaumont.com** – a summer camp covering south-
> east England.
> **www.kidstravel.co.uk** – bright and breezy design but it could
> have more content, still some good ideas and travelling tips for
> parents though biased to England.
> **www.pgl.co.uk/holidays** – activity holidays for children with lots
> of options.
> **www.thefamilytravelfiles.com** – a US oriented e-zine with lots
> of advice and links.
> **www.travellingwithchildren.co.uk** – good for ideas and advice,
> if you can put up with the adverts.
> **www.xkeys.co.uk** – specialist in residential camps for children
> of all ages, excellent web site with lots of information and
> references.

## Holiday cottages and B&B

**www.hidays.co.uk**                                           UK

> UK COTTAGES
> Hidays claims over 22,000 cottages in the UK, Ireland and
> France. The site is user friendly and you can search using
> numerous options from those who take pets, even cottages
> with pools.

T

**www.bedandbreakfast-directory.co.uk**                              UK

   BED AND BREAKFAST
   A regional directory of bed and breakfast places with a good
   search facility. Each entry has contact details, description and
   information such as whether online booking is available.

   *See also:*
   **www.cottagesdirect.com** – click on the interactive map and
   away you go, plenty of cottages to choose from.
   **www.hideaways.co.uk** – great for the south of England.
   **www.holidayrentals4you.com** – a wide range of properties to
   rent in UK, US and Europe.
   **www.nationaltrust.org.uk/cottages** – holiday cottages with
   a difference.
   **www.oas.co.uk/ukcottages** – over 1,000 cottages available
   throughout the UK.
   **www.preferredplaces.co.uk** – good site with a wide range
   of options.
   **www.seasidecottages.co.uk** – all within 10 miles of the sea.
   **www.selfcatering-directory.co.uk** – a very useful directory
   site listing hundreds of cottages with information and
   contact details.

# Cycling and touring

*The following are mostly UK specialists, but some cover further
afield too.*

**www.ctc.org.uk**                                                  UK

   WORKING FOR CYCLING
   The CTC have a great travel section with routes, tours, offers,
   links and directories, it's a great place to start your search for
   the perfect cycling holiday.

   *Also check out:*
   **www.bicycle-beano.co.uk** – Bicycle Beano have a good site
   covering cycling holidays in Wales and the borders.
   **www.bikemagic.com** – go to the travel pages for an excellent
   section where Bike Magic have got partners who'll supply flight
   deals for cyclists or rail travel and holidays.
   **www.byways-breaks.co.uk** – nice-looking site, Byways Breaks
   arrange cycling and walking holidays in the Peaks, Shropshire
   and Cheshire countryside.

**www.cycle-rides.co.uk** – a very good selection of biking tours through Europe and further afield.
**www.rough-tracks.co.uk** – wide range of active adventure holidays from beginners to experts.
**www.scotcycle.co.uk** – Scottish Cycling Holidays are specialists in cycling holidays in Scotland obviously. Nice site too.
**www.sustrans.co.uk** – the National Cycle Network is featured as part of this campaigning charity site.

# Camping and caravanning

*Many of the sites listed specialise in Britain but some have information on camp sites abroad too.*

## www.camp-sites.co.uk                                    UK

FIND A SITE
Excellent regional listing of the UK's campsites with comprehensive details on each site and links to other related directories.

*See also:*
**www.eurocampindependent.co.uk** – excellent site if you want to go camping in Europe, some special offers and you can chat about your experiences too.
**www.keycamp.co.uk** – European specialist with sites in seven countries.
**www.pjcamping.co.uk** – exhaustive selection of tents and camping equipment for sale, good info but still no online ordering.

## www.caravan.co.uk                                       UK

THE CARAVAN CLUB
Huge listing of sites, advice and practical help with details of over 200 sites and some 2,700 other certified locations where you can park up. There's also a European service. You can join the club on site and request any of the fifty or so leaflets they publish.

*See also:*
**http://camping.uk-directory.com** – a good regional sites directory, with retailing links, caravans for sale and conservation information.
**www.campingandcaravanningclub.co.uk** – an OK offering with information on sites and technical help and advice too.

**www.caravan-sitefinder.co.uk** - listing of over 3,500 caravan sites, with background information on a wide range of topics.
**www.clicreports.co.uk** - the Chat Line for Internet Campers offers loads of advice in a fun and informative way.

## Waterways

**www.britishwaterways.co.uk**                                          UK

BRITISH WATERWAYS
This organisation is responsible for maintaining a large part of Britain's waterways and this excellent site details their work. It contains interactive mapping of the routes with a great deal of background information, events listings and history.

*See also:*
**www.blakes.co.uk** – a boating holiday specialist.
**www.canalholidays.com** – an easy way to book your narrow boat holiday.
**www.canals.co.uk** – the biggest canal-related shop on the Internet, mainly videos, maps and books.
**www.gobarging.com** – luxury barging in Europe.
**www.hoseasons.co.uk** – great site from the specialists in boating holidays, you can book online too.
**www.waterways.org.uk** – Inland Waterways Association site, dedicated to keeping canals open and you can find out about their organised activities too.

## Adventure and activity

*Listed below are UK-oriented sites, see also page 427 for international adventure specialists.*

**www.activitiesonline.co.uk**                                          UK

ULTIMATE RESOURCE FOR LEISURE PURSUITS
A directory of adventure and activity holiday specialists covering everything from extreme sports to gardening. You get a description of the activity, then a list of relevant sites.

**www.sportbreak.co.uk**                                                UK

THE SPORTS BREAK DIRECTORY
A good directory, apart from sports it covers all activity holidays including leisure breaks, health clubs, even stag and hen parties. It's easy to use and the information is well put over.

*Other adventure holiday sites:*

**www.activityholsni.co.uk** – Activity Holidays in Northern
Ireland have a great site and lots to do.

**www.activitywales.co.uk** – break out and discover the real
Wales with Activity Wales. Use this well-constructed site to suss
out which activities to try.

**www.adventureholiday.com** – ProAdventure specialise in
activity holidays in North Wales.

**www.sportstoursinternational.co.uk** – sports holidays, mainly
running, cycling and swimming both UK and abroad.

**www.trailplus.com** – the ultimate adventure, offering lifestyle
experiences, adventure camps and much more.

# Walking and rambling

## www.ramblers.org.uk                                          UK

THE RAMBLERS' ASSOCIATION
News, strong views and plenty of advice on offer here, where
you can find out about the Association's activities and even join
a campaign. There are features on events and details of the
*Rambler* magazine, shopping and holidays.

## www.walkingbritain.co.uk                                     UK

BRITISH WALKS
Some 2,000 pages of information about walking in Britain,
it mainly covers the National Parks but it is expanding to
include less well-known areas. They provide decent route maps
and photos to guide you. There's also a list of handy links and
a good photo gallery.

## www.onedayhikes.com                                          US

WHERE DO YOU WANT TO HIKE TODAY?
A great site, which is basically a directory of hikes that you can
complete in a day, it's not just for the UK either, it covers the
whole world. There's excellent information on each hike plus
pictures and you get the chance to win a digital camera if you
send in a report of a hike you've done and it gets accepted.

T

### www.walkingworld.com                                    UK

OVER 2000 WALKS
Each walk has a detailed description and map and it's easy to
find a good one. In addition, there's advice on difficulty and
what you can expect to see. The walks cost £1.50 or you can
become a member for £14.95 per annum, then they're free.

*For more sites for hikers try:*
**www.bwf-ivv.org.uk** – the British Walking Federation organise a
wide range of activities and you can find out about them here.
**www.gelert.com** – equipment for sale, a good looking site well
worth a visit.
**www.ramblersholidays.co.uk** – Ramblers Holidays specialise in
escorted rambling holidays.

## Train, coach and ferry journeys

### www.pti.org.uk                                           UK

PUBLIC TRANSPORT INFORMATION
An incredibly useful site if you're a frequent user of public
transport or if you're using it to go somewhere you're not
familiar with. It categorises all the major forms of public
transport and lists for each area useful numbers, timetables,
web sites and interactive mapping to help you. It also includes
routes to Europe and Ireland.

### www.kizoom.co.uk                                         UK

TRAVEL SERVICE TO YOUR PHONE
Good quality travel information to your mobile phone sounds
great and this is a very well set up and easy-to-use site.
Unfortunately, it only works with a limited number of WAP
phones, so if you've one of those you're in luck.

### www.travelfusion.com                                     UK

THE TRAVEL COMPARISON PORTAL
A brilliant idea – pick a journey then compare whether it would
be best to go by coach, car, ferry or by air. It's simple to use,
but you have to register, then you can compare by price or
speed. It then connects you with the right operator if you want
to book.

# Railway travel

**www.rail.co.uk**                                                        UK

RAILWAY LINKS
A directory of useful links including timetables, operators and
associated businesses.

**www.nationalrail.co.uk**                                                UK

NATIONAL RAIL
National Rail's site has all the latest information, timetables and
links you need to plan a rail journey. It's very comprehensive
with up-to-the-minute information on what's going on.

**www.thetrainline.com**                                                  UK

BUY TRAIN TICKETS
You have to log in first but you can book a ticket for train travel,
whether business or leisure, (except sleeper, Motorail, Eurostar
and ferry services). They have an up-to-date timetable and the
tickets will be sent or you can collect. See also the fast working
**www.qjump.co.uk** which is similar. At both these sites there
are a bewildering number of options and prices, a little help
with what each ticket type and their relative costs wouldn't
go amiss.

*See also:*
**www.eurail.com** – details of the Eurailticket, information and
prices, and you can now buy online.
**www.eurostar.co.uk** – online booking plus timetables
and offers.
**www.eurotunnel.com** – online passenger bookings.
**www.greatrail.com** – escorted railway holidays, world-wide.
Well illustrated site.
**www.networkrail.co.uk** – what was Railtrack, some useful
information.
**www.trainpain.com** – the place to go to complain about trains!
**www.traintaxi.co.uk** – useful site if you need a taxi once you're
off the train, with taxi company contact details and advice on
whether there are usually taxis waiting.
**www.trainweb.com** – a huge train portal site; particularly good
for Amtrak in the US and Via Rail in Canada.

T

### www.thetube.com                                                     UK

LONDON UNDERGROUND
An excellent and informative site from London Underground
with lots of features, articles on visiting London and links to
related sites. There's a good journey planner and tube maps
too. See also the Tube Planner at **www.tubeplanner.com**
which is a straightforward journey planner and you could try
**http://owen.massey.net/tubemaps.html** a tube guide
and history.

## Coaches

### www.nationalexpress.com                                             UK

BOOK COACH TICKETS
Organise your journey with this easy-to-use web site from
National Express, and then book the tickets. Also offers an
airport service, transport to events and tours. See also
**www.stagecoachbus.com** where you can find information
about Stagecoach services and buy tickets and
**www.citylink.co.uk** for their Scottish Services.

## Ferries

### www.ferrysavers.com                                                 UK

BOOK YOUR CROSSING
Low cost ferry crossings and plenty of special offers on a
number of routes, you can book online but the price promise
seems to have disappeared.

*See also:*
**www.brittany-ferries.co.uk** – crossings to France and Spain
with online booking and special offers, also cruises and
holidays.
**www.dfdsseaways.co.uk** – details and offers on Scandinavian
routes.
**www.directferries.co.uk** – claims to offer the widest choice of
routes and crossings.
**www.drive-alive.com** – motoring holiday specialists who get
good rates on channel crossings as part of their package.
**www.ferry.co.uk** – great offers on selected crossings.
**www.ferrycrossings-uk.co.uk** – helpful site with offers and
links, shopping guide too.

**www.hoverspeed.com** – online booking and all the information you need to make the fastest channel and Irish Sea crossings.
**www.irishferries.ie** – excellent magazine-style site where amongst all the features you can find timetables and book tickets.
**www.posl.com** – P&O Stena Line with online booking, details of sailings and offers.
**www.seafrance.com** – bookings and information on their Calais-Dover service plus some special offers.

# Car hire

*It's probably best to go to a price comparison site before going to one of the car hire companies, that way you should get the best prices. One of the best is to be found at* **www.priceline.co.uk**

**www.holidaycars.co.uk**                                          UK

WORLD-WIDE CAR HIRE
Over 3,000 car hire locations throughout the world means that this site is well worth a visit on your quest, you can get an instant online quote and you can book too. Very good for the US. See also Holiday Autos who have a similar site at **www.holidayautos.co.uk** and also the competitive **www.pelicancarhire.co.uk** who specialise in Europe.

T

# Utilities

*Get the best prices on you gas, electricity and water and find out what the big suppliers are up to as well.*

**www.ofgem.gov.uk**                                                    UK

GAS AND ELECTRICITY SUPPLIER WATCHDOG
Data on the suppliers and companies providing comparison information makes for interesting reading. There's also background on how bills are made up, complaints and how energy reaches your home. Excellent.

**www.uswitch.com**                                                    UK

CUT YOUR BILLS – COMPARE PRICES
Take a few minutes to check the prices of the key utilities and see whether you can save on your current bills, its easy and quick. It also gives you the option to change to a green energy tariff. It also covers phones and loans, and there's also access to *Which?* Magazine's energy reports.

*See also:*
**www.servista.com** – straightforward and well-designed bill switching service
**www.theenergyshop.com** – very easy to use and fast results.
**www.unravelit.com** – savings on gas and electricity plus numerous other services.
**www.utilitydeal.com** – helps business users as well as home owners.

## Saving energy

**www.natenergy.org.uk**                                               UK

NATIONAL ENERGY FOUNDATION
Devoted to saving energy in order to benefit the environment. There's lots of advice and information to help save money too.

*See also:*
**www.energysaving.me.uk** – energy-saving lighting.
**www.est.org.uk** – a government trust set up to help fight against global warming.

U

# Electricity and gas

*Here are the main energy sites, who owns them at time of writing and the highlights of the site.*

**www.british-energy.com** – one of the largest electricity providers with a good-looking but not very useful site.

**www.calorgas.co.uk** – portability and gas with online ordering at £1.50 a delivery.

**www.centrica.co.uk** – owners of British Gas and the AA, this site aims to give information about the group, could be a lot more helpful.

**www.esb.ie** – good-looking site from an Irish supplier with online sign up available.

**www.gas.co.uk** – comprehensive service from British Gas with account viewing. Redirects you to **www.house.co.uk** but you still get info on gas.

**www.hydro.co.uk** – Scottish Hydro Electric has one of the sites most oriented to its customers.

**www.edfenergy.com** – a stylish site for London Electricity, SWEB Energy, Seeboard Energy and Virgin Home.

**www.nationalgrid.com/uk** – the National Grid, the Railtrack of power.

**www.nie.co.uk** – Northern Ireland Electricity with customer information on their service the rest is fairly corporate.

**www.npower.com** – nicely designed site with online application.

**www.powergen.co.uk** – Powergen has a neat site with calculators and a switching service.

**www.scottish-southern.co.uk** – owner of Swalec, site aimed at shareholders.

**www.swalec.co.uk** – Swalec, good house move planner.

**www.txuenergi.co.uk** – good service, helpful, much improved.

## www.transco.uk.com                                      UK
FOR GAS LEAKS
Transco doesn't sell gas, but maintains the 24-hour emergency service for stopping gas leaks – call 0800 111 999 to report one.

U

## www.corgi-gas-safety.com                                UK
COUNCIL OF REGISTERED GAS INSTALLERS
CORGI is the gas industry watchdog; the site has advice on gas installation and where to find a fitter or repairman.

**www.calorgas.co.uk** UK

CALOR GAS
Information on your nearest stockists, how best to use Calor
Gas and Autogas, there's also corporate background and
customer services too. You can also order it online with
payment collected on delivery.

# Water

**www.ofwat.gov.uk** UK

OFFICE OF WATER SERVICES
A very poor effort, especially when compared to the OFGEM
counterpart's site, however, you can find out about what they
do and you can contact them for advice.

*The following are the main water company sites:*
**www.nwl.co.uk** – nice lifestyle site with leisure information and
bill paying.
**www.nww.co.uk** – United Utilities, once North West Water has
a well-designed site with help, information and good advice for
consumers, with online access to your account. They now
supply electricity too.
**www.stwater.co.uk** – the consumer site of Severn Trent Water,
it's good looking and useful, you can even order a 'save a flush
bag' for your loo!
**www.swwater.co.uk** – lots of information and good advice,
bill paying online.
**www.thameswater.co.uk** – good information and advice.
**www.wessexwater.co.uk** – good site with bill paying facilities
and information, even which reservoirs you can fish in.

U

# Weather

### www.met-office.gov.uk
UK

EXCELLING IN WEATHER SERVICES
Comprehensive information on Britain's favourite topic of
conversation; easy to use with interactive maps. Includes details
on world weather and world weather news, UK weather
headlines and flash weather warnings, weather for aviators
and sailors and you can see what the weather is like on their
webcams. There's also a good selection of links and a mobile
phone service.

### www.bbc.co.uk/weather
UK

ANOTHER WINNER FROM THE BBC
Another page from the BBC site, it gives up-to-the-minute
forecasts, and is very clear and concise. It features: 5-day
forecasts by town, city or post code; specialist reports such
as ski resorts, pollution, sun index; world weather and the
shipping forecast. There's also a section dedicated to articles
on various aspects of the weather and details on making the
weather forecast programme.

*See also:*
**www.uk-weather.co.uk** – good for links.
**www.weather.com** – geared to the US, but has some really
good articles and features.
**www.weather.org.uk** – informative UK weather information site.

### www.weatherimages.org
US

SEE THE WORLD'S WEATHER – LIVE
Weatherimages is compiled by a true weather fan. Split into
twenty or so areas of interest, there is plenty of information and
there's loads to see. The best feature is the network of weather
cams from which you can see the best and worst of the world's
weather. See also the excellent **www.weather-photography.com**

*Other interesting and useful weather sites worth checking out:*
**www.chasingstorms.com** – home of the Storm Chasers and
Spotters Association.
**www.hurricaneadvisories.com** – American hurricane
information.

W

**www.hurricanes.net** – information on tropical storms and their effects.

**www.stormstock.com** – the world's premier storm footage library with some stunning clips, unfortunately they only supply in the US.

**www.stormtrack.org** – another US storm-tracking site, very comprehensive though.

**www.torro.org.uk** – the Tornado and Storm Research Organisation, an interesting UK-oriented site.

**www.tsunami.org** – the Pacific Tsunami Museum with some great stories, photos and links.

# Web Cameras

*One of the most fascinating aspects of the Internet is the ability to tap into some CCTV or specially set up web cameras from all around the world. Some sites will contain adult material.*

**www.camcentral.com**                                          US

WEB CAM CENTRAL
An excellent selection of cameras, chosen for quality rather than quantity; the wildlife ones are very good in particular but there's a good search facility too.

*See also:*
**www.camvista.com** – web cam shots of the UK and the US from a web cam manufacturer.

**www.webcam-index.com** – lists some 500 sites from around the world.

**www.webcamworld.com** – a big directory of web cams.

# Web Site Design

*As it's pretty expensive to get a site designed and built professionally, there's been an explosion in the number of books, software and sites dedicated to helping people put their own sites together. These web sites will help enormously and take you through the world of Hypertext Markup Language, Java and Flash.*

W

## http://hotwired.lycos.com/webmonkey

THE WEB MONKEY                                                US

A superb resource for web designers of all skill levels providing
everything from basic tutorials to articles from professional
designers. The 'How to' library is brilliant and, as you'd expect,
the site design is excellent too. See also **www.htmlgoodies.com**
who also offer tutorials and lots of tips for those times when
things don't go quite the way you want them to.

## www.codebeach.com                                        US

CODE BEACH

Code Beach describe their site as 'your complete guide to free
and open source code and tutorials for ASP, C++, ColdFusion,
Java, JavaScript, Palm, Perl, PHP, and Visual Basic' and it is.
Each language has a section with tutorials, downloads and
links for you to get your head around it all.

*Other essential sites:*

**http://cool.infi.net** – vote for the coolest sites and find out
which are considered the best. This has got very commercial
now, so lots of deals and adverts get in the way.

**http://webdeveloper.earthweb.com/webjs** - you're going to
need this site, it's a great source of those helpful little Java
programs you find on most sites. Why write your own when
you can download one for free.

**www.blogger.com** – a free web-publishing tool and
diary facility.

**www.blogs.com** – more blogs and blogging advice. See also
the section on page 41.

**www.cutandpastescripts.com** – a great time saving tool where
you can literally cut and paste bits of essential computer
graphics.

**www.desktoppublishing.com** – free web templates and original
clip art – excellent.

**www.dreamink.com** – very good online guide to web site
creation and design.

**www.dreamweaver.com** – home of one of the leading pieces of
web creation software, here you can download a trial version,
get lots of information and more downloads to improve
your site.

**www.flashkit.com** – animate your site, give it life here.

**www.fontfreak.com** – over 300 different and unusual fonts.

**www.homepagetools.com** – a really strong resource of tools
and services you can add to your site once you're up
and running.

W

**www.internet.com** – top tips, news and downloads – a comprehensive offering.

**www.jimtools.com** – OK, you're site is up and running, now promote it. This site tells you how, with lots of tips and a program that will send your new URL to lots of search engines.

**www.learnthenet.com** – web site construction made easy; senible, thorough and well designed.

**www.netforbeginners.about.com** – the beginners pages from About.com.

**www.port41.com** – manage and update your website the simple way.

**www.rnib.org.uk** – from the Royal National Institute for the Blind, here you can find information on how to make your web site more accessible for partially sighted and disabled people.

**www.spinwave.com** – free software to ensure that the pictures you choose fit the site, and load quickly and efficiently too.

**www.thecounter.com** – find out who visits your site and how often.

**www.ultimateresources.co.uk** – advice and information on how to make money from your site.

**www.useit.com** – great place to go for advice from a bone-fide web design guru.

**www.webaward.org** – so called the top awards for web design, annoying announcer to go with it.

**www.webbyawards.com** – an attractive and prominent site devoted to rewarding the best of what's on the Internet, learn from those who got it right.

**www.webpagesthatsuck.com** – examples of how not to do it, a chastening and humorous experience.

# Web Site Guides and Directories

*If you can't find the site you're looking for in this book then rather than use a search engine, check out one of these web site directories.*

**www.just35.com**                                                    UK

FIND IT THE EASY WAY
A very good directory site that is well categorised (maximum 35 sites in each category) and easy to use with each site reviewed and rated. You can also get the latest news and personalise the site.

### www.uk250.co.uk
UK

1,000S OF QUALITY SITES IN 250 CATEGORIES
Heavily advertised and hyped though this site has been, many
people seem to think that it consists of just the top 250 sites,
but it's actually a very comprehensive database of Britain's most
important and useful .co.uks and .coms. The sites listed are not
reviewed but a one-liner gives a brief description of what they
are about.

### www.thegoodwebguide.co.uk
UK

GOOD WEB GUIDE
The best web sites in several key categories are
comprehensively reviewed but you have to subscribe (£10-30
per annum) or buy the related book (subscription then free to
that subject area) to get the best out of it. It's a good site and
the books are good (if a little expensive), but the problem for
the Good Web Guide team is that you can get all the
information at reduced cost elsewhere.

### www.ukdirectory.co.uk
UK

DEFINITIVE GUIDES TO BRITISH SITES
A massive database of web sites conveniently categorised
into fifteen sections, they don't review, but there are brief
explanations provided by the site owners.

### www.bored.com
US

IF YOU'RE BORED
Basically a directory of unusual and humorous sites to occupy you
when you've nothing better to do, it's quite entertaining really.

## Weddings

### www.confetti.co.uk
UK

YOUR INTERACTIVE WEDDING GUIDE
A good looking and busy site, designed to help you through
every stage of your wedding with information for all
participants. There are gift guides, planning tools, advice,
a supplier directory and a shop. They don't miss much.

W

## www.wedding-service.co.uk UK

### UK'S LARGEST WEDDING AND BRIDE DIRECTORY

A huge list of suppliers, service providers and information by region, everything from balloons to speechwriters are listed. The site is not that easy on the eye and it takes a little while to find what you want.

## www.all-about-weddings.co.uk UK

### GETTING MARRIED IN THE UK

Excellent for basic information about planning weddings from the ceremony to the reception; it also has a good set of links to related and specialist supplier sites, a travel section and a shop. It's all wrapped up in suitably matrimonial design with love hearts flowing across the screen as you browse.

*Other good sites for weddings:*

**www.bridesuk.net** – excellent site from *Brides* magazine; get all the latest in bridal fashion and a guide to where to go on honeymoon.

**www.chauffeur-me.com** – a regional guide to chauffeured cars and limos throughout the UK.

**www.gwp-uk.co.uk** – home to the guild of wedding photographers with advice on choosing the right photographer for your wedding.

**www.hitched.co.uk** – another good all-rounder with the added feature of a discussion forum where you can swap wedding stories.

**www.lastnightoffreedom.co.uk** – everything you need to organise your stag or hen night.

**www.limoshop.co.uk** – reserve your stretch limo.

**www.partydomain.co.uk** – if you want to organise your own party then this is the site for you with some fairly naff offerings for hen and stag nights.

**www.pronuptia.co.uk** – details of the range and stores, not much else.

**www.theknot.com** – all (well nearly all) your wedding needs catered for, excellent and attractive design too.

**www.trading-direct.co.uk** – your wedding presents taken care of with an online wedding list service.

**www.webwedding.co.uk** – lots of expert advice and inspiration, a bit slow though.

**www.weddingguide.co.uk** – clean-looking site with shop, directory and advice plus a good search facility.

# Women

*The following are a few sites of particular interest to women.*

## Equality issues and politics

**www.womenandequalityunit.gov.uk**                    UK
THE WOMEN AND EQUALITY UNIT
Dedicated to promoting a 'vision of equality and opportunity for
all'. Politics aside, the site provides useful information on how
government policies impact on women's lives, covering hot
topics such as encouraging women to become more involved
in public life, balancing work and family, domestic violence,
money, health and equal opportunities. Worth visiting for the
useful links.

For information on what the UN is doing to promote gender
equality go to **www.un.org/womenwatch** where there is
information on all their initiatives and international treaties.
A dry but informative read.

**www.aviva.org**                    UK
INTERNATIONAL FEMINIST WEBZINE
If you want information on the political and social issues facing
women all over the world, this site has plenty of factual articles,
details of meetings and loads of links. There is a nice section
on international women's art too.

**www.savingwomenslives.org**                    US
A GLOBAL PERSPECTIVE
An excellent site to visit for a glimpse into the lives of women
throughout the world. There are heart-wrenching stories,
shocking facts, essays on issues and a newsroom. The US
foundation, The National Organisation for Women explore
similar issues at **www.now.org**

*See also:*
**www.poptel.org.uk/women-ww** – dedicated to supporting the
rights of women workers world-wide.
**www.womensaid.org.uk** – campaigns to end domestic violence
and assist abused women.

W

**www.fulltimemothers.org**                                      UK

FOR FULL-TIME MUMS
This organisation aims to promote the status of stay at home
mums and campaign for changes in the tax, benefit systems
and employment policy to give women more choice. There is
also information on how to join a local group, or set one up.
See also **www.workingmother.com** a campaigning e-zine for
working mothers from the US.

**www.womanstudent.co.uk**                                       UK

FOR WOMEN IN HIGH EDUCATION
Loads of information for UK and international students with
sections on money and careers, travel, health, leisure and
universities. Helpful section for overseas women planning to
come to British Universities.

## Working Women

**www.flametree.co.uk**                                          UK

INSPIRING SOLUTIONS TO BALANCE YOUR LIFE
This former magazine site now acts as a specialist consultancy
'working with organisations to respond effectively to the work-
life challenge'. If your company needs to improve their flexibility,
visit this site. Unfortunately they have abandoned the personal
section to concentrate on the corporate.

**www.resourceconnection.co.uk**                                 UK

FLEXIBLE WORKING SOLUTIONS
Although not exclusively for women, the flexible working
arrangements that are the site's lifeblood are particularly
attractive to women. Check out the flexible mum fact sheet,
get advice on how to convince your boss to co-operate, you can
also join their jobshare register. Send in your CV, you never
know what's out there.

**www.busygirl.co.uk**                                           US

AURORA WOMEN'S NETWORK
A more serious site than the its name suggests, their aim is to
advance women by supporting the business and career needs
of women. Amongst its services they offer classroom-based and
online IT training courses, women's investment clubs,
networking forums and a women-owned business directory.

W

### www.everywoman.co.uk
UK

NOT JUST FOR BUSINESS WOMEN
A really useful site aimed at women business owners, but the
'home' channel provides sound information on personal finance,
family and well-being for all women.

## Magazines

### www.handbag.com
UK

THE ISP FOR WOMEN
Described as the most useful place on the Internet for British
women, Handbag lives up to that with a mass of information
written in an informal style and aimed at helping you get
through life. There's shopping and competitions too. For some
it's a little too commercial though.

### www.ivillage.co.uk
UK

WHERE WOMEN FIND ANSWERS
All the sections you'd expect in a women's magazine, the
difference here is that they are trying to create a community
with a range of message boards, advice, a good section on
work, even a dating service.

### www.blackwomen.co.uk
UK

THE VOICE OF BLACK WOMEN
A serious magazine-style site that in addition provides a list of
services targeted at Black women living in the UK. See also
**www.blackliving.net** a good American magazine site with a
British interest; it has a .co.uk version under construction.

### www.bbc.co.uk/radio4/womanshour
UK

WOMAN'S HOUR
Excellent magazine spin-off from the popular Radio 4 program,
you can listen to programs, have your say and go to sections
such as those on food, health and history with it's timeline.

*Other general women's e-zines and portals:*
**http://womensissues.about.com** – features on a comprehensive
range of women's issues.
**www.allthatwomenwant.com** – a portal site that offers links
to sites covering a vast range of topics. It needs a search
engine though.

**www.cybergrrl.com** – a comprehensive American women's e-zine. Check out the sister site **www.femina.com** which is a useful search engine for women-friendly sites.

**www.icircle.co.uk** – part of the Freeserve network calling itself the Women's Channel.

**www.newwomanonline.co.uk** – good representation of the magazine.

## www.e-women.com                                                    UK

THE MULTICULTURAL WOMEN'S PORTAL

E-women aims to provide women world-wide with features and links which are relevant to their lives. There are lots of women's magazine-type features, a good range of forums, a shopping directory but less serious comment than when previously visited.

# Women's health

*Below are a few excellent sources of information on women's health issues, for more general health sites see page 200 and don't rely on websites, see a doctor if you are unwell.*

## www.healthywomen.org                                              US

EDUCATING WOMEN ABOUT THEMSELVES

The layout doesn't do justice to the quality of information on the site provided by the American-based National Women's Health Resource Center. Go to the 'health center' and use the pull-down menu to select a topic such as breast cancer, acupuncture or menopause. The aim is to provide women with good information to help them make informed decisions about their health.

## www.womens-health.co.uk                                           UK

OBS AND GYNAE EXPLAINED

A good starting point for information on obstetrics and gynaecology including pregnancy, infertility, complications and investigations. Has a good search facility and useful links.

W

## www.fpa.org.uk

FAMILY PLANNING

A really comprehensive web site from the Family Planning Association with information on all aspects of birth control written in a clear and helpful style. There is a useful page entitled 'I need help now' plus good links. For a more campaigning approach, try **www.mariestopes.org.uk** for a rundown on contraception choices and information on related topics such as health screening. You can even arrange for him to have a vasectomy online.

*See also:*

**www.ein.org** – Infertility Network with information and advice.
**www.menopausematters.co.uk** – excellent site giving the latest information on the menopause and how to live with it.
**www.miscarriageassociation.org.uk** – for miscarriage support and information.
**www.pms.org.uk** – National Association for Premenstrual Syndrome.
**www.pni.org.uk** – support for those suffering post-natal depression.

# Leisure

## www.journeywoman.com

PREMIER TRAVEL RESOURCE FOR WOMEN

Dedicated to ensuring safe travel for women, registering gets you access to the free newsletter plus lots of advice, guidance and tips from women who've travelled, traveller's tales and health warnings. See also **www.poshnosh.com** which is aimed at the 50+ traveller.

## www.womengamers.com

BECAUSE WOMEN DO PLAY

The aim is to provide a selection of reviews and games geared specifically to a female audience (although it doesn't stop this being an enjoyable site for men to visit). It has up-to-the-minute reviews, really well-written articles, lots of content and high quality design.

## www.wsf.org.uk                                                            UK

WOMEN'S SPORT FOUNDATION
The voice of women's sport is committed to improving and
promoting opportunities for women and girls in sport at every
level. It does this by lobbying and raising the awareness of the
importance of women in sport to the organisers and governing
bodies. Here you can find out how to get involved or get help.

## www.pinknoises.com                                                        UK

PROMOTING WOMEN'S MUSIC
Giving women a voice in the male-dominated international
electronic music scene by providing music, profiles of artists,
review, essays, a message board and comprehensive links.
Truly international in the artists it features and an invaluable
resource for women DJs and electronic music freaks.

## http://digital.library.upenn.edu/women                                    US

A CELEBRATION OF WOMEN WRITERS
A site with a passion for the work of women writers; the quality
and quantity of information on this site is tremendous with links
to biographical and bibliographical information about women
writers as well as providing complete books written by women.

*For other sites on women's arts see:*
**http://web.ukonline.co.uk/n.paradoxa** – feminist art journal
with good links to artists and women's art associations.
**http://womenwriters.net/links.htm** – a guide to Internet
resources as well as book reviews and features.
**www.blackwomenart.org.uk** – dedicated to black women in
fashion, design, crafts and the performing arts.
**www.distinguishedwomen.com** – biographies and women's
impact on history.
**www.the-womens-press.com**– for incisive feminist writing.

W

# Stop press....

*Here are some sites that came to us too late to make the main body of the book, we'll be sure to review them properly in the next edition.*

## Business

**www.plaxo.com** – keep up to date with your business contacts with this handy online service.

## Chat

**www.there.com** – amazing design concept, you create your personality (avatar) customizing everything from facial features to clothes, then join in conversations with everyone else in the 3-D world, you can even play games and go to parties!

## Children

**www.fffbi.com** – Animal Agents Fighting for Truth, Justice and Stuff Like That, an excellent site that uses games and stories to help children (8–13) learn about the world; great design and well thought out.

**www.lego.com** – very well designed and attractive site from Lego that offers information on products, games and links.

**www.puzzlepirates.com** – an interactive pirate role playing game, very appealing graphics and it looks good fun too.

## E-Mail

**http://spamarrest.com/** – excellent spam reduction program, prices start at $19.95 for 3 months usage.

## Games

**www.gamer.tv** – an above average games site, the one to try if you have broadband.

## Gay

**www.hrc.org** – a bold activist site aimed at campaigning for gay, lesbian and transgender rights, it really shows the way to use a site as a campaigning vehicle.

## Greeting Cards

**www.talkintoons.com** – a very funny selection of animated greetings cards, great design too.

# Health

**www.cancerfacts.com** – an outstanding site aimed at giving accurate information on many different types of cancers, it's also got a good links section if more information is needed.

**www.kidshealth.org** – an engaging American site with three areas, one for parents, one for kids and one for teenagers with each having their content adjusted accordingly. The kids' section is particularly effective with even quite complex illnesses explained well.

**www.medicaltourism.co.uk** – if you don't want to use the NHS for whatever reason, here you can organise your operation or check-up and have a holiday as well.

# History

**www.napoleonguide.com** – all you need to know about Napoleon, not the greatest design but very authoritative.

**www.eternalegypt.org** – a stunning site both in terms of design and what you get in terms of interactivity, the quality of the photos is exceptional and it contains all you need to know about Egyptian civilization.

# Hobbies

**www.readymademag.com** – almost unclassifiable, this is a magazine site and store devoted to making just about anything, a combination of the bizarre and the useful.

# Humour

**www.engrish.com** – a great collection of mainly Japanese misinterpretations and misuse of the English language on everything from signs to products.

# Movies

**www.ifilm.com** – great if you have broadband; you can download clips, trailers and much more. There is some adult-oriented content though.

# Music

**www.azlyrics.com** – an excellent lyrics database site, you can browse by artist, song or album.

**www.musicoftheday.com** – more lyrics well archived and you can hear them too.

**www.napster.com** – Napster is back, this time as a proper commercial music site with over 700,000 songs to choose from. New releases every Tuesday and you can try it free for a limited period.

**www.vh1.com** – best known as a music TV channel, here you can watch videos and get the latest news. In the interactive section there are games to play or you can test your knowledge in the music quizzes.

# News

**www.newsisfree.com** – build your own tailor-made news site using this excellent portal which is updated every 15 minutes.

# Reference

**www.everything2.com** – a messy site containing hundreds of contributions on hundreds of topics, it's not exactly user friendly but it makes for a very interesting browse.

**www.wikipedia.org** – a growing and more to the point free encyclopedia with over 250,000 entries.

# Travel

**www.luxurylink.com** – an American travel site that concentrates on the more luxurious side of travel.

**www.gocitykids.com** – a guide to the major US cities aimed at parents, helping them find activities for their children.

**www.UK.map24.com** – a good-looking and efficient mapping tool.

# Web Design

**www.freewebs.com** – free website building program.

# INDEX